CINCPAC

COMMAND HISTORY

1975

Appendix VI — The SS MAYAGUEZ Incident

Classified by CINCPAC

~~Not Releasable To~~

~~Foreign Nationals~~

COPY __1__ OF __65__ COPIES

APPENDIX C

COMMANDER IN CHIEF PACIFIC COMMAND HISTORY

1975

Appendix VI — The SS MAYAGUEZ Incident

Prepared by the Command History Branch

Office of the Joint Secretary

Headquarters CINCPAC, FPO San Francisco 96610

CAMP H. M. SMITH, HAWAII

1976

TABLE OF CONTENTS

APPENDIX VI

THE SS MAYAGUEZ INCIDENT

SECTION I--INTRODUCTION

(U)   The Cambodian seizure of the United States vessel, MAYAGUEZ, on 12 May 1975 was a significant incident viewed in the context of the international situation when it occurred. Cambodia and Vietnam had just fallen to communist control the previous month and the PUEBLO incident of 1968 was still a fresh memory. It was apparent, at the time, to national leadership from the President on down that this test of United States willpower called for quick, firm, and decisive action which would help to reaffirm America's determination in the eyes of her opponents and allies as well as the American public. Admiral Noel Gayler, Commander in Chief Pacific at the time of the incident, commented on the successful joint Service recovery operation:[1]

> Cambodian adventurism tested the United States with the seizure of the merchant ship MAYAGUEZ on the high seas in May. The recovery operation has left no doubt as to our resolve and capabilities in that part of the world. Our Marines, sailors and airmen again met the challenge. Stories of their courage abound - from the Marine who directed air strikes while swimming off-shore after his helicopter was shot down, to the sailors in the motor whaleboat who took on dug-in heavy weapons with small arms, to the Air Force pilots who forced their way into the landing zones while taking hits.

During the period immediately following the incident, detailed reports were prepared independently by participants up to and including the Joint Chiefs of Staff. In addition, every aspect of the incident was subjected to exhaustive Congressional scrutiny to include a full-scale General Accounting Office (GAO) investigation, the unclassified findings of which were released to the public in October 1976. Although these findings were critical of certain aspects of MAYAGUEZ recovery operations, overall military participation was described as follows:[2]

----

1. <u>CINCPAC Command History 1975</u>, Vol. I, p. v.
2. <u>The Seizure of the MAYAGUEZ--A Case Study of Crisis Management</u>, Report of *The* Comptroller General of the United States, May 11, 1976, p. 56, hereinafter referred to as The Comptroller General MAYAGUEZ Report.

1

• Finally, assembling, under severe time constraints, the various military assets scattered throughout the Pacific area was generally accomplished in an efficient and effective manner.

o Comnand and control of, and communications between, multiservice assets was established expeditiously. The performance of U.S. Forces was inspiring.

(U)   This monograph will not attempt to recount all the details of the MAYAGUEZ operation already available in existing reports. Instead, it will attempt to tie together loose ends and present an overview of the MAYAGUEZ operation from the CINCPAC unified command level. This overview will stress the important military aspects of the operation to include command and control, intelligence/reconnaissance, and planning and execution. In covering these aspects, further emphasis will be placed on CINCPAC's "lessons learned," which should provide valuable insight, and hopefully foresight, for reference in coping with possible future crisis action situations. As CINCPAC has noted, "...with full benefit of hindsight we could have done a number of things better. Life is like that, and there is no reason we should not acknowledge it."[1]

---

1. CINCPAC 131338Z Feb 76.

SECTION If--NOTIFICATION

Cambodia had fallen to the communists on 17 April' 1975 and the fall of the Republic of Vietnam followed closely behind on 30 April 1975. On 12 May 1975 the American Embassy in Vientiane advised that the Pathet Lao had moved quickly to exploit the virtual disappearance of the Vientiane side and to exert control over government operations, commercial activities, and movement of persons there. In the wake of these events, most United States Forces had departed the immediate area except for those in Thailand. In'the midst of this situation, the MAYAGUEZ incident tested the United States crisis action capabilities. 1

(U) It was 0718 Zulu (Z) hours on 12 Kay 1975 when Mr. John Neal of Delta Exploration Company in Jakarta, Indonesia received a "Mayday" (distress) call from the United States merchant ship MAYAGUEZ:2

'Have been fired upon and boarded by Cambodian armed forces at 9 degrees 48 minutes north/102 degrees 53 minutes east. Ship is being towed to unknown Cambodian port.

(C) CINCPAC received this information at 09142 hours 12 Hay 1975 in a . message from the American Embassy, Jakarta. This notification was similarly received by the White House, the National Security Agency (NSA), the Central Intelligence Agency (CIA), the Defense Intelligence Agency (DIA), and the National Military Command Center (NMCC) at the Pentagon. Based on the message, CINCPAC contacted the Joint Chiefs of Staff (JCS) and discussed assets available to reconnoiter the scene of the incident; thus. initial preparations for the MAYAGUEZ operation were begun, pending the outcome of State Department attempts to make contact through diplomatic channels. As the situation developed, diplomatic channels were determined at executive level to be unsatisfactory and military means were employed to recover the MAYAGUEZ and release her crew.3

(C) The MAYAGUEZ seizure, which began the chain of events leading to military action, was not a totally isolated incident, lacking any indications as to its possible occurrence. CINCPAC observed that adequate and timely warning was provided)

1. CINCPAC Command History 1975,-Vol. 11, pp. 607, 609, 617.
2. Op. Cit., The Comptroller General MAYAGUEZ Report, p. 89. [All times will be shown in Greenwich Mean or Zulu time; for Cambodian (G) time, add 7 hours; for Hawaii (W) time. subtract 10 hours.]
3. 'Jakarta 0356/120903Z May 75.

Communist acts against foreign shipping.

----

1. CINCPAC 191623Z Jun 75 (EX)...

SECTION III--COMMAND AND CONTROL

Command Relationships

(the communications aspects of command and control will be discussed in detail later in this section).

. In conference, the local on-scene commander, who was Commander, U.S. Support Activities Group/7th Air Force (COMUSSAG/7AF), assumed the responsibility for planning and directing operations to recover the MAYAGUEZ and cause the release of her crew. Based upon this understanding, COMUSSAG/7AF, in his initial planning guidance to subordinate and supporting units, interpreted command and control relationships as follows:[1]

...The international implications of this operation make restraint imperative. Complete command and control must be maintained by COMUSSAG/7AF, who will be acting upon direction from the National Military Command Center.. ..

. CINCPAC's execution message, authorizing implementation of COMUSSAG/7AF's initial planning guidance, clarified the command and control relationship as it was to apply throughout, the MAYAGUEZ operation until its termination on 15 May 1975:[2]

...Command and control will be maintained by CINCPAC, who will be acting under direction from JCS (NMCC).

. In accordance with this relationship, COMUSSAG/7AF, under CINCPAC's operational command, planned and directed MAYAGUEZ operations on the scene. Air Force and Marine assets were placed under the operational control of, and Naval assets (minus the Marines) supported, COMUSSAG/7AF. Command relationships were again spelled out, using different wording, in COMUSSAG/7AF's final operation plan:[3]

...overall control of the operation will be as directed by CINCPAC and approved by the JCS. CINCPAC will have

----

1. COMUSSAG/7AF 1317482 May 75.
2. CINCPAC 1320512 May 75 and 1523302 May 75.
3. .COMUSSAG/7AF 1417302 May 75 (EX).

operational control over all PACOM designated forces.
CINCSAC will have operational control over the B-52 strike
force. COMUSSAG/7AF will act as the coordinating authority
for the operations of supporting forces.

Command relationships are depicted on the following chart.

(U)   Although Naval forces committed to the MAYAGUEZ operation were not
under the operational control of COMUSSAG/7AF, it was noted that no requests
made by the local command were denied by these forces. . As the Commander in
Chief Pacific Fleet (CINCPACFLT) noted, "the execution requirements for
MAYAGUEZ did not provide sufficient time to prepare'and promulgate a detailed
OPORDER..."; however, CINCPACFLT did advise that "unless otherwise birected,
task force units assigned to subject operation in Gulf of Thailand should plan
on operating in support of COMUSSAG/7AF with direct liaison authorized all
concerned." The Commander, Seventh Fleet further passed on CINCPACFLT
instructions for participating task force units to respond to directions and.
tasking from COMUSSAG/7AF.[1]

Communications

---

1. Ibid.; CINCPACFLT '1318572 May 75 and 1405052 Jun 75 (EX); COMSEVENFLT
   1423262 May 75.
2. J3 Discussion Topic, undated, Issue: Lessons Learned Recent Contingency
   Operations. for discussion at CINC conference held 14 Aug 75 at LANTCOM.

COMMAND RELATIONSHIPS

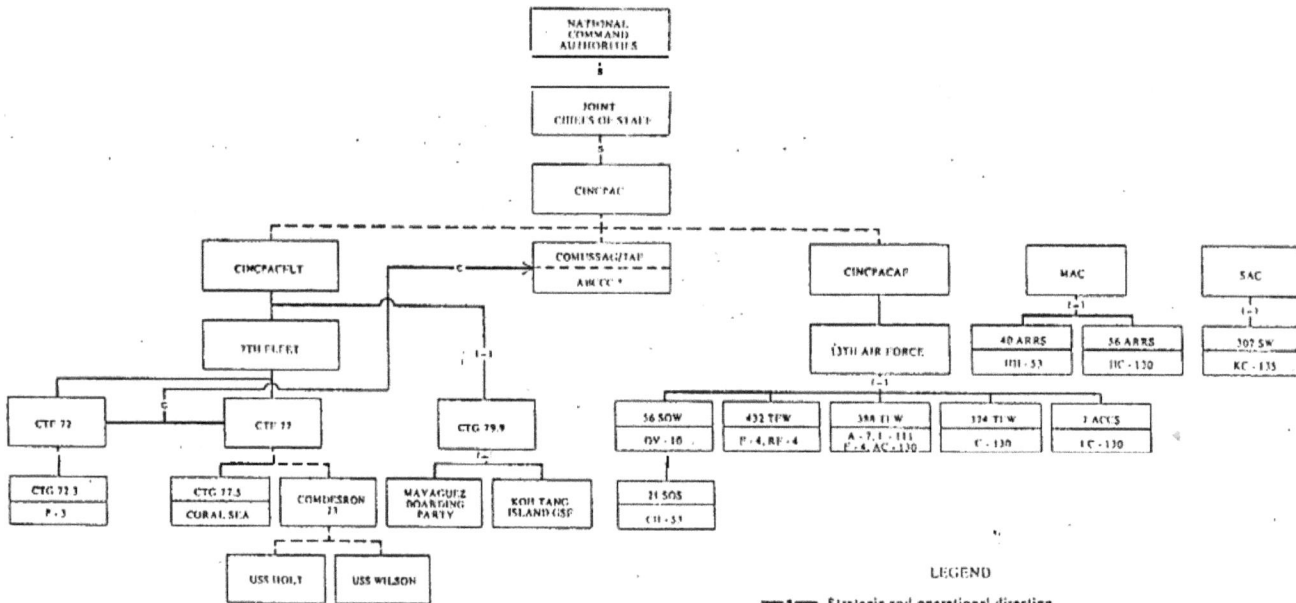

Constructed from the following sources:
CINCPACFLT 131857Z May 75, 142326Z May 75
USSAG/7AF and JCRC History, 1 Apr - 30 Jun 75, p. 100
Discussions with representatives of CINCPACAF and
CINCPACFLT History offices

LEGEND

— s — Strategic and operational direction
— — — Operational Command (Unified Command
         level)/Control (below Unified Command)
———— Command
— I-I — Command less operational control.
         All units in this status were placed under
         operational control of COMUSSAG/7AF
— c —→ Direct coordination and support
   •   Airborne Command and Control
         Center for operational coordination only

in Hawaii; and COMUSSAG/7AF in Thailand. This arrangement emphasized operational control and real time reporting and information gathering.[1]

(S) The communications conference permitted direct control by Washington decision-makers over events halfway, around the world. On the other hand, [7] An example was COMUSSAG/7AF's interpretation of command and control relationships in his initial planning guidance. Furthermore,

(S) The PACOM Required Operational Capabilities for Secure Voice and Data Conferencing and Communications for Remote Force/Joint Task Force Operations, included in the PACOM Command and Control System Master Plan submitted to the JCS on 29 January 1975, recommended use of inherent satellite broadcast capability to satisfy conferencing requirements and proposed that an operational test bed be established in PACOM to resolve operational and technical questions. The experience gained through extensive use during the EAGLE PULL, FREQUENT WIND, and MAYAGUEZ operations led CINCPAC to further emphasize the following requirements:[3]

(S) Tactical communications established between the on-scene commander and subordinate and supporting units during the MAYAGUEZ operation were characterized

---

1. CINCPAC 1313382 Feb 76.
2. Op. Cit., The Comptroller General MAYAGUEZ Report, pp. 33-35; J6/Memo/ 0027-75 of 11 Jun 75, Subj: Lessons Learned-SS MAYAGUEZ/Koh Tang Island; J3/Memo/00566-75 of 8 Sep 75, Subj: SS MAYAGUEZ & Koh Tang Island Operation.
3. J6/Memo/0027-75 of 11 Jun 75, Subj: Lessons Learned-SS MAYAGUEZ/Koh Tang Island; CINCPAC 1916232 Jun 75 (EX).

It was monitored

, and patched ___   . Enemy forces could just
as easily have monitored the same 'net.

                                                                    capability did
_exist from the ABCCC to USSAG, and to Naval units only, through the

(C)   The Marine Ground Security Force (GSF), landed on Koh Tang Island to
free the MAYAGUEZ crew, lost its   capability in a helicopter crash,
and thus its   Therefore, the GSF
was forced to

(C)   As a result of the.
      during the MAYAGUEZ operation, CINCPAC further emphasized the following
requirements:[4]

_____

1. Ibid.
2. Ibid.
3. CINCPAC 1916232 Jun 75 (EX).
4. Ibid.

(U)   Communications nets involved in the MAYAGUEZ operation are depicted on the following chart.

(S)   In commenting to the JCS on interrelated command, and control and communications requirements for further contingency/noncombatant emergency evacuation (NEMVAC) operations, CINCPAC noted that, in the case of the MAYAGUEZ operation,

thus providing a clearer tactical picture to the on-scene commanders.   The plot could have easily been remoted to the rear echelon headquarters and the,

Reporting

(S)   The existence of unilateral Service reporting channels to the JCS during the MAYAGUEZ operation permitted the forwarding of conflicting reports, which had to be referred back to CINCPAC for resolution.   The primary example of this was casualty reporting, where receipt and release of fragmentary and unverified information at Office of the Secretary of Defense level gave the appearance of inaccurate casualty reporting.   This problem was partially related to the nature of the   means of communication in use (for details see communications section), which, lacking specific procedures, allowed for ad hoc inquiries from higher authority and discrepancies between voice and hard copy reporting.*

(S)   Interface between intelligence and operational reporting was an area that witnessed highly effective innovations as well as need for refinement (for details see communications and intelligence/reconnaissance sections).

(S)   In addition to report-related observations found in the communications and intelligence/reconnaissance sections of this monograph, CINCPAC noted, in general, that   channels must go through the unified commander to insure coordinated and accurate reporting to all concerned.   CINCPAC, realizing that official casualty figures had to be reported through Service channels,

----

1.   Ibid.; J6/Memo/0027-75 of 11 Jun 75, Subj: Lessons Learned-SS MAYAGUEZ/ Koh Tang Island Operation.
2.   J1/Memo/311-75 of 18 Jul 75, Subj: SS MAYAGUEZ/Koh Tang Island Operation; CINCPAC 1916232 Jun 75 (EX).

COMMUNICATIONS

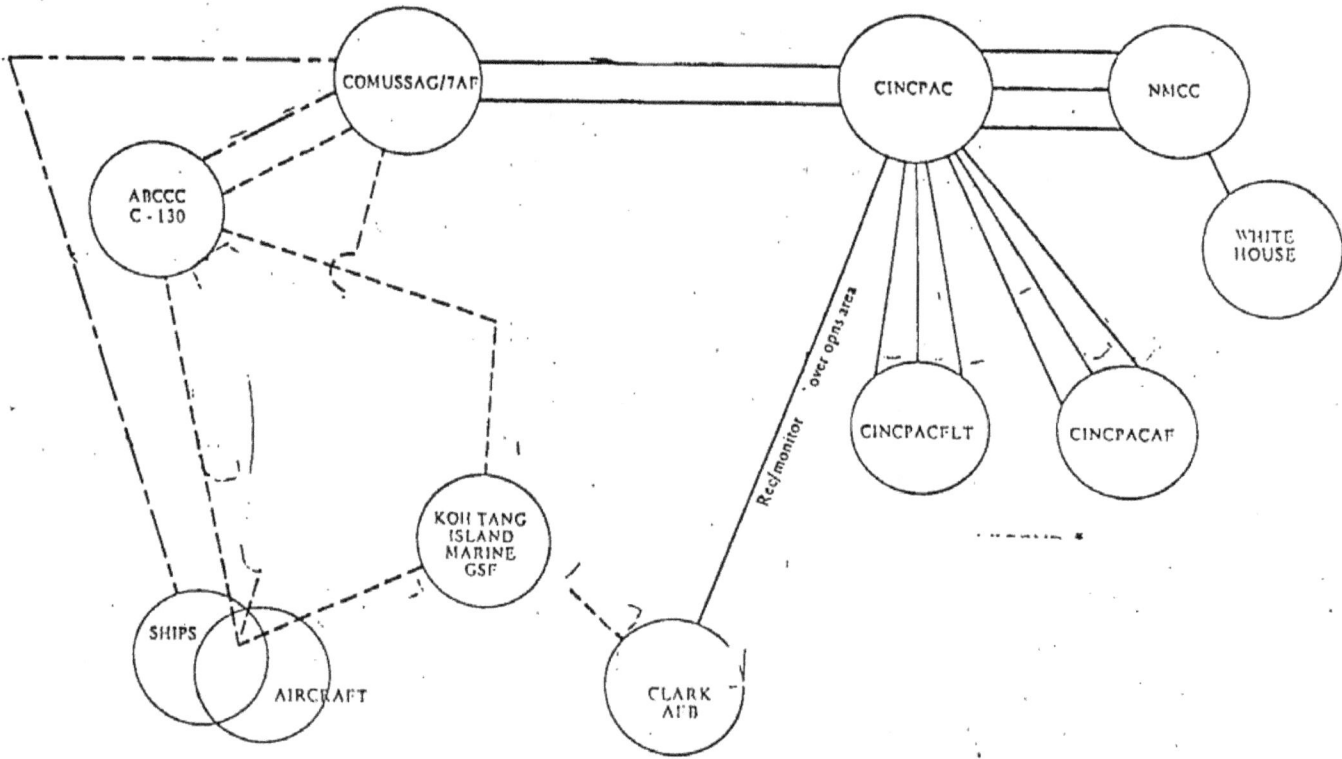

Adapted from 1620 Chart dated 8 Jul 76 and J6 Memo/0027-75,
11 Jun 75, Subj: SS/Mayaguez/Koh Tang island Operation.

recommended a change to JCS Publication 6 to provide force status and identity (FORSTAT) casualty reporting from unit level to the unified command to allow monitoring. [1]

V

---

1. J1/Memo/311-75 of 18 Jul 75, Subj: SS MAYAGUEZ/Koh Tang Island Operation.

SECTION IV--INTELLIGENCE/RECONNAISSANCE

(S) Upon notification of the MAYAGUEZ incident, the Deputy Director for Operations, National Military Command Center requested CIIKPAC to launch reconnaissance aircraft from U-Tapao, Thailand. This initial request was followed by further guidance:]

- CINCPAC provide continuous. P-3 surveillance over the Gulf of Siam north of 8 degrees north and east of 101 degrees east, no closer than 12 nautical miles to the Cambodian-mainland, islands excluded,

- CINCPAC provide photo coverage of Phnom Penh, Sihanoukville, and the islands of Poulo Wai at first satisfactory light, regardless of cloud cover. (The platform was not specified.)

- _____ provide (OLYMPIC MEET) coverage of Poulo Wai at _____ also within the 12 nautical mile restriction.

From this guidance, CINCPAC further instructed CINCPACFLT to report sightings of Cambodian naval units as well as the captured MAYAGUEZ, and obtain photos of Cambodian naval units as feasible. This mission was, in turn, passed to the Commander, Philippine Air Patrol Group (CTG 72.3), who had P-3 aircraft located at his primary base of operations, Cubi Point, Republic of the Philippines, and at his logistic base and refueling. stop, U-Tapao Royal Thai Naval Air Station, Thailand. At 0166Z hours, 13 May a P-3 aircraft reported positive identification of the MAYAGUEZ at 9°56' N, 102°58' E.[2]

(S) The platform, mechanics of film processing, and exploitation procedures for photo reconnaissance were not addressed by the JCS. but after a telephone exchange between CINCPAC J2 and the Defense Intelligence Agency (DIA) the DIA provided processing, duplicating, and disseminating instructions to CINCPAC, SAC, and the SAC Reconnaissance Center, with information copies to Air Force

------

1. After Action Report, US Military Operations, SS MAYAGUEZ/Koh Tana Island, 12-15 May 1975, prepared by the JCS, Tab D, Encl 9, p. 1 (hereinafter referred to as JCS After Action Report); JCS 8233/121944Z May 75.
2. U.S. Naval Institute Proceedings,. Vol. 102/11/885, Nov 76, p. 94, "'Mayday' for the MAYAGUEZ," by Commander J.A. Messegee, USN (hereinafter referred to as Proceedings); Op. Cit., JCS After Action Report, Tab D, Encl 9, p. 1; CINCPAC 1221042 May 75.

headquarters, COMUSSAG, CINCPACAF, and the 432d Tactical Fighter Wing (TFW) at Udorn, Thailand. The DIA message cited the JCS message as having directed ___ (OLYMPIC MEET) and ___ (FACE VALUE) missions against Cambodian targets; the FACE VALUE missions were to be processed and exploited by the 432d TFW at Udorn, while OLYMPIC MEET mission materials were to be delivered to the ___ The remainder of the DIA message named specific exploitation objectives, but did not address the JCS-directed P-3 reconnaissance.[1]

(S) This omission was apparently resolved (possibly through operational channels) because, approximately three hours after the DIA message, CINCPAC J2 directed COMUSSAG, CINCPACAF, and CINCPACFLT to follow the DIA instructions for processing and distributing the FACE VALUE and OLYMPIC MEET missions. CINCPAC also directed CINCPACFLT to forward unprocessed P-3 mission imagery to the 432d Reconnaissance Technical Squadron (RTS) at Udorn for initial processing and rapid readout. The 432d RTS was to prepare the Initial Photo Interpretation Report (IPIR) and dispatch it to specified addressees as "Special USN P-3 Coverage." A duplicate positive was to be sent to the Fleet Air Intelligence Service Center (FAISC) Pacific, and the original negative to Fleet Intelligence Center Pacific in Hawaii.[2]

(S) Because the Navy P-3 unit at U-Tapao, Thailand had not been an addressee on the CINCPAC message. COMUSSAG retransmitted the message to the U-Tapao-based P-3 unit, but apparently too late. A little more than six hours after the dispatch of the CINCPAC message, COMUSSAG was informed that the first P-3 film had been sent to the FAISC Pacific at Cubi Point, Philippines for processing.[3]

(S) Subsequent imagery was handled as instructed, however, and, when the operation to recover the MAYAGUEZ and her crew was authorized, CINCPAC provided film handling instructions for fleet tactical aerial photo reconnaissance operations. When IPIRs of Koh Tang Island indicated possible helicopter crash imagery, CINCPAC directed COMUSSAG to provide the most recent photography to the Commander Task Unit 72.3.5 (P-3s) at U-Tapao for possible resumption of Marine personnel recovery operations. Throughout the MAYAGUEZ operation, flash precedence COMPASS LINK ___ was employed. Expedited Armed Forces Courier Service, requested by CINCPAC on 13 May 1975,

....

1. 523 HistSum May 75, with 12 attached msgs, second of which was JCS 8223/ 1219442 May 75; DIA (DC-SC) 05216/122108Z May 75 (BOM).
2. CINCPAC 1302392 May 75.
3. COMUSSAG/7AF 1312532 May 75, which cited several undated phonecons and COMUSSAG INCR 130755Z May 75.

was cancelled on 20 May, and on 21 May CINCPAC directed CINCPACFLT, CINCPACAF, and COMUSSAG to revert to normal film handling procedures. 1

(S) With the photo reconnaissance platform specified as RF-4C, CINCPAC instructed COMUSSAG/7AF *to* provide' photo coverage of Phnom Penh, Sihanoukville, Hon Panjang Island (09°18' N, 103°28' E), and the island groups in the vicinity of 09°58' N, 102°53' E (Poulo Wai). Flights over Phnom Penh and Sihanoukville were restricted to a minimum altitude of 6,000 feet, while flights over the islands were restricted to a minimum of 4,500 feet. The Essential Elements of Information (EEI) included merchant ships, naval craft, and paratroop landing/ drop zones. After the MAYAGUEZ was located and under observation, CINCPAC requested initial imagery of Koh Tang Island and daily coverage until after the execution of contemplated recovery operations. Flights in the vicinity of Koh Tang Island were restricted to a minimum altitude of 6,500 feet. The EEI now included:[2]

- Pier facilities.

- Gun emplacements.

- Fortifications.

- Small boat locations.

- Troop concentrations.

- Evidence of ship/shore personnel movement to/from MAYAGUEZ.

- One-time readout of building locations/helicopter landing areas.

(S) Photo reconnaissance instructions were subsequently amended, as required, and included RF-4C coverage following each tactical air strike in support of recovery operations as well as Navy missions over the Konpong Som area. In both cases the minimum altitude restriction of 6,500 feet applied.[3]

(S) In the midst of this reconnaissance activity, the location of the MAYAGUEZ crew was of crucial importance to operational decisions. The

----

1. J23 HistSum May 75; CINCPAC 1302412 May 75, 1421452 May 75, 1523332 May 75, 1615112 May 75, 1622262 May 75, 2000372 May 75, and 2101132 May 75.
2. CINCPAC 1221372 May 75 and 1323462 May 75.
3. CINCPAC 1403252 May 75, 1421102 May 75, 1500402 May 75, and 1500452 May 75.

above-listed EEI included the requirement to report evidence of personnel movement to/from the MAYAGUEZ and, in conjunction with preliminary actions to isolate Koh Tang Island and the MAYAGUEZ, the JCS emphasized that:[1]

> It is particularly important to get maximum information on any outgoing boat to determine if there are Americans aboard and to report such when requesting authority to sink, although this will be difficult to accomplish. Deck loading probably will be required on the small boats as they did in taking personnel, believed to be Americans, from the ship to the island.

(S) The knowledge that personnel, believed to be Americans, had been taken from the MAYAGUEZ to Koh Tang Island was based on P-3 aircraft (LY499) reports that one gunboat and one tugboat were observed along side the MAYAGUEZ and that personnel were being transferred from the MAYAGUEZ to the tugboat. The P-3 further reported that the gunboat and tug with personnel on board departed the MAYAGUEZ heading toward shore, and that the personnel seated on deck with heads on knees appeared to be Caucasian. COMUSSAG/7AF followed the progress of this movement:[2]

Time	Observation
1310182 May	Boat which had been tied to starboard side of MAYAGUEZ has started to move toward the island with a lot of people on board.
1310242 May	Small fishing-type vessel which was tied to port side of MAYAGUEZ is now-moving toward island. The boat appears to have Caucasian personnel on board. ...
1310332 May	Ground fire was received by JUMBO 01 as he made low visual reconnaissance pass near the island. No hits. Personnel are disembarking on the island.
1311152 May	Report from KING 22, HC-130. Two small boats off-loading personnel on island and they are moving toward the interior of the island.

---

1. JCS 9376/131905Z May 75.
2. PATRON FOUR 131024Z May 75; CTG 72.3 131050Z May 75; COMUSSAG/7AF 131105Z May 75, 131115Z May 75, 131118Z May 75, 131135Z May 75, and 131245Z May 75.

1312272 May   Summary of situation. The MAYAGUEZ is still in the
                water. All personnel appear to have been transferred
                to the island...both small boats are at the island....

   (U)   The above indications, which led to the conclusion that the MAYAGUEZ
crew was being held on Koh Tang Island, prompted the actions taken to isolate
the island and the MAYAGUEZ. The objective was to prevent the crew and ship
from being taken to mainland Cambodia, thus avoiding a situation similar to
the PUEBLO affair of 1968.[1]

   (S)   The only other indication as to the possible location of the
MAYAGUEZ crew during the incident, prior to their release, came about 01032
hours 14 May, when a P-3 observed a "...fishing boat, with possible Caucasians
huddled in the bow..." heading from Koh Tang Island toward the Cambodian
mainland. Other United States Forces in the area at that time, which had also
observed the boat, included four A-7, two F-4, one C-130, two F-111, and one
KC-135.[2]

   (S)   The flight of A-7s from the 347th TFW was directed to orbit and
maintain contact with what they described as "...a fishing vessel of approximately 40 foot length with approximately 30-40 people of undetermined race
aboard, seated on deck." They remained on station for two hours and tracked
the vessel until it entered the harbor around Kompong Som and docked at 03152
hours 14 May. At the same time, the flight of F-4s from the 388th TFW
reported observing the A-7s attempting to impede the progress of a boat
carrying 30-40 people on deck "...thought possible to be Caucasians...." The
F-4s were forced to leave the area early to refuel, but not before they had
attempted to turn the boat by firing in front of it. COMUSSAG/7AF reported
that "...one thirty foot craft with approximately 40 people aboard..." was
maintaining course toward Kompong Som harbor in spite of attempts to turn it
by firing in front of it and making multiple CBU-30 (riot control agent)
passes over it. This boat "...was not taken under direct attack because of
the probability of Americans being aboard...."[3]

   (S)   In summary, the MAYAGUEZ crew was not positively identified until
they came alongside the USS WILSON in a Thai fishing boat about 03082 on
15 May during the assault on Koh Tang Island. The balance of indications
favoring the existence of at least some of the crew remaining on the island

----

1. Op. Cit., JCS After Action Report, p. 1.
2. PATRON FOUR 1401402 May 75.
3. 347TFW 1407072 May 75; 388TFW 1403552 May 75, 1405352 May 75, 1405502
    May 75; PATRON FOUR 1402422 May 75, 1403232 May 75; USSAG/7AF 1402352
    May 75; Op. Cit., JCS After Action Report, p. 2.

was weighted by "...an intelligence source of higher classification..." which indicated that the Khmer Communists intended to take them to Koh Tang Island. The subsequent Koh Tang Island phase of the MAYAGUEZ operation was based on this conclusion.[1]

(U) On the afternoon of 14 May Marine Major Randall Austin, who led the assault on Koh Tang Island, conducted an aerial, reconnaissance of the island in a U.S. Army U-21 aircraft, but he noted, "unfortunately, we were limited to a minimum altitude of 6,000 feet and could not see the necessary detail;" This restriction was apparently locally established. Evidence leading to this conclusion can be found in Navy Commander J.A. Messegee's (CTG 72.3) recollections of the 'initial P-3 reconnaissance to locate the MAYAGUEZ:[2]

 • * * * *

> In addition to no air cover, we also were concerned about the antiaircraft (AA) armament on the Cambodian gunboats, inasmuch as we had lost a P-3 to this type of boat during the Vietnam War. Although our best intelligence indicated the boats' heaviest weapons were 20mm, one publication indicated they had 40mm. This discrepancy caused me to set a 6,000-foot minimum altitude restriction on our aircraft when in the vicinity of a possible gunboat and to require a one-mile minimum offset. We were to learn that these restrictions did not hamper our ability to visually monitor gunboat movements, except during periods of low cloudiness. At these minimums, however, we could not discern specific details, such as the lettering on the bow and stern of the MAYAGUEZ.

(U) Commander Messegee went on to say, however, that he later directed passes as low as 300 feet, and there was no indication that a 6,000-foot minimum remained in effect for P-3s beyond the initial sortie cited.[3]

(S) Also important was the need for accurate information on the enemy situation, both on Koh Tang Island and on the Cambodian mainland. CINCPAC observed that, to this end, photo reconnaissance provided little order of

---

1. CINCPAC 1313382 Feb 76; PATRON FOUR 150258Z May 75 and 150327Z May 75.
2. NAVY TIMES, 27 Aug 75, p. 15, "The Assault on Koh Tang"; Draft narrative of interview by Colonel Savoy with Major Austin, undated, Subj: Koh Tang Assault/Operation MAYAGUEZ; USSAG/7AF & JCRC History, 1 Apr-30 Jun 1975, dated 22 Aug 75, p. 91; Op. Cit., Proceedings, p. 94.
3. Op. Cit., Proceedings, p. 95.

battle (OB) information on the island because of the dense jungle cover. Photo reconnaissance by   was not timely enough for use in such a fast-moving situation. As noted above, the Marine GSF commander's visual reconnaissance proved unsatisfactory to obtain OB information, and _ _ . .   collection resources provided no OB intelligence due to a

(S)   Intelligence. shortly after the fall of Cambodia (17 April 1975) reported the existence of 18-20 people on the island at that time. IPAC disseminated this information by an intelligence spot report (SPOTREP) on 13 May. In a second SPOTREP, following closely behind the first, IPAC estimated the maximum of one Khmer Communist company (90-100 men) reinforced with a heavy weapons squad to be on the island; however, this report apparently did not reach the Marine GSF commander prior to the assault on the island, although it did reach the transporting helicopter commander and others. According to Major J.B. Hendricks, Operations Officer of the Second Battalion of the Ninth Marine Regiment (2/9), from which the Koh Tang Island assault force was drawn,; their briefings informed them "...that there were 20-30 Khmer Rouge irregulars on the island, possibly reinforced by whatever naval support personnel that were there associated with the gunboats sighted in the area." A DIA appraisal which appeared in the JCS after action report on the incident estimated approximately 150-200 Khmer Communists on the island at the onset of the operation; however, there was no indication that this specific appraisal was generally available prior to the assault.[2]

(C)   Available maps were considered insufficient to plan an amphibious assault or direct naval gunfire in support of the Koh Tang Island phase of the MAYAGUEZ operation. Topographic maps at 1:50,000 or 1:100,000 scale did not extend to the island. The current nautical chart of the island was approximately 1:240,000 scale and there was a Joint Operations Graphic (JOG) at 1:250,000 scale. Standard Naval combat charts were only produced for high priority or training areas; however, other limited areas could have been mapped by the Defense Mapping Agency in 48 hours, exclusive of shipping time, for an amphibious assault.[3]

(S)   During the MAYAGUEZ operation the use of intelligence collection media for timely operational reporting (see also communications section) proved an important source of U.S. force data.

----

1. CINCPAC 1916232 Jun 75 (EX).
2. Op. Cit., Proceedings, p. 104, and JCS After Action Report, Tab B, pp. 1-2; COMIPAC 1318232 May 75 and 1321442 May 75; CINCPAC 1313382 Feb 76.
3. J3/Memo/00566-75 of 8 Sep 75, Subj: SS MAYAGUEZ/Koh Tang Island Operation; CINCPAC 1916232 Jun 75 (EX).

From there, CINCPAC received then
via operational communications, at tines well ahead of COMUSSAG/7AF voice
reports. There was some difficulty correlating operations and intelligence
reports because of this time differential

(S)   As a result of experience gained from the MAYAGUEZ operation, CINCPAC
directed a feedback system to ensure acknowledgement of critical intelligence
by commanders directly concerned, and further emphasized:[2]

      o

      e The need for accurate photos, charts, and maps of
the area for Naval gunfire, close air and assault support
forces.

      o The need to maintain tactical reconnaissance forces
in vital areas to provide timely coverage in fast-moving
situations.

      • The need for COMPASS LINK or a similar system to
                |to Washington, theater commanders,
and for possible press releases.

      • ,

      e The need to develop procedures to rapidly introduce
photography from various sources, such as P-3, into other
reconnaissance distribution systems in the immediate area
of operations.

....

1. J6/Memo/0027-75 of 11 Juri 75. Subj: Lessons Learned-SS MAYAGUEZ/Koh Tang
Island Operation.
2. J3 Discussion Topic, undated, Issue: · Lessons Learned Recent Contingency
Operations, for discussion at CINC conference held 14 Aug 75 at LANTCOM;
CINCPAC 1916232 Jun 75 (EX).

SECTION V--PLANNING AND EXECUTION

Planning

(S)   As CINCPAC's on-scene commander during the MAYAGUEZ operation, COMUSSAG/7AF was tasked to develop, submit for approval, and execute a multi-Service air, air assault, and surface plan for the recovery of the MAYAGUEZ and an assault on Koh Tang Island in little over 16 hours. Time constraints did not provide sufficient time for detailed operation orders. [1]

(S)   The initial operational concept involved use of the nearest available assets, Air Force security police. They were to make a helicopter assault directly on to the MAYAGUEZ at first light on 14 May; however, as the situation developed, incoming Marines replaced the security police in what was planned to be a simultaneously executed two-phase operation to recover the MAYAGUEZ and release her crew, supported by air strikes on mainland Cambodia.[2]

(S)   Actions taken at the direction of the JCS in support of the evolving operational concept included:[3]

- • CINCPAC move all available helicopter assets in Thailand to U-Tapao.

- • CINCPAC move 75 USAF security police from Nakhon Phanom to U-Tapao.

- o CINCPAC move two reinforced platoons of Marines from Cubi Point to U-Tapao via MAC airlift.

- o CINCPAC place one Okinawa-based Marine battalion on advanced deployability posture for movement to U-Tapao via MAC airlift.

- o CSAF task MAC to provide appropriate support to CINCPAC as required and move appropriate MAC airlift to Kadena AB in preparation to lift Okinawa-based Marines.

----

1. J5/Memo/0031-75 of 17 Jul 75, Subj: SS MAYAGUEZ/Koh Tang Island Operation.
2. USSAG/7AF and JCRC History, 1 Apr-30 Jun 1975, dated 22 Aug 75, pp. 87-89.
3. JCS 9179/131610Z May 75.

(S) Based on these JCS instructions, CINCPAC further tasked COMUSSAG/7AF to move the helicopter assets and security police in Thailand to U-Tapao; CINCPACFLT to move the Marines from Cubi Point and Okinawa to U-Tapao; and CINCPACAF to preposition the required airlift in Okinawa. In addition, the following taskings had already been directed:[1]

   o USS CORAL SEA [CVA-43] and escorts (TG 77.5) from the vicinity of Indonesia (about 950 miles away) to the vicinity of Kompong Som.

   o USS HOLT, Destroyer Escort (DE-1074), and USS VEGA from about 100 miles off the Philippine coast (southwest of Subic Bay) to the scene of the incident.

   o USS WILSON, Guided-Missile Destroyer (DDG-7), enroute from Kaohsiung, Republic of China, bound for Subic Bay, Republic of the Philippines to the vicinity of Koh Tang Island.

   o USS OKINAWA, enroute to Okinawa, return to the Philippines to reconstitute an Amphibious Ready Group (ARG) (USS OKINAWA, USS DULUTH, USS BARBOUR COUNTY, and USS MT. VERNON) and prepare to proceed to the scene. (This unit was not deployed.)

(S) The essence of COMUSSAG/7AF's initial operational concept was as follows:[2]

   o Arrive on station at first light, 2300Z 13 May/ 0600G 14 May.

   o Effect recovery of the ship and, if possible, the ship's crew. .

   o USAF tactical aircraft air-drop riot control agents (RCA) on the ship to immobilize any personnel on board.

   o Use all CH-53 helicopter assets available in Thailand and all but two of the available HH-53 assets.

----

1. Op. Cit., JCS After Action Report, Tab D, Encl 9, p. 1; The Comptroller General MAYAGUEZ Report, pp. 36-38; and Proceedings, pp. 97, 108; CINCPAC 1317372 May 75.
2. COMUSSAG/7AF 1317482 May 75.

• At ten minute intervals, in a single helo-lift, offload, from a hover, 125 USAF security police, 2 explosive ordnance personnel, 2 paramedics, and 1 Army captain interpreter onto the MAYAGUEZ.

(S) During the deployment of helicopters and 100 USAF security police from Nakhon Phanom to U-Tapao, which began at 1300Z hours 13 May, one CH-53 crashed because of mechanical failure, killing 18 security police and 5 crew members.]

(S) At 2051Z hours 13 May, CINCPAC directed COMUSSAG/7AF to modify the concept by substituting USMC Ground Security Force (GSF) personnel for the USAF security police, and emphasized that command and control would be maintained by CINCPAC. No execute order was issued.[2]

(TS) At 0645Z hours 14 May the JCS notified CINCPAC:[3]

Higher authority has directed that all necessary preparations be made for potential execution early on the 15th to seize the MAYAGUEZ, occupy Koh Tang Island, conduct 8-52 strikes against the port of Kompong Som and Ream Airfield, and sink all Cambodian small craft in target areas.

(TS) CINCPAC was now tasked to plan for and execute, when directed, the following operations:[4]

• USS HAROLD E. HOLT seize SS MAYAGUEZ using ships company and or augmenting Marines at U-Tapao.

o Occupy Koh Tang Island with Marine forces at U-Tapao supported by Air Force helo assets and tactical air and naval gunfire support as available and required.

o Sink all Cambodian small craft in the target areas of Koh Tang, Poulo Wai, Kompong Som, and Ream.

(TS) CINCSAC was tasked to conduct conventional B-52 strikes against the port of Kompong Som and Ream Airfield from Guam.[5]

---

1. USSAG/7AF & JCRC History, 1 Apr-30 Jun 1975, dated 22 Aug 75, p. 88.
2. CINCPAC 132051Z May 75.
3. JCS 1109/140645Z May 75 (EX).
4. Ibid.
5. Ibid.

(TS) CINCPAC then tasked COMUSSAG/7AF to provide the detailed plans required by the JCS by 1300Z hours 14 May. CINCPAC further specified that, in planning, maximum emphasis should be placed on use of the USS CORAL SEA for close air support and minimum reliance on the availability of Thai-based strategic and tactical air. Although not mentioned, this specification was probably in deference to Thai sensitivities; however, as the situation actually evolved, this specification was not adhered to.[1]

(TS) During the new planning phase, participating units provided input to the plan that was finally submitted. There was general agreement on the need for simultaneously boarding the MAYAGUEZ and helo assaulting Koh Tang Island; however, views differed on the method for boarding the MAYAGUEZ. CINCPACFLT's concept, which was finally executed, was to transfer the boarding party by helicopter to the USS HOLT. The Marine task force commander (CTF 79.9) and COMUSSAG/7AF initially envisioned inserting the boarding party by helicopter directly onto the MAYAGUEZ in a manner similar to COMUSSAG/7AF's previous concept (see page 23). The concept submitted in COMUSSAG/7AF's final plan agreed with CINCPACFLT on the method for boarding the MAYAGUEZ; but, in an apparent oversight in the employment paragraph to the same plan, insertion on the MAYAGUEZ was specified to be by helicopter. CINCPAC approved the final plan, subject to the boarding party boarding from the USS HOLT and clarification that supporting strategic air B-52D air strikes were to be as directed by the JCS. CINCPAC directed that the Marines be put aboard the HOLT and the HOLT brought alongside the MAYAGUEZ because it was unknown if any Cambodians were on the MAYAGUEZ. It was simpler, with fewer risks, to board the MAYAGUEZ from the HOLT than from helicopters.[2]

(TS) The following were the key elements of the final operational concept developed to recover the SS MAYAGUEZ and influence the outcome of U.S. initiatives to secure the release of the ship's crew:[3]

- Begin a simultaneous two-phase assault at sunrise 15 May local time (approximately 2300Z 14 May 1975).

- Using eight USAF CH/HH-53 helicopters, execute a combat assault on Koh Tang Island, with 175 Marines in the initial wave, subsequent buildup to a total of 625 Marines on the island, and rescue members of the SS MAYAGUEZ that may be found there.

---

1. CINCPAC 140750Z May 75.
2. CINCPACFLT 141254Z May 75; CTF 79.9 141400Z May 75; COMUSSAG 141515Z May 75; CINCPAC 142112Z May 75 and 131338Z Feb 76.
3. COMUSSAG/7AF 141730Z May 75 (EX).

e Using three USAF helicopters, insert 48 Marines, 12 USN/MSC personnel, and explosive ordnance team and a Cambodian linguist on the USS HOLT, close with the SS MAYAGUEZ, and board and secure her.

e Close air support and area coverage against all Cambodian small craft would be provided by USAF and USN tactical air. Naval gunfire support would be available, and 8-52 strikes or Naval tactical air would be directed against possible reinforcing mainland Cambodian targets.

(S) Subsequent operations followed this concept closely; with tactical air from the USS CORAL SEA being substituted for B-52s in the mainland strikes.

(S) Experience gained in planning for the MAYAGUEZ operation highlighted the need to maintain and follow adequate, current crisis action procedures in responding to quick-breaking situations. Realizing the impracticality of attempting to prepare explicit plans for every possible crisis situation, and the fact that sufficient planning time would hardly ever be available, CINCPAC observed that those options most likely to be executed should be clearly identified early in the planning process to prevent subordinate commands from "spinning their wheels," planning for options that had little likelihood of being executed. Overall, the requirement for U.S. military assets worldwide to be strategically mobile and instantly responsive was emphasized.[2]

(S) Observing the interrelated plans and operations process, CINCPAC stressed the need to increase the number of joint incident exercises with more imaginative and realistic scenarios, commencing with PACOM Command Post Exercises (CPXs), moving, with JCS concurrence, to higher-level politico-military games (possibly inter-departmental). and then frequent, full-fledged exercises with force participation.[3]

Execution

The MAYAGUEZ/Koh Tang Island Operation

(S) The operation began with the first insertion of Marines on Koh Tang Island at about 22552 14 May (0555G 15 May) and the landing of the boarding

---

1. Op. Cit., JCS After Action Report, Tab A, p. 2.
2. J5/Memo/00131-75 of 17 Jul 75, Subj: SS MAYAGUEZ/Koh Tang Island Operation.
3. CINCPAC 1916232 Jun 75 (EX).

party on the USS HAROLD E. HOLT at about 2305Z 14 May (0605G 15 May). Although the USS HOLT met no opposition, and the boarding party was in complete control of the MAYAGUEZ within about two hours (0128Z 15 May), the Marine GSF and transporting USAF helicopters met fierce opposition from the beginning. Their ordeal lasted about 14 hours (last Marines extracted at about 1310Z 15 May). The MAYAGUEZ crew had been identified as safe aboard the USS WILSON within about 4 hours (0308Z 15 May) after the initial assault on the island; however, because of the strong enemy opposition encountered on the island, reinforcements were required to stabilize the situation and successfully extract the Marines.[1]

(S) During the initial insertion of Marines on Koh Tang Island, concern for the safety of the MAYAGUEZ crew, believed to be on the island, precluded landing zone preparation by air strikes or naval gunfire. Even after confirmation of the crew's recovery, fast A-7 Forward Air Controllers (FACs) were unable to pinpoint locations of friendly units and suppress enemy fire because of the confines of, and confusing situation on, the battlefield. It was not until 0930Z 15 May that two OV-10 "Nail" slow FACs, with loitering ability, were on station to pinpoint friendly positions for effective close air support. Also, it was not until 0735Z 15 May that the first helicopter was able to recover to the CORAL SEA rather than return to U-Tapao (helicopters used were a mix of HH-53 air-refuelable "Jolly Green," and CH-53 non-air-refuelable "Knife" aircraft).[2]

(S) In summary, the Koh Tang Island phase of the MAYAGUEZ operation involved the insertion of 231 Marines and subsequent evacuation of 227 (there were three missing in action and one killed in action left on the island) in the face of severe enemy fire. A total of 15 USMC, USAF, and USN personnel were killed in action, 49 wounded in action, and 3 Marines missing in action. Participating USAF helicopters incurred three combat losses, four were severely damaged, and six received minor damage.[3]

(S) As a result of the experience gained from executing the Koh Tang Island phase of the MAYAGUEZ operation, CINCPAC made the following additional observations relative to the means available to support the assault:[4]

---

1. Assault on Koh Tang, DCS/Plans and Operations, HQ PACAF, 23 Jun 75, pp. 23, 1-1, 1-3; PATRON FOUR 1503272 May 75; COMUSSAG/7AF 1502152 May 75.
2. Assault on Koh Tang, DCS/Plans and Operations, HQ PACAF, 23 Jun 75, pp. 2, 4, 18, 28, 29, 1-2.
3. Ibid., USSAG/7AF & JCRC History, 1 Apr-30 Jun 1975, dated 22 Aug 75, p. 99.
4. J3/Memo/00566-75 of 8 Sep 75, Subj: SS MAYAGUEZ/Koh Tang Island Operation; CINCPAC 1916232 Jun 75 (EX).

• Helicopter availability dictated the size and composition of forces; thus, the initial insertion was marginal in size, and rapid buildup ashore was not possible due to limited lift capability. Once the CORAL SEA was within 10 miles of the .island, and shuttle distance was reduced, adequate support was available for the extraction' phase. As we approach reduced force levels in the theater, particular attention must be paid to airmobile support from all services which provides flexibility to force composition.

• Troop lift helicopters should be air refuelable and equipped with fire preventive foam in external fuel tanks, as well as other hardening measures (losses were greater among CH-53s).

• We should use helicopters and low speed FACs to coordinate tactical air assets whenever the tactical environnent permits.

Supportive Air Strikes Against the Cambodian Mainland

Air strikes in support of the MAYAGUEZ operation were conducted against mainland Cambodian targets as directed by the JCS, the final decisions resting with higher authority. Cyclic strikes from the USS CORAL SEA against targets in the Kompong Som area were scheduled with first time-on-target about 0045Z 15 May, which closely coincided with the recovery of the MAYAGUEZ. In the midst of the initial execution of the operation, a Foreign Broadcast Information Service report out of Bangkok quoted a Cambodian Government press release to the effect that they intended to release the MAYAGUEZ and crew. This was being discussed by CINCPAC and the NMCC when, about 0044Z 15 May, word was received from the White House to cancel the CORAL SEA strike; however, by 0052Z 15 May word was received to again proceed with the CORAL SEA strikes as planned. The first wave did not expend any ordnance. Then, right after the MAYAGUEZ had been searched and found empty, CINCPAC received information from an unknown Cambodian station saying, "Let the Americans go. We do not want to become prisoners ourselves." This supported the belief that at least some Americans could still be on Koh Tong Island, and shortly after this, the second wave of CORAL SEA aircraft arrived over the mainland to attack Ream Airfield. By 0308Z 15 May the release of the MAYAGUEZ crew had been confirmed and at 0329Z 15 May CINCPAC reported to the NMCC that the crew members had told the WILSON personnel that as a "condition for release they promised air strikes would cease." CINCPAC now queried the JCS as to whether or not the third wave should continue on course. The Chairman, JCS discussed this with the Secretary of Defense, and the third and final strike was directed and carried out.[1]

(S) Finally, at 04552 15 May, the JCS notified all participants in the MAYAGUEZ operation:[2]

> Immediately cease all offensive operations against Khmer Republic related to seizure of MAYAGUEZ. Disengage and withdraw all forces from operation area as soon as possible consistent with safety/self-defense.

(S) CINCPAC noted that "...the threat of bombing of the Cambodian mainland did, in fact, influence the Cambodian's decision to release the crew..." as was verified by the captain of the MAYAGUEZ.[3]

----

1. JCS Report, <u>Strike Operations Against Mainland Targets During Operations to Recover SS MAYAGUEZ and Crew</u>, dated 19 May 1975.
2. JCS 2396/150455Z May 75.
3. CINCPAC 1313382 Feb 76.

SECTION VI—SUPPLEMENTARY BIBLIOGRAPHY

(U)   The following are additional references which; though not cited, helped to provide the full breadth of perspective necessary to write this monograph.

Carlile, Donald E., LTC, USA, "The MAYAGUEZ Incident--Crisis Management," Military Review, Vol. LVI, No. 10, October 1976, pp. 3-14.

Commander in Chief U.S. Pacific Fleet, Command-History of the Commander in Chief U.S. Pacific Fleet, 1 January 1975-31 December 1975, Makalapa, Hawaii, 7 September 1976. (SECRET)

Headquarters, 1st Battalion, 4th Marines, 3rd Marine Division (-)(Rein), FMF, After Action Report, Recovery of the SS MAYAGUEZ, 12 November 1975. (CONFIDENTIAL)

Headquarters, Pacific Air Force, History of Pacific Air Forces, 1 July 1974-31 December 1975, Vol. I, Hickam AFB, Hawaii:Office of PACAF History, 30 July 1976. (TOP SECRET)

Rowan, Roy, The Four Days of MAYAGUEZ, New York:W.W. Norton and Co., Inc., 1975.

Smith, James E., LTC, USAF, "The MAYAGUEZ Incident," a case study submitted to the faculty of the Air War College, Maxwell AFB, Alabama, April 1976. Defense Supply Agency, Defense Documentation Center file number ADC006284. (SECRET)

U.S. House of Representatives, Seizure of the MAYAGUEZ, Part I, Hearings before the Committee on International Relations and its Subcommittee on International Political and Military Affairs, 94th Congress, First Session, May 14 and 15, 1975. Washington:U.S. Government Printing Office, 1975.

U.S. House of Representatives, Seizure of the MAYAGUEZ, Part II, Hearings before the Subcommittee on International Political and Military Affairs of the Committee on International Relations, 94th Congress, First Session, June 19 and 25, and July 25, 1975. Washington:U.S. Government Printing Office, 1975.

UNCLASSIFIED

U.S. House of Representatives, <u>Seizure of the MAYAGUEZ</u>,
<u>Part 111</u>, Hearings before the Subcommittee on International
Political and Military Affairs of the Committee on International
Relations, 94th Congress, First Session, July 31 and September 12,
1975. Washington:U.S. Government Printing Office, 1975.

U.S. House of Representatives, <u>Seizure of the MAYAGUEZ,</u>
<u>Part IV</u>, Reports of the Comptroller General of the United
States submitted to the Subcommittee on International Political
and Military Affairs, Committee on International Relations,
94th Congress, Second Session, October 4, 1976. Washington:
U.S. Government Printing Office, 1976.

98-E-4?
c.1

NATIONAL DEFENSE UNIVERSITY

NATIONAL WAR COLLEGE

LOOKING FEROCIOUS:
THE FORD ADMINISTRATION'S MANAGEMENT OF THE MAYAGUEZ
AFFAIR

CAROL VAN VOORST/CLASS OF 1998
COURSE 5603: NATIONAL SECURITY POLICY PROCESS

FACULTY LEADER: DR. MELVIN GOODMAN

FACULTY ADVISOR: DR. MELVIN GOODMAN

Report Documentation Page

Form Approved
OMB No. 0704-0188

1. REPORT DATE **1998**	2. REPORT TYPE	3. DATES COVERED **00-00-1998 to 00-00-1998**	
4. TITLE AND SUBTITLE **Looking Ferocious: The Ford Administration's Management of the Mayaguez Affair**		5a. CONTRACT NUMBER	
		5b. GRANT NUMBER	
		5c. PROGRAM ELEMENT NUMBER	
6. AUTHOR(S)		5d. PROJECT NUMBER	
		5e. TASK NUMBER	
		5f. WORK UNIT NUMBER	
7. PERFORMING ORGANIZATION NAME(S) AND ADDRESS(ES) **National War College,300 5th Avenue,Fort Lesley J. McNair,Washington,DC,20319-6000**		8. PERFORMING ORGANIZATION REPORT NUMBER	
9. SPONSORING/MONITORING AGENCY NAME(S) AND ADDRESS(ES)		10. SPONSOR/MONITOR'S ACRONYM(S)	
		11. SPONSOR/MONITOR'S REPORT NUMBER(S)	

12. DISTRIBUTION/AVAILABILITY STATEMENT
Approved for public release; distribution unlimited

13. SUPPLEMENTARY NOTES

14. ABSTRACT
see report

15. SUBJECT TERMS

16. SECURITY CLASSIFICATION OF:			17. LIMITATION OF ABSTRACT	18. NUMBER OF PAGES **15**	19a. NAME OF RESPONSIBLE PERSON
a. REPORT **unclassified**	b. ABSTRACT **unclassified**	c. THIS PAGE **unclassified**			

Standard Form 298 (Rev. 8-98)
Prescribed by ANSI Std Z39-18

"Let's look ferocious!"

> -- Secretary of State Henry Kissinger, May 15, 1995, advising
> President Ford to continue with air strikes on the Cambodian
> mainland although the *Mayaguez* and its crew were already free[1]

President Ford considered the May 12-15, 1975 *Mayaguez* affair his most significant

foreign policy decision and one of the highlights of his presidency He asserted in his

memoirs that the administration's decisive and responsible management of the incident

had achieved all its objectives three days after the seizure of the U S-registered

commercial container ship by a Khmer Rouge gunboat some 60 miles off the Cambodian

coast, the vessel and all 40 crewmembers were steaming safely towards their next port

More importantly, Ford was convinced, the administration's swift and aggressive

military response to the seizure had both bolstered the international prestige of the United

States and had given the sagging self-confidence of the American people a needed boost

Though Ford didn't mention it himself, others noted that his standing as president

improved in the immediate aftermath of the rescue, as a 12-point surge in his approval

rating underscored public approbation of the President's handling of the affair [11]

But was the *Mayaguez* affair really an example of the national security process working

in top form? Were all reasonable options scrutinized? Did the response the

administration chose suit the provocation? Were the national objectives identified by the

policy-makers reasonable?   Or, as some observers have suggested, did Ford and his

leading advisors bring to the table a particular mindset -- a way of interpreting the specific incident itself in the context of global and regional developments -- that funneled

them willy-nilly towards a military response and impeded consideration of alternative

actions? The record does indeed suggest that the Ford national security team, its

collective sensitivities raw following several foreign policy disasters, interpreted what

under other circumstances would have been a medium-level bilateral tussle as a "crisis"

in international confidence in the U S The Ford administration then attempted to

resolve the "crisis" by application of brute force, unfortunately with heavy casualties for

the United States In retrospect, the *Mayaguez* affair is less an example of good

decision-making under pressure than a testament to the missteps that can result when

fundamental assumptions about the nature of the problem are not critically vetted

Problem and Response

The President and his advisors acted quickly when word reached the White House early

on May 12, 1975, that a Khmer Rouge gunboat had seized the freighter *Mayaguez* in

coastal waters claimed by the Cambodian government The NSC team swiftly agreed

that U S objectives were (1) to free the ship and crew, and (2) to prove to a doubting

world that America's resolve to keep its commitments and resist adversaries remained

intact In the absence of diplomatic relations with the new Khmer Rouge government,

which had just captured Phnom Penh a few weeks before, the United States attempted to

send a diplomatic protest through the PRC The President also ordered the preparation of

an imposing military rescue effort Reconnaissance planes were sent to track the

Mayaguez's movements, U S naval ships were sent to the Gulf of Thailand, and 1,100

Marines were dispatched to U S installations in Thailand to prepare to take back the ship and crew by force

Although the ship itself was located fairly early on, planning for the rescue of the crew was impeded by uncertainty regarding their whereabouts   Intelligence sources and air surveillance on May 12-14 were unable to confirm whether the crew was still on the ship (The Cambodians had in fact removed the 40 crewmembers early on May 13 and had transferred them to a series of shipboard and land holding sites)   Worried that the crew would be irretrievable should the Cambodians move them onto the mainland, the President ordered U S aircraft to forcibly interdict the movement of Cambodian patrol boats between the *Mayaguez* (then anchored off Koh Tang, an island 34 miles off the Cambodian coast) and the mainland   Three patrol boats were duly sunk and four were immobilized on May 14

On the afternoon of May 14, the President ordered the execution of the plan prepared by the JCS to recover the ship and its crew   Within hours, 131 Marines landed on Koh Tang (May 15 local time) but came under unexpectedly heavy groundfire   Concurrently, the Navy inserted Marines on board the *Mayaguez* (which turned out to be deserted), and air strikes were initiated against an oil depot and other military installations around Kompong Som harbor on the Cambodian mainland   Meanwhile, unbeknown to the U S but before the Marines landed on Koh Tang, the Khmer Rouge released the crew and put them all on a Thai fishing boat By mid-morning on May 15, all forty were safely transferred to a U S naval vessel The extraction of Marines from Koh Tang, however, proved to be extremely dangerous Casualties were serious More troops had to be sent

in to cover the withdrawal, and not until the early evening on May 15 (local time) were

all surviving U S combatants off the island [iii]

Post- Mortem

After the euphoria and hoopla of the rescue subsided, more details surfaced, inviting

scrutiny and raising questions that are still debated Critics taken aback by the human

cost of the operation attacked the assertions of President Ford and his major advisors that

the robust military response to the capture had been justified, prudent, and appropriate to

the provocation Early celebrants didn't know, and later administration supporters did

not emphasize, that 41 U S soldiers died and 50 Marines were injured in the attempt to

rescue 40 crewmembers and retrieve the freighter Operationally, critics observed, the

rescue mission hardly deserved the trumpeting the administration gave it [iv]

Other critics focused on the administration's determination to plan and proceed with a

risky military operation despite what decision-makers knew was faulty, tardy, and

insufficient intelligence Bad information on the capacities of the Cambodian defense

forces on Koh Tang was largely responsible for the high death toll among the attacking

Marines Equally dubious intelligence combined with aggressive military action nearly

cost the lives of the *Mayaguez* crew, who came under fire from U S planes when being

ferried about by the Cambodians It was clear that luck, rather than the competence of the military rescuers, had a great deal to do with the successful return of the crew and that the whole operation was very nearly a disaster [v]

Others -- and not just U S observers -- were disturbed that Washington had been so quick to go to a High Noon scenario, provoking and staking all on a military confrontation while shortchanging the opportunities for a diplomatic resolution These critics pointed out that the U S had given up very easily when early efforts to communicate with the Cambodian government through the Chinese had not worked out The U S had ignored the U N Secretary General's appeal to exhaust diplomatic resolutions before reaching for a military resolution Washington's ultimatums had also forced a timetable on the Cambodians which that government, new and disorganized, could not meet. [vi]

Then there were those uncomfortable with what they saw as the latest demonstration of the U S propensity for high-handed behavior in Southeast Asia   A chief complaint on this score was the Ford administration's violation of Thai sovereignty   Over the explicit and vocal objections of the Thai government, the U S rescue mission was run out of a U S base in Thailand   Although the Thais were (at least officially) mollified by a U S apology immediately after the event, Washington's willingness to run roughshod over the Thai government was interpreted by critics as a blow to U S credibility as an honest partner in Asia [vii]

Domestically, Ford's decisions to attack Cambodian naval ships and to bomb the Cambodian mainland were questioned by supporters of the 1973 War Powers Act, who argued that the President had violated the spirit if not the letter of the act by failing to consult fully with the Congressional leadership before ordering troops into action [viii] In fact, Ford or other administration representatives had briefed members of the House and Senate several times during May 13-14 and the President had even met with the bipartisan leadership late on May 14   Sure that the War Powers resolution did not apply to the *Mayaguez* case, however, the President did not ask for Congressional concurrence with any of his decisions, he simply explained them   Although he dismissed later complaints from "liberals in the press and Congress" that he had violated the War Powers Act, the President did decide to send a report on the operation to the leaders of the House and Senate immediately at the end of the incident [ix]

Having anticipated much of the criticism later leveled at them for their management of the *Mayaguez* challenge, President Ford and his national security team dealt were relatively unperturbed by the post-incident bleats   The operational and tactical aspects of the U S response had, after all, been thoroughly discussed during the course of four formal NSC meetings and numerous one-on-one discussions between May 12 and May 15   The President and his inner circle (Secretary of State Kissinger, Secretary of Defense James Schlesinger, and Deputy National Security Advisor Brent Scowcroft) had consulted experts and high-level representatives from the military and other pertinent agencies before refining the details of the military operation   All knew very well that the operation was risky   the JCS had estimated there would be between 20 and 40 casualties [x]   Though unhappy with the lack of intelligence information, and frustrated by the slow flow of news from the action site to Washington (the 11-hour time difference did not help), the President accepted that making important decisions with incomplete information was part of his executive responsibilities [xi] He also did not "give a damn about offending" the sensibilities of the Thais and thought their protests were pro forma [xii]

The administration argued that diplomatic solutions had not been neglected – they had just not been effective given the perceived necessity for a speedy retrieval of the crew Not only had the U S attempted to send a message demanding the release of the ship to the Cambodians through the PRC the first day of the crisis, the State Department had tried to deliver a similar message through Beijing on the second day   On the afternoon of May 14, the U S had also formally requested U N assistance in securing the release of the ship and its crew [xiii] Ford pointed out that he had authorized the issuance of a last minute public statement offering to cease military operations on receipt of a firm Cambodian promise to release the crew [xiv]

Mindset over Matter

Operational issues aside, the real question to be asked concerning the Ford administration's handling of the *Mayaguez* affair is how the decision-makers came to interpret the seizure of a rusty freighter as a major threat to overall U S security interests The answer to this question is key to understanding the White House's immediate, almost gut-instinct decision to go for a Great Power military response, it explains as well the President's fixation on an offensive military engagement despite its serious problems and unavoidable risks What the record indicates is that the reactions of the President and Secretary of State Kissinger in particular were very much determined by a mindset that virtually ruled out any real effort to find a resolution on terms other than a military zero sum victory In the *Mayaguez* case, the military tool was chosen less because it suited the immediate task of freeing the ship and crew than because it projected to the world an image of the United States that served what the White House, State Department, and NSC saw as the U S 's broader foreign policy goals [xv]

It was the special timing of the seizure that determined the shape of the Ford team's response What at a later or earlier period might have been seen as a pesky problem for the State Department to iron out -- after all, the Cambodian navy had intercepted and temporarily held a number of ships from various countries before the *Mayaguez* was taken -- became a showdown that the President, Kissinger, and apparently much of the inner circle were convinced would have international ramifications of the most serious kind

Ford's aides also knew that, handled as a demonstration of presidential authority and grit, the *Mayaguez* affair could have positive domestic repercussions for Ford's credibility as Commander-in-Chief Ford had an image problem He had been in office only nine months when the *Mayaguez* was seized As the only non-elected president in U S history, he lacked a personal mandate to govern His capacity to lead the country had been famously questioned by such well-known detractors as Lyndon Johnson Ford's public image was a likeable but bumbling guy of mediocre intelligence His advisors saw, as one noted, that the *Mayaguez* was his "first acid test" as Commander in Chief [xvi]

Ford also saw the incident as an opportunity for Americans to "view another side of their

President " [xvii] Ford appears to have been predisposed to an aggressive, photo-op

response that showed him firmly in charge, diplomatic finesse or other quiet resolution of

the problem wouldn't have had the same effect in changing the President's image

Even more important in shaping administration thinking, however, was the international

context of the capture Less than two weeks before the incident, the last Americans had

ignominiously fled Saigon as the city finally fell to the North Vietnamese The scenes of

panic and raw *sauve qui peut* despair shot on the roof of the U S embassy in Saigon were

beamed around the world This humiliation followed almost directly on the heels of the

U S evacuation of Phnom Penh when the Khmer Rouge seized control of the Cambodian

capital April 17 Ford and Kissinger were convinced that the last sorry chapter of the

ten-year U S debacle in Southeast Asia had severely damaged U S international prestige

and undercut American credibility around the world Kissinger predicted dourly that the

surrender had "ushered in a period of American humiliation" across the globe [xviii] Ford

was concerned that the defeat in Vietnam and Cambodia had led even good friends like

the British and Israelis to doubt the "resolve" of the United States to stand by its overseas

commitments The President was determined "not to permit our setbacks to become a

license for others to fish in troubled waters" and was equally resolved to prove that

America would stand firm with more than rhetoric [xix]

Both the President and Kissinger agreed that the *Mayaguez* incident provided an opportunity to provide that proof. During the first NSC meeting on May 12, Kissinger had emotionally argued that what was at stake was far more than the seizure of a ship it was the international perception of U S resolve and will Ford agreed when Kissinger said the U S response had to be strong and firm, the U S had to draw the line and show that it could not be pushed around The whole world was watching to see if the withdrawal in Southeast Asia meant the U S had lost its resolve to stand up against aggression [xx] In the May 13 NSC meeting, Kissinger again took the same line, arguing for a dramatic show of force on the grounds that a sensational move would help restore the tainted U S credibility Worried about North Korean intentions on the peninsula, the Secretary also thought that a forceful U S response might deter the North Koreans from launching an offensive against the south [xxi]

Apparently alone among the NSC members, Defense Secretary Schlesinger focused on the *Mayaguez* as a specific problem rather than as a symbol of American resolve to wave in front of a skeptical world (Note Schlesinger seems to have made his disagreement count later in the rescue, when the Pentagon quietly neglected to carry out all the bombing raids ordered by the President) [xxii] The rest of the major decision-makers saw the *Mayaguez* principally in terms of a specific Big Picture interpretation of recent events in the region the capture of the *Mayaguez* was an international crisis for the United States, it was a deliberate challenge that demanded a quick and tough response, and the right response was to flex military muscle From the first NSC meeting on, an aggressive and forceful response was the only one seriously considered, subsequent decisions mainly concerned the type, timing, and details of the military response The conviction

that the world was intently watching and judging America's future actions by its behavior

in the *Mayaguez* made a swift response imperative -- no time to wait for diplomatic

wheels to grind, no waiting for the U N or other friends to be helpful, no hold-ups for

intelligence reports to come in -- and a hard, robust military response the only option

worth serious consideration From this point of view, the potential costs of inserting U S

military into a dangerously uncertain situation were absolutely justified on national

security grounds This kind of thinking made it possible for the national security team to

give serious consideration to massive retaliatory and punitive B-52 strikes against the

Cambodian mainland

A second preconception was crucial in shaping the President's assessment of the

challenge and his choice of response Ford immediately drew an analogy between the

seizure of the *Mayaguez* and the 1968 *Pueblo* incident, in which the North Koreans

captured a U S naval intelligence ship, killed a sailor, and imprisoned and mistreated the

crew for nearly a year. [xxiii] Ford considered the *Pueblo* incident a "benchmark" for his

handling of the *Mayaguez* challenge His repeated references to the *Pueblo* indicate the

degree to which that experience colored his decisions with *Mayaguez* The *Pueblo* case

was raised during the first NSC meeting, and Ford recalls in his memoirs that he

discussed the fate of the navy ship and its crew with Schlesinger early on May 13 He

told Schlesinger he would not allow history to repeat itself by losing control of the crew

The President's order to the Pentagon to do what it took to ensure that movement between Koh Tang and the coast was interdicted was issued specifically to prevent the transfer of the *Mayaguez*'s crew to the mainland [xxiv]

However, the analogy between the *Pueblo* and the *Mayaguez* wasn't all that tight, and comparing the two – and framing options accordingly – did little to help the NSC assess the *Mayaguez* situation on its own merits [xxv] The *Mayaguez* was a privately owned freighter, not a Navy vessel filled with sensitive gear, its crew did not have classified knowledge of interest to hostile governments In contrast to the men on the intelligence ship, the *Mayaguez's* crew had limited value as hostages Additionally, the specific role the Cambodian government played in masterminding the capture of the *Mayaguez*, as well as the intentions of those who decided to seize the American vessel, were and remain unclear

In a stunningly telling passage, Ford relates in his memoirs that, during the final NSC meeting on May 14, White House photographer David Hume Kennerly broke into the middle of a discussion on airstrikes against the Cambodian mainland to ask whether anyone had considered that the seizure might simply be an act of piracy by the local commander rather than the execution of orders from Phnom Penh [xxvi] The answer was no Kennerly had put his finger on the central flaw of the Ford team's management of the *Mayaguez* preconceptions and unquestioned assumptions inhibited thorough analysis of the problem at hand The question of the identity and intentions of the perpetrators of the seizure was one of several issues that should have been raised at the first, not the last, NSC meeting Given the chaos in Cambodia and the lack of intelligence concerning the new government, Ford should have been less hasty to (1) take it as a given that the Khmer Rouge central command was behind the capture of the Mayaguez, and (2) interpret the seizure as a deliberate kick in the pants to a wounded giant [xxvii] Had he been less seized with what he thought were the lessons of the *Pueblo* analogy, Ford might have taken more time to explore diplomatic options – which were in fact looking rather promising by May 15 -- or to wait for better intelligence before directing the Marines at risky and useless targets Had Ford and Kissinger been less blinkered by the humiliation in Vietnam, less consumed by the imperative to send rah-rah signals to all those Doubting Thomas nations, they might have been more open to explore ways to resolve the *Mayaguez* problem by finesse rather than ferocity, and to impress enemies and friends with U S brains rather than brawn

[i] Ron Nessen, *It Sure Looks Different from the Inside* (Chicago Simon & Schuster, 1978). 129

[ii] The President's approval rating went up from 39% to 51% Nessen, *It Sure Looks Different*, 129-131, Gerald Ford, *A Time to Heal* (New York Harper and Row, 1979), 283-84, Walter Isaacson *Kissinger A Biography* (New York Simon & Schuster, 1992), 651

[iii] A detailed account of the movements of the crew and the Mayaguez is in Roy Rowan, *The Four Days of Mayaguez* (New York W W Norton & Co , 1975) For descriptions of the Washington decision-making process, see Ford, *A Time*, Isaacson, *Kissinger*, Richard G Head, Frisco W Short, and Robert C McFarlane, *Crisis Resolution Presidential Decision-Making in the Mayaguez and Korean Confrontations* (Boulder, Co WestView Press, 1978), and Christopher Jon Lamb, *Belief Systems and Decision Making in the Mayaguez Crisis* (Gainesville, Florida The University of Florida Press, 1989), and Kennedy School of Government, *The Mayaguez Incident* (Mss , Harvard College, 1983)

[iv] 23 Marines were killed in a helicopter crash in Thailand, 18 Marines were killed in action or missing in ground fighting in Cambodia Lamb, *Belief Systems*, 29-31

[v] Several crewmembers were hit by shrapnel Rowan, *Four Days*, 133-137

[vi] Kennedy School, *Mayaguez*, 19 A GAO study commissioned by the Senate agreed that insufficient time and attention had been given to diplomacy See Head. *Crisis Resolution*, 144

[vii] See, for instance, Michael Morrow "Ford Fastest Gun in the East," *Far Eastern Economic Review*, May 30, 1975, 10-11, William Shawcross, "Making the Most of Mayaguez," *Far Eastern Economic Review*, May 30, 1975, 11-12, Norman Peagam, "Thailand's Turn to Protest," *Far Eastern Economic Review*, May 30, 1975, 12-13

[viii] Senators Harry Byrd and Mike Mansfield were particularly upset, Senator Tom Eagleton demanded a GAO study of the administration's handling of the Mayaguez in June Kennedy School, *Mayaguez*, 18

[ix] Ford, *Time to Heal*, 280-81, Kennedy School, *Mayaguez*, 17-19

[x] Oddly, the question about possible casualties was not raised until late in planning, and then was not raised by one of the principals Robert T Hartmann, *Palace Politics An Inside Account of the Ford Years* (New York McGraw-Hill, 1980), 327

[xi] Nessen, *It Sure Looks Different*, 131

[xii] Ford, *Time to Heal*, 276-277

[xiii] Kennedy School, *Mayaguez*, 14

[xiv] Nessen, *It Sure Looks Different*, 125-26

[xv] Secretary of Defense Schlesinger did not share this view, which explains his disinclination for a robust military response Ford, *Time to Heal*, 279

[xvi] Hartmann, *Palace Politics*, 324

[xvii] Ford, *Time to Heal*, 276

[xviii] Isaacson, *Kissinger*, 647

[xix] Ford, *Time to Heal*, 275

[xx] Ford, Ibid , 276, Isaacson, *Kissinger*, 649, Nessen, *It Sure Looks Different*, 118

[xxi] Kennedy Schook, *Mayaguez*, 12, Isaacson, *Kissinger*, 649

[xxii] The JSC was also hesitant to use force, but mainly because they wanted more time to plan a successful operation Isaacson, *Kissinger*, 649-50, Kennedy School, *Mayaguez*, 12

[xxiii] Ford, *Time to Heal*, 277

[xxiv] Ibid , 277

[xxv] An excellent discussion of the President's emphasis on the Pueblo as the analogy to the Mayaguez, and the differences between the two, can be found in Richard E Neustadt and Ernest R May, *Thinking in Time The Uses of History for Decision-Makers* (New York The Free Press, 1986), 58-66

[xxvi] Ford, *Time to Heal*, 279-80

[xxvii] It is worth noting, for instance, that *Mayaguez* was not flying identification flags when taken Rowan, *Four Days*, 198

NAVAL WAR COLLEGE
Newport, R.I.

THE MAYAGUEZ INCIDENT
A Failure in Operational Leadership

by

Glenn T. Starnes

Major, United States Marine Corps

Accesion For

NTIS CRA&I	✗
DTIC TAB	☑
Unannounced	☐
Justification	

By ....
Distribution /

Availability Codes

| Dist | Avail and / or Special |

A-1

A paper submitted to the Faculty of the College of Naval Command and Staff in partial satisfaction of the requirements of the Department of Operations.

The contents of this paper reflect my own personal views and are not necessarily endorsed by the Naval War College or the Department of the Navy.

Signature: _Glenn T. Starnes_

16 June 1995

DTIC
SELECTED
APR 1 8 1995
G

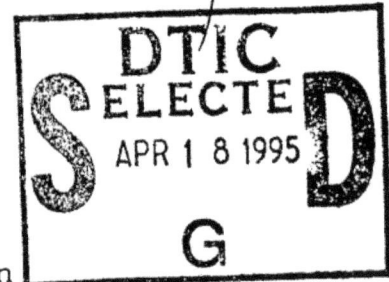

Paper directed by Captain D. Watson
Chairman, Joint Military Operations Department
Commander Robert P. Schoultz, USN

_____   136695
Faculty Advisor   Date

19950417 048

REPORT DOCUMENTATION PAGE

1. Report Security Classification: Unclassified	
2. Security Classification Authority:	
3. Declassification/Downgrading Schedule:	
4. Distribution/Availability of Report:	DISTRIBUTION STATEMENT A: APPROVED FOR PUBLIC RELEASE; DISTRIBUTION IS UNLIMITED.
5. Name of Performing Organization: Joint Military Operations Department	

6. Office Symbol: 1C	**7. Address:** Naval War College 686 Cushing Rd. Newport, RI 02841-5010

8. Title (Include Security Classification): The Mayaguez Incident : A Failure in Operational Leadership (U)

9. Personal Authors: Starnes, Glenn T., MAJ, USMC

10. Type of Report: Final	**11. Date of Report:** 950213

12. Page Count: 28

13. Supplementary Notation: A paper submitted to the Faculty of the Naval War College in partial satisfaction of the requirements of the Joint Military Operations Department. The contents of this paper reflect my own personal views and are not necessarily endorsed by the Naval War College or the Department of the Navy.

14. Ten key words that relate to your paper: Mayaguez, Hostage Rescue, Cambodia, Southeast Asia, President Ford, Kissinger, Operational Leadership, USSAG/7thAF, NSC and Crisis Action, Heliborne Assaults

15. Abstract: On 15 May 1975, the United States successfully conducted a hostage rescue mission off the coast of Cambodia. The tactical forces recaptured the Mayaguez, a U.S. cargo container ship, and rescued the forty-man crew. The success and political euphoria of the Mayaguez crisis resolution championed this relatively small tactical mission encompassing strategic implications. Unfortunately, the euphoria hid a number of failure at the operational level of war. Heroic tactical actions and pure "good luck" overcame these failures in planning, coordination, and execution/supervision to achieve success. Through research and operational analysis, this paper examines these faiures. Military rescue missions, more often than not, have strategic implications because of the threat to national or international prestige. The art of command and leadership at the operational level is an essential element to ensure successful strategic/tactical mission accomplishment. The intervening twenty years since Mayaguez have seen a greater emphasis placed on operational art, yet the execution of operational leadership must constantly be studied to ensure proper application. The Mayaguez incident provides an excellent example for the study of operational leadership in strategic/tactcal missions.

16. Distribution/ Availability of Abstract:	Unclassified XX	Same As Rpt	DTIC Users

18. Abstract Security Classification: Unclassified

19. Name of Responsible Individual: Chairman, Joint Military Operations Department

20. Telephone: (401) 841-3414/4120	**21. Office Symbol:** 1C

Abstract of

THE MAYAGUEZ INCIDENT
A Failure in Operational Leadership

On 15 May 1975, the United States successfully conducted a hostage rescue mission off the coast of Cambodia. The tactical forces recaptured the Mayaguez, a U.S. cargo container ship, and rescued the forty-man crew. The success and political euphoria of the Mayaguez crisis resolution championed this relatively small tactical mission encompassing strategic implications. Unfortunately, the euphoria hid a number of failures at the operational level of war. Heroic tactical actions and pure "good luck" overcame these failures in planning, coordination and execution/supervision to achieve success. Through research and operational analysis, this paper examines these failures. Military rescue missions, more often than not, have strategic implications because of the threat to national or international prestige. The art of command and leadership at the operational level is an essential element to ensure successful strategic/ tactical mission accomplishment. The intervening twenty years since Mayaguez have seen a greater emphasis placed on operational art, yet the execution of operational leadership must constantly be studied to ensure proper application. The Mayaguez incident provides an excellent example for the study of operational leadership in strategic/tactical missions.

Preface

I began this study intending to show how the U.S. military has improved its ability to conduct strategic/ tactical missions in the twenty years since the Mayaguez incident. I knew problems had occurred during the mission in May 1975. I did not realize the magnitude of the failures at the operational level. The scope of my paper quickly changed from a comparison of twenty years of rescue missions to an analysis of operational failures during the Mayaguez crisis. Unexplored in this paper is the question, "Has the military improved and/or corrected the numerous operational failures present at Mayaguez?" I believe the military has improved its ability to conduct operational art. But that improvement was not a result of Mayaguez. It took the Desert One disaster, growing pains in Urgent Fury and Congressional directives to start the military on the road to improvement. I believe a comparison study of these events with the failures at Mayaguez would show that had the military conducted a proper analysis of Mayaguez in 1975, they could have started on the road to improvement five years earlier. That comparison study is beyond the scope of this paper. I have laid the foundation. Someone else can build the bridge.

Table of Contents

INTRODUCTION

At face value, military rescue missions appear to be tactical in nature. Nothing could be further from the truth if the mission affects strategic policy or national prestige. Terrorists and/or third world nationalist/ethnic forces use the seizure of hostages to embarrass, humiliate or affect their target country's prestige or international standing. The resolution of a hostage crisis elevates a tactical military rescue to a strategic/tactical mission. The requirement for operational command and leadership is essential to translate strategic desires into tactical objectives, as well as plan, coordinate and execute/supervise the strategic/tactical mission. If the operational effort fails to meet its requirements, the success of the mission is left to luck or chance. During the Mayaguez incident in 1975, luck saved an operational fiasco. Personnel working at the operational level need to study the many failures in this "lucky" success. In the absence of luck, military leaders must possess carefully honed skills at the operational level to achieve victory.

BACKGROUND SUMMARY

On 12 May 1975, Khmer Rouge forces fired upon, boarded and seized a U.S. commercial cargo ship, the S.S. Mayaguez, as she traversed international waters. Cambodian gunboats escorted the cargo ship to the nearby island of Koh Tang. The Cambodians took the forty-man crew off the ship and later transferred them to a different island. Within hours of notification (via a distress signal) of the seizure of the Mayaguez, President

Gerald Ford convened a meeting of the National Security Council (NSC) to discuss a response to the Cambodian piracy. Over the next 60 hours, the NSC met three additional times. (Appendix A provides a timeline relating actions and events to the time span involved.) At this first meeting, the president directed Secretary of State Henry Kissinger explore diplomatic channels to obtain the release of the ship and her crew. He also directed the NSC develop a military contingency plan.

When diplomatic efforts proved fruitless, President Ford ordered the immediate execution of the contingency plan. At 0615 (local) 15 May, Marines (pre-staged at an airbase in Utapao, Thailand) conducted a heliborne assault of Koh Tang, believing the Mayaguez crew was on the island. A second group of Marines boarded the anchored and surprisingly vacant Mayaguez from a Navy destroyer.

The assault on Koh Tang encountered a regular, well-armed Cambodian force numbering nearly 200 strong (five times the intelligence estimates). The Marines found themselves out-numbered and out-gunned. Air Force aircraft provided close air support fires for the assault forces while carrier-based Navy aircraft bombed NSC-approved targets on the Cambodian mainland to prevent enemy reinforcement. Enroute to Koh Tang to provide naval gunfire support, the U.S.S. Wilson encountered the crew of the Mayaguez, free, unharmed and aboard a Thai fishing boat. With both the cargo ship and her crew safely retrieved, President Ford ordered a halt to offensive actions.

The Marines on Koh Tang could not disengage or attempt a helicopter extract without additional combat forces aboard a scheduled second assault wave. With their arrival, the Marines eventually stabilized their defenses. Enemy fire damaged most of the available helicopters during the two assault waves. By late afternoon, only 4 of 13 available aircraft remained operational. The extraction began at 1520. The last Marines departed Koh Tang (still under intense enemy fire) at 2015. Total casualties amounted to 15 killed in action, 50 wounded and 3 Marines missing. Of the 13 helicopters involved, 2 crashed on Koh Tang and the remaining 9 aircraft were severely damaged by enemy fire.[1]

President Ford and his advisors rejoiced at the successful accomplishment of the rescue mission. Newspapers and magazines proclaimed a strong comeback for American prestige in the Far East. Some criticisms and analytical observations of the mission surfaced initially but were quickly subjugated to a file drawer. If military and political leaders identified the numerous failures at the operational level, they soon forgot or left them unanswered.

UNITY OF COMMAND

Even though Mayaguez was a relatively small tactical mission, there existed a definite need for an operational level command structure to provide unity of command. (Appendix B provides the ad hoc command relationships formed for the Mayaguez mission.) The military contingency plan developed by

3

the NSC tasked Admiral Noel Gaylor, Commander-in-Chief Pacific Forces (CinCPac), to prepare forces for a forceful rescue mission. Admiral Gaylor assigned Lieutenant General John Burns, Chief of the U.S. Support Activities Group and Commander of the 7th Air Force (USSAG/7thAF) in Thailand, as the "on-scene commander" (which roughly equates to Commander Joint Task Force). The selection of LtGen Burns ensured the tactical forces would receive the aviation assets needed to conduct the mission.

Contrary to standard practice, neither the Joint Chiefs of Staff (JCS) nor CinCPac assigned responsibility for the mission in message format.[2] This led to problems in planning and coordinating the mission. Lieutenant General Burns believed he had "received command of all inbound ships and planes, with full authority to call on more." In fact, the on-scene commander never received operational control of Navy and Marine forces. Admiral Gaylor directed Navy and Marine commands in the Pacific "to respond to the direction and tasking of USSAG/7thAF and to conduct contingency operations as directed by CinCPac and USSAG/7thAF." Of particular note, the carrier-based aircraft providing operational fires, never came under USSAG\7thAF control.[3] From the beginning, the rescue mission lacked the primary element of operational leadership, unity of command.

LACK OF GROUND REPRESENTATION

Lieutenant General Burns organized an ad hoc, joint force for the rescue mission. He utilized his USSAG/7thAF staff (all

4

Air Force) for operational planning and execution. He realized time constraints would eliminate any chance for coordination and inhibit information flow to the tactical forces. Accordingly, he asked for a senior Marine to serve as overall commander of ground forces.

Colonel John Johnson, USMC, assumed the role of ground forces commander (TG 79.9). Charged with establishing a liaison between the tactical forces and the operational staff, Col Johnson chose to remain with the tactical forces at Utapao, Thailand. He relied on communication assets to execute any coordination/liaison with USSAG/7thAF in Nakhon Phanon, Thailand. His presence enhanced the planning for the helicopter assault but coordination with USSAG/7thAF and execution of the entire rescue mission suffered. Marine representation was nonexistent at the operational level and led to a breakdown in the flow of vital information to the tactical forces. Colonel Johnson failed to provide required advisory knowledge to the operational staff to assist in decision making.[4]

Colonel Johnson wanted to participate in the assault on Koh Tang. Lack of helicopters demanded he and his staff remain at Utapao. Mistakenly believing he could control all ground force actions from Koh Tang, he elected not to place a Marine representative on the Airborne Command, Control and Communication (ABCCC) aircraft which LtGen Burns had designated the focal point for all rescue mission activities. Colonel Johnson communicated with USSAG/7thAF in Nakhon Phanon by telephone. He planned on communicating with the assault forces on Koh Tang via the ABCCC. For unknown reasons, the ABCCC never established the communications link to Utapao.[5] Colonel Johnson's self-imposed isolation at Utapao effectively turned over operational control of all ground forces to the Air Force's on scene coordinator. The senior Marine for the Mayaguez mission became an irrelevant bystander.

INFORMATION FLOW

Several lapses in the flow of information to the tactical forces occurred at the operational level. Lieutenant Colonel Randall Austin, commander of the assault forces on Koh Tang, embarked on the first assault wave with the assumption pre-assault fires would engage and neutralize the island's defenses. Enemy forces had previously fired on reconnaissance aircraft. Pilots referred to the anti-aircraft defenses as "pretty good" and "a sure thing." An AC-130 Spectra gunship was on station, prepared to deliver accurate, pre-assault fire support. Although CinCPac had authorized such fires and LtCol Austin had requested them, LtGen Burns decided against pre-assault fires, fearing endangerment of the Mayaguez crew. Neither he nor his staff informed the assault forces of his decision. Enemy fire damaged 7 of 8 helicopters in the first assault wave. All but one friendly battle death occurred during the insert of the assault forces.[6]

Lieutenant Colonel Austin also departed for Koh Tang with inadequate intelligence estimates. During operational planning sessions, several estimates of enemy strength surfaced. Reports of enemy forces on Koh Tang ranged from 20 to 30 people without leadership to 90 or 100 soldiers with a few heavy weapons. A Defense Intelligence Agency (DIA) report estimated 200 regular soldiers with sufficient fire power and anti-aircraft weapons defended the island.[7] During post mission interviews, more than one USSAG/7thAF staff officer indicated "estimates of enemy strength were not of particular concern to them."[8] The designated Mayaguez operational staff failed to reconcile the wide disparages in the estimates of enemy strength. They never passed on the DIA estimate to the tactical planners at Utapao.[9]

OPERATIONAL PLANNING

Lack of a well organized and fully representative operational staff led to failures in operational planning, specifically the employment of naval and air forces and lack of operational reconnaissance. Although the USSAG/7thAF staff lacked Navy representation, they planned the employment of expected naval warships. Their plan called for two destroyers, the U.S.S. Holt and Wilson, to provide gunfire and search and rescue (SAR) support. They also directed the Holt assist in the seizure of the Mayaguez. This task effectively kept the destroyer occupied during the first ten hours of the Koh Tang assault. Although the assault was scheduled for 0615, the second destroyer, Wilson, was not scheduled to arrive until 0730. Upon Wilson's arrival, CinCPac directed her to intercept a Thai fishing boat spotted by Air Force pilots. The boat had

7

the Mayaguez crew aboard. Finally, when the commander of Destroyer Squadron 23 (DESRON 23), in charge of Holt and Wilson, contacted the ABCCC for mission assignments and tasking, the ABCCC failed to task DESRON 23 with providing naval gunfire support. The designated on scene operational coordinator never even informed the Navy component command of the Koh Tang assault plans.[10]

When Adm Gaylor assigned LtGen Burns the Mayaguez mission, he directed the USSAG/7thAF commander "provide detailed plans for, among other things, employment of TacAir . . . ." The operational staff failed to assume and plan airborne forward air control (FAC) and SAR responsibilities. After action reports showed that during the first 8 hours of the assault, 10 different airborne FACs were used with at least 14 different turnovers. Although OV-10s, the aircraft best suited to perform the airborne FAC and SAR duties, were available, the USSAG/7thAF staff neither requested nor planned their utilization.

Even more inconceivable than poor air support planning was the staff's failure to use all means available to protect the finite number of helicopters available for the mission. Knowing the threat of anti-aircraft fire existed, the operational staff allowed the troop helicopters to conduct the assault without escort gunships.[11] The absence of pre-assault fires made escort suppressive fire an imperative.

Finally, in developing the enemy situation and the operational plan, the USSAG/7thAF staff failed to conduct a detailed pre-assault reconnaissance of Koh Tang. Apparently, the Air Force staff cared little about beach defenses, enemy positions and locations of the captive Mayaguez crewmen. The time and assets existed to conduct a reconnaissance, yet the operational staff never requested the forces. Pilot reconnaissance reports of 13 May indicated a Cambodian gunboat transported 30 to 40 caucasians to the mainland.[12] As with other incongruent reports, the USSAG/7thAF staff seems to have ignored this report since it did not support their plan.

FAILURES IN EXECUTION

Failures in unity of command, information flow and operational planning paved the way for additional problems at the operational level during execution of the rescue mission. The Marines on Koh Tang constantly updated their situation to the ABCCC. Unfortunately, the ABCCC failed to keep the Marines informed as to the status of the entire Mayaguez mission. Four hours after the initial assault found the Marines trying to consolidate and hold their defensive positions, desperately awaiting reinforcements. Known in the ABCCC but not relayed to LtCol Austin, LtGen Burns (possibly at the direction of CinCPac) had cancelled the scheduled second assault wave because the Mayaguez crew had turned up safe and unharmed. Apparently, the ABCCC (the only asset talking to the forces on Koh Tang) was not accurately reporting the status of the assault forces to the operational commander. Eventually, the second wave reinforced LtCol Austin's men. The ABCCC never explained the delay to the

Marines on Koh Tang. Lieutenant Colonel Austin learned of the crew's rescue from the Marines on the second wave.[13]

The flaws in operational command and leadership that led to the previously discussed failures also allowed actions at the national/strategic level to affect the tactical mission. I want to concentrate on two specific areas: the overabundance of decision making at the strategic level on matters of an operational and tactical nature; and, the failure at the operational level to properly translate the strategic intent or primary objective of this tactical mission encompassing strategic implications.

OVERABUNDANCE OF DECISION MAKING

Citing the Government Accounting Office (GAO) report of the Mayaguez incident, Christopher Lamb stated, "Washington had better communications with the tactical fighting forces than did the local commander. . . . So centrally controlled were the military operations that the president could make on-the-spot decisions" concerning the mission.[14] The unique communications capabilities of the Command Center in the White House provided the strategic decision makers the ability to bypass the operational commander and affect tactical decisions and actions during the Mayaguez crisis. Unfortunately, the operational command was not strong enough to exert its authority and intercept this strategic interference.

The National Security Council considered five military options proposed by the JCS and chose a coordinated rescue plan.

The mission consisted of a heliborne assault of Koh Tang by one Marine force, the seizure of the Mayaguez by a separate Marine boarding party, and the bombing of mainland targets to prevent enemy reinforcement. The NSC wanted the operational fires (the mainland bombings) to coincide with the seizure and the assault. LtCol Austin wanted to conduct a night assault of Koh Tang to achieve an element of surprise. The NSC denied his request since the boarding party required daylight to search the Mayaguez.

The NSC must have had a strategic or political reason for requiring simultaneous actions. Unfortunately, they failed to communicate their reason to subordinate echelons. A last minute change in the tactical employment of forces, ordered by CinCPac, delayed the seizure of the ship and the mainland bombings.[15] If the USSAG/7thAF commander had understood the NSC's intent, he could have delayed the assault of Koh Tang.

The ad hoc operational command structure employed by LtGen Burns enabled CinCPac to easily affect tactical actions. On 15 May, Adm Gaylor bypassed both LtGen Burns and Col Johnson by ordering LtCol Austin on Koh Tang to neither "hazard his force" nor "take offensive action without waiting for reinforcements." This led to confusion at the tactical level. As the fighting continued on Koh Tang, Adm Gaylor grew anxious and fearful of the Cambodians overrunning the Marine positions. Without consulting or even informing the Marines, he directed the employment of the 15,000 pound BLU-82, the largest conventional bomb in the U.S. arsenal, on the enemy defenses at Koh Tang. He wanted to "apply maximum psychological pressure against [the] Cambodian soldiers." The Marines saw the parachute-delivered bomb deploy and believed it was a resupply attempt that missed the drop zone. After recovering from the explosion's concussion, they were glad the "resupply" missed the drop zone.[16]

Failures in operational leadership also allowed President Ford to affect actions at the tactical level with decisions made hastily at the strategic level. During the execution of the mission, he ordered the carrier, the U.S.S. Coral Sea, to delay the first of four strike packages aimed at operational targets on the mainland after the aircraft had already launched. Although he rescinded his order five minutes later, the strike aircraft were unable to act and react fast enough and failed to hit their targets.[17]

The capability for instant communications between the strategic decision makers and the "trigger pullers" consistently left the USSAG/7thAF staff and LtGen Burns in the dark. The operational commander failed to divorce the NSC, JCS and CinCPac from the tactical action. Asked whether an overabundance of supervision of the rescue mission existed, a Pentagon general said, "Let's say there was enough."[18] Reading between the lines, I would say "enough" was too much supervision at the strategic level. That interference endangered the tactical mission and the lives of every fighting participant.

TRANSLATING STRATEGIC INTENT

President Ford and the members of the NSC approached the Mayaguez incident as a final test of U.S. foreign policy in Southeast Asia. During the previous month, U.S. forces had conducted the final military evacuations of both Cambodia and South Vietnam. American prestige in the Far East region was at an all time low in May 1975. The abandonment of former allies, plus the diplomatic humiliation the United States had suffered over North Korea's seizure of the U.S.S. Pueblo in 1968, influenced the national leaders' decision making ability.

In the absence of a speedy diplomatic solution, America's response to the seizure of the Mayaguez had to be quick and forceful. President Ford commented later, the United States had to "dispel doubts about U.S. will and its capacity to respond to provocation." The force must be sufficient enough to send a proper message of intent to the Far East.[19] At the first meeting of the NSC on 12 May, the members "quickly agreed on the two foremost U.S. objectives: to recover the ship and its crew; and, to do so in such a way as to demonstrate firmly to the international community that the United States could and would act with firmness to protect its interests . . . ."[20]

Although the State Department and the White House explored diplomatic channels in an attempt to solve the crisis, the NSC proceeded with the development of a forceful military response. They approved the basic strategy of a simultaneous, two pronged, Marine assault and the bombing of Cambodia at their third meeting on the night of 13 May. The president and many of his advisors believed the size of the force must be overwhelming. According to Secretary Kissinger, "The excessive use of force [would] demonstrate that there are limits beyond which the U.S. will not be pushed."[21]

In his analysis of the crisis, Daniel Bolger determined three strategic objectives existed for the Mayaguez mission: secure the crew of the Mayaguez; secure the Mayaguez; and, prevent Khmer Rouge reinforcement.[22] While the objectives listed above are more appropriately operational/tactical objectives, Bolger's analysis parallels the mission analysis performed by the USSAG\7thAF staff. Like Bolger, LtGen Burns and his staff failed to recognize the primary strategic objective of the Mayaguez crisis. As Christopher Lamb pointed out, the rescue of the ship and its crew was secondary to the need to demonstrate American resolve and forcefulness. Secretary Kissinger all but admitted this fact during the crisis when he remarked, "The lives of crewmen must, unfortunately, be a secondary consideration."[23]

National prestige is normally a paramount concern and quite possibly the number one priority governing all diplomatic and military efforts during a crisis. Understanding the priority of strategic goals and translating them into tactical objectives falls within the realm of operational leadership. While the NSC failed to articulate their strategic intent in the Mayaguez crisis, the USSAG/7thAF staff failed to properly analyze their

14

mission. They were unable to determine the primary strategic goal and translate that goal into operational/tactical objectives. These failures, at the strategic and more importantly at the operational level, led to confusion and near disaster at the tactical level. "If national prestige had been more clearly established as the top priority, avoiding failure even if it meant increasing [the] risk to the hostages would have guided the military planners."[24]

CONCLUSION

History shows America's actions during the Mayaguez crisis proved conclusive. "For the first time in several years, the utility of force was demonstrated in a successful U.S. military operation. That success generated a moral uplift for the American people, restored a belief in American credibility and demonstrated a strategic resolve worthy of a great power."[25] Yet, as I have shown, numerous problems existed at the operational level in command and leadership. An ad hoc command organization whose operational staff was purely Air Force led to tremendous problems in unity of command as well as planning, coordination, and execution. The lack of Marine and Navy representation on the USSAG/7thAF operational staff magnified these problems. Advanced communications technology and ineffective operational leadership enabled decision makers at the strategic level (NSC, JCS and CinCPac) to adversely affect the tactical and operational execution of the mission. Possibly the greatest operational failure was the inability at the

15

operational level to translate strategic intent into operational/tactical planning and execution.

In his article "Raids and National Command," Peter Kelly wrote, once the "decision to use force is made--planning and execution should be the responsibility" of the operational/ tactical commander. The president cannot become a tactical commander. The JCS cannot solve operational problems. Neither the NSC nor the JCS should "allow Washington to function as a super tactical operations center, greatly increasing the risk of failure and unnecessary casualties."[26]

The requirement for well-executed, operational leadership in tactical missions encompassing strategic implications is as strong as the requirement for operational leadership in a major operation or campaign. In the Mayaguez incident, the failures in operational command and leadership could have led to mission failure. To determine whether the military has learned from the operational fiasco at Mayaguez, the reader should study later strategic/tactical mission like the aborted Iranian hostage rescue mission or the Grenada mission. While a study of this kind is beyond the scope of this paper, I believe the reader would find some operational failures corrected and others left unresolved. The lessons of Mayaguez must be studied and not forgotten, if the military is to continue to improve command and leadership at the operational level of war.

APPENDIX A

Mayaguez Incident Timeline

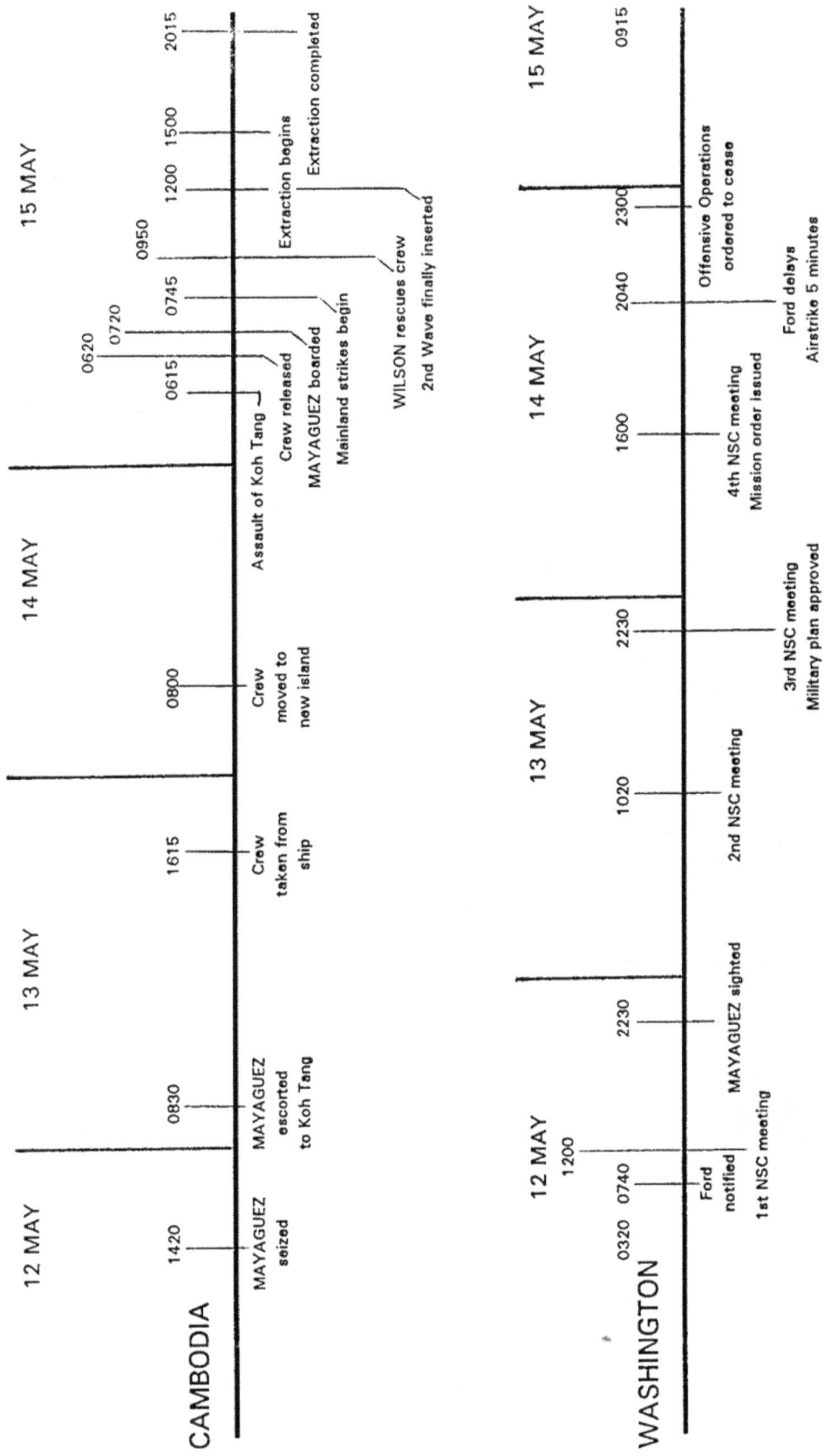

CAMBODIA

12 MAY	13 MAY	14 MAY	15 MAY

- 1420 — MAYAGUEZ seized
- 0830 — MAYAGUEZ escorted to Koh Tang
- 1615 — Crew taken from ship
- 0800 — Crew moved to new island
- 0615 — Assault of Koh Tang
- 0620 — Crew released
- 0720 — MAYAGUEZ boarded
- 0745 — Mainland strikes begin
- 0950 — WILSON rescues crew
- 1200 — 2nd Wave finally inserted
- 1500 — Extraction begins
- 2015 — Extraction completed

WASHINGTON

12 MAY	13 MAY	14 MAY	15 MAY

- 0320 0740 — Ford notified / 1st NSC meeting
- 1200 —
- 2230 — MAYAGUEZ sighted
- 1020 — 2nd NSC meeting
- 2230 — 3rd NSC meeting / Military plan approved
- 1600 — 4th NSC meeting / Mission order issued
- 2040 — Offensive Operations ordered to cease
- 2300 — Ford delays Airstrike 5 minutes
- 0915

* 11 Hours difference between Cambodia and Washington

** Not to Scale; Times approximate to nearest five minutes

APPENDIX B

COMMAND RELATIONSHIPS

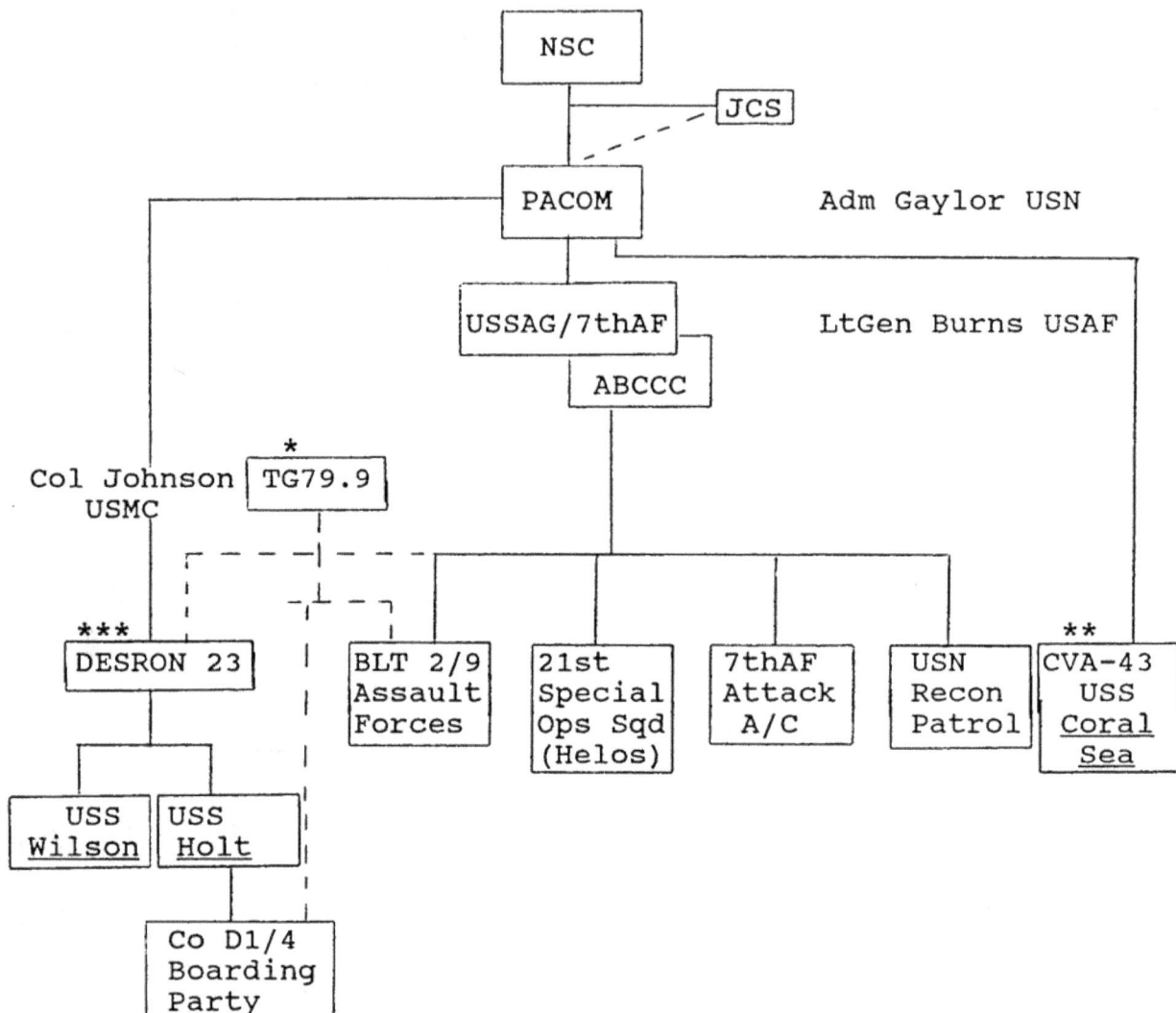

```
                          ┌──────┐
                          │ NSC  │
                          └──────┘
                              │        ┌─────┐
                              │    ┌ ─ ─│ JCS │
                              │   ╱     └─────┘
                          ┌────────┐
                          │ PACOM  │          Adm Gaylor USN
                          └────────┘
                              │
                          ┌──────────────┐
                          │ USSAG/7thAF  │    LtGen Burns USAF
                          └──────────────┘
                              │ ┌────────┐
                              └─│ ABCCC  │
                                └────────┘
                     *
    Col Johnson  ┌─────────┐
    USMC         │ TG79.9  │
                 └─────────┘
                      ┊
    ***         ┌──────────┐┌──────────┐┌──────────┐┌──────────┐┌──────────┐┌──────────┐
  ┌───────────┐ │ BLT 2/9  ││ 21st     ││ 7thAF    ││ USN      ││ **       │
  │ DESRON 23 │ │ Assault  ││ Special  ││ Attack   ││ Recon    ││ CVA-43   │
  └───────────┘ │ Forces   ││ Ops Sqd  ││ A/C      ││ Patrol   ││ USS      │
                │          ││ (Helos)  ││          ││          ││ Coral    │
                │          ││          ││          ││          ││ Sea      │
                └──────────┘└──────────┘└──────────┘└──────────┘└──────────┘
  ┌───────┐┌───────┐
  │ USS   ││ USS   │
  │ Wilson││ Holt  │
  └───────┘└───────┘
          ┌─────────┐
          │ Co D1/4 │
          │ Boarding│
          │ Party   │
          └─────────┘
```

*   Colonel Johnson of TG79.9 became irrelevant when he failed to establish liaison with USSAG/7thAF.   Communications problems forced the USMC forces to fall under operational control of the USAF on scene coordinator in the ABCCC.

**   Although the Coral Sea established contact with the ABCCC and delivered operational fires in support of the assault on Koh Tang, command and control remained with CinCPac and the NSC.

*** DESRON 23 and its assets participated in the mission at the direction of CinCPac. The ABCCC never provided tasking.

NOTES

1. Roy Rowan, <u>The Four Days of Mayaguez</u>, (New York: W Norton & Co., Inc., 1975), 20-22, 40, 45, 66-69, 87-88, 199; Christopher Lamb, <u>Belief Systems and Decision Making in the Mayaguez Crisis</u>, (Gainesville, Fl.: University of Florida Press, 1989), 86; and <u>U.S. Low-Intensity Conflicts, 1899-1990</u>, Congressional Research Service, Library of Congress, (Washington, D.C.: Government Printing Office, 1990), 173-174.

2. Daniel P. Bolger, <u>Americans at War: An Era of Violent Peace, 1975 -1986</u>, (Novato, Ca.: Presido Press, 1988), 32-34; and Urey W. Patrick, <u>The Mayaguez Operation</u>, (Washington, D.C.: Center For Naval Analysis, 1977), 42.

3. Patrick, 8.

4. J.M. Johnson, R.W. Austin, and D.A. Quinlan, "Individual Heroism Overcame Awkward Command Relationships, Confusion and Bad Information off the Cambodian Coast", <u>Marine Corps Gazette</u>, October 1977, 26-28; Bolger, 87-88; and Lamb, 130-131.

5. Johnson, 29; and Patrick, 47, 51.

6. Patrick, 92-93, 102; and Rowan, 102.

7. Bolger, 50-51.

8. Lamb, 132.

9. Richard G. Head, Frisco W. Short, and Robert C. McFarlane, <u>Crisis Resolution: Presidential Decision Making in the Mayaguez and Korean Confrontations</u>, (Boulder, Co.: Westview Press, 1978), 120; Bolger, 47; and Patrick, 8.

10. Patrick, 15, 97.

11. Ibid., 74, 89-91, 93.

12. Bolger, 47, 89-90.

13. J.A. Messegee, Robert A. Peterson, Walter J. Wood, J.B. Hendricks, and Michael J Rodger, "Mayday for the Mayaguez", <u>United States Naval Institute Proceedings</u>, November 1976, 106; Bolger, 76; and Patrick, 663, 107.

14. Lamb, 236.

15. Bolger, 43; and Patrick, 9, 101.

16. Lamb, 27-28, 97, 114; and Messegee, 107.

17.   Bolger, 73; and Rowan, 219.

18.   Bolger, 88; and "The Mayaguez - What Went Right, Wrong", 29.

19.   Rowan, 68, 141-142.

20.   Head, 110.

21.   William Shawcross, "Making the Most of Mayaguez", <u>Far Eastern Economic Review</u>, 30 May 1975, 11.

22.   Bolger, 49.

23.   Lamb, 266.

24.   Ibid., 182-183, 266.

25.   Head, 148.

26.   Peter A. Kelly, "Raids and National Command: Mutually Exclusive!", <u>Military Review</u>, April 1980, 24-25; and Richard F. Brauer Jr., <u>A Critical Examination of Planning Imperatives Applicable to Hostage Rescue Operations</u>, (Carlisle Barracks, Pa.: U.S. Army War College, 1984), 9.

WORKS CITED

Bolger, Daniel P. _Americans at War: An Era of Violent Peace, 1975 - 1986_. Novato, Ca.: Presido Press, 1988.

Brauer, Richard F. Jr,. _A Critical Examination of Planning Imperatives Applicable to Hostage Rescue Operations_. Carlisle Barracks, Pa.: U.S. Army War College, 1984

Head, Richard G., Frisco W. Short, and Robert C. McFarlane, _Crisis Resolution: Presidential Decision Making in the Mayaguez and Korean Confrontations_. Boulder, Co: Westview Press, 1978.

Johnson, J.M., R.W. Austin, and D.A. Quinlan. "Individual Heroism Overcame Awkward Command Relationships, Confusion and Bad Information off the Cambodian Coast." _Marine Corps Gazette_. October 1977.

Kelly, Peter A. "Raids and National Command : Mutually Exclusive!" _Military Review_. April 1980.

Lamb, Christopher J. _Belief Systems and Decision Making in the Mayaguez Crisis_. Gainesville, Fl.: University of Florida Press, 1989.

"The Mayaguez - What Went Right, Wrong." _US News and World Report_. 2 June 1975.

Messegee, J.A., Robert A. Peterson, Walter J. Wood, J.B. Hendricks, and Michael J. Rodger. "Mayday for the Mayaguez." _United States Naval Institute Proceedings_. November 1976.

Patrick, Urey W. _The Mayaguez Operation_. Center For Naval Analysis. April 1977.

Rowan, Roy. _The Four Days of Mayaguez_. New York: W Norton & Co., Inc., 1975.

Shawcross, William. "Making the Most of Mayaguez." _Far Eastern Economic Review_. 30 May 1975.

U.S. Low-Intensity Conflicts, 1899-1990. Congressional Research Service Library of Congress. Washington, D.C.: Government Printing Office, 1990.

BIBLIOGRAPHY

Bartlett, Tom. "Mayaguez." Leatherneck Magazine.
    September 1975.

Bauer, Charles J. "Military Crisis Management at the National
    Level." Military Review. August 1975.

Bennett, Charles F. "The Mayaguez Re-Examined: Misperceptions
    in an Information Shortage." Fletcher Forum 1. Fall 1976.

Bolger, Daniel P. Americans at War: An Era of Violent Peace,
    1975 - 1986. Novato, Ca.: Presido Press, 1988.

Brauer, Richard F. Jr,. A Critical Examination of Planning
    Imperatives Applicable to Hostage Rescue Operations.
    Carlisle Barracks, Pa.: U.S. Army War College, 1984

Carlile, LtCol Donald E. "The Mayaguez Incident: Crisis
    Management." Military Review. October 1976.

Hamm, Michael J. "The Pueblo and Mayaguez Incidents: A study
    of Flexible Response and Decision Making." Asian Survey.
    June 1977.

Head, Richard G., Frisco W. Short, and Robert C. McFarlane,
    Crisis Resolution: Presidential Decision Making in the
    Mayaguez and Korean Confrontations. Boulder, Co: Westview
    Press, 1978.

Johnson, J.M., R.W. Austin, and D.A. Quinlan. "Individual
    Heroism Overcame Awkward Command Relationships, Confusion
    and Bad Information off the Cambodian Coast." Marine
    Corps Gazette. October 1977.

Kelly, Peter A. "Raids and National Command : Mutually
    Exclusive!" Military Review. April 1980.

Lamb, Christopher J. Belief Systems and Decision Making in the
    Mayaguez Crisis. Gainesville, Fl.: University of Florida
    Press, 1989.

"Mayaguez, the President and History." Armed Forces Journal
    International. June 1975.

"The Mayaguez - What Went Right, Wrong." US News and World
    Report. 2 June 1975.

Messegee, J.A., Robert A. Peterson, Walter J. Wood, J.B. Hendricks, and Michael J. Rodger. "Mayday for the Mayaguez." _United States Naval Institute Proceedings_. November 1976.

New York Times. 11 May - 30 Jun 1975.

_____. 8 Oct 1976.

_____. 28 May 1979.

Osbourne, David and Fred Houk. "Mayaguez: The Fiasco Behind Ford's Finest Hour." _Rolling Stone_. December 1977.

Patrick, Urey W. _The Mayaguez Operation_. Center For Naval Analysis. April 1977.

Rowan, Roy. _The Four Days of Mayaguez_. New York: W Norton & Co., Inc., 1975.

Sandefer, Howard L. "Proper Prior Planning and the Next Mayaguez." _U.S. Naval Institute Proceedings_. August 1975.

Scali, John, "US Recovers Merchant Ship Seized by Cambodian Navy." _Department of State Bulletin_. Vol. 62, No 1876, 9 June 1975.

Shani, Joshua. "Airborne Raids." _Air University Press_. March - April 1985.

Shawcross, William. "Making the Most of Mayaguez." _Far Eastern Economic Review_. 30 May 1975.

Summers, Laura. "Consolidating the Cambodian Revolution." _Current History_. Vol 69, No 411, December 1975.

"Using a Big Stick on Cambodia." _Newsday_. 15 May 1975.

U.S. Low-Intensity Conflicts, 1899-1990. Congressional Research Service Library of Congress. Washington, D.C.: Government Printing Office, 1990.

Washington Post. 14 - 19 and 26 May 1975.

_____. 22 Feb 1979.

_____. 30 Jun and 14 Jul 1985.

_____. 28 Feb 1988.

The *Mayaguez* Incident: Near Disaster at Koh Tang

CSC 1998

Subject Area - History

EXECUTIVE SUMMARY

<u>Title</u>: The *Mayaguez* Incident: Near Disaster at Koh Tang

<u>Author</u>: Major Mark J. Toal

<u>Thesis</u>: The tactical leadership, initiative, and individual heroism at Koh Tang overcame poor operational command and control to narrowly avert a strategic disaster.

<u>Discussion</u>: The *Mayaguez* incident is a clear example in which the tactical, operational, and strategic level of war merged: where tactical actions had strategic implications. The strategic objectives determined by the National Command Authorities were to recover the ship and crew and in doing so demonstrate U.S. strength and resolve. Discussions in the National Security Council meetings clearly prioritized the objectives, the most important of which was to demonstrate to the world that the U.S. remained an international power willing and able to defend its overseas interests.

Poor operational command and control during planning created real problems that would plague the operations until its conclusion. From an execution point of view, these problems were developed by a combination of several factors that included:
    1. A joint task force, composed of units from three different services, was hastily formed and tasked to rapidly conduct a complex operation with strategic implications.
    2. Command and control failures during planning caused by the absence of centralized leadership to unify the effort and form a cohesive task force.
    3. Faulty dissemination of crucial intelligence to the tactical planners and operators which resulted in a flawed scheme of maneuver.
These factors created a planning environment characterized by chaos and confusion which accentuated the fog and friction of the operation which nearly resulted in defeat.

Chaotic, confused, and incomplete planning based on faulty intelligence proved to be a recipe for disaster. During the operation, the same problems of command and control that plagued it during planning were present to a greater degree and accentuated the fog and friction of the battle. At the operational level, there was little situational awareness, and no one was in command or coordinating the battlespace. Throughout the fight, there were occasions when the Marines were nearly overrun by the numerically superior, well-trained, and disciplined enemy force. During the fourteen hour battle seemingly minor tactical events influenced the outcome. The tactical leadership, initiative, and individual heroism of countless servicemen overcame significant command and control obstacles to prevent tactical defeat and strategic failure.

Report Documentation Page

Form Approved
OMB No. 0704-0188

Public reporting burden for the collection of information is estimated to average 1 hour per response, including the time for reviewing instructions, searching existing data sources, gathering and maintaining the data needed, and completing and reviewing the collection of information. Send comments regarding this burden estimate or any other aspect of this collection of information, including suggestions for reducing this burden, to Washington Headquarters Services, Directorate for Information Operations and Reports, 1215 Jefferson Davis Highway, Suite 1204, Arlington VA 22202-4302. Respondents should be aware that notwithstanding any other provision of law, no person shall be subject to a penalty for failing to comply with a collection of information if it does not display a currently valid OMB control number.

1. REPORT DATE **1998**	2. REPORT TYPE	3. DATES COVERED **00-00-1998 to 00-00-1998**

4. TITLE AND SUBTITLE **The Mayaguez Incident: Near Disaster at Koh Tang**	5a. CONTRACT NUMBER
	5b. GRANT NUMBER
	5c. PROGRAM ELEMENT NUMBER
6. AUTHOR(S)	5d. PROJECT NUMBER
	5e. TASK NUMBER
	5f. WORK UNIT NUMBER
7. PERFORMING ORGANIZATION NAME(S) AND ADDRESS(ES) **Marine Corps War College,Marine Corps Combat Development Command,Quantico,VA,22134-5067**	8. PERFORMING ORGANIZATION REPORT NUMBER
9. SPONSORING/MONITORING AGENCY NAME(S) AND ADDRESS(ES)	10. SPONSOR/MONITOR'S ACRONYM(S)
	11. SPONSOR/MONITOR'S REPORT NUMBER(S)

12. DISTRIBUTION/AVAILABILITY STATEMENT **Approved for public release; distribution unlimited**

13. SUPPLEMENTARY NOTES

14. ABSTRACT

15. SUBJECT TERMS

16. SECURITY CLASSIFICATION OF:			17. LIMITATION OF ABSTRACT	18. NUMBER OF PAGES	19a. NAME OF RESPONSIBLE PERSON
a. REPORT **unclassified**	b. ABSTRACT **unclassified**	c. THIS PAGE **unclassified**	**Same as Report (SAR)**	**53**	

Standard Form 298 (Rev. 8-98)
Prescribed by ANSI Std Z39-18

Superior technology and firepower did not dominate the battlefield at Koh Tang. The fighting ability, courage, and steadfast determination of Marines and airmen prevailed to achieve strategic objectives. Technology cannot replace the intangible factors that influence all levels of war.

TABLE OF CONTENTS

AN IMPORTANT SUCCESS

Inscribed on the 140 black granite panels of the Vietnam War Memorial are the names of 58,183 Americans who sacrificed their lives in the service of their country. The last eighteen names are those who died in the final combat action in the long and bitter war in Southeast Asia and are unknown to most Americans. These eighteen servicemen did not actually die in Vietnam but rather on a small and jungled island in the Gulf of Thailand named Koh Tang, where a small, forgotten, and yet savage battle was fought to achieve geopolitical objectives. On 12 May 1975, Cambodian naval forces seized a U.S. merchant ship, the *SS Mayaguez*, along with its unarmed civilian crew of forty men. The U.S. responded with swift military action that resulted in a ferocious fourteen hour battle on Koh Tang and the successful recovery of the ship and all crew members. After failure in Southeast Asia, a successful military operation was important to the U.S. As the authors of *Crisis Resolution: Presidential Decision Making in the Mayaguez and Korean Confrontations* observed, "For the first time in several years, the utility of force was demonstrated in a successful U.S. military operation. That success generated a moral uplift for the American people, restored a belief in American credibility, and demonstrated a strategic resolve worthy of a great power."[1] Across the nation, media accounts declared victory. The *Atlanta Journal* opined, "There seems to be a feeling of joy that at last we have won one."[2] *The New York Times* announced a "domestic and foreign triumph."[3] *Time* stated that the military resolution of the *Mayaguez* incident "significantly changed the image of U.S. power in the world...."[4] *U.S. News and World Report* responded, "President Ford's fast and forceful response to a challenge...was meant as a signal to U.S. allies and adversaries. In essence: Don't take us lightly."[5] What was omitted from these media accounts was how narrowly the Marines on Koh

---

[1] Richard J. Head, Frisco W. Short, and Robert C. McFarlane, *Crisis Resolution: Presidential Decision Making in the Mayaguez and Korean Confrontations* (Boulder CO: Westview Press, 1978), 148.

[2] Atlanta Journal quoted in "A Strong but Risky Show of Force," *Time*, 26 May 1975, 18.

[3] The New York Times May 16, 1975 , quoted in "A Strong but Risky Show of Force," *Time*, 26 May 1975, May 16, 1975.

[4] "A Strong but Risky Show of Force," *Time*, 26 May 1975, 9.

[5] "New Test For U.S. Why Ford Moved So Fast," *U.S. News and World Report*, 19 May 1975, 19-22.

Tang escaped defeat in fighting against a well-disciplined, tough, and numerically superior force. At one point in the battle, the Marines were so close to being overrun that a company commander turned to his company gunnery sergeant and said, "Gunny, I think we've had it."[6] One can only speculate the media accounts, the domestic and international reaction, and the strategic implications had a Marine company been overrun, and its members either killed or taken hostage by a military force viewed as "fourth rate." Although the strategic objectives were accomplished, at the tactical level it was a very close fight that nearly resulted in defeat and thus strategic failure. The *Mayaguez* incident is a clear example of a situation in which the tactical, operational, and strategic levels of war merged; where tactical actions had strategic implications. The purpose of this paper is to illustrate that the tactical leadership, initiative, and individual heroism at Koh Tang overcame poor operational command and control to narrowly avert a strategic disaster.

---

[6]   James H. Davis quoted from an interview with John F. Guilmartin, Jr., *A Very Short War. The Mayaguez and the Battle of Koh Tang* (College Station, TX: Texas A&M University Press, 1995), 133.

SETTING THE STAGE

On 12 May 1975, the U.S. merchant ship, *SS Mayaguez*, was enroute from Hong Kong to Sattahip, Thailand, with a containerized cargo of commercial products to include food, clothing, medical supplies and other general cargo.[7] The ship was transiting a customary sea lane and trade route through international waters approximately sixty miles southwest of the Cambodian port of Kompong Som in the vicinity of the Cambodian island of Poulo Wai. At 1410 local time (0310 Eastern Standard Time [EST]) the *Mayaguez* was challenged by a Cambodian gunboat with several rounds across the starboard bow. Minutes later the ship was boarded by seven armed men carrying AK-47s and rocket propelled grenade launchers (RPGs).[8] The Cambodians seized the ship and took the unharmed crew prisoner. At 1418 (0318 EST) the *Mayaguez* radioed a mayday distress call which stated, "Have been fired upon and boarded by Cambodian armed forces at 9 degrees 48 minutes N and 102 degrees 52 minutes E. Ship is being towed to an unknown Cambodian port."[9] Mr. John Neal of the Delta Exploration Company in Jakarta, Indonesia, received the distress call and forwarded the information to the American Embassy Jakarta. At 1612 (0512 EST) the National Military Command Center (NMCC) in Washington D.C. received its initial report from the American Embassy Jakarta.

After the seizure a Cambodian gunboat led the *Mayaguez* to an island, Poulo Wai, where it anchored for the night. The next morning the *Mayaguez* set sail toward Cambodia and anchored a mile off the northeast tip of Koh Tang, located approximately thirty miles south of Kompong Som, Cambodia. (Figure 1 and 2)

---

[7]   Head, Short, and McFarlane, 101.

[8]   Major George R.Dunham, and Colonel David A. Quinlan, *U.S. Marines in Vietnam: The Bitter End* (Washington D.C: History and Museums Division, Headquarters, U.S. Marine Corps, 1990), 238.

[9]   US Congress, House, Subcommittee on International Political and Military Affairs, Committee on International Relations, *Seizure of the Mayaguez,* Hearings on the *Mayaguez* Incident, pt. 4, *Report of the Comptroller General of the United States*, 94th Cong., 2d sess., October 4, 1976, 16. (Hereafter referred to as *GAO Report*)

Cambodian Intentions

Cambodian motives to seize the *Mayaguez* were unclear during the crisis and remain so today. On 17 April 1975, the radical communist Khmer Rouge overthrew the Lon Nol government and seized the capitol, Phnom Penh. With the exception of the mass executions occurring in Cambodia, little was known about the Khmer Rouge. The U.S. did not recognize the newly established government and did not know the identity of the actual leaders.[10] It was also not known whether the ship was seized by order of the Khmer Rouge or on the initiative of a local commander. [11]

There were indications that the Khmer Rouge wanted to establish their nationalist credentials and legitimacy by extending their territorial waters ninety miles offshore to include several contested islands in the Gulf of Thailand which Cambodia had historically claimed.[12] These islands included Poulo Wai and Koh Tang. Just days before the *Mayaguez* seizure, there were four incidents of Cambodian aggression against foreign vessels in international waters:
  May 2: Capture and subsequent release of several Thai fishing boats
  May 4: Firing upon and attempt to board a South Korean ship
  May 6: Seizure of several South Vietnamese small craft
  May 7: Detention of a Panamanian ship for 36 hours.[13]

These incidents against vessels of various countries support the notion that Cambodian aggression was not aimed exclusively at the U.S.

While Cambodian intentions were unclear, the Ford Administration generally believed the *Mayaguez* seizure was an act of provocation and intimidation aimed at humiliating the U.S. Senator Barry Goldwater captured the feeling when he referred to the incident as a "little half-assed country...taking a shot at us."[14] In his book, *A Very Short War*, John Guilmartin makes the

---

[10] Head, Short, and McFarlane, 103.
[11] Lamb, 91. The idea of a local commander taking action without governmental sponsorship was proposed by White House photographer David Kennerly during a National Security Council meeting.
[12] GAO Report, 16.
[13] Head, Short, and McFarlane, 103.
[14] "A Strong but Risky Show of Force," *Time*, 26 May 1975, 18.

following point that suggests the Khmer Rouge would have preferred to avoid conflict with the U.S.:

As Marxist-Leninist revolutionaries, the new rulers of Cambodia no doubt welcomed an opportunity to embarrass the United States. But having captured Phnom Penh less than a month before, they were surely preoccupied with consolidating their power. It is therefore unlikely that the leaders were willing to go to any great trouble or run any great risk to do so.[15]

Even if the motives were unclear, it was clear that the Khmer Rouge took subsequent control of the ship and crew and showed no indication of freeing them. The captain of the *Mayaguez*, Captain Charles T. Miller, stated later in congressional testimony that once it became apparent that the crew and ship were American, the Cambodians received orders by direct radio link with the authorities in Phnom Penh.[16] The Khmer Rouge accused the ship of spying and ordered the captors to transport the crew to the Cambodian mainland. President Ford and his advisors correctly assumed that the Khmer Rouge would oppose with military force any efforts to retake the ship and crew.[17]

The Strategic Environment

From a current perspective, the seizure of the *Mayaguez* may not appear to have major strategic implications. However, taken in the context of the events of the time, the situation loomed much larger. In the global arena, U.S. reliability as an ally and its ability to play a positive leadership role in the international affairs were being questioned domestically and internationally alike.[18] The prestige and credibility of the U.S. as a superpower was challenged. In general, America's morale was low.

The U.S. had just concluded an exhaustive and controversial ten year conflict in Southeast Asia that had divided the American people. On 17 April 1975, the Cambodian capital of Phnom Penh fell to the communist Khmer Rouge regime, and just two weeks later on 30 April the South

---

[15]   John F. Guilmartin, Jr., *A Very Short War. The Mayaguez and the Battle of Koh Tang* (College Station, TX: Texas A&M University Press, 1995), 35-36.
[16]   Lamb, 188.
[17]   Guilmartin, 36.
[18]   Head, Short, and McFarlane, 102.

5

Vietnamese capital of Saigon was overrun by North Vietnamese forces. U.S. military forces conducted consecutive operations to evacuate Americans and allied personnel from both capitals with Operations Eagle Pull and Frequent Wind respectfully. Although these operations were successful, the American retreat from two third world countries overrun by communist forces was a humiliating blow to national prestige. The Phnom Penh and Saigon evacuations virtually ended the presence of the U.S. in Indochina and marked an end to thirty years of determined efforts by successive U.S. presidents to keep Indochina noncommunist. The U.S. had clearly suffered a strategic loss.

In the spring of 1975, tensions with the belligerent North Koreans were rising, and the U.S. was concerned about the likelihood of conflict on the Korean Peninsula. During April 1975, the South Koreans had discovered and destroyed several tunnels constructed by the North Koreans under the Demilitarized Zone. The South Korean President Park Chung Hee, as well as the Japanese, predicted a North Korean invasion before 1976. The North Korean dictator, Kim Il Sung, believed that U.S. resolve was weak based upon previous U.S. responses to North Korean aggression.[19] In January 1968, the North Koreans had seized the *USS Pueblo* and its crew. In April 1969, North Korea shot down an American EC-121 surveillance aircraft in international waters/airspace killing all aboard. In both cases, the U.S. responded with diplomacy and little resolve. In his memoirs, Henry Kissinger expressed the opinion that the U.S. response to the EC-121 crisis was weak and indecisive which "demoralized friends and emboldened adversaries."[20]

During 1975, the U.S. was also focused on the Mideast peace process and attempted to broker an agreement for the disengagement of Israeli and Egyptian forces in the Sinai. The 1973 OPEC oil embargo and the resultant escalation of oil prices had pushed most Western economies into a recession. Additionally, the U.S. continued to be fully engaged in the Cold War against the Soviet Union, China, and North Korea.

---

[19]   Lamb, 72.

[20]   Henry Kissinger, *White House Years*, (Boston: Little, Brown & Co., 1979), 316, 318, 321.

On the domestic front, the country was still reeling from Watergate, and only nine months had passed since the resignation of President Nixon. Consequently, Gerald R. Ford became the first president appointed to office who did not have a political mandate from the people.[21] The public confidence and the prestige of the Office of the President of the United States was arguably the lowest since the Civil War, and Ford knew that it would be an enormous task to restore confidence in the presidency at home and abroad.[22]

The seizure of the *Mayaguez* offered an opportunity for the US to make a political statement to the world with a tough response. With recent setbacks in Indochina and the Middle East and rising tensions on the Korean Peninsula, Ford had sought an opportunity to demonstrate to the world that the U.S. was not a paper tiger and was willing and able to defend its overseas interests.[23] Ford was determined not to preside over another humiliation.[24] Even before the seizure of the *Mayaguez, Time* quoted an unnamed U.S. government policy planner as stating, "There's quite a bit of agreement around here that it wouldn't be a bad thing if the other side goes a step or two too far in trying to kick us while we're down. It would give us a chance to kick them back - hard."[25] The *Mayaguez* incident gave the Ford Administration the opportunity they sought. With U.S. political and military credibility at stake, there was substantial risk of serious damage with strategic implications. As Guilmartin said, "Although the scale of the action was not, the stakes were high."[26]

---

[21]   Head, Short, and McFarlane, 102.
[22]   Ibid, 71.
[23]   "A Strong but Risky Show of Force," *Time*, 26 May 1975, 9.
[24]   Head, Short, and McFarlane, 71.
[25]   "A Strong but Risky Show of Force," *Time*, 26 May 1975, 9.
[26]   Guilmartin, 3.

12-14 MAY 1975:
AN ISSUE OF NATIONAL PRESTIGE

On Monday 12 May 1975, at 0512 Eastern Standard Time (1612 12 May, Thailand time) the NMCC in Washington, D.C., was alerted by the initial report from the American Embassy Jakarta on the *Mayaguez* seizure. This report initiated a flurry of activity at the National Command Authority (NCA) and started a chain of events that would conclude about 100 hours later. At 0530 Lieutenant General Brent Skowcroft, USAF, Deputy Assistant for National Security Affairs, notified Ford. At 0646 the acting Chairman of the Joint Chiefs of Staff (CJCS), General David Jones, USAF, was contacted. The Chairman, General George S. Brown, was in Europe at the time. By 0730 reconnaissance aircraft were ordered by Joint Chiefs of Staff (JCS) to search for the *Mayaguez,* and within 90 minutes P-3 surveillance aircraft from Thailand and the Philippines were launched. The nearest surface ships were also ordered to proceed to the area and soon afterward the escort destroyer *USS Harold E. Holt* and the supply ship *USS Vega* were steaming at best speed west to the Gulf of Thailand. At 0740 Skowcroft and a Central Intelligence Agency representative briefed Ford at his usual daily morning intelligence brief. The Secretary of State and National Security Advisor, Dr. Henry Kissinger, was notified at his 0800 staff meeting and immediately called the president. At 0923 Ford, Kissinger, and Skowcroft met in the Oval Office to discuss the situation. During this meeting, Ford called for the National Security Council (NSC) to meet at 1205, almost nine hours after the seizure.

It is important to note that Ford implicitly understood the seriousness of the *Mayaguez* seizure before the first scheduled NSC meeting. Ford stated in an interview after the crisis, "My feeling that the seizure of a U.S. vessel and crew, especially by a country which had so humiliated us, was a very serious matter."[27] Ford was well aware of the similarities of the current crisis and the North Korean seizure of the U.S. intelligence-gathering ship *Pueblo*. On 23 January 1968, when North Korean gunboats seized the *Pueblo*, local US military forces were present but were not used promptly. By the time the Johnson Administration had acted, the ship was in a North Korean port and the crew were being held at an unknown location in North Korea. As Guilmartin noted, "The deep humiliation inflicted by brutal North Korean exploitation of *Pueblo's* crew and the diplomatic price of securing their release had left their mark." [28] In dealing with the *Mayaguez* incident, Ford, Kissinger, and Skowcroft were foremost influenced by the *Pueblo* incident and subsequent acts of North Korean aggression. During all four NSC meetings that were held during the *Mayaguez* crisis, North Korea was a frequently discussed topic. Ford believed if the *Mayaguez* crew were taken to the Cambodian mainland, they would be virtually irretrievable by military action. It was clear that the feasibility of a military response was decreasing with time. Personally taking charge of the situation, Ford understood that immediate action was necessary to resolve the crisis favorably. He wanted to prevent another *Pueblo* incident and to demonstrate to the world, especially North Korea, that the U.S. was still a superpower and that aggression would not go unpunished.[29]

The NSC met at 1205 with eleven participants.[30] During the meeting, Kissinger was adamant that the greatest issue was not international piracy, but the global perceptions of American power and resolve.[31] In the meeting, Kissinger was quoted as stating, "At some point the United States

---

27   Lamb, 68.

28   Guilmartin, 37.

29   Lamb, 84, 245-286.

30   Ibid, 80. The participants included the President, Vice President Nelson D. Rockerfeller, Henry Kissinger, Secretary of State; James Schlesinger, Secretary of Defense; William Colby, Director of the Central Intelligence Agency; LtGen Skowcroft, Deputy Assistant for National Security Affairs; Robert Ingersoll, Deputy Secretary of State; William Clemens, Deputy Secretary of Defense; Donald Rumsfield, Assistant to the President; and W. Richard Smyser, senior National Security Council staff officer for East Asia.

31   Ibid, 81.

must draw the line. This is not our idea of the best situation. It is not our choice. But we must act upon it now, and act firmly."[32]

During the initial NCS meeting, the president directed the following:
1. Deliver a strong diplomatic protest to the Cambodian government via the People's Republic of China.
2. Redirect the USS Coral Sea, enroute to Australia, to the area of seizure.
3. Assemble an Amphibious Task Force in Philippines.
4. Maintain continuous photo reconnaissance of the area.
5. Issue a public statement (designed to reach the Khmer Rouge) reporting the facts and noting the US demand for the immediate return of the ship and crew.

Most importantly, the strategic objectives were determined in the initial NSC meeting to be: (1) to recover of the ship and its crew; (2) to avoid the possibility of a hostage negotiation (i.e., prevent a reenactment of the *Pueblo* incident); and (3) to demonstrate American power and resolution with a forceful response as an example to the international community that the U.S. has the capability and firm resolve to protect its interests.[33] Participants noted that the first two objectives could be contradictory. Ford summed up the dilemma when he asked his press secretary, Ron Nesson, a hypothetical question, "Would you go in there and bomb the Cambodian boat and take a chance with Americans being killed?"[34] Kissinger seemed to prioritize the strategic objectives when he was quoted as stating that the lives of the *Mayaguez* crew "must unfortunately be a second consideration."[35] The Ford Administration actions suggest that the foremost objective was to demonstrate American power with a forceful response at the expense of the crew's safety, if necessary. [36]

At 2116 a P-3 positively identified the *Mayaguez* anchored near Poulo Wai. Once located, it remained under constant surveillance throughout the crisis. Thirty minutes after the initial sighting, the ship was observed to weigh anchor and proceed toward Kompong Som.

---

32   Kissinger quoted in Gerald R. Ford, *A Time to Heal,* (New York: Harper & Row Publishers, 1979), 276.
33   Guilmartin states that another objective was to "avoid the possibility of a hostage negotiations," 38.
34   Ron Nesson, *It Sure Looks Different from the Inside* (Chicago: Playboy Press, 1978), 118.
35   "Ford's Rescue Operations." *Newsweek,* 26 May 1975, 16.
36   Lamb, 164.

Tuesday, 13 May

On 13 May CINPACFLT ordered the aircraft carrier *USS Coral Sea* and the guided missile destroyer *USS Henry W. Wilson* to join the *Holt* and *Vega* in the waters of Kompong Som. As the NCA received reports of the *Mayaguez's* movement, there was serious concern that the ship and crew would be taken to the Cambodian mainland. At 0230 Scowcroft requested permission to conduct interdiction efforts to isolate the *Mayaguez* from the mainland. Ford authorized these interdiction efforts and the use of riot control agents and gunfire by Thailand-based U.S. aircraft to prevent the ship from reaching Cambodia. At approximately 0218 it was observed to anchor about a mile off the northeast coast of Koh Tang. At 0552 Secretary of Defense James R. Schlesinger, briefed Ford that the ship was anchored off the island of Koh Tang. Ford instructed Schlesinger not to allow another "*Pueblo*" to take place and to quarantine the *Mayaguez* from the mainland. At 1717 (0617 EST) JCS ordered the Commander-in-Chief, Pacific Command (CINCPAC) to quarantine the ship in order to prevent the transfer of the crew to mainland Cambodia. Within the hour after the order was transmitted, pilots observing the *Mayaguez* reported that the crew members were being transferred to Koh Tang.

The second NSC meeting was held at 1030 and lasted 56 minutes. Kissinger was not present at this meeting due to an engagement in Kansas City. During the meeting, the director of the CIA, William Colby, briefed that the *Mayaguez* was anchored near Koh Tang and the crew had been most likely transferred to the island. Concerning the diplomatic efforts, there was no Cambodian reaction from the released U.S. statement, and the Chinese refused to deliver the note of protest to the Khmer Rouge. Additionally, the Thai government had stated it would not permit the use of its bases for U.S. action against Cambodia. The second NSC meeting discussed the following courses of action:
1. The use of diplomacy with the Peoples Republic of China (PRC), Khmer Rouge, and the United Nations in an attempt to return ship and crew
2. Conduct a military show of force operation
3. Seize an island in retaliation
4. Conduct a heliborne landing on the *Mayaguez*
5. Conduct a ship to ship boarding operation

6. Conduct a Marine heliborne assault at Koh Tang
7. Attack Kompong Som with carrier air strikes
8. Conduct B-52 strikes at Kompong Som. [37]

Upon conclusion of the meeting, Ford understood the urgency to deploy US forces to the area and ordered the following actions:

1. Position the second aircraft carrier *USS Hancock,* which embarked with a Marine Amphibious Unit (MAU) from the Philippines in the area
2. Isolate the *Mayaguez* and Koh Tang from the mainland by use of Thailand-based Air Force assets which included F-4, F-111, and A-7 tactical aircraft
3. Move a Marine Battalion from Okinawa to Utapao, Thailand, to provide the capability of a heliborne assault by Thursday morning, 15 May (Wednesday evening, 14 May ETA).

At 1200 JCS ordered CINCPAC to isolate both the *Mayaguez* and Koh Tang from the mainland. Additionally, JCS ordered that any interception of Cambodian gunboats must be reported to Washington, where the decision of whether to sink them would be made. Between 2010 and 2151, with orders relayed from Ford, three gunboats were sunk and four were immobilized. By the second NSC meeting, strategic planners and decision makers were discussing operational and tactical courses of action as well as making tactical decisions. At the initial stages of the *Mayaguez* operation, the tactical, operational and strategic level of war were already merging together.

The third NSC meeting was held at 2240. Kissinger was present at this meeting and continued to forcefully advocate the use of military action "to have an impact on President Kim Il-Sung and the North Koreans."[38] During the meeting, Ford was briefed on the progress of diplomatic activity which had produced no success to date. He also received operational reports concerning the efforts to isolate Koh Tang and the status of military forces converging on the area. During this meeting, Ford was notified that a Cambodian patrol boat followed by a fishing boat had departed Koh Tang and was heading toward Kompong Som. Under NCA orders, the patrol boat was sunk; however, the fishing boat continued its course. A pilot reported observing a number of caucasians, possibly the *Mayaguez* crew, on the fishing boat. After some

---

37   Head, Short, and McFarlane, 114-115.
38   Roy Rowan, *The Four Days of Mayaguez* (New York; Norton & Co, 1975), 141-142.

discussion, Ford ordered the pilots "to do everything possible to turn the boat around, but not to sink it."[39] U.S. aircraft used bombs, rockets, tear gas, and cannon fire in an attempt to turn the boat, but it continued its course toward Kompong Som.

After Jones presented military options and courses of action, Ford agreed to the following sequence:

1. Attack Koh Tang on Thursday morning May 15, Thailand time (Wednesday evening EST, May 14). From a staging area in Thailand, Marines will simultaneously recapture the *Mayaguez* with a boarding operation from the *Holt* and conduct a heliborne assault on Koh Tang.
2. Conduct naval air attacks against mainland targets to prevent reinforcements from Cambodia. In order to isolate Koh Tang and the *Mayaguez* from mainland Cambodia, small vessels will not be permitted to transit between Koh Tang and the Cambodian coast.
3. B-52 bombers will be put on alert for deployment against targets on the Cambodian mainland to prevent reinforcements from Cambodia, demonstrate U.S. power, and punish Cambodia for their aggression.
4. The State Department will deliver a letter to the United Nations Secretary General seeking assistance in securing the release of the ship and crew.[40]

After deciding on the specific actions, Ford asked Jones if the schedule could possibly be advanced one day. Jones responded that the JCS could not recommend an earlier assault because forces were still converging into the area and further coordination was required.[41]

Upon conclusion of the third NSC meeting, the JCS met in the Pentagon to review the timing of the operation. The gathering was uneasy and those present questioned that there was enough time to establish effective command and control of the widely dispersed forces converging on the area. The JCS reached a consensus that an extra day would provide a higher assurance of success but agreed that the urgency of the situation overcame the degree of risk associated with a rapid military operation.[42]

---

[39]   Ford, 278.

[40]   Head, Short, and McFarlane, 118.

[41]   Rowan, 142-143.

[42]   Lamb, 121-122.

Wednesday, 14 May

The fourth and final NSC meeting occurred at 1552. In Thailand, the time was 0252 15 May, less than ninety minutes before American assault helicopters were scheduled to launch from Utapao. During the meeting, Colby reported that some of the *Mayaguez* crew were most likely on the mainland and their location was unknown. Jones conducted a detailed brief of the overall operational and tactical plans. In doing so, he emphasized that postponing military action another 24 hours would increase the ability of the forces to conduct a well-coordinated attack.[43] Ford continued to feel that if immediate action was not taken, a *"Pueblo"* scenario would be repeated and quickly dismissed any suggestion of postponement. Between 1645 and 1710, (0345 and 0410, 15 May, Thailand time) and with helicopters loaded and waiting to launch at Utapao, the president issued orders to execute the recovery plan.

In summary, the strategic objectives determined by the NCA were to recover the ship and crew and in doing so demonstrate U.S. strength and resolve. Discussions in the NSC meetings clearly prioritized the objectives, the most important of which was to demonstrate to the world that the U.S. remained an international power willing *and able* to defend its interests.

---

[43]   Ibid, 90.

A TRAIN WRECK IN THE MAKING

Poor operational command and control during planning created real problems that would plague the operation until its conclusion. From an execution point of view, these problems were developed by a combination of several factors that included:

1. A joint task force, composed of units from three different services, was hastily formed and tasked to rapidly plan and conduct a complex operation with strategic implications.
2. Command and control failures during planning caused by the absence of centralized leadership to unify the effort and form a cohesive task force.
3. Faulty dissemination of crucial intelligence to the tactical planners and operators.

These factors created a planning environment characterized by chaos and confusion which accentuated the friction of the battlefield.

Organizing the Joint Task Force

Because of the immediacy of the situation, forces from different services were quickly formed to execute the operation. When the *Mayaguez* was seized, only two U.S. Navy ships were within 24 hours steaming time.[44] Just two weeks earlier, a large armada of U.S. ships had participated in Operation Frequent Wind but were now scattered throughout the Pacific. On 13 May the *Holt, Vega,* destroyer *USS Wilson,* and the aircraft carrier *USS Coral Sea* were ordered to proceed immediately to the waters off Kompong Som.[45] These naval forces were the only ships that could arrive at the objective area prior to the morning of 15 May (Thailand time), the date operations would commence as directed by the NCA. The amphibious ready groups that had been involved in Operation Frequent Wind were returning Marines to Okinawa and Japan and

---

[44] J.M. Johnson, Jr., R.W. Austin, and D.A. Quinlan, "Individual Heroism Overcame Awkward Command Relationships, Confusion, and Bad Information off the Cambodian Coast." *Marine Corps Gazette*, October 1977, 25.
[45] Ibid, 25.

15

their distance from Koh Tang rendered these forces unavailable for a rapid response. As a result, the Air Contingency Battalion Landing Team (ACBLT), Battalion Landing Team (BLT) 2/9 located in Okinawa, and a reinforced company from 1st Battalion, 4th Marine Regiment (D 1/4) located in Subic Bay, were ordered to Utapao to take part in the recovery operation. When BLT 2/9 received its movement orders at 2030 13 May (Thailand time), all four of its rifle companies were conducting field training in Okinawa. By 0530 14 May, only seven hours after receiving the movement order, lead elements of BLT 2/9 were enroute to Utapao. D 1/4 departed Naval Air Station Cubi Point, Philippines at 0115 14 May and arrived at Utapao at 0505.[46] Less than 24 hours later, USAF assault helicopters carrying Marines would be enroute to Koh Tang.

The USAF ordered all the CH-53 and HH-53 heavy helicopters in the 7th Air Force to Utapao from Korat and Nakhon Phanom Air Bases in Thailand. Utapao was the closest allied military facility at 190 nautical miles from Koh Tang. Seventh Air Force's heavy helicopters included CH-53s from the 21st Special Operations Squadron and HH-53s from the 40th Aerospace Rescue and Recovery Squadron.[47] There were a total of thirteen heavy helicopters at Utapao available for the operation. Two were designated as search and rescue (SAR) aircraft and eleven helicopters (6 HH-53s and 5 CH-53s) were dedicated to the assault. USAF tactical aircraft which included F-4s, A-7Ds, OV-10s, and AC-130s supported the operation from Korat and Nakhon Phanom.

As the incident unfolded, various units and commands from the USAF, Navy, and the Marine Corps were rapidly converging on Utapao and the waters off of Kompong Som to form a joint task force. All U.S. forces in Asia were under the command of Admiral Noel A. M. Gaylor, CINCPAC, who was located in Hawaii. Gaylor designated the Commander, US Support Activities Group/7th Air Force (COMUSSAG/7th), Lieutenant General John J. Burns, Jr, USAF, as the "on scene operational commander and the central coordinating authority."[48] In effect,

---

[46]   Ibid, 25.

[47]   HH-53s carry more armor than the CH-53 and have inflight refueling capability. CH-53s have external fuel tanks. Both are capable of extended air operations.

[48]   Johnson, Austin, and Quinlan, 26.

Burns was designated as the Commander of the Joint Task Force (CJTF). USSAG Headquarters, located in Nakhon Phanom, was the closest US military headquarters to Cambodia and had been heavily involved in Operations Frequent Wind and Eagle Pull. Burns had also been the operational commander for Operation Eagle Pull.[49]

Burns selected Brigadier General Walter H. Baxter, USAF, Commander of the 17th Air Division, to act as his deputy and supervise the planning. With the 7th Air Force's heavy helicopters moving to Utapao, Burns selected Colonel Loyd J. Anders, USAF, Deputy Commander for Operations, 56th Special Operations Wing as the helicopter mission commander.[50] It is ironic that Burns, Baxter, and Anders, each with fixed-wing aircraft backgrounds and no helicopter experience, were now tasked with planning and conducting a heliborne operation.[51]

On 13 May Major General Carl W. Hoffman, Commanding General, III Marine Amphibious Force, received notice to provide an ACBLT and other support to COMUSSAG. Hoffman formed a command group of five officers from his staff and designated Colonel John M. Johnson Jr. as the commander of the ACBLT (Task Group 79.9). In essence, Johnson was the Marine Corps service component commander to the CJTF/COMUSSAG. In addition to Johnson and his small staff, Task Group 79.9 consisted of BLT 2/9 (Task Unit 79.9.1), commanded by Lieutenant Colonel Randal W. Austin, and D 1/4 reinforced with a small command element from 1/4 (Task Unit 79.9.2). Task Unit 79.9.2 was commanded by 1/4 Executive Officer Major Raymond E. Porter and Company D's Commanding Officer was Captain Walter A. Wood.

During the execution of the operation, Burns determined that the operational control of the Marine forces and USAF tactical aircraft would be exercised by COMUSSAG through an Airborne Mission Commander (AMC) and battle staff located in an Airborne Battlefield Command and Control Center (ABCCC). Inherent to the plan, the AMC would be the on-scene

---

[49]   Lucien S. Vandenbroucke, *Perilous Options. Special Operations as an Instrument of Foreign Policy,* (Oxford: Oxford University Press, 1993), 95.
[50]   Guilmartin, 46.
[51]   Ibid, 47.

commander operating under the direction of COMUSSAG in Nakhon Phanom. Burns had used this command and control arrangement when he commanded operation Eagle Pull a month earlier. Aboard a specially equipped EC-130, the ABCCC would orbit approximately 90 miles northeast of Koh Tang in order to be within communication range of both Koh Tang and Nakhon Phanom. (Figure 3)

The various forces that merged together to form a joint task force possessed all the tools necessary to conduct a successful operation. What was critically required but missing was a leader to pull these forces together and direct everyone's efforts in the same direction.

Command and Control

Failures of command and control in the operational planning were primarily caused by the physical separation of planning cells and the absence of centralized leadership to unify the effort. A senior USAF officer described the planning atmosphere when he recalled that "preparations at Utapao lacked coordination and leadership. No one seemed to be in charge."[52] Intrusive micromanagement from higher headquarters only exacerbated the situation.

Although Burns was the CJTF, he elected to remain in Nakhon Phanom and tasked his deputy, Baxter, to oversee the planning of the Marines and USAF helicopter units at Utapao. Under this arrangement, COMUSSAG would be physically separated by 160 miles from his subordinate commanders and planners. One flag officer commented, "it was quite clear that the on-scene commander was not on scene."[53] Additionally, Baxter never took charge of the planning process and did not provide any central direction. An after-action report by BLT 2/9 stated that Baxter was present at planning meetings but his "exact role was unknown to 2/9 personnel."[54] Bottom line: No one took charge of the planning process at Utapao. The absence of centralized authority and direction was the source of confusion in the planning phase. Compounding this situation, the USAF and Marine commanders were assigned to different

---

[52]   Colonel George A Dugard, USAF, quoted in Vandenbroucke, 98.
[53]   Major George R.Dunham and Colonel David A. Quinlan, *U.S. Marines in Vietnam: The Bitter End* (Washington D.C.: History and Museums Division, Headquarters, U.S. Marine Corps, 1990)
[54]   Vandenbroucke, 98.

command posts that were physically separated from each other within the air base at Utapao. As a result, the Marines and USAF personnel planned independently. The physical separation of the commanders throughout the chain of command accentuated the disjointed planning.

The disjointed atmosphere was evident when key participants to the operation were absent from planning meetings and briefs. The final planning conference took place at 1900 14 May, about just nine hours before the scheduled helicopter launch time. Key participants included Anders, Johnson, Baxter, Austin, and Wood. Missing from the conference were all the helicopter crews who were in crew rest as well as the AMC and battle staff. Tasked with controlling the battle under the direction of COMUSSAG, the AMC and battle staff were available for the meeting but for some unknown reason were not present. Most likely the crew was not aware of the meeting, and their absence was a serious omission considering their key role in the operation.

The final planning meeting occurred at 0100 15 May, just three hours before the anticipated departure time of 0405. This was the first and only chance that most of the tactical commanders could personally interact and work out any problems in the plan. In effect, it was a confirmation brief. The atmosphere of the meeting was described as casual and relaxed, and the briefing was an impromptu affair conducted in a room without chairs or tables.[55] The helicopter crews, Marine commanders, and staff were present; however, the AMC and battle staff were again absent because they were preparing for a aircraft launch time of 0315. At 0430 the AMC and battle staff were finally briefed of the plan by radio as they were airborne in the ABCCC. Although COMUSSAG was to control the operation through the AMC in the ABCCC, COMUSSAG and the AMC were not aware of details of the plan, since neither had participated in any of the mission briefings. As the battle was about to begin, the AMC knew the general scheme of maneuver but was unaware of the friendly order of battle and essential

---

[55]   Guilmartin, 84.

19

communications information, such as call signs and frequencies. This situation was a source of tremendous friction throughout the battle.

From the start of the crisis, Burns and his planners were the recipients of simultaneous micromanagement from the JCS via the National Military Command Center (NMCC) at the Pentagon as well as from CINCPAC in Hawaii. By-passing CINCPAC, NMCC became increasingly intrusive and directive during the planning and usually communicated directly with Burns or his subordinate planners in Utapao. As a result, two higher echelons of command were simultaneously making the same information demands or providing redundant information and prescriptive directives to the planners. COMUSSAG was forced to simultaneously answer CINCPAC in Hawaii and the JCS at the NMCC. The NMCC and CINCPAC provided COMUSSAG specific guidance and demanded briefbacks of tactical and operational plans to ensure that preparations conformed with the president's intent.[56] Not only did the higher headquarters became actively involved in the tactical planning, but JCS and CINCPAC's "thirst for information was unquenchable."[57] They demanded continuous updates in extraordinary detail to include tail numbers and call signs of aircraft.[58] Johnson stated that the reporting requirements became a distraction to the planners and "simply interfered with any efforts to effectively carry out the planning for the task that faced us.[59]

The NMCC and CINCPAC simultaneously offered directives, advice, and redundant information that applied to the tactical level. For example, the JCS directed COMUSSAG that the assault would occur at 0542. The JCS specified the exact time of the assault to the minute; a detail usually left decided by the operational and tactical planners. During the planning, the NMCC and CINCPAC frequently contacted tactical planners at Utapao with irrelevant information. Johnson was personally contacted by a major general in the NMCC just to be

---

[56] Vandenbroucke, 95.
[57] Ibid, 96.
[58] Ibid, 96.
[59] Ibid, 97.

informed that there were no snakes on Koh Tang.[60] In his book *Perilous Options,*
LucienVandenbrouke summarizes the situation when he stated, "By imposing excessive
reporting requirements, inundating the planners with a flood of at times useless information, and
trying to direct local actions in the smallest detail, the Pentagon and CINCPAC greatly
complicated USSAG's task."[61]

Poor Dissemination of Intelligence

USSAG headquarters in Nakhon Phanom possessed accurate intelligence from several
sources concerning enemy strength and disposition at Koh Tang. Aerial photographs and other
imagery was also available but none of this crucial intelligence was ever disseminated to the
tactical planners at Utapao. The physical separation and flawed coordination between USSAG
headquarters and the planners at Utapao had a devastating effect on the dissemination of
intelligence.

USSAG headquarters in Nakhon Phanom received accurate intelligence from several sources
concerning enemy troop strengths and dispositions. A report by CINCPAC's intelligence branch,
Commander, Intelligence Pacific (IPAC), indicated that Koh Tang was defended by
approximately 100 infantry supported by heavy weapons to include mortars, recoilless rifles,
machine guns, and RPGs. A separate Defense Intelligence Agency (DIA) report indicated an
understrength Khmer Rouge infantry battalion of 150-200 troops supported with a robust
complement of heavy weapons. Using IPAC and DIA estimates, USSAG's own estimate was
100-300 enemy troops. Vandenbrouke states that, "USSAG forwarded these estimates to the
U.S. Air Force 307th Strategic Wing at Utapao. But USSAG neither gave the information to the
Marines who were to assault Koh Tang nor instructed the 307th Strategic Wing to do so. "[62] The
end result was that the planners at Utapao never received these enemy estimates.

USSAG also had information concerning the employment and disposition of the Cambodian

---

60   Ibid, 97.
61   Ibid, 98.
62   Ibid, 99.

forces. USAF reconnaissance aircraft had reported to USSAG no fewer that eleven incidents of antiaircraft fire from Koh Tang.[63] During the evening of 13-14 May, an AC-130 gunship received antiaircraft fire and using scanning devices located and reported several gun emplacements oriented on the beaches that were planned as Landing Zones (LZs).

Accurate intelligence was available at the operational level but was never disseminated to the tactical planners and operators. The only information the assault forces received concerning enemy strength at Koh Tang included a preliminary report from IPAC estimating twenty soldiers and a former Cambodian naval officer's estimate of no more than eighteen to thirty irregulars. During most of the planning, Marines were using outline maps of Koh Tang prepared from U2 imagery. The only aerial photograph of Koh Tang the Marines possessed was taken from a personal camera at 4,500 feet during a visual reconnaissance.[64] The pictures were of limited use except to confirm that the beaches were narrow and the island was covered by dense jungle.

After-action reports proved that intelligence estimates by both IPAC and DIA were extremely accurate. There is evidence to suggest that the Cambodian troops on Koh Tang were expecting a heliborne assault and had positioned their forces accordingly, covering the only two possible LZs on the island. Oriented on the landing zones, enemy infantry reinforced with heavy weapons were dug into covered and concealed positions that indicated signs of recent construction.[65] (Figure 4) Although the intelligence estimates failed to be disseminated to the planners and executors at Utapao, the information was available to the USSAG staff to include Burns. Burns and his staff were also aware of the planned scheme of maneuver.[66] Timely intelligence is imperative to develop an effective plan. With knowledge of a large and well-armed enemy force on Koh Tang, it seems unusual that no one at USSAG questioned the plan that was developed at Utapao.

---

63   Ibid, 99.
64   Guilmartin, 72.
65   Ibid, 82.
66   Vanderbrouke, 98.

Scheme of Maneuver

With inaccurate intelligence concerning enemy strength and dispositions, the planners at Utapao developed operational and tactical plans for the recovery of the *Mayaguez* and crew. BLT 2/9 was tasked to conduct a heliborne assault to "seize, occupy, and defend the island of Koh Tang, hold the island indefinitely, (for a minimum of 48 hours) and to rescue any of the crew members of *Mayaguez*..."[67] A boarding party from D 1/4, consisting of 48 Marines and six sailors were given the mission to recover the *Mayaguez* and any crew members on board.[68] (Figure 5) On 1900 14 May, a planning conference determined the scheme of maneuver. Shortly after midnight on 15 May, about four hours before the assault force was scheduled to launch, the final plan was completed. The boarding party would be inserted on the *Holt* from USAF helicopters. Following *Holt's* closure on the *Mayaguez* and after USAF tactical air laid riot control agents on the ship, D 1/4 would conduct a ship to ship boarding.[69] Dictated by the JCS, the boarding of the *Mayaguez* and the assault on Koh Tang were planned to occur nearly simultaneously at 0542. USAF tactical aircraft were tasked with supporting the Marines at Koh Tang and to also interdict any attempts to move *Mayaguez* or crew to Cambodia. During the assault and boarding operations, Navy tactical aircraft from the *Coral Sea* would interdict Cambodia naval and air

bases to prevent reinforcements from Cambodia.

The scheme of maneuver called for eight USAF helicopters to insert 180 members of BLT 2/9 on Koh Tang. This wave would consist of G Company, a section of 81mm mortars, and the BLT "Alpha" command group. One reinforced platoon would land at the western LZ and the remainder of the company, the 81 mm mortar section and the BLT command group would all land in the larger eastern LZ. The platoon in the western LZ would establish a blocking position, while the remainder of the company would push west from the eastern LZ. For the second and

---

[67]   Johnson, Austin, and Quinlan, 25.

[68]   Six Maritime Sea Command civilian personnel were also attached to the boarding party.

[69]   The original plan called for a heliborne landing on the *Mayaguez*, but there was concern about landing helicopters and disembarking Marines on the containerized cargo.

subsequent waves, an availability of twelve helicopters was planned with a four and one-half hour turn-around time between waves. The second wave would consist of Captain Mykle E. Stahl's reinforced Company E and follow-on waves would be comprised of the remainder of BLT 2/9 and Johnson's command group.[70] The fire support plan contained an "on-call" plan for continuous close air support (CAS) and naval gunfire support.[71] There was no preplanned preparation fires because of concern for the safety of any crew members that may be on the island.

If the intelligence were to have been disseminated, tactical plans would have changed significantly. Because the intelligence information and enemy situation were the foundation of the plan, faulty information resulted in an ineffective plan. If the planners had been aware of the intelligence reports that indicated a battalion-sized force in prepared defensive positions covering the LZs, the scheme of maneuver and fire support would have been modified. Under the assumption that there were only eighteen to thirty irregular forces on the island, the plan to conduct a heliborne assault against a well armed, numerically superior, and entrenched force with no preparatory fires was not tactically sound. Guilmartin summarized the situation when he observed, "If ever an infantry unit was set up to by circumstances for failure, 2/9 was it. Yet 2/9 did not fail. The same point applies to the two helicopter squadrons."[72] The progressive failure of poor command and control, continuing inaccurate intelligence, and a flawed plan created chaos and near defeat during the execution of the operation.

---

[70] Johnson, Austin, and Quinlan, 28. Because of the limited availability of helicopters, Johnson decided to remain at Utapao during the initial waves and planned to insert into Koh Tang on a subesequent wave.

[71] Ibid, 28.

[72] Guilmartin, 42.

15 MAY 1975:
A FIERCE BATTLE AND NEAR DISASTER

Chaotic, confused, and incomplete planning based on faulty intelligence proved to be a recipe for disaster. During the execution phase of the operation, the same problems of command and control that plagued it during planning were present to a greater degree and accentuated the fog and friction of the battle. As the helicopters approached Koh Tang, the operation began to immediately go wrong.

First Wave

At 0414 the assault force launched from Utapao. At 0602 Jolly Green (JG, HH-53s) 11, 12, and 13 began putting Porter's boarding force on the *Holt*.[73] Friction began immediately; neither the helicopters nor the ABCCC had the radio frequency for the *Holt*. As a result of the disjointed planning, this was the first of many communications problems to come during the day. Finally at 0631 the boarding party was safely aboard the *Holt*.

At approximately 0603 the first helicopter Knife 21 (K-21, a CH-53), landed at Koh Tang in the western LZ and was followed by K-22. As Second Lieutenant James McDaniel's 1st platoon of Company G were disembarking K-21, the jungle erupted with small arms and automatic weapons fire along with RPGs and mortar fire. At 0605 the call of "Hot LZ!" was transmitted on the UHF helicopter control frequency. K-21 and K-22 were both hit hard. K-21 immediately lost an engine and ditched three-quarters of a mile off the beach in the ocean and immediately flipped over. One crewman disappeared with the sinking aircraft and three other crewman were recovered a short time later. K-22, carrying Davis, the company commander, aborted the landing and provided fire to cover K-21's withdrawal. K-22, with one destroyed engine and a severe fuel leak, limped back to the coast of Thailand. A SAR helicopter picked up the heliteam and returned them to Utapao.

---

[73] Different sources contain different timelines in reference to the events during the battle. To remain consistent, I have used the times presented in Guilmartin's *A Very Short War*.

On the eastern LZ, the largest LZ which was to receive the bulk of the forces, the first two helicopters were shot down as they entered the landing zone. K-23 was touching down when intense fire erupted and destroyed an engine and shot off the tail pylon. The pilot managed to land the helicopter despite the loss of control and Second Lieutenant Michael Cicere's third platoon of Company G (G/3), sprinted for the treeline north of the LZ. Moments later, the crew evacuated the helicopter and joined the Marines. In the treeline, the small force set up a perimeter and dug in. K-31 was following K-23 into the zone when it began to take sustained automatic weapons and RPG hits from the jungle bordering the beach. As the helicopter was trying to gain altitude to abort the landing, a RPG impacted the cockpit and killed the co-pilot. Seconds later, another RPG impacted the aircraft causing the port external fuel tank to explode engulfing the helicopter in a ball of flame. K-31 crash landed in four feet of water approximately fifty meters from the beach. Seven Marines and two Navy corpsman were killed in the helicopter, and three Marines were killed as they made their way to the beach and charged the treeline. The remaining ten Marines and three USAF crewman swam seaward. One of the survivors in the water was the forward air controller (FAC), First Lieutenant Terry Tonkin. At 0620 using an USAF survival radio, he was able to direct firing runs from USAF A-7s on enemy positions surrounding the eastern LZ.[74]

In the first twenty minutes of the assault, three helicopters were shot down and one sustained severe damage. On the western LZ, McDaniel and nineteen Marines were under continuous fire but managed to push into the treeline and overran an enemy 60 mm mortar position in the process[75]. On the eastern LZ, Cicere and twenty Marines were isolated and pinned down. At this time, the AMC directed the remaining four helicopters to divert their landing from the eastern LZ to the western LZ. This decision probably prevented more helicopters from being destroyed in the heavily defended eastern LZ. K-32 diverted from the eastern LZ and landed thirteen Marines at the western LZ to increase the force there from twenty to 33 Marines. During

---

74   Johnson, Austin, and Quinlan, 30.

75   Guilmartin, 89.

the insertion, K-32 sustained heavy damage including a RPG hit in the tail section. Although severely damaged, the helicopter was able to return to Utapao. At 0626 JG-42 carrying First Lieutenant Dick Kieth, Executive Officer of Company G, and 29 Marines landed at the western LZ. JG-42 sustained heavy damage but made it back to Utapao. Neither aircraft was able to fly again. JG-43, carrying Austin, the BLT command group and a section of 81 mm mortars, attempted to land in the western LZ but was driven off by gunfire. On a second attempt, JG-43 landed the 29 Marines between 900 and 1,200 meters south of the western LZ. This group of Marines were isolated and particularly vulnerable because most carried only .45 caliber pistols as sidearms.

At 0630 the situation at Koh Tang was grim. Fourteen Americans were dead. Of the 180 Marines and sailors in the first wave, only 109 were ashore in three isolated positions. Sixty personnel of Company G were in the western LZ fighting against tough enemy resistance while establishing and expanding their perimeter. Twenty personnel from G/3 (not including five USAF crewman) were defending an isolated position near the eastern LZ and 29 personnel from the BLT command group and a section of 81mm mortars were about 1,000 meters south of the western LZ and working their way north against enemy resistance. There were also thirteen survivors swimming seaward from the eastern LZ. (Figure 6)

As the Marines were battling the Cambodians, USAF tactical air was not able to provide CAS. The situation on the ground was confusing, and the pilots were unaware of the location either of friendlies or the enemy. Because the jungle was so dense, the fighting was extremely close. Smoke to mark positions was difficult to see through the jungle and the Marines were running low on pyrotechnics. The loss of Tonkin, the BLT FAC, also eliminated the UHF link. Air-ground communications were made over the VHF tactical nets which were already overburdened with radio traffic.

At 0712 Austin was able to make radio contact with the main body in the western LZ and began to formulate a link up plan. At 0800 Kieth ordered McDaniel to take a patrol south of the LZ to link up with Austin's isolated group. The patrol entered the jungle and quickly ran into strong enemy fire. One Marine was killed and four were wounded to include McDaniel. As the patrol withdrew to the perimeter, the enemy conducted a fierce counterattack on the heels of the patrol. The Marines, fighting bravely, repulsed the attack.

As the Marines on Koh Tang were fighting for their lives, the recovery of the *Mayaguez* was proceeding as planned. With the boarding party safely staged on the *Holt*, the ship steamed toward the *Mayaguez*. At 0714 USAF A-7s engulfed the *Mayaguez* with riot control agents, and ten minutes later the *Holt* pulled alongside. At 0725 Wood and the Marines of D 1/4, boarded the *Mayaguez* and quickly seized it. The *Mayaguez* had been abandoned, and the Marines declared the ship secure at 0822. At 0958 the *Holt* began towing the *Mayaguez* to international waters as three Maritime Sea Command personnel prepared to get it underway on its own power.

At 0720 the destroyer, *Wilson,* arrived off the east coast of Koh Tang. Its commanding officer, Commander Mike Rodgers, immediately sensed the confusion of the battle after he contacted the ABCCC. He was asked by the ABCCC what kind of aircraft he was and assigned an orbit of 10,000 feet.[76] Moments later a lookout on the *Wilson* spotted swimmers in the ocean, quickly discovered that these were thirteen survivors of JG-31, and began rescue operations. Due to an oversight caused by the rapid and chaotic events, the ABCCC never informed the *Wilson* of friendlies in the water. The unexpected events of the opening rounds of the battle overwhelmed the ABCCC battle staff. No one was in command or coordinating of the battle. After rescuing the swimmers, the *Wilson* was ordered by the ABCCC to intercept a small boat heading toward Koh Tang from Kompong Som. As the *Wilson* closed on the small boat, caucasians and a white flag were spotted. As it turned out, the entire *Mayaguez* crew was aboard. At 1005 the crew of the *Mayaguez* was safely aboard the *Wilson* and Washington was immediately notified. Due to another oversight by the ABCCC, the Marines at Koh Tang, tasked with rescuing the crew members on the island, were never informed that the crew had been

---

[76]   Michael J.Rodgers from an interview with Guilmartin, 98.

recovered. About 1200 Austin was finally informed by Marines from the second wave that the crew was rescued

At 1005 the strategic objectives of recovering the *Mayaguez* and crew had been accomplished; however, at the operational and tactical level this was irrelevant. At Koh Tang 114 Americans were fighting for their lives against a tenacious enemy who had no intention of quitting.[77] Reinforcements would have to be put on the island to avoid a tactical defeat. Isolated in small perimeters, the Marines were in a perilous situation. The commanders at the strategic and operational level were unaware of this development. The ABCCC and COMUSSAG had little situational awareness and did not comprehend the tactical situation. Johnson at Utapao was receiving information from the returning helicopter crews and inherently understood the urgent need to reinforce the island. Johnson was probably the only one not at Koh Tang who understood the urgent requirement for additional troops.

After 0900 Kieth established communications with an USAF airborne tactical air controller (TACA) overhead. At 0938 an AC-130 gunship, Spectre 61, began to provide effective CAS in support of the Marines in the western LZ. Three hours after landing in a hot LZ, the Marines were finally receiving effective fire support. After three aborted insertion attempts and two aerial refuelings, JG-41 was able to finally land Second Lieutenant Richard H. Zales and his 24 Marines of 2d Platoon, Company G (2/G) in the western LZ. The additional firepower and ammunition was crucial in defending the perimeter. JG-41 was shot up, and while it returned to Utapao, it was not to fly again.

Second Wave

Of the eleven helicopters in the first wave, only four were still operable. Three had crashed and four were out of commission due to severe damage. Two helicopters (K-51, 52) in Nakhon Phanom had completed maintenance and were now available. With one helicopter dedicated to SAR, only five helicopters were available for the second wave. The five helicopters in the

---

77   Guilmartin, 99.

second wave launched from Utapao between 0900 and 1000. Aboard K-52, K-32, JG-11, JG-12, and JG-43, were 127 reinforcements that included Davis and the remainder of Company G as well as elements of Company E.

With the recovery of the *Mayaguez* and crew, Ford wanted to disengage as quickly as possible. At 1155 JCS sent a message to CINCPAC directing "all concerned to immediately cease all offensive operations against the Khmer Republic...[and to] disengage and withdraw all forces from operating area as soon as possible."[78] This order passed through the chain of command until it reached the ABCCC. The AMC ordered the second wave to return to Utapao. After vehement protests from Johnson, Austin, and various helicopter pilots, the second wave continued toward Koh Tang. This is further indication that COMUSSAG or the AMC did not have a grasp of the battle.

As the second wave was inbound, the command group and mortar section continued to move north to link up with the main force in the western LZ. At around 1030 Austin's group was close to the perimeter. Austin and Kieth decided to task Zale's second platoon to conduct a link up attack to the south. Supported by CAS and 81mm mortar fire, G/2 attacked south and the link up was complete around 1200.

At 1150 JG-11 and JG-12, landed at the western LZ, off-loaded their Marines and took four wounded Marines aboard. After previously diverting helicopters from the eastern LZ, the AMC, mistakenly ordered K-52, JG-43, and K-51 to insert on the eastern LZ. K-52 was hit hard by enemy fire, aborted the landing, and barely made it back to the Thai coast.[79] K-51 and JG-43 diverted to the western beach and successfully inserted shortly after 1200. The main perimeter in the western LZ now had an effective force of 205 Marines.

G/3 and five Airmen on the eastern LZ were still isolated. After the second wave insertions, JG-43 and JG-11 were held in orbit for an attempt to rescue the isolated group. At approximately 1400 A-7's laid riot control agents in the vicinity of the eastern LZ and JG-43

---

[78]   Ibid, 107.
[79]   Ibid, 114.

30

attempted to land. The helicopter received heavy enemy gunfire, lost an engine and was forced to abort. Followed by JG-11, JG-43 returned to the *Coral Sea* for repairs. After this unsuccessful attempt to extract the eastern LZ, only three of the second wave helicopters were flyable.[80]

After completing rescue operations of the thirteen swimmers, the *Wilson* had returned to Koh Tang shortly after 1300. Coordinating with the ABCCC and A-7s, the *Wilson* initiated and provided naval surface fires support and engaged targets near the eastern LZ. The naval gunfire was controlled by A-7's who had spotted enemy positions during JG-13's unsuccessful rescue attempt. The *Wilson*, located about 1,000 meters off the east coast of Koh Tang, fired 176 rounds of 5-inch fire in support of the isolated Marines. Seven hours after landing at Koh Tang, the Marines finally had their first naval gunfire support.

At 1500 the Marines in the western LZ were consolidating their defensive perimeter. Austin requested guidance from higher headquarters- should they dig in, seize the island, or extract? He never received an answer from the AMC or COMUSSAG. At 1620 two OV-10s arrived at Koh Tang; Major Undorf in Nail 68 and his wingman Captain Richard Roehrkasse in Nail 47. They arrived to a chaotic situation with no one commanding or coordinating the battlespace. This was the turning point in the battle. The fire support coordination arrangements were not working to support the Marines. During the planning, the Marines had requested but were denied OV-10s to support the assault. Unlike A-7s, OV-10s had the endurance to remain on station to provide operational continuity and the capability to maintain continuous eye contact on ground targets. The pilots were also trained as airborne FACs and TACAs. Once he arrived on station, Undorf quickly contacted the Marines on both the eastern and western LZs to establish friendly positions. Using the OV-10's smoke rockets to mark targets, he quickly controlled A-7 and F-4 air strikes. Just minutes after the OV-10s arrived, Undorf began to orchestrate the battle and

---

[80] Ibid, 117.

began to impose order to the chaotic situation. This was the first time since the Marines landed that someone was coordinating the battle and effective fire support.

After being briefed of the criticality of the situation on the eastern LZ, Undorf directed his attention to extracting the isolated group. There was a partly sunken Cambodian swift boat with twin-mounted .50 caliber machine guns still in operation and covering the eastern LZ. These machine guns had caused much of the damage to JG-43 in the aborted attempt to extract G/3. The *Wilson*, monitoring the tactical communication nets, volunteered naval gunfire support. In coordination with Undorf, the *Wilson* at 1655 completely destroyed the swift boat with 5" naval guns. The *Wilson* also made its gig available to provide close-in .50 caliber machine gun fire and to serve as an emergency extract and a surface search and rescue craft.

The Extraction

At 1630 there were only four helicopters available to extract the Marines: JG-11, JG-12, K-51, and K-52. JG-43 had been rapidly repaired on the *Coral Sea* and at 1710 was launched to make a total of five helicopters for extract. At 1736 Spectre 11 and 21 were orbiting Koh Tang, and at 1813 Undorf began to control fire missions for Spectre 11. Under the cover of gunship fires and machine gun fire from both the *Wilson's* gig and the OV-10s, JG-11 landed on the eastern LZ at 1820. The Marines and airmen fought their way back into the helicopter as enemy soldiers came within hand grenade range. USAF helicopter crew members and Marines knocked out the helicopters windows with rifle butts and fired through the openings.[81] One minute after sunset, at 1823 JG-11 lifted off with 20 Marines and five Airman safely aboard. Moments after the eastern LZ was evacuated, a C-130 dropped a 15,000 pound bomb (BLU-82) in the center of the island. This drop was not coordinated with the Marines on the island. As the bomb floated down on a crate from a parachute, the Marines believed it was a misdirected resupply effort and were amazed when it exploded.

---

[81]   Ibid, 124.

The successful extraction of the eastern LZ relieved the most critical tactical problem. However, it was unclear as to what should happen next, to extract or reinforce? Undorf contacted Austin for guidance. Austin made it clear that the situation was critical. Unable to obtain orders or guidance from the AMC, Undorf contacted Austin and told him to make the call. Undorf told him he was confident he could control the helicopters and coordinate the fire support to extract his Marines but was unsure about the status of bringing in reinforcements. Austin decided to extract the force. With the decision to extract, the forces at Koh Tang began to execute one of the toughest tactical scenarios: a helicopter extraction in the midst of intense enemy fires during darkness.

As the forces prepared for extraction, the Marines in the western LZ began to reduce their perimeter. As Company E was retrograding from the perimeter under enemy fire, a machine gun team was left behind. These three Marines were not discovered missing until the extraction was completed and were declared missing in action and presumed dead. Another helicopter, JG-44 had been repaired and was now enroute to Koh Tang, adding the available helicopters to six. The *Holt* had completed her mission of towing the *Mayaguez* to international waters and was now in support off the west coast of Koh Tang. With no advance warning of an inbound helicopter, the Marines were surprised when K-51 landed at about 1840. The enemy illuminated the LZ with mortar rounds and poured heavy fire at the helicopter. Moments later, K-51 took off with 54 Marines aboard. Following K-51, JG-43 landed at 1847 and embarked 54 Marines as mortar rounds were impacting the beach. While JG-43 was still in the LZ, JG 44 (piloted by First Lieutenent Robert D. Blough) entered the tiny zone and nearly collided with JG-43.[82] A near disaster! After JG-43 cleared the LZ, JG-44 made a second attempt to land but was driven off by heavy fire. On the third try, JG-44 landed at 1854 and departed with 40 Marines. Instead of returning to the *Coral Sea*, Blough decided to drop off the Marines on the *Holt* saving precious time.

---

[82]   High tide had decreased the size of the LZ.

There were now only 73 Marines left on the dark island fighting a numerically superior enemy. At this most crucial moment, the coordination of the battle had to be transferred to another OV-10. Running low on fuel, Undorf and his wingman expertly conducted a battle hand-off to Captain Seth Wilson in Nail 69 and First Lieutenant Will Carroll in Nail 51. Spectre 11 also had to depart because of low fuel and ammunition but was soon replaced by Spectre 21. During the battle handover, radio contact with the Marines was initially lost, and the OV-10 did a low flyover with landing lights on to make sure they were not overrun. Adding to the drama, Wilson's gig had only 1,000 rounds of ammunition remaining. The extraction was going to be a very close call.

Wilson and Carroll went to work controlling the helicopters and coordinating fires. Because of Blough's initiative to disembark the Marines on the *Holt*, JG-44 was inbound to take a second load just fourteen minutes after his first pick-up. At 1915 with Spectre 21 providing effective fires, JG-44 landed and picked up 34 Marines. JG-44 recieved heavy enemy fire, lost an engine, and was forced to land on the *Coral Sea*. In command of the 28 Marines remaining on the island, Davis, reported at 1929 that they were in danger of being overrun. Spectre 21 continued to provide CAS as K-51 was inbound to the LZ. Because of the darkness, battlefield smoke, and the reflection of flares and illumination off the surf and water, K-51 aborted landing attempts three times. At 1950, on the fourth try and guided by the outgoing tracers of the Marines, K-51 landed in the tight horseshoe perimeter with landing lights ablaze. The perimeter was so tight that the Marines were anchored in the waters edge and under intense enemy fire. After all Marines were on-board, a quick check of area was made by the crew chief, Technical Sergeant Wayne L. Fisk, to ensure no one was left in the small zone. Fisk, a veteran of the Son Tay raid, made his way back on the helicopter and fired his GAU-5 making him the last U.S. ground combatant of the Vietnam War. K-51 lifted off at 2000 ending the small war at Koh Tang. At the end of the day, friendly casualities included fifteen killed in action, 48 wounded in action, and three missing in action and presumed dead.

The U.S. strategic objectives had been accomplished but the battle had been a very close call. Uncoordinated and chaotic planning resulted in an uncoordinated and chaotic battle. At the operational level, there was little situational awareness, and no one was in command or coordinating the battlespace. Throughout the fight, there were occasions when the Marines were nearly overrun by the numerically superior, well-trained, and disciplined enemy force. In spite of the operational command and control failures, the ferocious battle was resolved by a narrow margin through competant tactical leadership, initiative, and individual heroism.

TACTICAL LEADERSHIP
AND BRAVERY PREVENTS DISASTER

At Koh Tang U.S. forces approached the brink of tactical and operational disaster with strategic implications that can only be described as bleak.[83] The loss of an entire unit would have been a dramatic blow to national prestige and credibility, especially following the U.S. policy failures in Southeast Asia. Throughout the fourteen hour battle seemingly minor tactical events influenced the outcome. The tactical leadership, initiative, and individual heroism of countless servicemen overcame significant command and control obstacles to prevent tactical defeat and strategic failure.

Command and Control Obstacles

The same command and control failures that plagued the planning resulted in a chaotic battle where friction and confusion reigned. The most significant command and control obstacle was the inability to effectively communicate and coordinate fire support during the battle. Tasked with controlling the battle under direction from COMUSSAG, the AMC was ineffective and at best monitored rather than coordinated the battle. In spite of the technologically advanced, long range communications systems, COMUSSAG and the AMC were not able to command or even gain situational awareness through most of the battle. The AMC and battle staff were overwhelmed by unexpected events and could not react to the tempo of operations to make timely and accurate decisions. The communication system of radio nets tying higher echelons of command to tactical units created tremendous friction. Most of the nets were channeled through the ABCCC. As a result, the ABCCC was inundated with radio traffic and messages from tactical units and three echelons of higher command. Within the first minutes of combat after UHF radios were destroyed in helicopter crashes, the remaining VHF nets were used to coordinate actions between units on the ground and to coordinate CAS. These VHF nets were saturated to the point where they were barely usable. Compounding the problem was micromanagment from higher headquarters, which added friction and increased the burden on

---

[83]   Guilmartin, 150.

the already stressed ABCCC. There was a constant and sometimes simultaneous demand of battle reports as well as tactical direction from both COMUSSAG, CINCPAC, and the NMCC. CINCPAC not only demanded continuous battle reports and casualty counts, but also attempted to control the tactics of helicopters and the Marines.[84] At one critical point in the battle when Marines were coordinating an AC-130 fire mission to support a helicopter insert, USSAG demanded to know if the Marines had a Khmer linguist and a bullhorn with them. [85] From the opening shots of the battle the ABCCC became a bottleneck in the information flow and as a result was overwhelmed, confused, and gained little situational awareness. Meanwhile, the battle raged with little coordination or direction from the AMC.

There was sufficient firepower to provide continuous support of the USAF helicopters and Marines at Koh Tang; however, there was no workable plan to coordinate fire support. Because the tactical planners were briefed that the *Mayaguez* crew members were being held by only a platoon of irregular forces on the island, no preparatory fires were planned.   As the first inbound helicopters received withering fire in the LZs, there was no immediate fire support available. An AC-130 gunship was on station, but minutes before the helicopters began their descent into the LZs, it left station to refuel. With A-7s on station, no one at the battlefield could accurately direct any CAS. The ABCCC was unaware of the freindly locations and A-7s could not identify Marine positions. Because UHF radio links were severed, the Marines could not initially communicate with CAS aircraft but later established contact over the clogged VHF nets. To facilitate the coordination of CAS, a fighter pilot was designated as the airborne tactical air controller (TACA). The TACA was the on-scene commander of the tactical aircraft to direct CAS and to serve as the link between the ABCCC and tactical air elements. Because of high fuel consumption and short loiter times of the fast moving jets, TACAs were continuously changing. With each new TACA, the Marines had to brief the pilot on an over-burdened VHF net. After the pilots were finally fully briefed, the fighters only had time for a couple strikes and

---

84 Vandenbroouke, 107.
85 Guilmartin, 108.

then would leave station to be refueled. Between 0530 and 0630 during the first wave inserts, there were four different TACAs. During the fourteen hour battle, there was a turnover of fourteen different TACAs which severely hampered the desperately needed fire support and increased the friction of the battle.[86]

Breaking Through the Friction

Tactical command and control exhibited through exemplary combat leadership on Koh Tang proved to be the most significant factor in overcaming operational command and control problems. The leadership of the BLT commander, company commanders, and small unit leaders was absolutely outstanding. Very few of the Marines in BLT 2/9 had any combat experience, and yet they performed magnificently. Individual acts of heroism were commonplace and are too numerous to cite. The Marines, outnumbered and facing a tenacious enemy, were able to quickly organize and react to unexpected and changing tactical situations.[87] Initially fighting from three isolated positions, the Marines were in danger of being overrun and defeated in detail, but the fighting ability of the individual riflemen and their leaders saved the day. The USAF helicopter pilots and crews displayed the same courage and tenacity during the harrowing inserts and extracts under intense enemy fires.

There are many instances where individual decisions and initiative affected the outcome of the battle. It appears from different accounts that a number of officers, Marines and USAF helicopter pilots alike, vehemently protested when the inbound second wave was initially aborted. The second wave of Marines and the ammunition resupply they brought with them provided the critical combat power and ammunition to prevent tactical defeat. Austin's decision to extract his forces instead of remaining overnight was a bold and correct decision. Without reinforcements, it is debatable whether the Marines could have defended their position through the evening, as their ammunition was running low. Blough, piloting JG-44, extracted two loads of Marines from the western LZ. After his first pick-up of forty Marines, he decided to

---

86 Vandenbrouke, 104.

87 Guilmartin, 153.

disembark them on the *Holt* rather than flying fifteen minutes further to the *Coral Sea*. Because of his quick perception of battle dynamics, Blough and JG-44 were revisiting the LZ just fourteen minutes later. Blough's critical action speeded the extraction during a time when the small number of Marines remaining in the LZ were almost being overrun.

To overcome fire support coordination problems, resourceful actions were initiated at the tactical level. After surviving a helicopter crash and while swimming in the ocean, Tonkin used a USAF survival radio to call in air strikes on the eastern LZ. Another example of resourceful action was demonstrated during the link up between Austin's isolated group and the Marines in the western LZ. Two officers in separate postions, Kieth in the western LZ and Captain Barry Cassidy located with the BLT command group, were able to direct effective CAS onto enemy positions located within a closing gap between converging friendly forces. Over a VHF net, Keith and Cassidy collectively controlled precision air strikes in a shrinking area by verbally guiding pilots onto the target. Simultaneously, Cassidy also controlled effective AC-130 fire missions. Once employed, the firepower of the AC-130s were critical to the survival of the Marines.

During the battle, Commander Rodgers, the captain of the *Wilson,* was monitoring tactical nets and initiated naval gunfire support. With an A-7 controlling naval gunfire, the ship provided 176 rounds in support of the Marines on the eastern LZ. Additionally, *Wilson's* gig provided close-in machine gun fires that proved critical during the extraction. Rodgers and his crew's situational awareness, initiative, and skill, led to effective fire support for the forces at Koh Tang. The first time that there was any control of the battle was shortly after Undorf and the OV-10s came on station at 1600; about ten hours after the battle began.[88] Coordinating maneuver with fires, Undorf personally imposed order on a chaotic situation. He also conducted a thorough and expert battle handover to a new OV-10 crew at a very critical point during the

---

[88]   The Marines had requested OV-10 support from the Air Force early in the planning phase but were denied.

extraction. His tactical and technical competence, initiative, and leadership made a significant difference in the outcome of the battle.

The battle at Koh Tang was an extremely close call. There are a myriad of minor individual actions that collectively or separately may have changed its outcome. The intangible characteristics of the Marines and other servicemen at Koh Tang to include leadership, discipline, bravery, improvisation, dogged determination, and espirit de corps, were the most significant factors in overcoming friction of battle.

LOOKING INTO THE FUTURE

As Guilmartin observed, "Koh Tang was both a small war and the last battle of a larger one"[89] The *Mayaguez* incident and subsequent battle at Koh Tang represented the closing chapter in a long and unpopular war in Southeast Asia . In the same instance, it also provided a glimpse to the future. The *Mayaguez* incident resulted in a rapid response, joint military operation and was also a prelude to the type of conflict the U.S. would face in the future. The U.S. would begin to see conflict initiated with asymmetrical acts against non-combatants and/or property by well-armed combatants whose governmental sponsorship may or may not be known. In 1979 just over four years after the *Mayaguez* was seized, Iranians captured the U.S. Embassy in Iran and held 58 Americans hostage for over a year. This asymmetrical act resulted in a failed rescue attempt and a crippled presidency. On Sunday morning 23 October 1983, the Marine barracks in Beirut was attacked by a suicide bomber with a truck packed with explosives. Two hundred forty three Americans were killed, and the course of U.S. policy in Lebanon was altered. In 1993 using unarmed Somali civilians as cover and concealment, gunmen battled U.S. Army Rangers, killing eighteen and taking one prisoner. U.S. policy was again altered. The above listed are all examples in which the tactical, operational, and strategic levels merge together into one. In each case they were like the *Mayaguez* incident. Events at the tactical level involving small units of battalion size or smaller had strategic implications.

The *Mayaguez* incident also marked a change in the technological character of war. During the crisis, national and military leaders possessed and exercised global communications assets and capabilities to control and direct military forces at the operational and tactical levels of war. With the advanced communications resources available today, military and civilian leaders have an even greater capability. The *Mayaguez* incident illustrated that global communications can be a "double-edged sword." They have the potential to enhance command and control and reduce the fog and friction of war. Conversely, their misuse through intrusive micromanagement can

---

[89]   Ibid, 151.

41

degrade command and control and significantly increased the fog and friction of war. Technology also provides a means to collect intelligence. As exemplified in the *Mayaguez* incident, accurate and timely intelligence is not effective unless disseminated.

Superior technology and firepower did not dominate the battlefield at Koh Tang. The fighting ability, courage, and steadfast determination of Marines and airmen prevailed to achieved strategic objectives. The value of competent leadership and the fighting ability of an individual Marine or serviceman cannot be overemphasized. Technology cannot replace the intangible factors that influence all levels of war.

FIGURE 1:
LOCATION OF MAYAGUEZ AND CREW 12-15 MAY 1975

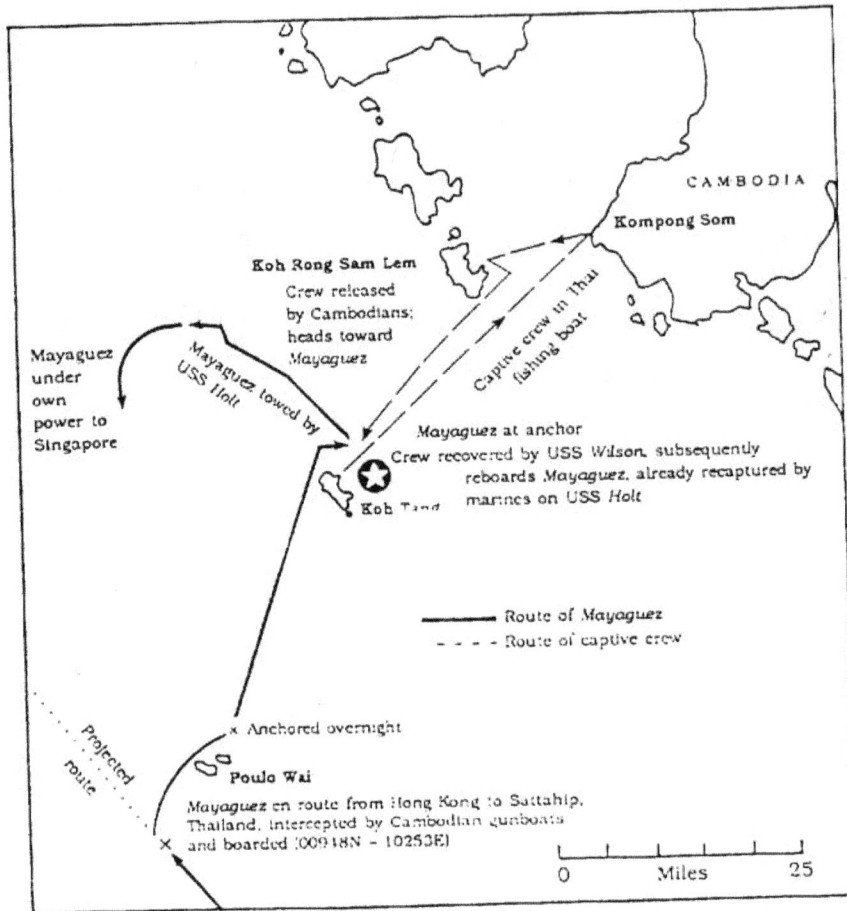

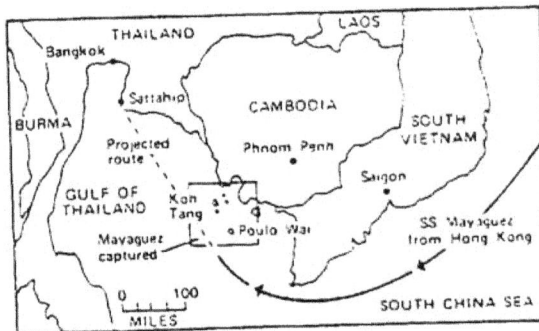

Source: GAO Report, 64.

FIGURE 2:
MAP OF KOH TANG

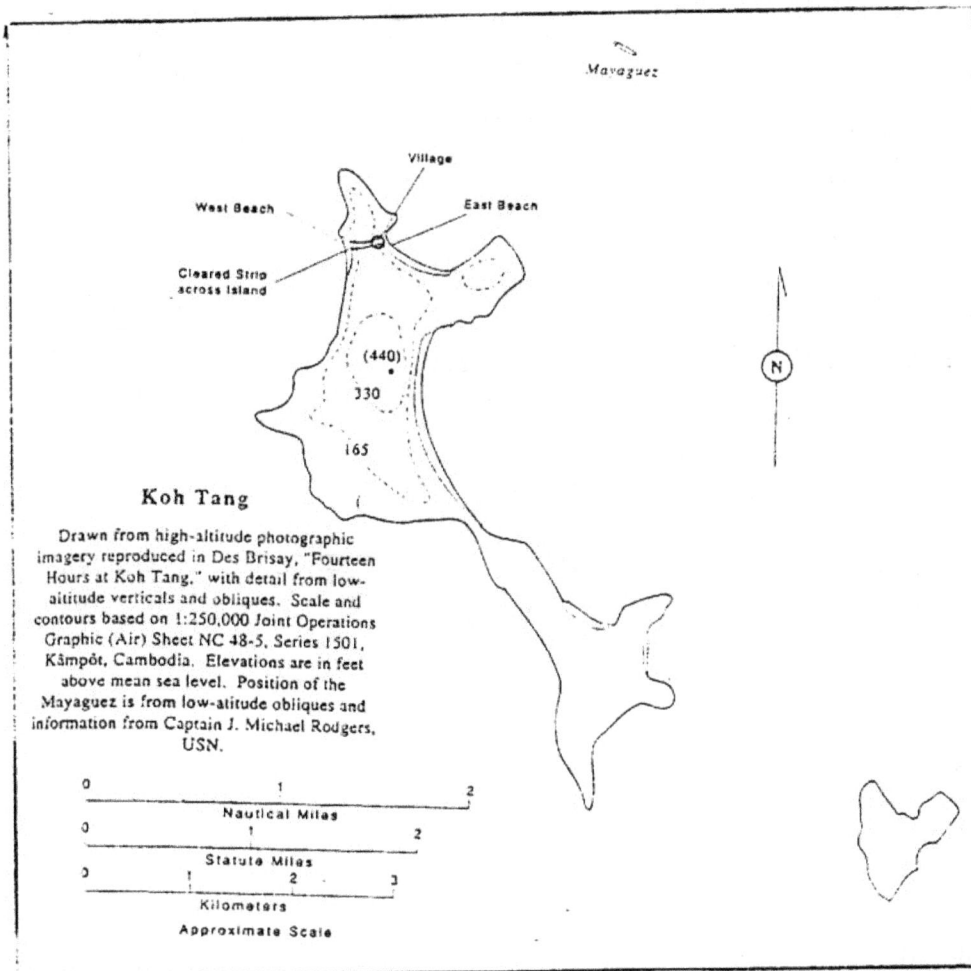

Mavaguez

Village

West Beach

East Beach

Cleared Strip
across Island

(440)

330

165

Koh Tang

Drawn from high-altitude photographic
imagery reproduced in Des Brisay, "Fourteen
Hours at Koh Tang," with detail from low-
altitude verticals and obliques. Scale and
contours based on 1:250,000 Joint Operations
Graphic (Air) Sheet NC 48-5, Series 1501,
Kâmpôt, Cambodia. Elevations are in feet
above mean sea level. Position of the
Mayaguez is from low-altitude obliques and
information from Captain J. Michael Rodgers,
USN.

Nautical Miles

Statute Miles

Kilometers

Approximate Scale

Source: Guilmartin, 71.

FIGURE 3:
MILITARY CHAIN OF COMMAND

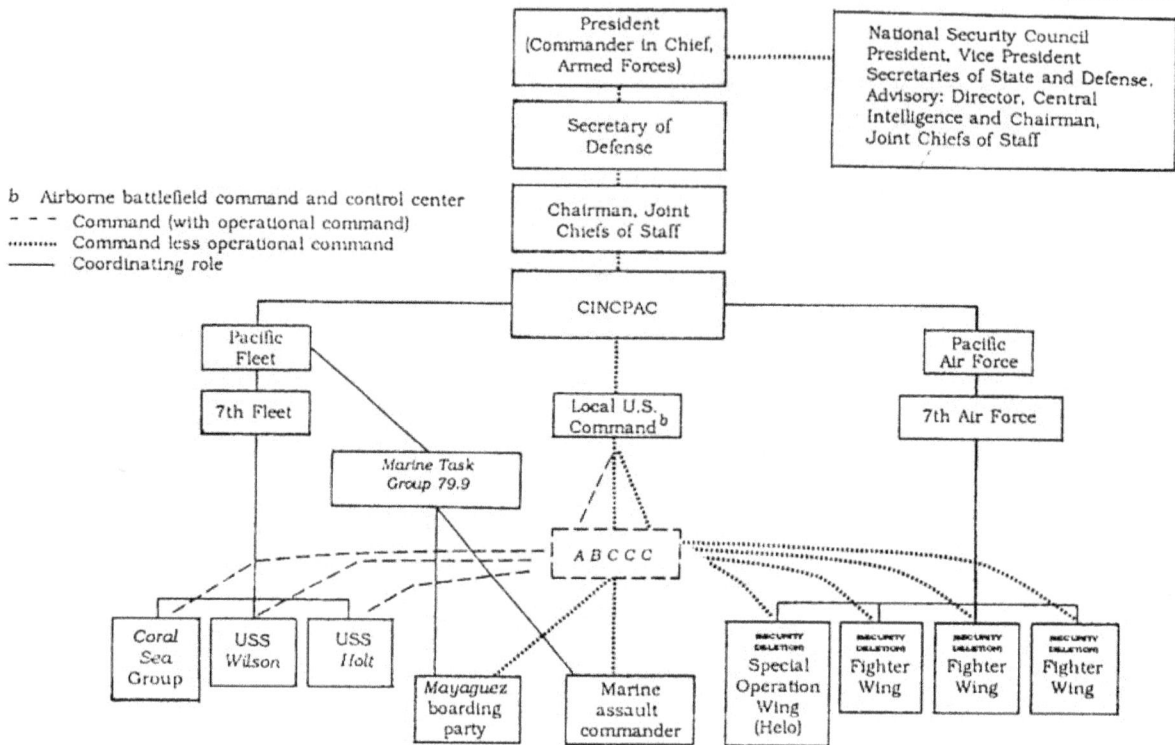

Source: GAO Report, 86.

FIGURE 4:
SCHEME OF MANEUVER

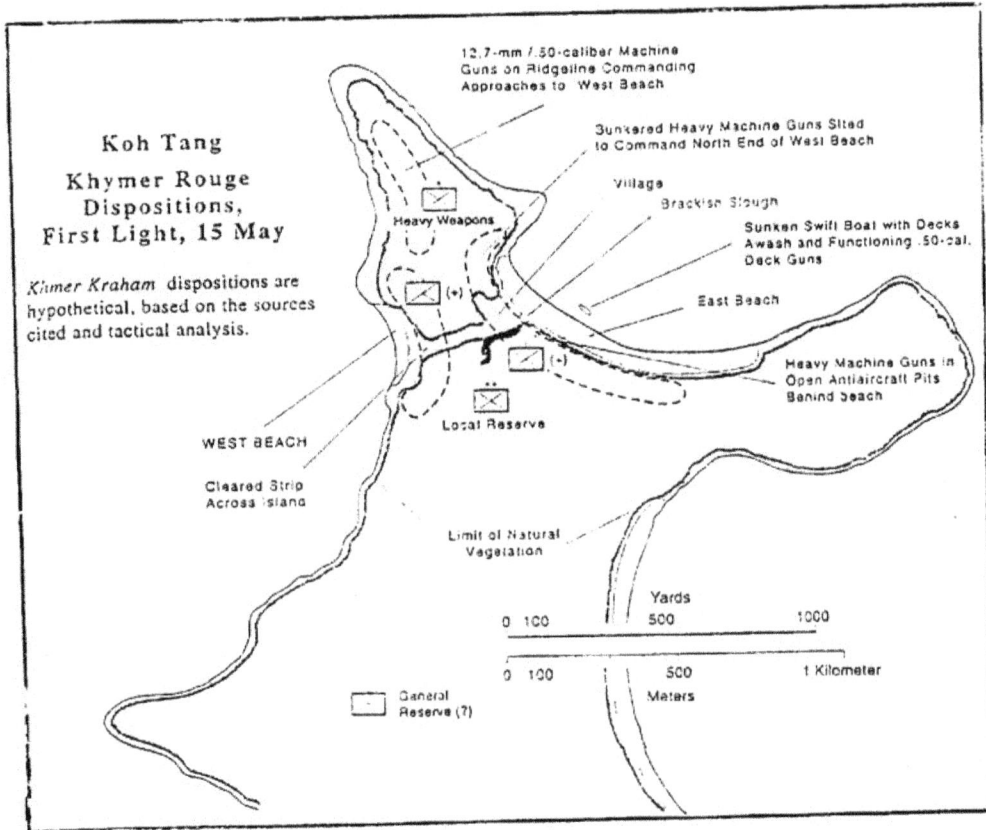

Koh Tang
Khymer Rouge
Dispositions,
First Light, 15 May

Khmer Kraham dispositions are
hypothetical, based on the sources
cited and tactical analysis.

12.7-mm /.50-caliber Machine
Guns on Ridgeline Commanding
Approaches to West Beach

Bunkered Heavy Machine Guns Sited
to Command North End of West Beach

Village
Brackish Slough

Sunken Swift Boat with Decks
Awash and Functioning .50-cal.
Deck Guns

East Beach

Heavy Machine Guns in
Open Antiaircraft Pits
Behind Beach

Heavy Weapons

WEST BEACH

Cleared Strip
Across Island

Local Reserve

Limit of Natural
Vegetation

Yards
0 100   500   1000

0 100   500   1 Kilometer
Meters

General
Reserve (?)

Source: Guilmartin, 78

46

FIGURE 5:
ENEMY DISPOSITION 15 MAY 1975

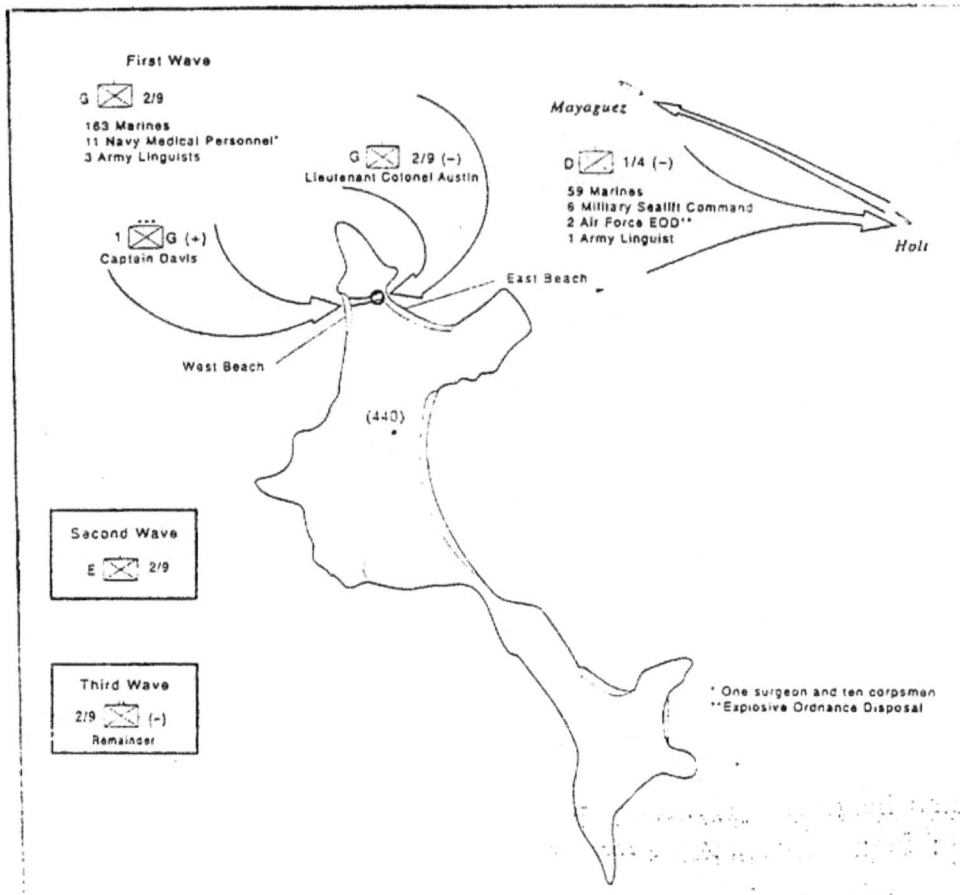

Source: Guilmartin, 83

47

FIGURE 6:
KOH TANG RESCUE OPERATIONS

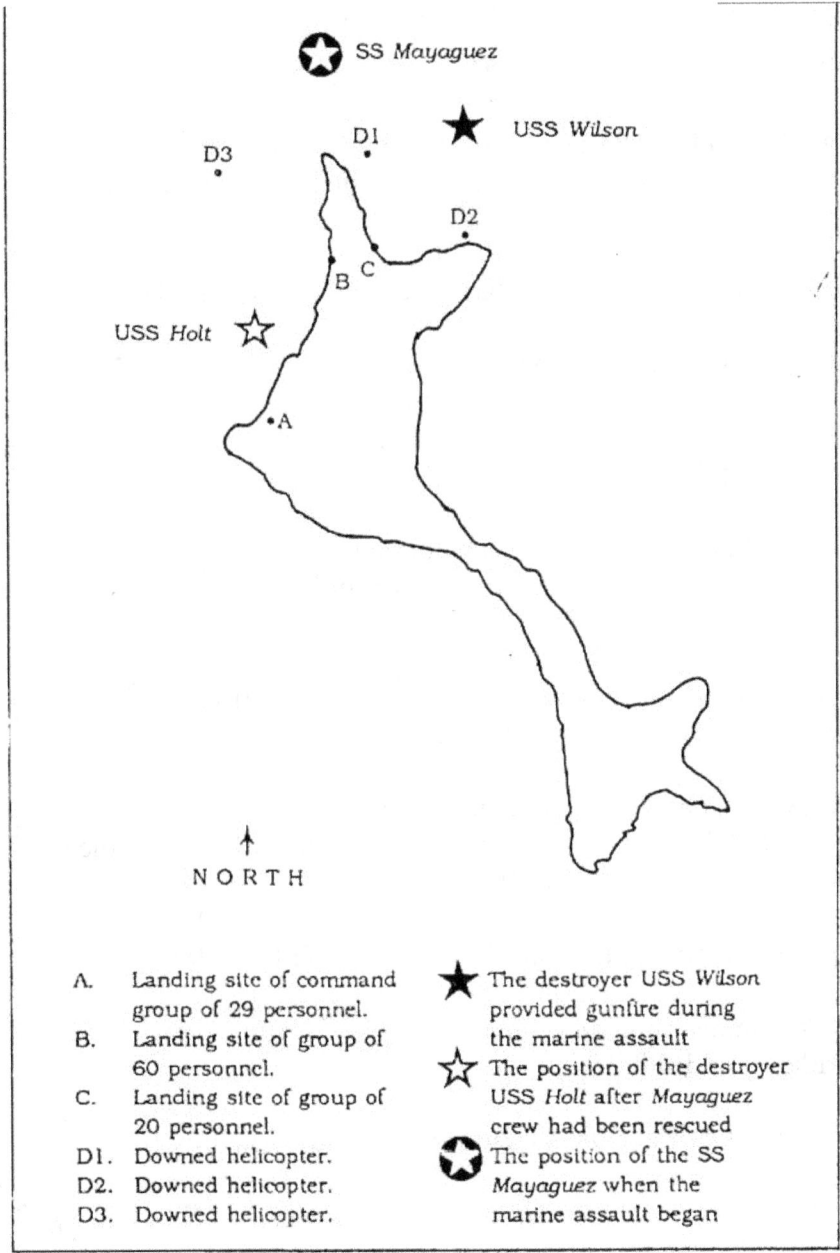

A. Landing site of command group of 29 personnel.
B. Landing site of group of 60 personnel.
C. Landing site of group of 20 personnel.
D1. Downed helicopter.
D2. Downed helicopter.
D3. Downed helicopter.

★ The destroyer USS *Wilson* provided gunfire during the marine assault
☆ The position of the destroyer USS *Holt* after *Mayaguez* crew had been rescued
✪ The position of the SS *Mayaguez* when the marine assault began

Source: GAO Report, 93.

BIBLIOGRAPHY

"A Strong but Risky Show of Force." *Time*, 26 May 1975, 9-18

Dunham, Major George R., and Colonel David A. Quinlan *U.S. Marines in Vietnam: The Bitter End.* Washington D.C.: History and Museums Division, Headquarters, U.S. Marine Corps, 1990

Ford, Gerald R. *A Time to Heal.* New York: Harper & Row Publishers, 1979.

"Ford's Rescue Operations." *Newsweek*, 26 May 1975, 16-18

Guilmartin, John F., Jr. *A Very Short War. The Mayaguez and the Battle of Koh Tang.* College Station, TX: Texas A&M University Press, 1995

Head, Richard J., Frisco W. Short, and Robert C. McFarlane. *Crisis Resolution: Presidential Decision Making in the Mayaguez and Korean Confrontations.* Boulder CO: Westview Press, 1978.

Hendricks, J. B. "'Mayday' for the *Mayaguez:* The Battalion Operations Officer." *U.S. Naval Institute Proceedings,* November, 1976, 104-108.

Johnson J.M., Jr., R.W. Austin, and D.A. Quinlan. "Individual Heroism Overcame Awkward Command Relationships, Confusion, and Bad Information off the Cambodian Coast." *Marine Corps Gazette*, October 1977, 24-34.

Kissinger, Henry. *White House Years.* Boston: Little, Brown & Co., 1979.

Lamb, Christopher. *Belief Systems and Decision Making in the Mayaguez Crisis.* Gainesville, University of Florida Press, 1989.

Nesson, Ron. *It Sure Looks Different from the Inside.* Chicago: Playboy Press, 1978.

"New Test For U.S. Why Ford Moved So Fast." *U.S. New and World Report*, 19 May 1975, 19-22.

Rodgers, J. Michael. "'Mayday' for the *Mayaguez:* The Guided-Missile Destroyer's Skipper." *U.S. Naval Institute Proceedings,* November, 1976, 100-104.

Rowan Roy. *The Four Days of Mayaguez.* New York: Norton & Co, 1975.

Vandenbrouke, Lucien S. *Perilous Options. Special Operations as an Instrument of Foreign Policy.* Oxford: Oxford University Press, 1993.

Wood, Walter J. "'Mayday' for the *Mayaguez:* The Company Commander." *U.S. Naval Institute Proceedings,* November, 1976, 100-104.

U.S. Congress, House, Subcommittee, on International Relations. *Seizure of the Mayaguez.* Hearings before the Committee on International Relations and its Subcommitte on International Political and Military Affairs. 94th Cong., 1st sess., 1975

U.S. Congress, House, Subcommittee on International Political and Military Affairs, Committee on International Relations, *Seizure of the Mayaguez,* Hearings on the *Mayaguez* Incident, pt.4, *Report of the Comptroller General of the United States*, 94th Cong., 2d sess., October 4, 1976.

NAVAL
POSTGRADUATE
SCHOOL

MONTEREY, CALIFORNIA

THESIS

THE *MAYAGUEZ* INCIDENT:
AN ORGANIZATIONAL THEORY ANALYSIS

by

Edward J. Lengel
Charles R. Rambo
Shelley A. Rodriguez
Michael D. Tyynismaa

September 2006

| Thesis Advisor: | Erik Jansen |
| Second Reader: | Brian H. Greenshields |

THIS PAGE INTENTIONALLY LEFT BLANK

REPORT DOCUMENTATION PAGE		*Form Approved OMB No. 0704-0188*

Public reporting burden for this collection of information is estimated to average 1 hour per response, including the time for reviewing instruction, searching existing data sources, gathering and maintaining the data needed, and completing and reviewing the collection of information. Send comments regarding this burden estimate or any other aspect of this collection of information, including suggestions for reducing this burden, to Washington headquarters Services, Directorate for Information Operations and Reports, 1215 Jefferson Davis Highway, Suite 1204, Arlington, VA 22202-4302, and to the Office of Management and Budget, Paperwork Reduction Project (0704-0188) Washington DC 20503.

1. AGENCY USE ONLY *(Leave blank)*	2. REPORT DATE September 2006	3. REPORT TYPE AND DATES COVERED Master's Thesis	
4. TITLE AND SUBTITLE: The *Mayaguez* Incident: An Organizational Theory Analysis		**5. FUNDING NUMBERS**	
6. AUTHORS Edward J. Lengel, Shelley A. Rodriguez, Michael D. Tyynismaa and Charles R. Rambo			
7. PERFORMING ORGANIZATION NAME(S) AND ADDRESS(ES) Naval Postgraduate School Monterey, CA 93943-5000		**8. PERFORMING ORGANIZATION REPORT NUMBER**	
9. SPONSORING /MONITORING AGENCY NAME(S) AND ADDRESS(ES) N/A		**10. SPONSORING/MONITORING AGENCY REPORT NUMBER**	

11. SUPPLEMENTARY NOTES The views expressed in this thesis are those of the author and do not reflect the official policy or position of the Department of Defense or the U.S. Government.

12a. DISTRIBUTION / AVAILABILITY STATEMENT Approved for public release; distribution is unlimited	12b. DISTRIBUTION CODE A

13. ABSTRACT (maximum 200 words)

Applying selected concepts of organizational theory to the *Mayaguez* incident of 1975 leads to a more comprehensive understanding of events and more accurate lessons learned. Application of organizational theory to the *Mayaguez* incident demonstrates the decision processes at the executive level left the military operation vulnerable to failure. Henry Mintzberg's structural contingency model and Lee Bowman and Terrence Deal's frames model are used and are applied to executive-level decisions. The rationale behind focusing on the executive level is twofold: first, it is where final critical decisions are made and second, military operations cannot take place without an executive-level authorization. The *Mayaguez* crisis was rife with potential pitfalls and, though President Ford was equipped with an organization of intelligent, competent personnel, the result was unnecessary loss of life. Publicly, the operation was a success and President Ford the savior of the *Mayaguez* crew. To the military, the operation was an embarrassment because of failures in the organizational structure and decision making. Application of organizational theory provides an avenue for analysis of the military operation within the *Mayaguez* rescue.

14. SUBJECT TERMS *Mayaguez*, Organizational Theory, President Ford, decision making, executive level, frames, Mintzberg, Structure in Five, coordination mechanisms, organizational design, divisionalized form	15. NUMBER OF PAGES 197
	16. PRICE CODE

17. SECURITY CLASSIFICATION OF REPORT Unclassified	18. SECURITY CLASSIFICATION OF THIS PAGE Unclassified	19. SECURITY CLASSIFICATION OF ABSTRACT Unclassified	20. LIMITATION OF ABSTRACT UL

NSN 7540-01-280-5500

Standard Form 298 (Rev. 2-89)
Prescribed by ANSI Std. 239-18

i

THIS PAGE INTENTIONALLY LEFT BLANK

THE *MAYAGUEZ* INCIDENT: AN ORGANIZATIONAL THEORY ANALYSIS

Edward J. Lengel, Major, United States Air Force
B.S., United States Air Force Academy, 1992

Charles R. Rambo, Major, United States Army
B.S., East Tennessee State, 1994

Shelley A. Rodriguez, Major, United States Air Force
B.S., United States Air Force Academy, 1992
M.B.A., Touro University, 2000

Michael D. Tyynismaa, Major, United States Air Force
B.S., North Carolina State University, 1991
M.A. George Washington University, 2000

Submitted in partial fulfillment of the
requirements for the degree of

MASTER OF SCIENCE IN DEFENSE ANALYSIS

from the

**NAVAL POSTGRADUATE SCHOOL
September 2006**

Author: Edward J. Lengel   Charles R. Rambo

                 Shelley A. Rodriguez   Michael D. Tyynismaa

Approved by: Erik Jansen
                Thesis Advisor

                Col. Brian H. Greenshields
                Second Reader/Co-Advisor

                Gordon McCormick
                Chairman, Department of Defense Analysis

THIS PAGE INTENTIONALLY LEFT BLANK

ABSTRACT

Applying selected concepts of organizational theory to the *Mayaguez* incident of 1975 leads to a more comprehensive understanding of events and more accurate lessons learned. Application of organizational theory demonstrates the decision processes at the executive level left the military operation vulnerable to failure. Henry Mintzberg's structural contingency model and Lee Bowman and Terrence Deal's frames model within organizational theory are used and are applied to executive-level decisions. The rationale behind focusing on the executive level is twofold: First, it is where final critical decisions were made, and second, military operations cannot take place without an executive-level authorization. The *Mayaguez* crisis was rife with potential pitfalls and, though President Ford was equipped with an excellent organization of intelligent, competent personnel, the result was unnecessary loss of life. Publicly, the operation was a success and President Ford the savior of the *Mayaguez* crew. To the military, the operation was an embarrassment—all because of failures within the organizational structure and poor decision making. Application of organizational theory provides an avenue for analysis of the military operation within the *Mayaguez* rescue.

THIS PAGE INTENTIONALLY LEFT BLANK

TABLE OF CONTENTS

THIS PAGE INTENTIONALLY LEFT BLANK

LIST OF FIGURES

THIS PAGE INTENTIONALLY LEFT BLANK

LIST OF TABLES

THIS PAGE INTENTIONALLY LEFT BLANK

ACKNOWLEDGMENTS

Most importantly, we thank Dr. John F. Guilmartin Jr., professor of history at Ohio State University and author of *A Very Short War: The Mayaguez and the Battle of Koh Tang* (College Station, Texas: Texas A&M Press, 1995). His firsthand knowledge as a participant in the *Mayaguez* incident greatly facilitated our research. He graciously donated his time to our seemingly endless questions. Dr. Guilmartin still lives by the motto of the Air Force combat rescue community: *"These things we do…that others may live."*

Our group also thanks the survivors of Koh Tang Island who interviewed with us via email and telephone communication. Specifically, Col. (Ret.) James Davis, Mr. Bob Blough, Mr. Dan Hoffman, and Mr. Larry Barnett all contributed to our research efforts on the Mayaguez incident. Without their firsthand accounts and invaluable insight, we would not have been able to draw the correct conclusions for our analysis. We are grateful for the opportunity to learn from the nation's veterans, those who are eager to instruct and continue the education process of the military community. We are indebted to them not only for their contribution to our thesis, but for their military service to this great nation.

THIS PAGE INTENTIONALLY LEFT BLANK

I. INTRODUCTION

On 12 May 1975, an American merchant ship, SS *Mayaguez*, was seized by the Cambodian government in what President Gerald Ford believed was a threatening show of force by the relatively new Khmer Rouge government. The United States government responded swiftly by sending a full military package to rescue the Mayaguez and her crew. In the end, President Ford publicly declared the operation a success, but for the military, it was an abysmal failure. A full report was produced to summarize the events. After reviewing the report, Congress requested, and the Government Accounting Office (GAO) conducted, an investigation to clarify incongruous statements and events listed in the incident report.

This thesis is based on the hypothesis that by applying selected concepts of organizational theory to the Mayaguez incident of 1975, one can gain a more comprehensive understanding of events and more accurate lessons learned. Specifically, application of organizational theory to the Mayaguez incident demonstrates that the decision processes at the executive level left the military operation vulnerable to failure. To conduct this analysis, the authors used Henry Mintzberg's structural contingency model and Lee Bowman and Terrence Deal's frames of reference model within organizational theory. In particular, the models are applied to the highest levels of the National Command Authority and Department of Defense organizations, focusing on the executive-level decisions rather than the entire structure itself. This thesis defines the executive level during the Mayaguez incident as the National Security Council principal members: president, secretary of state, and secretary of defense. The rationale behind focusing on the executive level is twofold: First, it is where final critical decisions were (and still are) made, and second, military operations did not and cannot take place without an executive-level decision.

A. PURPOSE:

The purpose of this thesis is to reexamine the events and published lessons learned of 12–15 May 1975 through the lenses of organizational theory. Because there is no single, cohesive organizational theory per se, the task of examining organizations becomes complicated, requiring integration of a web of different theories and approaches. However, by combining select theories within a larger frame of reference model, a clearer picture of the organization, actors, and its effectiveness is obtained. Applying organizational theory to the *Mayaguez* incident demonstrates that decision processes at the executive level made the military operation vulnerable to failure.

Although the Government Accounting Office (GAO) published a full report of the Mayaguez incident, it was both incomplete and inaccurate in terms of analysis. The report merely consolidated information from various sources within the government, to include the military, rather than applying analysis to the events themselves. Unfortunately for the military, the GAO report was, and still is, the only source of information for lessons learned. Since inaccurate or incomplete, the lessons derived from the information presented left the military vulnerable to committing the same mistakes in future operations. If an analysis of the errors made in the planning and execution of the Mayaguez incident resulted in a more comprehensive review of the organization as well as its actions, perhaps subsequent missions such as the hostage rescue attempt in Iran— Operation EAGLE CLAW, or more commonly, Desert One—would not have failed. While the GAO report reviews events that were not executed as planned, it fails to *analyze or explain* shortcomings within the organization itself that also attributed or were causal to the mistakes made. The report seems to only assign blame to individuals rather than examine failed processes, structures, and systems; it actually misses the analytical process altogether. In fact, nothing was stated about the failures of the organization except in the case of failed communications. In the absence of analysis, the recommendations for correcting the problems are then flawed.

For an organization to operate efficiently and effectively, careful attention must be paid to every aspect of the organization, its environment, and the mission it intends to accomplish. Several methods could be used to analyze the Mayaguez incident, but perhaps the most telling is that of organizational theory. In this thesis, the focus is on the executive level. Applying organizational theory to the executive decision makers involved in the *Mayaguez* incident reveals that the decision processes of the individuals—specifically President Ford—were flawed, causing the entire military operation to fail.

B.   BACKGROUND

The following chapter is an adaptation from Dr. John Guilmartin's book, *A Very Short War: The Mayaguez and the Battle of Koh Tang.* Although other sources were consulted and are available on the subject, Dr. Guilmartin's book appeared to be the most succinct and accurate account of the events that transpired. He is recognized as the foremost authority on the *Mayaguez* incident not only because he researched and authored his book, but also because he piloted one of the helicopters during the operation, thus enabling firsthand accounts of the action.

On 12 May 1975, two weeks after the fall of Saigon, Cambodia's Navy seized the U.S.-owned container ship SS *Mayaguez*, along with its crew. The intentions of the Cambodian government were unknown when the ship was seized, largely because leadership in Washington, D.C., did not recognize and would not communicate with the new Cambodian government, comprised of the Khmer Rouge. President Gerald Ford quickly came under intense pressure to recover the crew and ship. In 1968, North Korea seized the *USS Pueblo*, resulting in eleven months of captivity of the crew and embarrassment to the United States. With this event in mind, President Ford acted decisively to recover the *Mayaguez* and crew. What should have been an easy operation against a small, unorganized and officially unrecognized country was anything but.

The United States, having recalled forces after the Vietnam conflict, still had sufficient airpower based at U-Tapao Royal Thai Navy Base, Thailand, to launch an operation, but needed a ground force to aid in the recovery of the *Mayaguez* crew. Unfortunately, ground troops were stationed elsewhere; some of them still exiting Vietnam, some in Thailand, and some in Okinawa, Japan. The president requested troops to meet the strict timeline he imposed for recovery of the *Mayaguez* and crew, going as far as to return troops who had just left the battlefields of Vietnam. Late that night, on the evening of May 12, 1975, the *Mayaguez* was located, anchored off of Koh Tang

Island in the Gulf of Siam. Based on the assumption the crew was on the island, the command structure planned the operation as a rescue of the *Mayaguez* crew and recapture of the ship as United States' sovereign property. The Marines would deploy to U-Tapao and board Air Force special-operations and rescue CH/HH-53s based in Thailand to take the beach at Koh Tang Island on May 15, 1975. The military also was tasked to recapture the actual ship, SS *Mayaguez*. This would be the Air Force's first helicopter assault operation.[1] After recovery of the crew, the helicopters would transport the crew to the aviation-ready frigate USS Henry Holt, already in seas nearby.

Unbeknownst to the Marine forces and Air Force crews, the island harbored an estimated 100–300 armed, combat-hardened Khmer Rouge forces placed there to protect Koh Tang from occupation by Vietnam. An old political dispute over sovereign rights to Koh Tang Island had escalated between Cambodia and Vietnam in recent months, causing the Cambodians to station combat-ready troops and weaponry on the island. Because diplomatic relations between the United States and Vietnam were strained and diplomacy with the Cambodians was virtually non-existent, the United States government failed to accurately assess the island's inhabitants and importance to the region. Instead, the intelligence community estimated a total of only 18 to 40 persons on Koh Tang Island, including both the lightly armed militia and indigenous population. This would be only one of many major mistakes made in the *Mayaguez* incident.

On the approach to the island, the Air Force helicopter crews were the first to suffer the consequences of previous intelligence and diplomatic failures as the Khmer Rouge shot down three of the first four helicopters approaching the island. Intelligence was both inadequate and unavailable for the mission and diplomatic efforts, notably limited in nature, had failed to secure the release of the *Mayaguez* and crew. Unfortunately for the operation, the second helicopter carried the Marine Forward Air Controller (FAC) team, and the fourth helicopter was so badly damaged it had to abort and return to U-Tapao. Eventually, Marines were inserted successfully via other helicopters. Regrettably, the Air Force A-7s failed to locate the Marines, leaving them

---

[1] The previous assaults done with Special Operations Forces, e.g. Son Tay, were still classified at the time of the Mayaguez Operation.

without fire support. The Marines continued to fight valiantly as they waited for the remaining helicopters to fly through enemy fire to deliver reinforcements, their motivation waning from the offensive beach assault to mere survival. Unfortunately, the enemy continued to fire on and destroy most of the remaining helicopters leaving the Marines with few options to return. In fact, only three of the helicopters that landed in U-Tapao would be able to continue and return to Koh Tang to recover the ground forces.

Finally, with the assault still waging, a Marine boarding party brought in by Air Force helicopters embarked the *Mayaguez* expecting to find the ship under siege. To the contrary, the ship was deserted because the Khmer Rouge had taken the *Mayaguez* crew to the Cambodian mainland two days earlier. President Ford ordered air strikes on the Cambodian port and vessels in the surrounding waters to protect the military forces and preclude the SS *Mayaguez* from being taken to the mainland. Unbeknownst to the military forces involved in the operations, the Khmer Rouge were constantly moving the crew during the operation not as a practice of deception but merely to get the crew to a location suitable for release.

The reason behind moving the *Mayaguez* crew is unclear. It is possible the Khmer Rouge did not want to complicate the dispute with Vietnam over the island by involving the United States, or it may be that the U.S.' retaliatory strikes on the Cambodian mainland influenced the Khmer Rouge. Regardless of the reason, the Khmer Rouge released the crew, sending them out to sea in a Thai fishing boat. Fortunately, the USS Henry G. Wilson had just arrived in the area and was able to recover the *Mayaguez* crew after spotting Caucasians waving white flags on the deck of a Thai fishing vessel.[2] The recovery of the *Mayaguez* crew resulted in a Presidential order to cease assault operations on Koh Tang Island, saving a second wave of Marines from possible fatalities as the Khmer Rouge were far more prepared than our fighting forces.

After the *Mayaguez* crew was recovered, the assault operation was transformed into a rescue operation to extract the remaining Marines off the island. An AC-130 Spectre Gunship provided firepower while an air-rescue HH-53 Jolly Green and two OV-

---

[2] Commander in Chief Pacific Command. *The SS Mayaguez Incident.* Command History Branch, Office of the Joint Secretary, Appendix VI. San Francisco, CA. 1976.

10 Forward Air Controllers (FACs) coordinated in the air to save the remaining Marines. It was the FACs, and not the chain of command, that initiated the rescue of the battered Marines. When the rescue operations began, night already had fallen, but the Khmer Rouge had not relented with its assault against U.S. forces. Despite only four HH-53s being flight capable, the rescue force launched to recover the Marines. Of course, within seconds of approach to the island, all HH-53s were fired upon, rendering one of them unable to complete the mission. As the night progressed, one more helicopter was able to return to the rescue operation, achieving only marginal success.

At the end of the night, as the last helicopter approached, the ground commander was asked to take a final head count of his Marines to ensure it would be the helicopter's last run and no one would be left behind. The commander concluded all Marines were accounted for and the helicopter extracted the Marines to the USS Holt. Once aboard the Holt, a final headcount was taken and the mood drastically soured with the news: E Company was missing three Marines. Those Marines were declared as Killed in Action (KIA) by the United States government who stands by its declaration even today. However, recently uncovered eye-witness accounts and interviews of the soldiers on the beach revealed the Marines were, in fact, left behind fighting for their lives.[3]

In the GAO report of the *Mayaguez* incident as well as President Ford's assessment, the mission was considered a success despite the contrary opinion of those involved in the operation below the executive level. Military losses went largely unnoticed with the announcement of the successful recovery of the SS *Mayaguez* and her crew by President Ford. Forty-one military men lost their lives attempting to save the *SS Mayaguez* and her 39 crewmembers. Unknown to the president and cabinet, and before the first shot was fired on Koh Tang Island, the *Mayaguez* crew had been released to a Thai fishing vessel. The entire beach assault was executed needlessly. Row Rowan, in *The Four Days of Mayaguez*, writes:

> At 7:29 A.M., the very minute United States Marines were seizing his ship, and Gerald Ford was being informed by Henry Kissinger of Phnom Penh's intent to release it anyway, the captain and crew of the *Mayaguez*

---

[3] United States Department of Defense News Release. "MIA Marines Identified from the Mayaguez Incident." http://www.defenselink.mil/releases/2000/b05182000_bt260-00.html.

were setting out in a fishing boat from the Cambodian shore—a fact which would have amazed the president, the secretary of state, and all the Marines fighting and dying on Koh Tang.[4]

By applying select concepts of organizational theory, this thesis concludes the GAO report was incomplete in analysis and consequently formed the basis for learning the wrong lessons. Unfortunately even today, lessons learned are often generated but rarely studied or analyzed before or after issuance. Faulty information and lack of analysis provide for erroneous results and can lead to future failures. Organizational theory provides a new perspective to the *Mayaguez* incident, producing drastically different results and conclusions than previously published material. In fact, it is possible that had President Ford understood or applied some aspect of organizational theory in his analysis, he might have prevented the failures experienced by the military and ultimately, saved the lives of the men who fought on Koh Tang.

C. METHODOLOGY AND CHAPTER REVIEW

This thesis is derived from a project assigned by Dr. Erik Jansen to analyze an organization using the principles taught in his graduate classes at the Naval Postgraduate School in Monterey, California. Dr. John Guilmartin's book, *A Very Short War*, served as the impetus for the detailed research of the organizations involved in the *Mayaguez* incident and because of recently declassified National Security Council (NSC) minutes, the project quickly honed in on decision making at the executive level. Subsequently, the discoveries concluded in the assignment gained the interest of Dr. Guilmartin. At his request, the findings were presented at the Mershon Center at Ohio State University. From there, this thesis evolved.

In addition to Dr. Guilmartin's book, several others were accessed in researching the incident. Ralph Wetterhahn's *The Last Battle: The Mayaguez Incident and the End of the Vietnam War* provided a similar account of the incident but focused more on the failure to account for all Marines when exiting Koh Tang Island rather than the executive

---

[4] Rowen, Roy. *The Four Days of the Mayaguez.* New York: W.W. Norton & Company, 1975.

level of operational structure during the incident.[5] Another work by Roy Rowan, *The Four Days of the Mayaguez*, provides a historical account of the Mayaguez incident and though published in 1975 (the same year in which the incident took place), still offers an insightful account of some of the executive-level problems. Finally, Christopher Lamb's *Belief Systems and Decision Making in the Mayaguez Crisis* offered an expanse of researched aimed directly at the executive level of the *Mayaguez* incident. His approach, while also based on concepts within organizational theory, varies from the premise of this work. The supposition that President Ford either consciously or subconsciously altered the structure of the organization by essentially becoming the sole actor within the strategic apex is unique to this thesis. Again, this is largely due to the application of diverse concepts that fall under the umbrella of organizational theory.

Besides authored books, a diverse collection of government and military resources were accessed. The Marines publication on military command and control, memorandums issued during the incident, the GAO report, and NSC minutes were all researched in detail. The GAO report, when coupled with the recently declassified NSC minutes, revealed information not previously published in other accounts of the *Mayaguez* incident with the exception of one. Brian Kelly's documentary released in 2000, *Seized at Sea: Situation Critical (The Story of the Mayaguez Incident)*, cited some of the references in the NSC minutes, relating them directly to executive-level decisions. However, while the account is compelling, it only exposes the decisions and still does not address the reasons behind the failures at the executive level. Particularly valuable to this thesis, however, are Mr. Kelly's interviews of former President Ford, then Secretary of State Henry Kissinger, and then Secretary of Defense James Schlesinger.

In addition to the interviews supplied by Mr. Kelly's documentary and Dr. Guilmartin himself, other participants were also consulted. Colonel (Ret.) Jim Davis, ground commander of the Marines during the incident; then First Lieutenant Bob Blough, a HH-53 pilot during the rescue, and Dr. Guilmartin all provided insight gained over the

---

[5] It should be noted Dr. Guilmartin found discrepancies in Mr. Wetterhahn's facts, leading Dr. Guilmartin to question Mr. Wetterhahn's account of the Marines left behind. In interviews conducted with Dr. Guilmartin during the trip to Ohio State University, November 12-14, 2006, he refuted some of the facts in Mr. Wetterhahn's book because of his personal involvement in the events cited.

years since the incident. Additionally, electronic mail was received from then Second Lieutenant Dan Hoffman, Marine ground troop who provided a first-hand account of the heavy ground fighting on Koh Tang as well as Larry Barnett, also part of the Marine assault force who provided yet another perspective of the ground account. While strongly opinionated, the interviews helped examine the frames through which participants viewed the event. Although the thesis ultimately focuses on the executive-level, specifically President Ford, the interviews were compelling accounts of how influential the concepts of frames of reference are in the body of organizational theory.

Because there is no single, unified organizational theory but rather a vast number of complementary, and sometimes competing, theories, much research was accomplished to determine those most applicable to the analysis of the *Mayaguez* incident. It was determined the most relevant works in organizational theory for this particular analysis are Henry Mintzberg's structure in fives theory and Larry Bolman and Terrence Deal's work on frames. The structural theory easily dominated the research done on the organization because of particular importance to the thesis is the structure itself. Mintzberg's discussion of coordination mechanisms and communication within the organization helped to define areas of failure previously not addressed by the GAO reports. Bolman and Deal's work on frames was especially critical to understanding the failures caused by executive-level decision making. By combining the two concepts within organizational theory, the proposal that President Ford became the sole member of the strategic apex which resulted in a changed and ineffective organizational structure was developed. Simply applying organizational theory to the *Mayaguez* incident demonstrates the decision processes at the executive level left the military operation vulnerable to failure.

D.   CHAPTER REVIEW

In Chapter I, the basic story of the *Mayaguez* was revealed. In Chapter II, the thesis provides a review of organizational theory and discusses key concepts of configuration and frames. In Chapter III, Mintzberg's structural theory is applied to the executive level actors in the *Mayaguez* incident and in Chapter IV, application of

9

Bowman and Deal's frames theory further reveals problems in the executive-level decision making. In Chapter V, the findings are consolidated and the true value of the critical analysis of executive-level decisions is revealed. The thesis concludes with Chapter VI and provides implications and recommendations for future study. Finally, appendices of the NSC minutes, the GAO report, and other works serve to enhance the analysis achieved.

II.   ORGANIZATIONAL THEORY

A.   INTRODUCTION TO ORGANIZATIONAL THEORY

The goal of this chapter is to introduce key concepts and terms that are used in the analysis of the *Mayaguez* incident. The published lessons learned from this incident, while important, were produced with little or no analysis.[6] The major thrust of this chapter is derived from Lee Bolman and Terrence Deal's book, *Reframing Organizations* and from Henry Mintzberg, a noted authority among organizational theorists. Both approaches have synthesized a diverse body of organizational theory and while they are not the only approaches, they were most revealing in analyzing the *Mayaguez* incident.

Bolman and Deal's model of framing is used to define what frames represent, how they are derived, and their value in analysis. Secondly, frames can be used to better understand organizations and the decisions made by their leaders. Using the frames presented by Bolman and Deal, Mintzberg's models of organizational structure are interlaced to develop the critical analyses, especially within the structural frame.

B.   FRAMES

"As a mental map, a frame is a set of ideas or assumptions you carry in your head. It helps you understand and negotiate a particular territory. The territory isn't necessarily defined by geography."[7] People develop frames to conduct everyday life. Some are built subconsciously while others involve a deliberate process. Framing is a way to sort through large volumes of information expeditiously, enabling a decision maker to discern important information from merely peripheral details. It is a way to sort and classify information into distinct categories, thereby resulting in a frame. Because it is often a personal perspective when sorting the information, the frame sometimes implies values for judging a situation. Different people who observe the same situation may actually frame it differently based on their personal perspectives and prior experiences. The message is, "what looks reasonable, or ridiculous, depends on the context— on how it is

---

[6] See Appendix D

[7] Bolman, Larry G. and Terrence E. Deal. *Reframing Organizations: Artistry, Choice, and Leadership.* 3rd Ed. San Francisco: Jossey-Bass, 2003, 12.

framed [by] what has preceded it and the language used to present it."[8] Regardless of the perspective, the goal of framing is to organize information.

Bolman and Deal provide organizational frames of reference to assist in understanding organizations as open systems and make it easier to navigate among the complexity of the organization. To achieve this, they have categorized different disciplines into four frames: Structural, Human Resource, Political, and Symbolic.[9] Each of these frames emphasizes the perspective associated with a major discipline such as sociology, psychology, political science and anthropology. By categorizing the disciplines, multiple approaches to organizational theory can be packaged into frames that hold concepts more easily applied to organizations. In the case of the *Mayaguez*, frames would have provided multiple perspectives of the problem at hand for President Ford and his staff.

A key part of the application process with the four frames is the understanding that each frame has specific strengths and weaknesses associated with it. Just like any common mechanical tool, understanding which tool is needed and appreciating the capabilities of that tool is necessary. For example, one can use a hammer to drive in a screw, but a screwdriver would probably produce much better results, especially in the long term. In addition, Bolman and Deal's four frames are meant to be multiplicative in nature. "Effective managers need multiple tools, the skill to use each of them, and the wisdom to match frames to situations."[10] Balancing the tools should always be an objective for any manager dealing with a complex problem. President Ford's limited international experience as a naval officer likely produced a different frame through which he viewed the *Mayaguez* incident than that of his Secretary of State, Henry Kissinger, a man whose entire background involved foreign policy.

---

[8] Pfeffer, Jeffrey. *Managing with Power: Politics and Influence in Organizations.* Boston, MA: Harvard Business School Press, 1992, 190.

[9] Bolman and Deal, 14-15.

[10] Ibid., 18.

C.   STRUCTURAL FRAME

With its roots in "sociology and management science, the structural frame emphasizes goals, specialized roles, and formal relationships."[11] Military members are keenly aware of this frame because members are trained to understand their formal organizational chart and their chain of command. "The organizational structure determines where formal power and authority are located."[12] Every individual is assigned a role and is required to understand their responsibilities and tasks. In addition every move a service member makes is governed by rules, regulations, policies and procedures. To this end, "the best structure is the one that helps the organizations achieve its strategy" and utilize its resources efficiently.[13] This belief takes into account six assumptions that Bolman and Deal identify as forming the structural frame foundation:[14]

- Organizations exist to achieve established goals and objectives.
- Organizations increase efficiency and enhance performance through specializations and a clear division of labor.
- Appropriate forms of coordination and control ensure that diverse efforts of individuals and units mesh.
- Organizations work best when rationality prevails over personal preferences and extraneous pressures.
- Structures must be designed to fit an organization's circumstances (including its goals, technology, workforce, and environment).
- Problems and performance gaps arise from structural deficiencies and can be remedied through analysis and restructuring.

Scanning through this list, it is apparent that the focus is on the needs of the organization and not the individual worker. In the military, although leadership works to mitigate risks, there is often a requirement to put the needs of the mission and the state above the individual member.

Bolman and Deal state that organizational structure is a blueprint for establishing formal roles and expectations; it defines internal and external interactions of the

---

[11] Bolman and Deal, 14.

[12] Galbraith, Jay R., Diane Downey and Amy Kates. *Designing Dynamic Organizations: A Hands on Guide for Leaders at All Levels.* New York: American Management Association, 2002, 3.

[13] Galbraith, Downey and Kates. 60.

[14] Bolman and Deal, 45.

organization and its members. In addition, this blueprint can be designed in numerous ways and should consider such forces as the environment, job specialization, coordination mechanisms and control measures. The factors that influence organizational architecture are better explained by Henry Mintzberg's extensive work in the area of structural configurations.[15] This work is based on Mintzberg's Structure in Fives and is used as the basis of analysis within the structural frame.

D.   MINTZBERG'S STRUCTURE IN FIVES

In Mintzberg's Structure of Fives, there are five types of organizations: Simple Structure, Machine Bureaucracy, Professional Bureaucracy, Divisionalized Form, and Adhocracy. All organizations consist of five components: the Strategic Apex, Middle Line, Technostructure, Support Staff, and Operating Core. For each part to communicate, organizations use some or all of the five coordination mechanisms to synchronize the differentiated components within the organization: Direct Supervision, Standardization of Work Processes, Standardization of Skills, Standardization of Outputs, and Mutual Adjustment. Mintzberg's five-sector diagram depicted below shows the major components of an organizational configuration and includes the Operating Core, Middle Line, Strategic Apex, Technostructure, and Support Staff.[16]

---

[15] Mintzberg, Henry. "Organization Design: Fashion or Fit?" *Harvard Business Review*, January–February (1981): 1–16.

[16] Ibid., 3.

Mintzberg – Five Parts

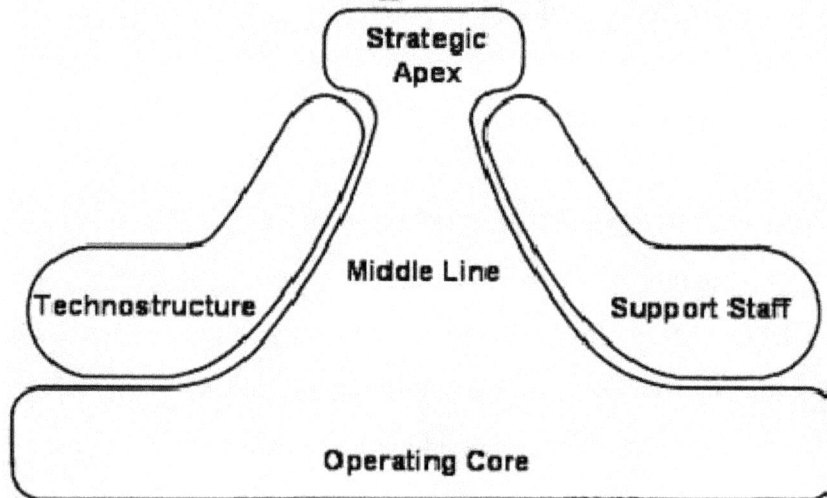

Figure 1. Mintzberg's Structure in Fives

These five parts describe organizational structures and how the organization may cope with its "environment, workforce, technology, and past structural commitments."[17] It is necessary to define each of the five parts to understand how they fit into the organizational structure and how they interact with one another. How the components fit and interact can determine the type of structure, and the inverse is also true: the type of structure can determine how the components fit and interact. Table 1 shows the relationship between the type of organization, the dominant parts, and the dominate mechanisms according to Mintzberg in his "Organization: Fashion or Fit" article.[18]

---

[17] Bolman and Deal, 72.

[18] Mintzberg, Henry. "Organization Design: Fashion or Fit?", 6

15

Table 1.   Structure, Coordinating Mechanism, and Dominant Part

Structure Type	Primary Coordinating Mechanism	Dominant Part
Simple structure	Direct supervision	Strategic apex
Machine bureaucracy	Standardization of work	Technostructure
Professional bureaucracy	Standardization of skills	Operating core
Divisionalized form	Standardization of outputs	Middle line
Adhocracy	Mutual adjustment	Support staff

First, the operating core consists of the main workforce, which consists of those hired to perform the "basic work of the organization".[19] In the *Mayaguez* incident, this would be the tactical elements tasked to execute the operation. Second, and above the operating core is the middle line, comprised of managers who supervise, control, and provide resources for the operators.[20] For the operation, the middle line consisted of units such as the Commander in Chief of Pacific Fleet and his Air Force counterpart commanders, essentially the military leadership of the DoD. The highest level of the structure is the senior management or the strategic apex; they are focused on the environment, the mission, and shaping the grand design of the organization.[21] In the *Mayaguez* operation, this consisted of the National Command Authority. The last two parts sit adjacent to the middle line and are the technostructure and support staff. For the *Mayaguez* incident, intelligence and logistical units filled these roles. The technostructure consists of specialists and professionals who standardize, measure, and inspect processes.[22] Examples of the technostructure are accounting departments, quality control, and standardization functions. Finally, the support staff performs indirect services that facilitate the work getting accomplished by all others in the organization.

---

[19] Ibid., 3

[20] Bolman and Deal, 73.

[21] Mintzberg, "Organization Design: Fashion or Fit?", 3.

[22] Ibid.

According to Mintzberg, the five types of organizations are dominated by a coordination mechanism. Martinez and Jarillo (1989) assessed research collected on coordination mechanisms used by multinational corporations. They define a coordination mechanism as, "any administrative tool for achieving integration among different units within an organization."[23] Mintzberg's coordination mechanisms within the organizational structure are: direct supervision, standardization of work processes, standardization of skills, standardization of outputs, and mutual adjustment.

Mintzberg describes the organizational environment in terms of stability and complexity. In a stable environment, change happens slowly. By contrast, an unstable or turbulent environment requires quick response from an organization to maintain its competitive edge. The environment of the organization can vary in complexity: the more complex, the more difficult it is for management to direct the organization leading to the need for decentralization.[24] Complexity describes the task that must be accomplished to generate the organization's product. (Producing a hamburger at McDonald's is a relatively simple task, where as a highly trained surgeon must execute complex tasks to perform an effective surgery.)

The way an organization communicates and operates relies on centralization or decentralization. Each method, particularly in decision making, affects the outcome of the structural design. Mintzberg describes vertical decentralization as "the extent to which decision making is delegated to managers down the middle line, while horizontal decentralization describes the extent to which non-managers . . . control decision processes."[25] The degree of vertical, horizontal, or any combination of the two types of decentralization will affect the coordination mechanism by which the structure is dominated by. Mintzberg's Fives is more easily understood by reviewing the following diagram:

[23] Martinez, J. Carlos, and Jon. C. Jarillo. "The evolution of research on coordinationmechanisms in multinational research." *Journal of International Business Studies*, 1989: 489–514, 490.

[24] Mintzberg, "*Organizational Design: Fashion or Fit?*", 16.

[25] Ibid., 15.

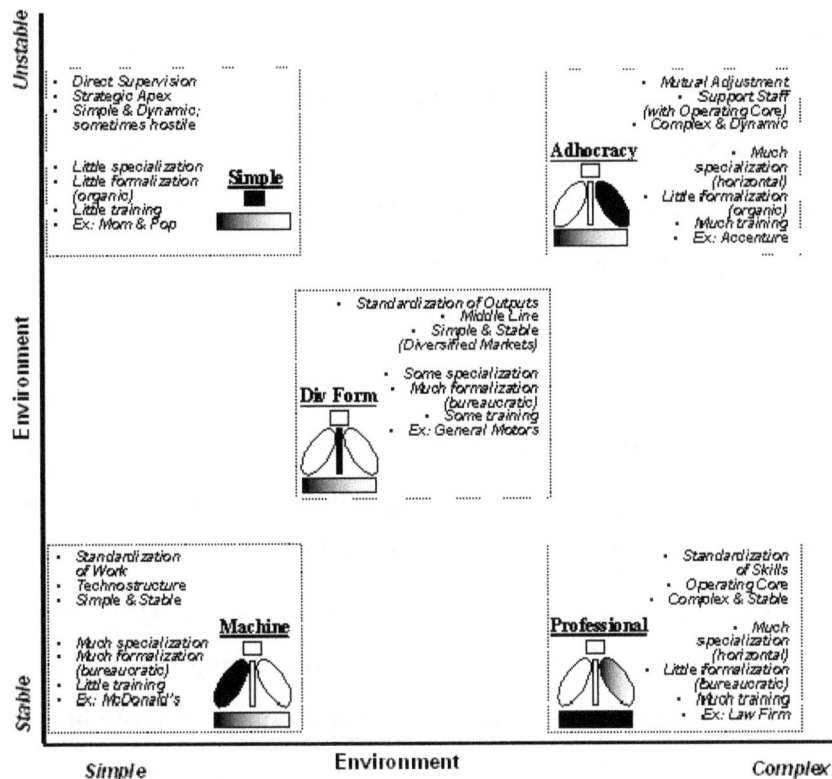

Figure 2. Mintzberg's Structure in Fives

The first of the five configurations is the Simple Structure. This configuration has two levels that include the strategic apex and operating core. This is typical of a start-up or small entrepreneurial company (commonly called "mom-and-pop" company) and it uses direct supervision by the strategic apex as its coordination mechanism. Its main strength is its capability to maneuver quickly in an unstable environment since the size is relatively small. In contrast, a limitation of the simple structure is the neglect of long-term strategy if the strategic apex gets too involved in the company's day-to-day activities.

The second of the five configurations is the Machine Bureaucracy, which is dominated by the technostructure. It standardizes the work processes as its coordination mechanism. This works because of the simple nature of the tasks and the stable organizational environment. In many ways this is the classic organizational structure, most commonly represented by businesses based on standard operating procedures (such

18

as McDonald's). These organizations have many levels of hierarchy topped by the strategic apex, which is concerned with long-term strategies, middle management working local level actions, and the operating core performing simple and repetitive tasks of producing food for customers. This setup allows the business to gain efficiency from the bureaucratic structure and puts the technostructure at the forefront since they are charged with standardizing processes and inspecting their performance. Because the work at the operator level is simple and often mundane, motivation is sometimes problematic.

The third of the five configurations is the Professional Bureaucracy. This configuration has a large operating core and usually has few managerial levels between the strategic apex and the operating core. University or law offices are two examples of this configuration. The primary coordination mechanism is the standardization of skills since most of the operating core is highly trained prior to entering the organization and each individual within the organization feels a certain amount of motivation to meet professional standards. These highly trained individuals execute complex tasks in a stable environment. This configuration creates some unique challenges. The operating core, because its individuals are highly specialized, can become isolated from the other parts of the organization. This causes difficulty in assessing quality control and also responding to a rapidly changing environment. "The result is a paradox: individual professionals may be at the forefront of their specialty, while the institutions as a whole changes at a glacial pace."[26]

The fourth of the five configurations is the Divisionalized Form. This configuration is characterized by a company like General Motors or a multi-specialty hospital with the middle line manager at the forefront of the organization. Because these organizations have diversified product lines, they can operate in moderately unstable environments and complete tasks that range from simple to complex. As a result, they use standardization of products as the coordination mechanism. It is readily evident that this configuration can be extremely difficult to manage effectively from the view of the strategic apex. The benefits to this configuration are much like a mutual fund in that

---

[26] Bolman and Deal, 77.

19

diversity can reduce risk and the company can benefit from ample resources. Some problem areas include competition between divisions or with the corporate headquarters. In addition, headquarters may find it difficult to stay in touch with all divisions and therefore must trust its division leaders to ensure success. However, this is the favored, or established, structural form of the United States military. As in the *Mayaguez* incident, communication through multiple layers in the divisionalized form is no easy accomplishment.

The fifth of the five configurations is Adhocracy. This "is a loose, flexible, self-renewing organic form tied together mostly through lateral means."[27] Examples include "think tanks" and advertising agencies that exist in turbulent environments requiring extreme flexibility. The support staff is the focal point of the organization and the primary coordination mechanism is mutual adjustment.[28] Mutual adjustment is a type of freewheeling and allows highly creative people to interact under an umbrella of ambiguity. The end result would likely be positive exploration that yields benefits to the organization. These organizations can survive in unstable environments that require complex tasks to be executed. A problem can arise if external pressures push them to formalize. If the environment requires them to be more formalized or standardized, the organization may not survive as it exists and may need to reconfigure which can cost the organization its workforce.

Mintzberg's Structure of Fives revealed structural problems as well as faulty coordination mechanisms between the parts of the organization involved in the *Mayaguez* incident. The predominant problem, however, was the strategic apex and its interaction with the remainder of the organization. This is further discussed in Chapter III.

E.   HUMAN RESOURCE FRAME

This frame emphasizes the study of psychological perspective of work. It views an organization as a large, extended family.[29] In contrast to the structural frame that

---

27 Bolman and Deal, 77.

28 Mintzberg, *"Organizational Design: Fashion or Fit?"*, 4.

29 Bolman and Deal, 14.

focused on the organization as a rational system of roles, the human resource frame sees many individuals who possess needs, emotions, capabilities and limitations. As a result, organizations and managers need to understand people and work to create a symbiotic relationship between workers and their work place. This linkage is further defined by the human resource frames core assumptions:[30]

- Organizations exist to serve human needs rather than the reverse.
- People and organizations need each other. Organizations need ideas, energy, and talent; people need careers, salaries, and opportunities.
- When the fit between individual and system is poor, one or both suffer. Individuals are exploited or exploit the organizations—or both become victims.
- A good fit benefits both. Individuals find meaningful and satisfying work, and organizations get the talent and energy they need to succeed.

The human resource frame is useful for analyzing often non-quantifiable human factors that affect the organization.

Three of the four core assumptions deal directly with establishing a true symbiotic relationship between the individual and the organization. Achieving this balance satisfies all parties and meets the needs of the individual while keeping the organization on track to succeed. A symbiotic balance such as this appears in nature between many animals and makes life better for each animal as a result. This is the goal of the human resource frame. However, a common problem is organizations are sometimes built with inherent conflict because an improper configuration exists from the start. This results in the needs of the individual not being met. Chris Argyris observed this conflict because the structure and method of management did not meet the needs of the individuals.[31] In addition, Argyris believed many organizations treated individuals like children and did not realize people have basic self-actualization tendencies. This mismatch of people and the organization must be understood and properly identified by management to reduce possible conflict.

To build and implement a strong human resource philosophy, Bolman and Deal provide some overall guidance and practices that should assist in achieving harmony

---

[30] Bolman and Deal, 115.

[31] Argyris, Chris. *Integrating the Individual and the Organization*, 32.

between individuals and the organization. The human resource table below summarizes the principles that should be part of any successful human resource strategy:[32]

Table 2.   Human Resource Principles and Practices.

Human Resource Principle	Specific Practices
Build and Implement a Human Resource Management Strategy	Develop a Shared Philosophy for Managing People Build Systems/Practices to Implement Philosophy
Hire the Right People	Know What You Want and Be selective
Keep Them	Reward Well and Protect Jobs Promote from Within and Share the Wealth
Invest in Them	Invest in Learning Create Development Opportunities
Empower Them	Provide Information and Support Encourage Autonomy and Participation Redesign Work and Foster Self-Managing Teams Promote Egalitarianism
Promote Diversity	Be Explicit and Consistent about the Organization's Delivery Philosophy Hold Managers Accountable

After reviewing the table, it is clear an organization must first commit to manage with human resources and nurture that relationship. A successful outcome would be reciprocation by the individuals to perform at their highest capability. In short, take care of the people's needs and they will take care of the organizational needs. In the *Mayaguez* incident, providing intelligence likely would have fostered confidence in the leadership dictating the operation. Because it was not provided or it was inaccurate if provided, this alienated the operators from the leadership. The operators no longer felt the keys to their success were supported at the executive level. Though the military is known for its fortitude and adaptability, President Ford's decision to combine units that had never worked together in a mission none of the units had attempted was extremely risky. Though one might think this conveyed utmost confidence in the troops by the

---

32 Bolman and Deal, 136.

executive level, it actually had the opposite effect as the troops felt they were operating in a vacuum, "left to fend for themselves."[33]

F.   POLITICAL FRAME

This frame, derived from political science, views an organization as a jungle or arena with a struggle for power and competition over scarce resources. The formation of coalitions is key and techniques such as bargaining, negotiation, coercion, and compromise are included in everyday activities. "Commitment . . . suggests that we can build alliances by getting others to do favors for us."[34] Favors typically lead to commitments which then lead to coalitions, as seen in government politics. This frame is typically represented by governmental structure. As issues arise, the sponsors of legislation work vigorously to build coalitions that support their position. During this process, individuals may try to leverage any power or influence they possess to develop support to attain resources to achieve their goals. This political process is said to be inevitable in any organization and managers need to understand how to use this frame to better understand their organization.

Bolman and Deal list five propositions to summarize the complex web of interactions between individuals and group interest:[35]

- Organizations are coalitions of diverse individuals and interest groups.
- There are enduring differences among coalition members in values, beliefs, information, interests, and perceptions of reality.
- Most important decisions involve allocating scarce resources—who gets what.
- Scarce resources and enduring differences make conflict central to organizational dynamics and underline power as the most important asset.
- Goals and decisions emerge from bargaining, negotiation, and jockeying for position among competing stakeholders.

The Department of Defense (DoD) exemplifies the above propositions. Each service component represents a coalition with special operations cutting across the services with its own coalition. Each coalition or group has unique interests such as

---

33 Col. (Ret.) James Davis, Interview with authors, August 30, 2005.

34 Pfeffer, Jeffrey. *Managing with Power*, 198.

35 Bolman and Deal, 186.

purchasing land-based equipment versus modernizing airframes. As each group jockeys for position, they defend their need to receive funding or the scarce resources of the DoD. When one party perceives another party is preventing attainment of its goals, conflict arises. "Each party forms its own interpretation of the situation," commonly referred to as conceptualization or framing.[36] Persons who have served in the Pentagon can attest to the conflicts that develop as resources are allocated to each group. On occasion, the joint process of acquisition or a political civilian leader may affect the decision process via negotiations, prioritization or are trumped by civilian use of power.

A key influence in the political frame is power. Each organization has a unique power distribution or lack thereof in some cases. According to Dr. Jeffrey Pfeffer, power is "the potential ability to influence behavior, to change the course of events, to overcome resistance, and to get people to do things they would not otherwise do."[37] Power in an organization is the ability to get things accomplished. This power can be derived from a coalition or an authority figure in the organization. Bolman and Deal list eight sources of power that have been derived by multiple sources: Position Power (authority), Information and Expertise, Control of Rewards, Coercive Power, Alliances and Networks, Access and Control of Agendas, Framing, and Personal Power.[38] Those who formally do not possess power in the organization or who exist at lower levels can use many of these power sources to overcome their position of disadvantage. Even when in a formal position of authority, one may find they do not possess the necessary power or influence to accomplish the job. John Kotter, a noted leadership expert, calls this a "power gap" and suggests that using the above list of power sources to close this gap as a manager.[39]

Power often can often be a source of conflict within an organization. Many people fear conflict or feel it is a negative, but this is not entirely true. Florence Heffron

---

[36] Heffron, Florence A. *Organization Theory and Public Organizations: The Political Connection.* NJ:Apprentice Hall, 1989, 184.

[37] Pfeffer, Jeffrey. *Managing with Power: Politics and Influence in Organizations.* Boston, MA: Harvard Business School Press, 1992, 30.

[38] Ibid., 195–6.

[39] Kotter, John P. *Power and Influence: Beyond Formal Authority.* New York: Free Press, 1985, 117.

states, "Conflict has benefits as well as costs. . . . Conflict challenges the status quo and stimulates interest and curiosity. It is the root of personal and social change, creativity, and innovation."[40] The real challenge in organizations is to properly manage this conflict. Poorly managed conflict brings negative outcomes to the organization instead of stimulating innovation and growth. Bolman and Deal identify key boundaries or interfaces, such as departments or levels in organizations as the most likely source of conflict. Congress and the NSC are naturally at odds (and thus, create a boundary) when it comes to military operations. Congress wants to be informed of every detail while the NSC requires the operational details be closely guarded.

Managers who seek to understand the political frame must be able to identify these areas of conflict and create the right environment allowing a positive outcome. Furthermore, their position alone will more than likely fail to provide the overarching power they expect. Instead, managers have to draw from the power sources listed by Bolman and Deal if they are to get the job done or effect the change they desire. President Ford, eager to prove himself worthy of the presidential position, likely was heavily influenced by the political frame. Combined with the symbolic frame, powerful influences affected his decisions during the *Mayaguez* incident.

G.   SYMBOLIC FRAME

The symbolic frame draws on social and cultural anthropology and views organizations as tribes or theaters.[41] The symbolic frame minimizes rationality and explains organizations in terms of cultures that are ripe in "rituals, ceremonies, stories, heroes, and myths than by rules, policies, and managerial authority."[42] Organizations may also be viewed as theaters where actors play specific roles in an organizational drama. "Problems arise when actors blow their parts, when symbols lose their meaning, or when ceremonies and rituals lose their potency." Furthermore, the use of symbols, myths, and magic may be used to rebuild lost spirit in the organization. A leader can influence an organization merely through his actions as he is a symbol of how to act, how

[40] Heffron, Florence A. *Organization Theory and Public Organizations*, 185.

[41] Bolman and Deal, p 15.

[42] Ibid., 15.

to dress, or how to lead. Symbolism works because they "appeal less to reason and more to [emotion]."[43] The objective of the symbolic frame is to understand how symbols in organizations become so powerful.

As mentioned in previous sections, frames are used to better package multidiscipline approaches to provide better understanding to a manager. The symbolic frame pulls from many resources and provides the following core assumptions:[44]

- What is most important is not what happens but what it means.
- Activity and meaning are loosely coupled; events have multiple meanings because people interpret experience differently.
- In the face of widespread uncertainty and ambiguity, people create symbols to resolve confusion, increase predictability, find direction, and anchor hope and faith.
- Many events and processes are more important for what is expressed than what is produced. They form a cultural tapestry of secular myths, heroes and heroines, rituals, ceremonies, and stories that help people find purpose and passion in their personal and work lives.
- Culture is the glue that holds an organization together and unites people around shared values and beliefs.

In the symbolic frame, perhaps the most significant assumption is that of culture and the effect it has on the organization. For this reason, culture is often synonymous with symbolic when using the frames approach to organizational theory. It is also representative of a more contemporary approach to organizational theory than that of traditional topics such as rational actors and objectivity. The importance of culture to an organization is profound. Culture can dictate every aspect of an organization to include its actions and outputs and the culture of the organization can also alter the individual's actions. "Culture both a product and a process."[45] "Symbols are powerful indicators of organizational dynamics" and "acquire meaning in the organization through recurring experiences."[46] Managers who understand the impact of culture and symbols on an organization can better apply their leadership and operate the organization effectively.

---

[43]Kotter, John P. *Power and Influence*, 91.

[44] Ibid., 242.

[45] Bolman and Deal, 243.

[46] Wilderom, Celeste P.M., Mark Peterson, and Neal Ashkanasy, eds. *Handbook of Organizational Culture and Climate*. Thousand Oaks, CA: Sage Publications, Inc., 2000, 73.

Symbols can simplify, clarify, and bring together an organization under even the most confusing of circumstance or environment.[47] "Symbolism not only affects how people perceive events, but it also influences actions."[48] For instance, the feeling the American flag imposes on a person ranges from freedom to simple patriotism, but most notably, it unifies them under a single movement acting in concert tied to emotion. (McDonald's golden arches unify all individual franchises under the umbrella of a single organization whether domestically or internationally located.) Symbols can range from myths, ceremonies, superheroes, to simple graphics such as Superman's "S". The use of symbols is so powerful that often in problem organizations, simply introducing an effective symbol for individuals to relate to can unify previously deeply divided components. The symbolic frame "offers powerful insight into fundamental issues of meaning and belief and possibilities for bonding people into a cohesive group with a shared mission."[49] President Ford did not perceive the strong influence upon him of the symbology of America as a weak superpower. Though he was aware he needed to improve America's image both domestically and internationally, he did not understand how this frame likely narrowed his perception of events, thereby making his decisions faulty.

Frames provide the leadership with a means to gather, process, and sort information critical to the organization's success. In the *Mayaguez* incident, President Ford's frames of reference dramatically affected and hastened the process of decision making. He felt political pressure because of the way he came into the presidency. He subverted the human resource frame by assuming the military could overcome shortages and inexperience. He felt pressured by the symbology of America as a weakened superpower. If the president had understood the effects framing and structure can have on decision making, it might have enabled him to include more information or allow more time to process the decision of an air assault campaign with an ill-equipped organization.

---

[47] Bolman and Deal, 269.

[48] Jones, Michael O. *Studying Organizational Symbolism: What, How, Why?* Thousand Oaks, CA: Sage Publications, 1996, 4.

[49] Bolman and Deal, 332.

THIS PAGE INTENTIONALLY LEFT BLANK

III. MINTZBERG'S STRUCTURE IN FIVES

Examining the *Mayaguez* Incident through the structural frame using Henry Mintzberg's theory of structural configuration provides one of many approaches to understanding the event. Mintzberg's theory, as described in Chapter II, describes how an organization fits within the context of the organization's environment and the organization's tasks. Success occurs when the organizational structure, decision authority, and coordination mechanisms match the environment and tasks.

In this document, the focus is on the strategic apex and how the chief decision maker's actions affected the structure and coordinating mechanisms of the organization. These changes in structure and coordinating mechanisms had a vital impact on the outcome of the military's mission.

A. DIVISIONALIZED FORM

The executive level of the United States government and the DoD most closely resembles Mintzberg's divisional form. In this structure, a single strategic apex controls multiple middle lines, each with their own specialized task. The president and close advisors (Cabinet members, Whitehouse staff) form the strategic apex and DoD makes up one of the substructures within divisionalized form. The Department of Defense, led by the Secretary of Defense and member of the NSC, has its own multiple divisions whose middle line managers include Geographic Combatant Commanders (GCC) and service chiefs. As discussed in Chapter II, the middle line directs the dominant mode of coordination, which is standardization of outputs.

The requirement for standardization of outputs is for the strategic apex to uniformly compare outputs of multiple organizations within the divisionalized structure. Standardization of outputs in a business context can be accomplished by comparing the net worth of separate divisions within the organization.[50] For the military, the output to be standardized is the ability for the division to utilize its resources to achieve its mission objective with acceptable losses.

---

[50] Mintzberg, *"Organization Design Fashion or Fit?"*, 10.

Each separate middle line manager is responsible for the personnel below him and is responsible for the outputs of his or her division (see Figure 3). Success of the organization relies somewhat on the autonomy of the division heads.[51] Prior to execution of hostilities in the *Mayaguez* incident, the middle line consisted of CINCPAC (Commander-in-Chief, Pacific Command), PACFLEET (Pacific Command Fleet), and PACAF (Commander, Pacific Command Air Force)[52]. Later, due to the actions of the president, the middle line was replaced by members of the strategic apex, rendering the established middle line ineffective.

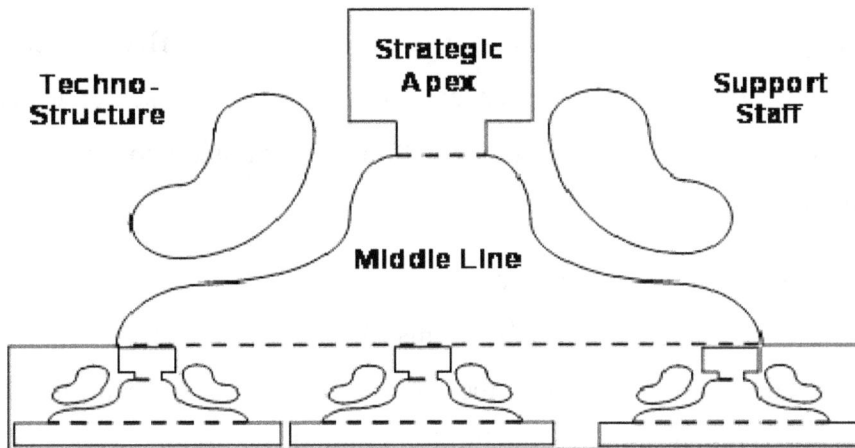

Figure 3. Mintzberg's Divisionalized Form

The strategic apex, with the president at the top, began in the traditional form as the NSC. The output sought by the strategic apex was an effective armed assault to recover the SS *Mayaguez* and her crew. The organization's ability to conduct the operation was severely hampered, however, when the president overstepped his boundaries within the strategic apex. It is unknown whether this was a conscious or subconscious maneuver, but nonetheless it is an obvious action as evidenced in the NSC

---

[51] Mintzberg, *"Organization Design Fashion or Fit?"*, 9.

[52] See Appendix G, CINCPAC Command Relationships.

minutes following the incident.[53] Again, the thesis focuses on examining the actions of the strategic apex throughout the ordeal, where the greatest insight into the failures of the operation is revealed.

The divisionalized structure works especially well for the armed forces. Each military specialty can organize, train and equip under a single chain of command. Air combat, ground combat and sea combat forces specialize to become effective in their individual arenas. The military can somewhat control the training situation or at least choose favorable timing for their training, creating a somewhat stable environment. The military in a training environment also can define the task or problem and attempt to keep the task from becoming too complex. When the environment is complex, training allows for timelines to be adjusted to allow for development of effective coordinating mechanisms. The result is a structure that passes directives from senior leaders to the middle line managers who implement them within their division to achieve a certain capability or output.

The Divisional Form can hold different types of structures from division to division within the overall organization. This design allows flexibility within the organization yet retains rigidity amongst the individual parts. For example, the Army, Navy, Air Force, and Marines all have flexibility in how they conduct operations but they are unyielding in how they use the chain of command. Some divisions, such as logistics units, are highly specialized and highly formalized much like a machine bureaucracy. Other divisions, such as task forces, are highly specialized and highly trained with little formalization. They are much like a professional bureaucracy, where the operators are given a goal and expected to provide a solution based on their training.[54] Hence, DoD operates as a divisionalized form consisting of a mixture of structures.

During wartime, DoD's typically conventional approach involves application of vast resources over a specified amount of time prior to an engagement. The divisionalized structure remains intact, allowing its leadership to rely on an established command and communication lines previously utilized and practiced in training.

---

[53] See all appendices of the National Security Council Minutes, May 12–15, 1975.

[54] Mintzberg, "*Organization Design Fashion or Fit?*", 6.

B. STRUCTURAL FORM DURING THE *MAYAGUEZ* INCIDENT

In peacetime, the military practices its job under coordination mechanisms that are structured to accomplish both complex and simple tasks in a relatively stable environment. During wartime or contingency operations, however, forces are normally detached from their organizing, training and equipping chains of command and realigned under a GCC. The intent of rearranging the command lines is to match the operating core of combat forces to a middle line whose focus is on applying combat power. The new chain of command additionally includes a large number of mission planners, intelligence specialists and personnel familiar with the area of operations. These specialists make up the support staff that is in place to aid the assigned combat force. The GCC is built to provide regional expertise and situational awareness.

Organizations use horizontal coordinating mechanisms to address complexity and instability. The operating core is empowered to "fuse experts drawn from different specialties into smoothly functioning, creative teams."[55] Organizations also use mutual adjustment through support staffs to deal with a complex task in an unstable environment. For the *Mayaguez* incident, the GCC that should have facilitated horizontal coordination and mutual adjustment was Commander-in-Chief, Pacific Command (CINCPAC). Unfortunately, CINCPAC did not fulfill this role because the president and his staff bypassed the middle line and directly supervised portions of the mission. This affected all operations, to include communications between the units. The units directly involved in the action needed to coordinate their movements, resupply, fire support, close air support and extraction but were not able to speak to each other due to the fact that each of the separate functions did not know what radio frequency the other units were using.[56] While this is not the fault of the executive level, it is resultant of the fact that the middle line was bypassed, so standard methods for coordinating communication were never executed. Mutual adjustment and horizontal coordination mechanisms are difficult to build during an operation if the support structure is disengaged.

---

[55] Mintzberg, *"Organization Design Fashion or Fit?"*, 10.

[56] Dan Hoffman, e-mail message to authors, August 30, 2005.

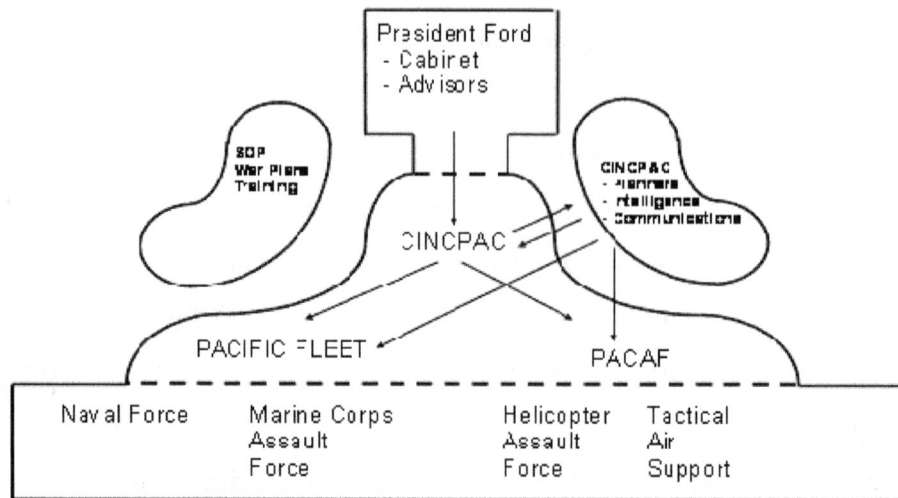

Figure 4. Mintzberg's Divisionalized Form During the *Mayaguez* Incident (ideal)

In some organizations, the way things are supposed to happen and the way they are executed are often not similar. Influences from other factors such as leadership, politics and external pressures can sway the organization away from its formally designed structure. During the *Mayaguez* incident, President Ford consolidated power at the strategic apex. Mintzberg notes that consolidation of power at the strategic apex is normal during periods of hostility.[57] But while consolidation is normal, this strengthening of power had far-reaching effects, changing the structure of the organization and mission execution.

The strategic apex in the United States military chain of command normally includes the president, vice president, director of the CIA, and secretaries of state and defense; however, based on the declassified NSC meeting minutes, President Ford specified his role as the sole decision maker.[58] This relegated the vice president, secretary of state, and director of the CIA to administrative functions, in effect placing them squarely in the middle line. The National Military Command Center (NMCC) shifted to the technostructure and became the conduit through which planning and

---

[57] Mintzberg, *"Organization Design Fashion or Fit?"*, 5.

[58] National Security Council Memorandum for the Record. Wednesday, May 14, 1975, 6:40pm-8:00pm. Gerald Ford Library.

standards for mission execution bypassed the organization. The SECDEF and CJCS also became part of the middle line, which already included the Local Command. In the beginning, the Local Command had direct control over the operating core—the units tasked with mission execution, USS Coral Sea, USS Holt, Boarding Party, Koh Tang Marine Assault Force, 41st Rescue and Recovery Wing, the tactical fighters, and 56th Special Operations Wing. As time progressed, the strategic apex centralized his power causing the middle line to grow and become ineffective. The original middle line— PACOM and its support staff— were demoted to an administrative staff role as well.

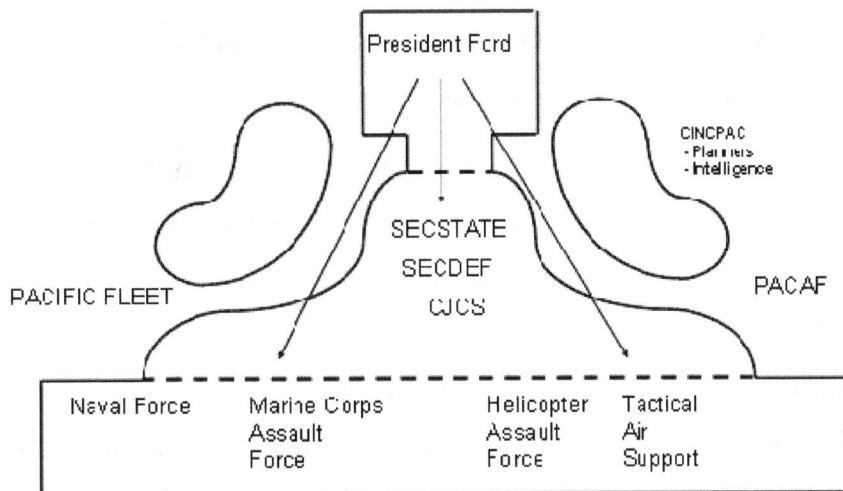

Figure 5. Mintzberg's Divisionalized Form During the *Mayaguez* Incident (in practice)

By forcing the middle line to take administrative staff roles, the president alienated those who were normally authorized to take action. This broke down the ability for the units involved to secure resources from their normal middle line support structures. With the president controlling the participants directly from the Whitehouse, the middle managers could not engage their support staffs to assist the assault force operating core.

The CINCPAC support staff was needed in the *Mayaguez* Operation to deal with the situational and organizational complexity. The Marine assault force needed a way to order resources and coordinate with the other units involved in the operation to include the helicopter squadron from the Air Force and the air support from both the Navy and the Air Force. When multiple requests for intelligence photos were denied or made unavailable essentially because the middle line had been bypassed, Col. (Ret.) James Davis, a Marine company commander who took his troops to Koh Tang Island, personally flew in a light observation aircraft with a handheld camera to get intelligence photos of the island before the attack. Because of altitude constraints, however, his photographs were of limited use. As he and his troops were preparing for takeoff aboard the running helicopters, he was finally handed the reconnaissance photographs he had requested much earlier. The photographs showed there were anti-aircraft weapons and large troop concentrations on the island that the assault force was totally unaware of until that point.[59] This greatly increased the risk and complexity of the mission.

Simple structures and vertical mechanisms of control work sufficiently well when there are simple tasks in an unstable environment, but complex tasks in an unstable environment often fail under the uncomplicated configuration. As in the Law of Requisite Variety, "the greater the variety within a system, the greater its ability to reduce variety in its environment through regulation."[60] In consolidating power, President Ford shifted the organization to look more like a simple rather than complex structure, similar to an autocracy.[61] A single decision maker, wielding the power to change and direct the workforce can have immediate impact on outputs. In the case of the *Mayaguez*, the output should have been an effective military operation to recover the ship and crew. However, the impact of President Ford's consolidation of power reduced the effectiveness to the point of output failure. The support staffs were essentially cut out of the designed structure. Figure 6 below shows Mintzberg's simple structure or autocracy.

---

[59] Col. (Ret.) James Davis, Interview with authors, August 30, 2005.

[60] Principia Cybernetica Web. http://pespmc1.vub.ac.be/ASC/LAW_VARIE.html

[61] Mintzberg, Henry. *Power In and Around Organizations.* Prentice-Hall:Englewood Cliffs, NJ, 1983.

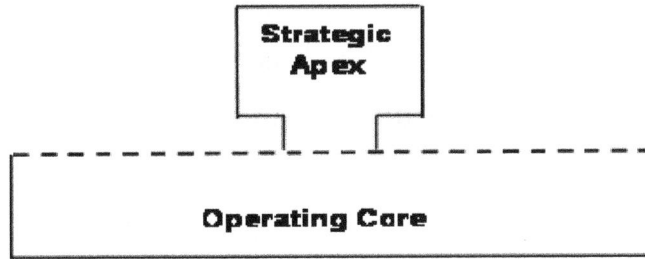

Figure 6. Mintzberg's Simple Structure or Autocracy

The weakness with a simple structure or autocracy is ". . . that when the CEO becomes . . . so wedded to his strategy that he cannot perceive the need to change it, the very survival of the organization becomes threatened."[62] In a complex environment a single leader cannot filter and process such massive amounts of information. Cultural factors for the Khmer Rouge, diplomatic factors, military capabilities and processes all flooding in within a short time period could not be accurately sorted by a single person. This was further amplified because that same person was preoccupied with relaying direct, tactical decisions to the operating core. In one case, President Ford spoke by radio directly with a fighter pilot flying over the waters near Cambodia.[63] This shows the incredible level that direct supervision was being used.

Direct supervision—the coordinating mechanisms during the final stages of the operation—was without any connectivity to the established organization. This was evident in every survivor interview; each stated they did not speak to one another but relied on the fact that things just happened and each component would do its job. Fortunately, the nature of the military is to be flexible and adaptive. In the case of the *Mayaguez*, it was the operating core that functioned as a well-trained team—mutually adjusting and deploying their skills in spite of the remainder of the organization. Of course, it functioned as a matter of survival rather than a matter of effective organizational structure.

---

[62] Mintzberg, Henry. *Power In and Around Organizations*, 358.

[63] *Seized at Sea: Situation Critical: The Story of the Mayaguez Crisis*. DVD. Produced, directed, and written by Brian Kelly. Alexandria, VA: Henninger Productions, 2000.

President Ford should have forwarded his objectives through the NSC to the middle line, which in turn, should have been conveyed to the operating core. (Need quote here about the importance of transmitting the organization's goal to the lowest levels.) Furthermore, the middle line should have been afforded the authority to act autonomously to achieve the organizational goal. In a divisionalized form, the "key assumption is that if the division managers are to be responsible for the performance of their divisions, they must have considerable autonomy to manage them as they see fit. Hence there is extensive delegation of authority from headquarters to the level of division manager."[64]

The essential organizational structures were in place at the onset of the *Mayaguez* incident but the president consolidated power in his own position at the strategic apex, thereby pushing down the Secretary of Defense to the middle line and relegating the true middle line to more of an administrative function. The simple structure he created did not fit in the complex environment. The operating core was left without an effective support staff and paid the price in casualties. President Ford's consolidation of power at the strategic apex may have been a response to perceived hostility but was likely also precipitated by other factors discussed in the frames chapter.

---

[64] Mintzberg, Henry. and Quinn, James B. *The Strategy Process: Cases, Concepts, Cases.* 2nd ed. Englewood Cliffs, NJ: Prentice Hall, 1991, 706.

THIS PAGE INTENTIONALLY LEFT BLANK

38

THIS PAGE INTENTIONALLY LEFT BLANK

IV. FRAMES

The difficult task when analyzing organizations and the actions of their leaders is choosing the correct frame(s) in which to view the occurrence or situation. In order to achieve the desired results of the organizational process, a suitable level of understanding is required when selecting the frame(s) through which to view an event. Bolman and Deal offer four interpretations (Structural, Human Resource, Political and Symbolic) of the frames analysis to facilitate selection of relevant frames. As previously discussed, frames are lenses through which observation is conducted in order to gain perspective and/or understanding of actions and responses.

In this chapter, analysis of the *Mayaguez* incident is concentrated at the executive level to help understand the democratic decision-making process at the strategic apex. Using the frames analysis will foster a larger perspective of a specific event in an extremely difficult and complex environment. Inappropriately framing an event or situation places the decision maker in a precarious situation with a low degree of fidelity. Additionally, trying to comprehend the exigency of the situation and choosing the correct frame can be extremely difficult.

Trying to match the correct frame to a particular situation can be demanding and can require an intricate understanding of the process. "For a given time and situation, one perspective may be more helpful than others. At a strategic crossroads, a rational process focused on gathering and analyzing information may be more helpful."[65] Selecting the perspective—or frame—is the art of framing and reframing situations to understand the meaning. To alleviate the confusion amongst the frames and cope with the uncertainty of deciding between them, Bolman and Deal developed a model for choosing the correct frame at the correct point in time. Table 3 poses questions to facilitate analysis and suggests the conditions under which a particular frame is likely to be most effective. In the case of the *Mayaguez* incident, framing and reframing the event using the table helps reduce ambiguity and bring together the analysis. The focal point of

---

[65] Bolman and Deal, 309

the frames analysis is the NSC and their individual commitment to the crisis, the technical quality of the decisions, degree of understanding, and the resources available for the operation.

Table 3.   Choosing a Frame

	YES	NO
Is individual commitment and motivation essential to success?	Human Resource Symbolic	Structural Political
Is the technical quality of the decision important?	Structural	Human Resource Political Symbolic
Is there a high level of ambiguity and uncertainty?	Political Symbolic	Structural Human Resource
Are conflict and scarce resources significant?	Political Symbolic	Structural Human Resource
Are you working from the bottom up?	Political Symbolic	Structural Human Resource

Several lines of recent research find that effective leaders and effective organizations rely on multiple frames. "[Leaders] can use frames as scenarios . . . to generate alternative approaches to challenging circumstances."[66] Using a frame, one can focus on a moment in time, a scene, or a set of ideas. Framing and reframing are a set of skills employed to one degree or another by the leader.

The essential tool of any manager is the ability to frame, particularly in a large, diversified or divisionalized structure. Using frames, a leader can make sense of a situation, subject, or object as well as judge its character and relative significance. In applying frames, a leader applies a particular meaning to the topic at hand. We define meaning when we ascertain that our interpretation is as valid as any other possible

---

66 Bolman and Deal, 333.

interpretation.[67] Even when frames are applied (consciously or subconsciously), people are inclined to use one frame over another to interpret a situation sometimes failing to make accurate or complete assessment of a situation. Knowledge of the frames approach should alert the leader to the importance of applying all possible frames in order to leverage the best possible solution.

For example, in a scenario in which employee morale is poor, the human relations frame might have more significance than the structural frame. "Rather than reorganize and restructure to improve production or conditions, it is likely more important to discover what is truly affecting the employees and include them in the process".[68] In the case of the *Mayaguez*, the structural frame was, at best, faulty. Although the brave men of the *Mayaguez* incident pulled the mission together with guts and determination, the organizational structure was highly suspicious from its inception. It was critical that the president use multiple frames of reference to view the situation through different perspectives. Using this approach, he would have likely made decisions based on more robust and properly contextualized information and then subsequently, develop an organization that could accomplish the mission.

A.   THE STRUCTURAL FRAME

As discussed in Chapter III, the organization became powerless as President Ford assumed the entire function of the NSC. By reserving sole decision-making authority, he removed a capable organization with a high degree of experience and hindered their ability to participate in the process. It is important to note that by assuming all decision-making capability, President Ford changed the structure of the organization, remaining alone atop the strategic apex. The president, feeling pressure from his environment, perceived an urgent need to move quickly to rescue the *Mayaguez* and her crew. He consolidated authority at the presidential level bypassing the middle line and senior staff, which limited the organization's ability to plan and organize effectively.

---

[67]Fairhurst, Gail T., and Robert A. Sarr. *The Art of Framing: Managing the Language of Leadership.* San Francisco: Jossey-Bass, 1996, 22.

[68] National Defense University. Strategic Leadership and Decision Making. http://www.au.af.mil/au/aw. Accessed April 1, 2006.

The major challenge for the president was to lead a large, complex set of activities and set goals under conditions of uncertainty.[69] While addressing the NSC, President Ford avouched, "as Commander-in-Chief, I have the right to use military force . . . and regardless of the 1973 law,[70] I have the authority to take action."[71] President Ford's perceived need to act decisively and quickly further exacerbated the complexity of the task and the instability of the environment in which the NSC was operating. Viewed through the structural frame, President Ford subconsciously changed the architecture of the organization and acting as the sole strategic apex member, he came to believe he was entitled to full and singular decision-making authority.

B.   THE HUMAN RESOURCE FRAME

"The human resource frame emphasizes an understanding of people, their strengths and weaknesses, reasons and emotions, desires and fears."[72] According to Kotter, a challenge of leadership is to "motivate, coordinate, and control a large group of subordinates."[73] Additionally, the human resource frame purports an existing strong linkage between the needs of the employee, the alignment of individual and organizational needs, interpersonal and group dynamics, and management approaches. A poor fit between the organization and its employees leads to ineffective performance.[74] In the case of the *Mayaguez*, the principles of the human resource frame were non-existent. Organizations exist to serve human needs.[75]

In an effort to bring the president's staff and organization in synchronization, Ford provided his vision of short and long-term goals and direction to rally his National Security Council (NSC). President Ford specified three objectives in the

---

[69] Kotter, John P. *The General Managers*. New York: Free Press, 1982, 20.

[70] President Ford is referring to the War Powers Act of 1973 that states the President shall consult with Congress before introducing Armed Forces into hostilities.

[71] National Security Council Memorandum for the Record. Wednesday, May 14, 1975, 6:40pm-8:00pm. Gerald Ford Library

[72] Bolman and Deal, 18.

[73] Kotter, *The General Managers*, 21.

[74] Bolman and Deal, 115.

[75] Ibid., 115.

Mayaguez crisis: "first, to recover the ship and crew; second to avoid the possibility of hostage negotiations; and third, to mount a demonstrative use of U.S. force to bolters America's international credibility."[76] The plan was to overwhelm a weaker enemy with superior force and rescue the hostages with lightning-fast precision. However, there were two human resource problems working against the president during the *Mayaguez*.

The first problem was the National Security Council and their devolving capability to influence the operation. The members of the NSC were operating under an extremely compressed timeline, and the president wanted quick results. Although President Ford hired competent and qualified people to serve on his staff, he failed to empower them and encourage autonomy to solve the *Mayaguez* crisis. If the staff had been empowered, they may have developed a more complete strategy with a shared philosophy, overcoming the narrow focus of the president. Additionally, including more personnel in the process might have produced alternative options not yet considered by President Ford. As seen in the NSC minutes in Appendix E, the president often stifled other suggestions made by members of the NSC to fulfill his interest in attacking the Cambodian mainland. When a president decides to exert his powers as Commander-in-Chief, he naturally interferes with standard operating procedures.[77]

The second failure within the human resource frame was President Ford's inability to manage the organizational conditions so that the people involved with the crisis could achieve their own goals and facilitate resolution of the incident.[78] "[Their] talent will be wasted if the structure, processes, and metrics dissipate their energy and

---

76 Guilmartin, John F., Jr. *A Very Short War: The Mayaguez and the Battle of Koh Tang.* College Station: Texas A&M University Press, 1995, 38.

77 Quinn, Kenneth. Mayaguez Paper. Kenneth Quinn to General Scowcroft. 25 Aug 75. "Mayaguez Performance Evaluation – Memoranda 6/75-10/75," Box 8. National Secruity Adviser Staff Assistant John K. Matheny Files. Gerald R. Ford Library.

78 Bolman and Deal, 119.

create barriers to their collective effectiveness."[79]   Centralizing all decision-making capability around him, President Ford essentially made managing the armed forces executing the rescue impossible.

By consolidating control, the president failed to allow the organization to function properly and achieve the correct mix of personnel for the job. Instead, he forced the hand of his middle line causing a violation of what Bolman and Deal call the Human Resource Principle, "hire the right people, be selective, and encourage autonomy and participation."[80] The soldiers chosen for the operation were those who were immediately available, not specifically trained or organized for the task at hand. The Marines were only six months out of boot camp and did not see any action in Vietnam; however, the Air Force enlisted flight crews were highly experienced (Telephone interview with Marine Ground Commander Colonel (Ret.) Jim Davis, August 29, 2005). The Air Force helicopters were comprised of few special operations helicopters but predominately a rescue unit that had never accomplished or even practiced an air assault prior to the *Mayaguez* crisis. In fact, because the raid on Son Tay still was classified at the time of the incident, no unit in the Air Force had officially planned or accomplished an air assault mission.[81]

C.   THE POLITICAL FRAME

"The political frame [references] organizations as competitive arenas characterized by scarce resources, competing interests, and struggles for power and advantage."[82] It is within this frame that decision making becomes an opportunity to gain or exercise power, to resolve conflict, and realign power if necessary. Because power, coalition, and conflict make up the core of the political frame, negative images usually come to mind when addressing politics. However, viewed through this frame, politics is simply the realistic process of making decisions and allocating resources in a

---

[79] Galbraith, Jay R., Diane Downey and Amy Kates. *Designing Dynamic Organizations: A Hands on Guide for Leaders at All Levels.* New York: American Management Association, 2002, 227.

[80] Bolman and Deal, 136.

[81] Robert Blough. Interview with authors. August 29, 2005.

[82] Bolman and Deal, 18.

context of scarcity and divergent interest. The challenge for President Ford during the *Mayaguez* operation was the scarcity of resources (limited number of trained military personnel and funding), diverging interests (selecting a diplomatic or military option) and proving himself as a worthy world leader.

President Gerald Ford assumed the Presidency in August of 1974 under extraordinary circumstances. He was the first vice president chosen under the terms of the 25th Amendment having been nominated by then President Richard Nixon to replace the resigned Vice President Spiro Agnew. When President Nixon resigned, it opened the door for Vice President Ford to assume the presidency. Not popularly elected to the office, it is possible President Ford felt a need to legitimize his actions and power. The *Mayaguez* incident was an excellent opportunity to restore the face of America after the Vietnam War via the hand of President Ford. However, the *Mayaguez* incident presented the president with an immediate challenge to his power base: Cambodia.

The Khmer Rouge regime achieved infamy by massacring millions through execution, starvation and forced labor. It was one of the most violent governments of the 20th century often compared to Adolf Hitler, Joseph Stalin, and Mao Zedong. For this reason, the United States refused to legitimize the government of Cambodia and, therefore, was reluctant to address them via diplomatic channels. President Ford strongly opposed direct contact with Cambodia to avoid giving credence to a brutal, communist government. Because he would not send a request for release of the *Mayaguez* and her crew directly to the Cambodian government, President Ford needed to build an international coalition to address the problem. China was available as a mediator for the incident, but the United States' treatment of Vietnamese citizens during the war dissuaded the Chinese from forging ties with the U.S. government. The U.S. issued a formal request to Cambodia through the Chinese demanding the release of the hostages; however, the Chinese Embassy refused to accept the message. After the incident—the U.S. discovered that the Chinese only verbally conveyed the message to Cambodia, but to what extent and reception is unknown.[83]

---

[83] National Security Council Memorandum for the Record. Wednesday, May 14, 1975, 6:40pm-8:00pm. Gerald Ford Library.

Another critical link in the international coalition was Thailand. The government of Thailand had made it known that if the United States intended to invade or conduct hostile acts against Cambodia over the *Mayaguez*, it would formally request removal of all American military troops. In the NSC minutes, President Ford acknowledged the Thai government would likely be upset at any U.S. military action against Cambodia, but that the Thais would be "reassured."[84] Failing to believe that the Thai government would follow through with its threat to demand the removal of American troops, President Ford again failed to forge a much-needed link in the international coalition. Using the international arena within the context of the political frame, President Ford could have realigned power from military to diplomatic channels, thereby relieving diverging interests and provide for safe return of the *Mayaguez* and crew.

Another critical aspect of the political frame is conflict. Because time was severely compressed and possibly because of President Ford's perceived need of proven legitimacy, conflict was relatively non-existent. Normally, conflict between the political bodies of the Department of Defense and the Department of State would be readily evident when the NSC considers military action. However, because President Ford had filled his staff with key supporters and because time was severely limited (by the president), the opportunity for conflict was initially reduced. One would think less conflict is healthy but according to Heffron, conflict is a necessary function within an organization. It "encourages new ideas and approaches to problems, stimulating innovation."[85] At one point during the NSC meeting over the *Mayaguez* crisis, Donald Rumsfeld, then Chief of Staff at the White House, said to President Ford, "From the political standpoint, we should get your friends and brief them, so that they can stand up for you."[86] This is a prime example of the president's efforts to limit conflict by surrounding himself with supporters to his cause.

President Ford sent troops into harm's way without a complete understanding of the situation in Koh Tang. President Ford had previously briefed congress on

---

[84] National Security Council Minutes. Tuesday, May 13, 1975, 10:40pm-12:25am. Gerald Ford Library.

[85] Heffron, Florence A. *Organization Theory and Public Organizations*, 185.

[86] National Security Council Minutes. Wednesday, May 14,1975, 3:52pm-5:42pm. Gerald Ford Library.

issues concerning Vietnam and the fall of Saigon in accordance with the War Powers Act.[87] During the *Mayaguez* incident however, President Ford felt he needed to use his presidential might to work outside the limits of the Act. This created turmoil amongst his staff and the Congress. Officially, Congress sent a response to the president through White House spokesman Robert Hartman that demanded consultation as required by the War Powers Act.[88]

D.   THE SYMBOLIC FRAME

"The symbolic frame focuses on issues of meaning and [interpretation]. It puts ritual, ceremony, story, play, and culture at the heart of organizational life."[89] Within the symbolic frame, it is necessary for a leader to develop and convey "credible strategic premises, identify and focus on core activities" and find the meaning behind the task at hand.[90] President Ford, while he developed credible strategy, failed to focus the organization on core activities to discover the purpose of the Cambodian seizure of the *SS Mayaguez*. Cambodia, in a long-standing war with Vietnam, had stationed combat-hardened troops on the island of Koh Tang to prevent its takeover from Vietnam. The Cambodians deemed the U.S. merchant ship SS *Mayaguez* a threat to the island because they feared the United States had sided with Vietnam. This story was unknown to the NSC and president and, if known, drastically would have altered the choices made at all levels of the organization— particularly the strategic apex that selected military action.

Meaning and interpretation are core components of the symbolic frame. The Vietnam War had just ended and the public viewed DoD, military, and administration as incompetent and fallible. The Vietnam War created a need to regain the public's trust

---

[87] Section 4 of the War Powers Act requires the President to report to Congress within 48 hours the basis for, facts surrounding, and estimated duration of the introduction of U.S. Armed Forces in hostilities. The War Powers Act is found as 50 USC S.1541-1548, passed in 1973 over the veto of President Nixon. It purports to spell out the situations under which he may deploy the Forces with and without a Congressional declaration of war. Under the War Powers Act, Ford cited Article II, Section 2 as his authority to send soldiers into combat. Ford made his report to Congress four hours before the expiration of the 48-hour window.

[88] National Security Council Minutes. Wednesday, May 14,1975, 3:52pm–5:42pm. Gerald Ford Library.

[89] Bolman and Deal, 19.

[90] Kotter, as cited in Bolman and Deal, Table 15.4, 316.

and confidence because the administration's ability to conduct and supervise war was non-existent. The Department of Defense wanted a chance to prove they could conduct successful operations and although the *Mayaguez* rescue was a small operation it became an avenue of great hope. The administration sought to alter the perception of the United States in the international arena by executing a swift, decisive military operation to bring home the *Mayaguez* and her crew. The success of this mission would immediately produce 39 heroes (the number of *Mayaguez* crew) for the American public to rally around. Looming in the back of their minds, however, was the previously unsuccessful attempt at hostage rescue on the *USS Pueblo*.

The *USS Pueblo* was a United States Navy vessel sent on an intelligence mission off the coast of North Korea. On January 23, 1968, North Korean naval vessels and MiG jets attacked the *USS Pueblo*, resulting in one soldier killed and several wounded in action. Subsequently, for the next eleven months, the eighty-two surviving crewmembers lived as captives in North Korea. After a series of military and diplomatic blunders by the United States, the North Koreans eventually released the *USS Pueblo* crew on their own accord. This event was a source of great embarrassment to the nation and still fresh in President Ford's mind, serving as an example of how the impact of an event can affect organizational perspective: the *USS Pueblo* became a symbol. Often times, this frame compels an organization to constantly search for its identity creating a need to draft another tale favorable in the public eye.

The people of the United States no longer felt the country was the great superpower it claimed to be. Globally the nation was perceived as weak and often deemed incapable of fulfilling its role as leader of the free world. President Ford felt that if America did not act quickly and decisively during the *Mayaguez* crisis and with sufficient force, it would confirm to Russia, North Korea, and China the United States was vulnerable to defeat. The symbology of a weak America was not acceptable or even believable to President Ford. It was inconceivable America could be anything but a symbol of great power and stature to Americans, but the rest of the world was starting to think otherwise. Both the *USS Pueblo* incident and the Vietnam War combined to threaten America's standing in world politics.

Since the Vietnam War ended only two weeks earlier, those involved in the *Mayaguez* crises seem to face insurmountable odds. Even the American military experienced feelings of tremendous defeat. Casualty numbers were unmentionable and often ambiguous, leading to further depleted levels of morale within the military. The culture within DoD and its political counterparts had become one of survival rather than domination. A great need emerged for the military to prove itself to not only the world, but to the American public and time would be of the essence in creating the new story by which to form the symbolic frame.

In reviewing the four frames of Bolman and Deal's frames of reference—structural, human resource, political, and symbolic—as well as Mintzberg's structure, the analysis of the *Mayaguez* incident is made clearer but still lacks full clarity. Other influences outside the applications of organizational theory can dramatically alter or influence the decisions of the executive level as well as the organization as a whole. However, in the *Mayaguez* incident, these influences do not change the thesis that President Ford altered the organizational structure by acting as the sole member of the strategic apex but merely add clarity to the crisis.

THIS PAGE INTENTIONALLY LEFT BLANK

V. FINDINGS

The *Mayaguez* incident, in terms of applied concepts of organizational theory, revealed many findings, the most predominant of which was the singularized form of the strategic apex. As previously stated, the traditional definition of the strategic apex is top management, meaning a body of persons collectively managing the organization. In the case of the United States government, top management (Mintzberg's strategic apex) is traditionally thought of as the NSC and the president. In simple organizations, the strategic apex is typically comprised of only one individual because the size of the organization is limited in terms of available personnel. In an organization the size of the United States government with a multitude of qualified and available personnel, it is not likely the strategic apex could operate successfully as a single individual. Additionally it is expected the organization, if it attempts to operate as such, will fail or as a minimum become ineffective. However, during the *Mayaguez* incident, the strategic apex quickly became a single person—the president. This thesis proposes the reason behind the failures encountered during the *Mayaguez* incident was that the organization, traditionally divisionalized, attempted to operate as a simple structure with the president as its sole actor in the strategic apex.

As previously stated, in a simple structure the dominant coordinating mechanism between the strategic apex and the remainder of the organization is based on direct supervision. In the divisionalized form (e.g. the government structure), the coordinating mechanism is standardization of outputs and the middle line accomplishes this by formalization—a task that cannot be created in a compressed timeline. During the *Mayaguez* operation, the president became focused on military action and gave little credence to other ideas proposed by the rest of the NSC. In effect, this isolated him as the sole decision maker who attempted to control the organization through direct supervision. This was exemplified by his direct contact with the fighter pilots (operating core) firing upon the vessels in the waters off of Cambodia.

By directing the fighter pilots, president Ford derailed established coordination mechanisms from the NSC down to the operating core, completely bypassing the middle line. This made the ability to accomplish or assign tasks difficult or in some cases, not possible, because established standard operating procedures normally executed by the middle line were circumvented. This further fueled the president's perception that he needed to directly intervene. According to Graham Allison and Philip Zelikow, the notion of one man leading a massive government and making decisions unilaterally is said to be an oversimplification of any national government.[91] Instead, a leader or "decision-maker" of national policy works as a joint member of a network that includes large organizations and multiple political actors. This argument is logical when the scope of a national government is matched with its dynamic environment. The task of collecting all the relevant information and possessing the needed expertise to make effective decisions as an individual seems unreachable. To add to the complexity, the president's actions were further affected by a phenomenon attributable to frames.

Normally, the Department of State and the Department of Defense have different frames through which they observe world events and possible responses. Instead of opposing one another in their framework, the Secretary of State, Dr. Henry Kissinger, and the Secretary of Defense, James Schlesinger, were in agreement for a proposed solution. Kissinger was known as a proponent of hard line foreign policy, often recommending military action in place of diplomatic action. Even when diplomatic action was the solution, it was associated with the possibility that decisive force would follow should the foreign body in question not comply. "Kissinger was emphatic on the use of force [in the *Mayaguez* incident]."[92] Collectively, their frames of reference complimented one another instead of providing opposing viewpoints for more comprehensively developed courses of action. "In a complex and uncertain world, senior managers can't be expected to always choose the alternative that in hindsight produces the best outcome. But good senior managers can be expected to ensure that . . . complex decisions are evaluated through a variety of alternative frames."[93]

---

91 Allison, Graham & Philip Zelikow. *Essence of Decision Making: Explaining the Cuban Missile Crisis.* 2nd Ed. New York: Addison-Wesley Educational Publishers, Inc., 1999, 3.

92 Rowen, Roy. *The Four Days of the Mayaguez.* New York: W.W. Norton & Company, 1975, 141.

93 Russo, J. Edward and Paul J.H. Schoemaker. *Decision Traps: Ten Barriers to Brilliant Decision-Making and How to Overcome Them.* New York: Doubleday, 1989, 58.

Reviewing the declassified documents shows the lack of fidelity President Ford possessed during this incident. The information pertaining to the threats on the island, the intentions of the Khmer Rouge, the location of the hostages, and the capabilities of the ad-hoc military forces severely impacted the capability of the president to possess enough situational awareness to act appropriately. The ability to collect both critical and timely information to make an effective decision is greatly influenced by those individuals directly surrounding the decision-maker as well as his preferences. This need for information highlights the necessity to develop and maintain clear channels of coordination in the organization. Effectively using the coordination mechanism(s) allows the decision-maker to stay well-informed. In the *Mayaguez* incident, President Ford not only chose to operate as the sole decision-maker, he also acted with limited situational awareness as events unfolded in the *Mayaguez* incident.

The middle line, especially in a divisionalized form, is traditionally most aware of the situation and most able to discern appropriate responses. Because President Ford essentially bypassed the middle line and thus the center of knowledge, he denied himself the situational awareness required for effective decision making. For example, the CIA was aware of the ongoing conflict between Vietnam and Cambodia over Koh Tang Island —a critical piece of information that might have led President Ford to explore a greater number of diplomatic channels rather than commit troops to a heavily fortified island. ". . . U.S. intelligence had a sound grasp of Khmer Rouge tactical capabilities on Koh Tang."[94] This vital piece of information might well have changed the entire outcome.

In addition to errors within the structure and the limited frames of reference through which President Ford viewed the initial *Mayaguez* recovery problem, several outside factors may have influenced his framing and decision making effort. Time and technology were determined to be the most significant outside influences that added to the complex environment in which President Ford operated. For example, though the situation at hand in the *Mayaguez* incident was complex, it was manageable until President Ford applied inordinate time constraints. This reduced the ability to separate the task of retrieving the crew from the perceived need for urgent military action.

---

94 Guilmartin, John F., Jr. *A Very Short War: The Mayaguez and the Battle of Koh Tang.* College Station: Texas A&M University Press, 1995, 36.

Time constraints—real or supposed—often cause conflict and pressure. Richard Nixon accurately observed that the American public would only allow a finite amount of time to accomplish a mission, something President Ford remembered well.[95] With Vietnam, the *USS Pueblo*, anti-war sentiment and deep concern for how the American public would view his actions, President Ford centralized the power and held all decision-making authority in the interest of saving time. However, his quick decisions were at the expense of planning, preparation, organization and human lives. If the Khmer Rouge moved the crew to mainland Cambodia, President Ford and his cabinet felt they would not be able to negotiate for their release. President Ford, in Rowan's book states, "I had to assume that if this fishing boat, with those crew member, got ashore, that the odds were against us in getting them back."[96] The Khmer Rouge did in fact transfer the crew to mainland Cambodia; however, they released them before first helicopter ever landed at Koh Tang Island.

Intelligence is critical to foreign operations as they often occur at great distances from the leadership in Washington, D.C. In the case of the *Mayaguez*, though the technology for intelligence was there, the outputs from that community were not routed through the proper channels. The military force obtained photos only seconds before takeoff and was unable to use the information given effectively. According to Bob Blough, the intelligence personnel assigned to the assault force were from the B-52 community—strategically focused rather than tactically oriented —and incapable of using the technology to their advantage. The photos and information required for a helicopter pilot flying below 5,000 feet was dramatically different than that of a B-52 pilot flying at 35,000 feet. Technology was not only a critical factor for the operating forces, but also for the president.

President Ford's ability to bypass the organization and reach directly to the operating core was directly enabled by technology. Through the radio connection established in the NMCC (National Military Command Center), he spoke directly several times to fighter pilots and the Airborne Command and Control Center during the strafing of the Cambodian waters. It is also likely that if the radio frequencies of

---

95 Borer, Douglas. The Clock is Ticking in Iraq, *San Francisco Chronicle*, October 7, 2005

96 Rowan, *Four Days of Mayaguez*, 143.

the assault force were known by the NMCC, he would have attempted contact with those participants as well. Though this seems advantageous, it is actually destructive in established divisionalized structures. The strategic apex should not have direct contact with the operating core as the apex lacks both the situational awareness and knowledge required for controlling the core's outputs. The middle line is critical to military operations, particularly in complex environments such as the *Mayaguez* incident. President Ford, eager to speak directly to the troops, completely changed the organizational structure and technology was the enabler.

Advancement of technology, while required and necessary, must be appreciated in the context in which it is used. Though President Ford's direct discussion with the troops seems an obvious mistake in the *Mayaguez* incident, it is unfortunately still common in today's military. In Robert's Ridge, for example, Secretary of Defense Donald Rumsfeld spoke directly to the MH-47 pilots executing an operation under fire in Afghanistan (personal interview with a participating MH-47 pilot, Captain Al Mack, USA, conducted May 2003), overriding the orders upon which the mission was executed. In fact, the orders were changing as the mission progressed and Secretary Rumsfeld directed the situation. The already dire situation was further complicated and the end result was unnecessary loss of life. Whether attributable in part or directly, the technology meant to provide perspective to the senior staff was causal to the accident because of misapplication by the strategic apex.

Time and technology, both outlying but influential factors in the *Mayaguez* incident, added to the complex environment. President Ford, unable to successfully navigate the complex environment, made decisions to execute based on incomplete and sometimes inaccurate information. Had the president not isolated himself as the single actor in the strategic apex, he may have found the complex environment more simple and straightforward. The frames of reference through which he attempted decision making were unfinished and often erroneous perspectives that limited his ability to execute effective action. Application of organizational theory to the *Mayaguez* incident demonstrates the decision processes at the executive level left the military operation vulnerable to failure despite perceived public success.

THIS PAGE INTENTIONALLY LEFT BLANK

VI. IMPLICATIONS FOR FUTURE STUDY AND CONCLUSION

Much can be learned from the *Mayaguez* incident using organizational theory as an analytical tool. The *Mayaguez* crisis was rife with potential pitfalls and though President Ford was equipped with an excellent organization of intelligent, competent personnel, the result was unnecessary loss of life. Sacrificing 41 military personnel for the recovery of 39 crewmembers is a major statement in terms of political and military objectives, despite the military responsibility of defending American lives no matter the cost. To the public, the operation was a success and President Ford the savior of the *Mayaguez* crew. To the military, the operation was an embarrassment of windfall proportions. What had begun as a major air assault operation had turned into a quest for survival—all because of failures within the organizational structure and poor decisions made through inappropriate or incomplete frames of reference. The magnitude of irony in the operation is unprecedented—even before the first shot was fired on the island of Koh Tang, the SS *Mayaguez* and her crew had been released. Had President Ford understood or applied even a single concept of organizational theory in his analysis of the situation, it would have provided the necessary perspective for critical decision making, saved lost lives, and prevented men being left behind.

A. IMPLICATIONS FOR FUTURE STUDY

Two areas of future study would enhance the proposal that application of the concepts within organizational theory serve to enhance analysis of lessons learned, specifically in the military or governmental environment. The first is to scrutinize the way in which information is gathered and analyzed for lessons learned. Contact with Joint Center for Operational Analysis to understand their process should be the starting point for further examination. The second area of future study is the development of a "tool" (e.g., checklist, flow diagram) for organizations to analyze their output and coordination mechanisms as well as structure. These two areas of study would greatly enhance the accuracy of lessons learned for organizations.

Proposal 1: Further examination of how lessons learned are analyzed is required to improve the resultant solutions.

The *Mayaguez* incident, while a single operation in the military's history, is stereotypical of how many operations occur. Because there is a predictable way military operations occur, there must be a way to alter or improve their actions. Yet the military has repeated the mistakes not only in the *Mayaguez* but also in operations prior to and after the *Mayaguez* incident, despite an entire center for lessons learned being established at the United States Joint Forces Command in Norfolk, Virginia. Named the Joint Center for Operational Analysis (JCOA), it exists to produce "compelling recommendations to change derived from direct observations and sound analysis of current joint operations, exercises and experiments."[97] It also maintains a "comprehensive database and archives of lessons and documents pertaining to previous and ongoing joint operations around the world." The irony is that the center was established in 1997—far too late when one considers the number of U.S. Military operations executed in the twentieth century. Better late than never, the center seeks to unify lessons learned across all services; unfortunately joint lessons are rarely analyzed outside of military channels.

"Failure to consciously define the problem in more ways that one" can lead to "undue influence by the frames of others."[98] Once again, the organization (the military in this case) views the problems through like-minded frames leading to erroneous or incomplete assumptions or actions. "Establishing the framework within which issues will be viewed and decided is often tantamount to determining the result."[99] Therefore, the resultant analysis is incomplete or inaccurate. Not only are the frames through which the analysts at JCOA view an operation limited, but the analysis itself is faulty. According to the website, JCOA gathers lessons learned from inputs entered by military members in the field. The center then repeats the mistakes and lessons learned in a war-gaming drill

---

[97] United States Joint Forces Command. *Joint Center for Operational Analysis.* http://www.jfcom.mil/about/fact_jcoa.htm.

[98] Russo and Schoemaker. *Decision Traps*, 39.

[99] Pfeffer, Jeffrey. *Managing with Power*, 203.

to produce a solution to the problem submitted. By using only single-source analysis, JCOA is limiting the military's possibilities for success, making them vulnerable to continued failure.

This thesis, by using concepts outside of the typical military war-game analysis, seeks to demonstrate the effectiveness of alternate analytical methods. Though organizational theory is more commonly associated with businesses, it has direct application to the military and government structures. In the case of the *Mayaguez*, an entirely different perspective of failure was achieved by exposing the president as the single-actor strategic apex. Though the president did not fail the operation, his decision making exposed the military to unnecessary risk. If one read only the GAO reports, it would be determined the military and in no way, the president, was entirely at fault for the mistakes committed.

War-gaming could include frames of reference as part of the final analysis. When used repetitively, it becomes second nature to view the events through different lenses, therefore allowing diverse analyses of the same experience, allowing for a shared understanding in a dynamic world. Organizational theory is not necessarily the answer, but it exemplifies the need to apply theories outside of typical military thought to expose the true problems and lessons learned in military operations.

Proposal 2: An organizational theory tool may be effective in alternative analysis of military lessons learned.

As exemplified by JCOA, the military lacks effective tools to properly analyze lessons learned. Instead, the lessons gathered through an online process are consolidated, reviewed, and then modeled by a war-game scenario. The center personnel design the game to simulate the same situation the forces were in, and then merely re-enact the event applying the lessons learned to "analyze" whether they are credible solutions. Though re-enacting the scenario with new material is somewhat effective, it hardly gains much more than a hindsight discussion. Again, the concern is the frame of reference through which the analysts examine the event *and the organization*. Unfortunately, the organization is rarely analyzed by any perspective other than the war-game. This thesis exemplifies the value of applying other academic theories when analyzing both organizations and events. Again, if frames of reference are incorporated, a shared understanding may result.

Though commanders often are laden with techniques, advice, and theories to take to battle, an organizational theory tool to use on the lessons learned may prove effective. Though it is not feasible in the heat of battle to pull out a checklist for analysis, it may be valuable in post-battle discussions. More importantly, JCOA would greatly benefit from the ability to apply theory rather than simulation or modeling to lessons learned. Varying theoretical perspectives serve to expand knowledge by providing different, even opposing views. As demonstrated in this thesis, application of organizational theory exposed organizational failures in the *Mayaguez* incident rather than simple lessons learned as published in the GAO analysis.

B. CONCLUSION

Applying selected concepts of organizational theory to the *Mayaguez* incident of 1975 leads to a more comprehensive understanding of events and more accurate lessons learned. Application of organizational theory to the *Mayaguez* incident demonstrates the decision processes at the executive level left the military operation vulnerable to failure. The *Mayaguez* crisis was rife with potential pitfalls and though President Ford was equipped with an excellent organization of intelligent, competent personnel, the result was unnecessary loss of life. Publicly, the operation was a success, however, to the military the operation was an embarrassment—all because of failures within the organizational structure and poor decision making. Application of the concepts within organizational theory facilitate comprehensive analysis rather than elementary lessons learned.

Future study should include both examination of the current process for collecting, analyzing, and publishing lessons learned as well as creation of a tool organizational leadership can use to analyze their processes, outputs, and design. It should be noted other organizational theorists suggest that while organizations can improve their processes and outputs, the improvement is often limited because the organization itself is resistant to change. Amy Zegart, in *Flawed by Design*, suggests, "Once [government agencies] arise, they become very difficult to change."[100] She observes that "the price of initial structural choices appears to be high . . . and [organizations] are created by political actors who must operate in a reality suffused with conflict, contention, and compromise..."[101] Though the theory challenges other theories that suggest organizations can change, it is also directly in line with the theory examined in this thesis—Bolman and Deal's framing theory. Regardless of the organizational theory, this thesis suggests application of *any* theory during analysis will prove more productive than current practices in governmental organizations.

---

[100] Zegart, Amy B. *Flawed by Design.* Stanford, CA: Stanford University Press, 1999, 5.

[101] Ibid., 53.

THIS PAGE INTENTIONALLY LEFT BLANK

APPENDIX A

LOCATION OF THE SS *MAYAGUEZ* AND AREA OF OPERATIONS

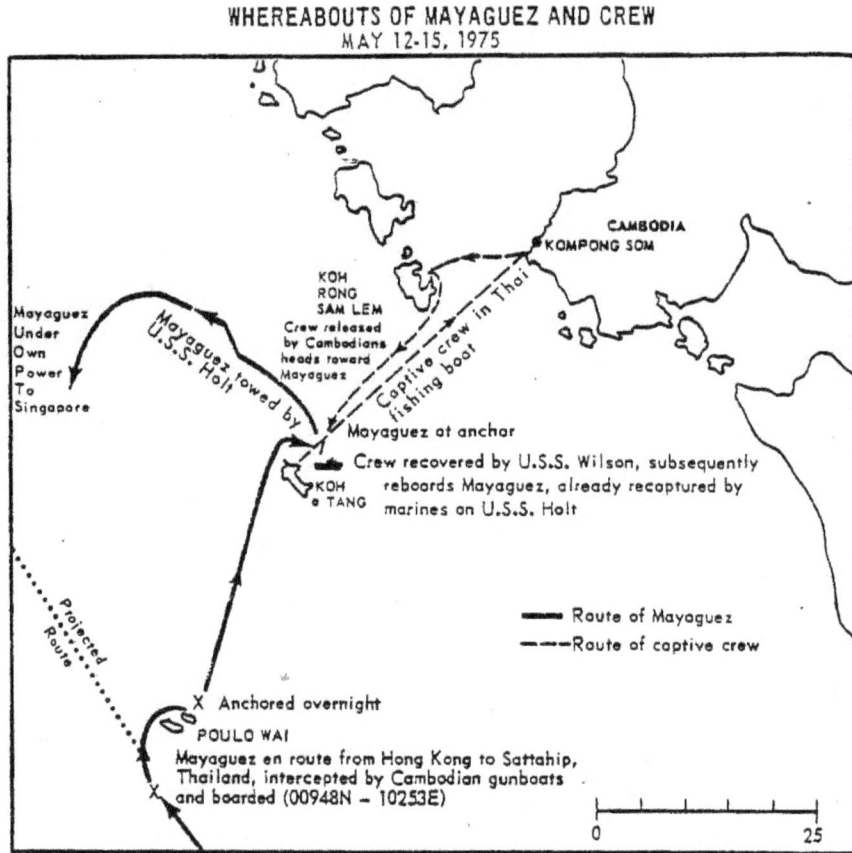

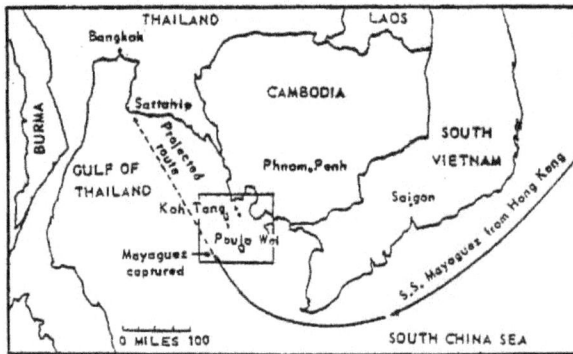

WHEREABOUTS OF MAYAGUEZ AND CREW
MAY 12-15, 1975

THIS PAGE INTENTIONALLY LEFT BLANK

APPENDIX B

MAYAGUEZ TIMELINE

May 12

3:18 a.m.—Mr. John Neal of the Delta Exploration Co. in Jakarta, Indonesia received a Mayday call from the *Mayaguez*. Messages stated "Have been fired upon and boarded by Cambodian armed forces at 9 degrees 48 minutes north/102 degrees 52 minutes east. Ship is being towed to unknown Cambodian port."

4:00 a.m. to 5:00 a.m.—Mr. Neal lost communication with the ship, gave up trying to reach the ship and informed the U.S. Embassy in Jakarta of the incident.

5:02 a.m.—U.S. Embassy in Jakarta informed Washington of the incident.

7:50 a.m.—Pentagon orders CINCPAC to send reconnaissance aircraft to find ship.

9:57 a.m.—U.S. reconnaissance aircraft were dispatched to the area to attempt to locate the ship and verify the report.

12:05 p.m.—The President chaired a meeting of the National Security Council.

1:50 p.m.—White House press briefing and statement concerning seizure of the ship and U.S. demands for its release.

4:30 p.m.—A representative of the Liaison Office of the People's Republic of China summoned to the State Department was given a message for the Cambodian authorities, demanding the release of the ship. The PRC representative refused to accept the message.

9:16 p.m.—U.S. reconnaissance aircraft made a positive identification of the ship and observed it being escorted by Cambodian gunboats. The aircraft was fired at and hit, sustaining minor damage.

May 13

12:10 a.m.—A representative of the United States Liaison Office in Peking delivered a message to the Cambodian Embassy there. A message was also delivered to the Foreign Ministry of the People's Republic of China.

1:25 a.m.—U.S. reconnaissance aircraft observed the *Mayaguez* anchoring one nautical mile north of Koh Tang Island. The aircraft was fired at but not hit.

6:04 a.m.—The *Mayaguez* crew was observed being transferred from the ship.

6:18 a.m.—The Pentagon ordered the Air Force to maintain surveillance of the *Mayaguez* and prevent its movement into port on the Cambodian mainland. Warning shots were fired across bow of *Mayaguez* to signal it not to move. Specific orders were given not to attack the Cambodian gunboats.

6:54 a.m.—White House press briefing on location of ship and U.S. surveillance effort.

7:35 a.m.—The crew is observed on the island but it cannot be ascertained how many men have been moved. Therefore, it is not certain that the entire crew has left the ship.

3:05 p.m.—A C-130 aircraft received small arms fire from the island.

3:20 p.m.—Four Cambodian gunboats at island fired anti-aircraft weapons at C-130.

5:50 p.m. to 6:35 p.m.—Congressional leadership contacted by telephone and advised that President had directed military actions to prevent the *Mayaguez* and its crew from being transferred to the Cambodian mainland and to prevent reinforcement from the mainland of Cambodian forces detaining the *Mayaguez* vessel and crew.

7:04 p.m.—Three patrol boats move from the island. Warning fire from USAF planes turns them back to Koh Tang.

9:43 p.m.—Cambodian patrol boat ignores warning fire from U.S. aircraft and continues to move. Boat is attacked and set afire.

9:52 p.m.—Patrol boat spotted with possible crew members on it. U.S. aircraft fires in front of it in order to turn it back. Boat continues to move toward the mainland.

10:03 p.m.—A different patrol boat moves and is engaged and set afire by air strikes.

10:40 p.m.—The President chaired a meeting of the National Security Council.

11:00 p.m.—The vessel believed to be carrying crew members reaches the mainland.

May 14

12:29 a.m.—Three other patrol boats are engaged by U.S. aircraft. One is sunk, other two damaged. A subsequent strike damages two other patrol boats.

7:15 a.m.—U.S. Liaison Office in Peking reported that PRC Foreign Ministry returned the message for the Cambodian authorities.

11:00 a.m.—USS *Harold E. Holt* arrives in the area.

11:00 a.m.—Congressional leadership notified by telephone that three Cambodian boats had been sunk and four damaged by U.S. air strikes.

11:50 a.m.—DOD press briefing and statement about U.S. attacks on Cambodian boats.

1:00 p.m. to 2:00 p.m.—A letter regarding this action was delivered to UN Secretary General Waldheim by Ambassador Scali, requesting UN Secretary General to take any steps in his ability to secure safe return of *Mayaguez* and crew.

2:00 to 5:00 p.m.—State Department officials briefed members of the House International Relations Committee, Senate Foreign Relations Committee and House Armed Services Committee.

3:52 p.m.—President chairs NSC meeting in the Cabinet Room.

4:45 p.m. to 5:10 p.m.—Orders are issued to begin the military operations for the recovery of the SS *Mayaguez* and crew including air attacks against military facilities near Kompong Som to prevent reinforcement and support from the mainland for Cambodian forces detaining the ship and its crew.

5:14 p.m. to 5:20 p.m.—U.S. assault forces take off from stations.

6:40 p.m. to 7:40 p.m.—President meets with Congressional leadership to inform them of the actions he has ordered to recover the ship and the crew.

7:00 p.m.—Marine assault force arrives at USS *Holt*.

7:07 p.m.—Phnom Penh domestic radio service carries a broadcast in Cambodian that states that the Cambodian Government will order the *Mayaguez* to withdraw from Cambodian territorial waters. No mention is made of the crew.

7:00 p.m.—Assault force arrives at Koh Tang Island and comes under fire.

7:15 p.m.—A helicopter in the assault force against Koh Tang Island is hit and downed.

7:45 p.m.—Another helicopter crashes on the island.

7:46 p.m.—Approximately 100 Marines are on Koh Tang Island.

8:06 p.m.—The Cambodian broadcast, monitored by the Foreign Broadcast Information Service and translated into English, was carried on the FBIS wire.

8:15 p.m.—Insertion of the first assault wave on Koh Tang Island was completed. 125 Marines now on beach.

8:15 p.m.—The President is informed of the FBIS wire report by Secretary Kissinger.

8:30 p.m.—White House press briefing and statement on the actions ordered by the President.

8:45 p.m.—Support aircraft arrive and commence operations against military installations near Kompong Som.

9:05 p.m.—Marines from the USS *Holt* board and take control of the SS *Mayaguez*. They find evidence that the vessel had been occupied until just before their arrival.

9:15 p.m.—White House issued press release on message being sent to Cambodian authorities offering to stop military operations if crew is released.
9:33 p.m.—*Mayaguez* is secured and U.S. colors are raised.
10:23 p.m.—A boat was reported near Koh Tang Island flying a white flag.
11:07 p.m.—The USS *Wilson* takes aboard the occupants of that boat. The occupants were determined to be the entire crew of the SS *Mayaguez*.
11:16 p.m.—The order was given to cease all offensive operations and begin to withdraw. The Commander of the forces on the island requests additional ground forces to provide security for a successful withdrawal.
11:21 p.m.—White House statement on recovery of ship.
11:45 p.m.—The additional ground security forces arrive at Koh Tang Island.

May 15

12:10 a.m.—Airstrikes at Kompong Som terminate.
12:25 a.m.—The *Mayaguez* crew is returned to its vessel.
12:30 a.m.—The President's statement on recovery of ship and crew.
12:45 a.m.—DOD press briefing on military actions.
1:21 a.m.—A helicopter is hit during effort to remove troops from the island.
2:00 a.m. to 2:30 a.m.—A report consistent with the War Powers Resolution from the President was transmitted to Speaker of the House and to President Pro Tempore of the Senate.
4:40 a.m.—*Mayaguez* underway.
6:15 a.m.—Commencement of operation to evacuate last elements of marines on Koh Tang Island using helicopters and USS *Wilson* and USS *Holt*.
7:17 a.m.—Final extraction of U.S. ground forces completed.
12:21 p.m.—Last aircraft departed the area.

THIS PAGE INTENTIONALLY LEFT BLANK

APPENDIX C

PICTORAL REPRESENTION OF TIMELINE

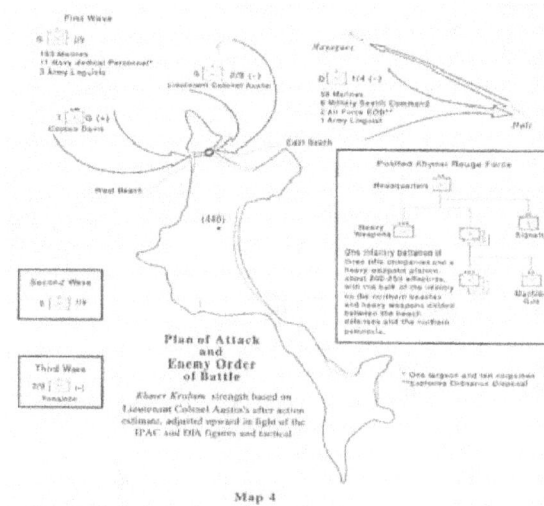

Map 4 — Plan of Attack and Enemy Order of Battle

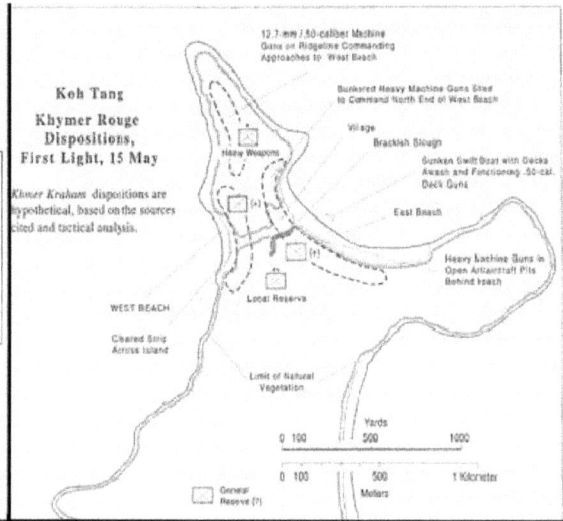

Koh Tang Khymer Rouge Dispositions, First Light, 15 May

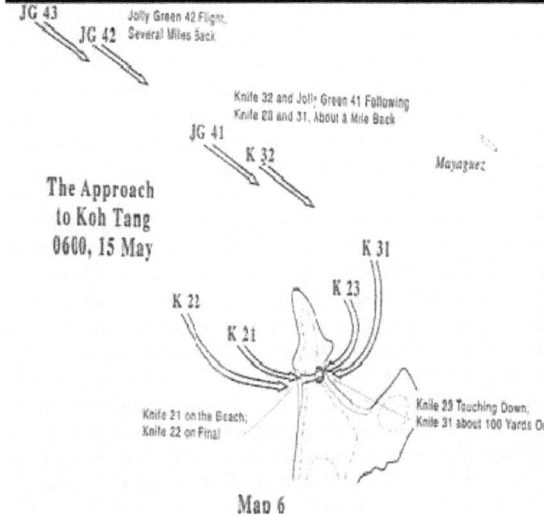

The Approach to Koh Tang 0600, 15 May

Map 6

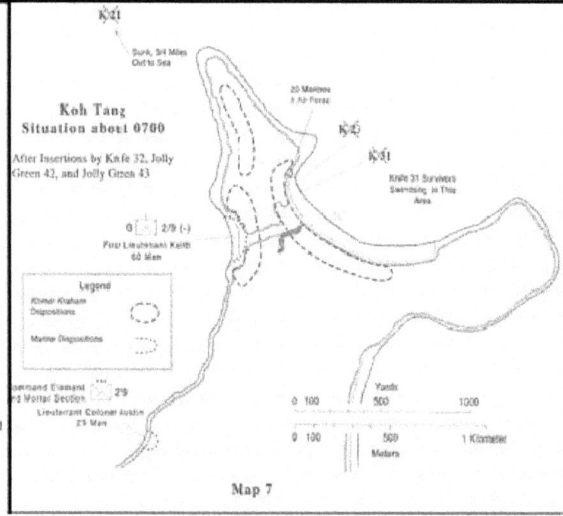

Koh Tang Situation about 0700

Map 7

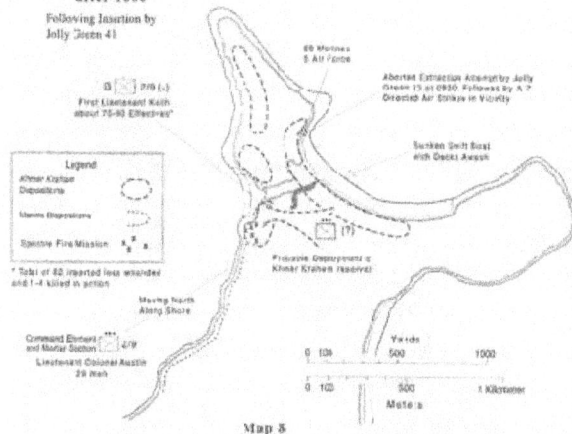

Koh Tang
**Situation Shortly
after 1000**

Following Insertion by
Jolly Green 41

Map 8

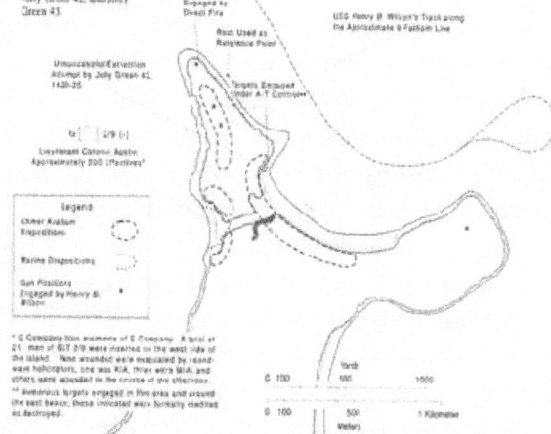

Koh Tang
Situation, 1330-1600

After Insertions by Knife 32,
Jolly Green 42, and Jolly
Green 43

Map 9

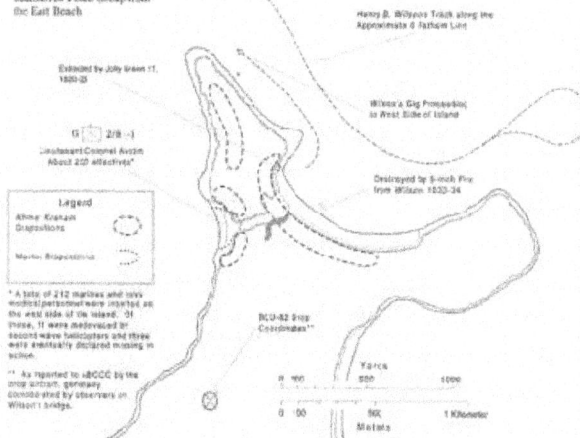

Koh Tang
Situation, 1820

Following Extraction of the
Marine/Air Force Group from
the East Beach

Map 10

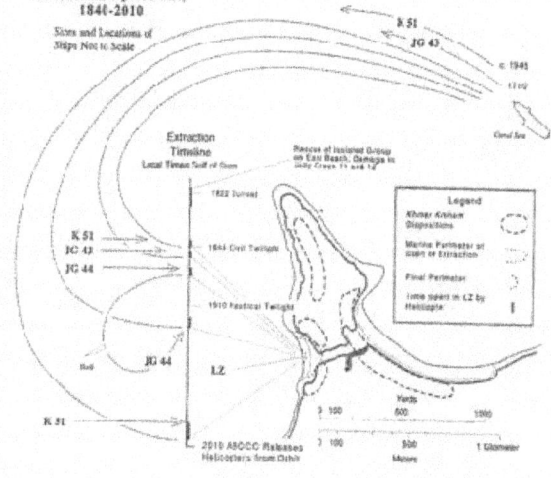

Koh Tang
**Extraction Operations,
1844-2010**

Sizes and Locations of
Ships Not to Scale

Map 11

APPENDIX D

GAO ANALYSIS

Chapter 7.—Agency Comments and Our Analysis

DEPARTMENT OF STATE

State did not challenge the facts in our report. However, in transmitting the Department's comments, the Deputy Under Secretary for Management expressed his personal view (see app. III) that the report was inadequate and misleading and that it attempted to second-guess the actions of officials acting under the constraints of time. He cited as an example of "weakness" in our reporting, that we ignored public statements of the Cambodian Deputy Prime Minister for Foreign Affairs.[1]

In drafting our report we very carefully reconstructed what factual information existed during the various stages of the incident. Care was taken not to introduce data which was out of the sequence of events and to weigh closely information which became available after the incident. For this reason, we purposely did not give much credence to the statements of the Deputy Premier of Cambodia which were made in September 1975, almost 4 months after the incident. Actually, the full September statements indicate that the seizure of the *Mayaguez* was initiated by a local commander, that authorities in Phnom Penh learned of it many hours later, and that poor communications between Phnom Penh and local authorities delayed the Cambodian response. Thus, these statements hardly support a view that expeditious military action was necessary to secure the release of the *Mayaguez* and its crew.

DEPARTMENT OF DEFENSE

Defense did not question the accuracy of our report but rather, in a few instances, our interpretation of the facts.

Defense maintained that "the report insists that the whereabouts of the crew could and should have been more accurately ascertained." This statement does not accurately reflect our position. Our report points out that additional assets were available to attempt to obtain better information but that these assets were not used. Defense agreed the use of these assets might have provided additional data during the incident. We pointed out that details as to the basis for suspecting caucasians had been moved to the mainland never reached the military command centers. These details lend credence to an interpretation that

---

[1] Actually the statements referred to were made by the Deputy Premier of Cambodia.

71

THIS PAGE INTENTIONALLY LEFT BLANK

APPENDIX E

NSC MEETING MINUTES

3539

THE WHITE HOUSE
WASHINGTON

~~TOP SECRET~~/SENSITIVE

MINUTES

NATIONAL SECURITY COUNCIL MEETING

Date:	Tuesday, May 13, 1975
Time:	10:40 p.m. to 12:25 a.m.
Place:	Cabinet Room, the White House
Subject:	Seizure of American Ship by Cambodian Authorities

Principals

The President
The Vice President
Secretary of State Henry A. Kissinger
Secretary of Defense James Schlesinger
Acting Chairman, Joint Chiefs of Staff Gen. David C. Jones
Director of Central Intelligence William Colby

Other Attendees

State: Deputy Secretary of State Robert Ingersoll

DOD: Deputy Secretary of Defense William Clements

WH: Donald Rumsfeld
           John Marsh
           Robert Hartmann
           Philip Buchen

NSC: Lt. Gen. Brent Scowcroft
           W. Richard Smyser

~~TOP SECRET~~/SENSITIVE - XGDS

President: Brent, can you tell us what the situation is?

Scowcroft: With regard to the boat that I told you about, we do not
                  have much time. Our aircraft has used riot control agents twice.
                  That has delayed the boat but it has not stopped it. It is now
                  about six miles from Kompong Som, according to the pilot.
                  The pilot is not at all sure that he can disable the boat without
                  sinking it.

President: I thought the first boat had reached the shore.

Schlesinger: It got to the island.

Jones: It was in range.

President: I understand we sank the second one. And the third one is the
                  one we are now talking about.

Scowcroft: That is correct. That boat is now six miles from Kompong
                  Som.

President: Did the pilot try riot control agents?

Scowcroft: They were tried and they did not work. Now the pilot is not
                  sure what to do next.

Schlesinger: He is not certain that there are Caucasians on board.

President: Let's look at it. If they got to shore, and we have done the
                  other things we are contemplating, there will not be much
                  opportunity for them anyway.

Kissinger: They will hold them for bargaining.

Hartmann: How can the pilot tell whether the men are Caucasians?

Schlesinger: By a number of signs, such as their size and the color of
                  their skin.

Scowcroft: It is not an easy identification. It is very tough.

Schlesinger: I would think that avoiding bargaining chips is less of an
                  objective than not being in a position where the Cambodians
                  can say that the F-4's killed our own men.

TOP SECRET/SENSITIVE   - XGDS

President: What do we do? Should we let them go into port?

Schlesinger: Let's continue to try to stop them with riot control agents.
                We understand there are 8 to 9 men on board who seem to
                be Americans. There are others below who may be
                Americans. The pilot thinks there may be more Americans.

President: What do you recommend?

Schlesinger: I recommend we sink the speedboats. I do not think we should
                sink the other boat but should rather continue to use the riot
                control agents.

Scowcroft: The pilot is reluctant to attack if he is under instructions not
                to sink the boat.

Schlesinger: That is true. He originally thought that he could disable the
                boat without sinking it. Then he became reluctant.

President: What do you think?

Kissinger: I have just come back into this problem, having been out of
                town all day. My instinct would have been as follows:

                We have two problems:

                -- First, the problem of the crew and the ship and of how we
                win their release.

                -- Second, our general posture which goes beyond the crew
                and the ship.

                But that sort of thing comes later.

                In the immediate situation, I think I agree with Jim. We will
                take a beating if we kill the Americans. At the same time,
                we must understand that we cannot negotiate for them once
                they are on the mainland. If you are willing to take that
                position, then I think we can let them go. We should not let
                them become bargaining chips.

Scowcroft: We have already done it on one.

Schlesinger:	There were no Caucasians on it.
Kissinger:	We have a pilot who thinks there may be Caucasians. It would have been a much better position for us to take that we will simply hit anything that leaves the island.
President:	Right.
Kissinger:	Now we are debating with the pilot.
President:	I gave the order at the meeting to stop all boats. I cannot understand what happened on that order, because I heard that it did not go out until 3:30
Schlesinger:	It went out by telephone within half an hour after you gave it.
Jones:	We talked to Burns, the Commander out there, immediately. The confirming order went out later. But our communications are so good that we can get all the information back here immediately to Washington in order to make the decisions from here.
President:	Was the order given, and at what time, not to permit any boats to leave the island or come into it? I was told it was not given until 3:30. That is inexcusable.
Jones:	That was the written order, not the verbal order.
President:	Let's find out when it was given.
Clements:	To assist General Jones, I was with him in the Situation Room when he gave the order even before he left the White House.
President:	Let's find out what happened. It is inexcusable to have such a delay. Now let us talk about the problem of the moment. It is a different situation, and I reluctantly agree with Jim and Henry.

TOP SECRET /SENSITIVE - XGDS

Schlesinger: I think we should destroy the boats that still remain at the island.

President: That is your recommendation. What do you think, Henry?

Kissinger: I'm afraid that if we do a few little steps every few hours, we are in trouble. I think we should go ahead with the island, Kompong Som, and the ship all at once. I think people should have the impression that we are potentially trigger-happy. I think that once we have our destroyer on station, that is ideal.

Schlesinger: I agree. It will go in at noon.

Kissinger: In the meantime, I think we should sink the boats that are at the island.

Rumsfeld: I thought the HOLT would get in at 8:00 a.m.

Schlesinger: We understand it is doing 21 knots, not 25.

Scowcroft: I have got to get the word out. What should I tell them?

President: Tell them to sink the boats near the island. On the other boat, use riot control agents or other methods, but do not attack it.

Marsh: Supposing the boats near the island have Americans on it. Should we send some order to use only riot control agents there?

Kissinger: I think the pilot should sink them. He should destroy the boats and not send situation reports.

President: On one boat, there is a possibility of Caucasians. On the others, we can't be sure.

Jones: Suppose we say in our order that they should hit all the boats in the cove, not just two.

Kissinger: We don't need to decide on the cove right now. We have some time.

President: Is it 11:00 o"clock there now?

Schlesinger: It is 10:00 o"clock.

President: How many hours away is the HOLT?

Kissinger: Fourteen hours.

Jones: (Raising a chart) I have tried to put all this in a chart,
               indicating when the key actions would take place. The HOLT,
               we expect, will arrive at 12:30 Washington time tomorrow.
               The CORAL SEA and the HANCOCK will arrive later. We
               are not sure of the latter's arrival time because it is having
               trouble with one propeller shaft.

               The Marines are all airborne. They are on the way to Utapao.
               That is the 1,000 Marines. The 150, with their helicopters,
               are already there and on the alert. The 1,000 Marines will
               arrive around 0300 tomorrow morning. That is the time for
               the first one. After that the others arrive every few hours.

President: Then the HOLT arrives at 11:30 Eastern Daylight time
               tomorrow. That is 2330 Cambodia time.

               And the CORAL SEA about 28 hours from now.

Jones: It is making 25 knots. The plots are pretty good. It is moving
               towards the spot.

President: That is not flank speed.

Jones: That is the best time that they can do.

President: Flank speed is 33 knots.

Jones: The Navy says that that is the best time that they can make.

Rumsfeld: The information this afternoon was that the HANCOCK would
               arrive on Friday.

Jones: This is very tenuous. They are working on one of the shafts.

Rumsfeld:	That is 2200, Friday, the 16th?
Jones:	No, the 15th.
Schlesinger:	We are in serious trouble on the mechanical side. One shaft is out on the HANCOCK. The OKINAWA has an oiler out. It is making only 10 knots. There has been a series of mishaps.
President:	What can be done before daylight ends over there today?
Schlesinger:	We have 11 choppers at Utapao. We can run operations against the vessel. In addition, we can land on the island with 120 Marines. We can support that with the force from Okinawa. All together, we would have 270 Marines. In all probability, we could take the island. The Marines estimate that there might be about 100 Cambodians on the island. We would prefer to land with 1,000.
President:	If you do not do it during this daylight, you have a delay. How long would it be?
Schlesinger:	24 hours. We do not have the HOLT there yet. The HOLT will arrive at noon tomorrow our time. If it is to do anything, I would prefer to wait until the first light on the 15th. Until the CORAL SEA arrives, all we can use are the helicopters at Utapao.
Kissinger:	How would the Marines get down?
Jones:	On ladders.
Schlesinger:	The helicopters would hover.
Kissinger:	But if there are 100 troops on the island, why do we not attack it?
President:	In this daylight cycle, you could put 120 on the ships, and 270 on the island?
Jones:	The total lift is 270. Our plan was to seize the ship with 120, and then to use the Marines from Okinawa to try to go on the island.

It is hazardous to go onto the island with this first group because you do not have time to recycle. We would have to let them remain there overnight, against a force that we do not know.

Kissinger: Does the CORAL SEA have helicopters?

Jones: No. It has only two or so that it uses itself. But we could take the Marines on to the CORAL SEA, and thus get them close to the island.

Kissinger: I understand we only have 11 choppers.

Colby: Couldn't the 270 protect themselves against the force on the island?

Jones: We have nothing to confirm the exact force on that island.

Kissinger: I do not see what we gain by going on with that force tonight. If you sink the boats in the area, and all who approach, it does not matter if we have anybody else on the island. At that point, nothing will be moving.

                My instinct would be to wait for the HOLT and the CORAL SEA. You can then work with the Marines from the CORAL SEA. Nothing can happen in the meantime. Then I would assemble a force and really move vigorously.

President: In other words, the time you gain in this cycle is not worth the gamble.

Kissinger: Later you can do more. It might work with the 270. But it is a risk. It should be decisive and it should look powerful.

Jones: But it cannot be in 24 hours, only in 48. Once you start cycling, it takes time.

Schlesinger: I think that Henry (Kissinger) is thinking of going tomorrow night.

Rumsfeld: But you have only a few hours left of daylight.

Jones: That would not be enough.

Schlesinger: We need the morning of the 16th for a coordinated assault.

Kissinger: We are talking about 48 hours.

President: In other words, you are talking about Thursday night our time.

Jones: On Wednesday night, the CORAL SEA will help a little with its fighters. But not with Marines. Maybe the HANCOCK will do it.

Kissinger: You also have the HOLT.

Jones: With the CORAL SEA, you have other vessels as well. You will have a total of five ships. You would have a good force, but it is very late at night to begin to cycle the Marines.

Colby: Our estimate was that there were 2,000 in Kompong Som. There is not a large force on the island.

President: Do you think we can figure with 100?

Colby: Yes. The KC have just arrived in power. They have probably not had time to man the island more fully.

Clements: In the time frame that you are talking about, there will not be an island worth taking. All the Americans will be gone.

President: Not if we knock out the boats. Unless, of course, they leave at night.

Clements: Right. I think they will get out. The HOLT will protect the ship. But that is not what matters. I doubt that there will be anything on the island.

Rumsfeld: Can we not use flares for this?

Jones: The main thing we use at night is infra-red. We can read it at night. The P-3's also have searchlights and flares.

TOP SECRET/SENSITIVE - XGDS

Rumsfeld: The P-3's should be good at keeping the boat under control.

Jones: Yes, unless the weather is bad.

Clements: The small boats can get through.   You cannot get control.

Colby: The KC may say something soon.

President: It seems that at a minimum we should wait for the next daylight
               cycle, with the HOLT getting there.

Kissinger: The HOLT will be there then.

President: Right.   Is it the unanimous view that we should withhold action
               until after the CORAL SEA has a full day there?

Schlesinger: I think you should wait.

Colby: This is not my business.   I do not think you should go tonight.
               But I worry about what might happen later.   If they get locked
               in, if they take reprisals, it would be very difficult for us.

Clements: I would like to take a middle position.   Once the HOLT gets
               there, we will have some control.   We can do a great deal.

Colby: I think that with the Marines, you have to go soon.

Kissinger: I am very leery about that operation using ladders.

Schlesinger: If there is token resistance on the island, the Marines can
               handle it.   If there is more, they can try to lock in and get
               more Marines to land the next day, with the HOLT for additional
               support.   It is a close call.   There are the pressures of time.
               It is also possible that the Cambodians will decide to execute
               our men.

Colby: Once we take that ship, the clock is ticking.

Clements: The HOLT can get them, by speaking to them with loud-
                speakers. It can let them know our position.

Kissinger: But that is not the issue. We should not look as though people
                can localize an issue. We have to use the opportunity to
                prove that others will be worse off if they tackle us, and not
                that they can return to the status quo.

                It is not just enough to get the ship's release. Using one
                aircraft carrier, one destroyer, and 1,000 Marines to get
                the ship out is not much. I think we should seize the island,
                seize the ship, and hit the mainland. I am thinking not of
                Cambodia, but of Korea and of the Soviet Union and of others.
                It will not help you with the Congress if they get the wrong
                impression of the way we will act under such circumstances.

                As for the 270 Marines, it had several components. There is
                an advantage in speed. The problem is if anything goes wrong,
                as often does. I think against 100 KC you would lose more
                Americans because you do not have overwhelming power. I
                am assuming we will not negotiate. We must have an uncon-
                ditional release. On balance, I would like to get a more
                reliable force.

Clements: If you want the ship and the Americans, why not let the HOLT
                do it? Let the HOLT broadcast that if the Americans are not
                released, all hell will break loose.

Kissinger: What would hell mean in a case like that?

President: Let's do an add-on to Colby's suggestion. The HOLT is there.
                You land 270 Marines. You bomb the airport at Sihanoukville.

Colby: My schedule is to land the Marines today.

Schlesinger: Until the CORAL SEA gets there, we have only the aircraft
                from Thailand. The inhibitions on the use of the aircraft from
                Thailand are greater.

President: No, you have the B-52's on Guam. They can be used.

Colby: If you knock out every boat, you have effectiveness.

TOP SECRET/SENSITIVE - XGDS

Kissinger:	That is still localizing it. We will not get that many chances.
	As Jim says, it would exacerbate the Thai problem.
President:	If we order the Marines to go from Utapao, we could get 270 in there.
Jones:	That was before we lost two helicopters on SAR. I would urge against going this daylight. The Marines would just be landing at Utapao. The helicopter pilots would be tired. Nobody would be mated up yet. It would be a difficult operation to be launching at that time, especially since we could not follow up the same day.
Kissinger:	If you were to give the orders now, Mr. President, there would still be some hours of delay before the messages were received and before the preparations were made. By then we would really only have three more hours of daylight left in order to conduct the operation.
President:	So we rule out any action on this daylight cycle. Then, on the next day, the HOLT gets there. We then have some more options. The CORAL SEA, however, doesn't get there until the next cycle.
Kissinger:	If you wait 24 more hours, you have the HOLT and you also have the fact that you can use 270 Marines.
Jones:	And, in fact, you have 250 more than you can put in. You also have the CORAL SEA.
Kissinger:	I am not sure that I would let the HOLT go up against the vessel. It may be best to keep the HOLT where it can blockade the island. Then we can seize the island.
Schlesinger:	I agree with Kissinger. But we have to keep in mind that there are forces on the island. That gives them time to prepare. It also gives them time to scuttle the ship.
Kissinger:	But they can still scuttle the ship, even with the HOLT alongside. If we could seize the ship quickly, I would agree. I did not know that the HOLT could board.
President:	Unless sailors are different now, they are not good boarders.

TOP SECRET/SENSITIVE - XGDS

Schlesinger:	Could any Marines do it?
Jones:	We could get the Marines on the ship, but then we could not use them for other things.
	The suggestion is to go with the first light on the 15th, to get the HOLT and to hold the island.
Kissinger:	My suggestion is to seize the island. We cannot do anything tonight. By tomorrow morning, we can put the Marines on the HOLT. They can operate. I would go for the island at daybreak of the 15th.
Schlesinger:	The problem with that is that the CORAL SEA will not be there. If you want an overwhelming force on the island, you should wait until the 16th.
Kissinger:	The ideal time for what I have in mind is the 16th. That would not just include the island but Kompong Som, the airport and boats.
President:	If you wait until the 16th, you have maximum capability. But the people in Utapao should be prepared to operate as soon as the HOLT gets there, at 11:30 tomorrow night. The Marines should be alerted.
Kissinger:	The HOLT gets there at noon tomorrow. So we can go from first light. We could seize the island and the ship. That, however, would not give us the CORAL SEA for such operations as we would wish to run against Kompong Som.
Schlesinger:	You can get 250 Marines in helicopters.
Colby:	That would mean 500 in two cycles.
President:	The operational orders should be set up so that the HOLT and the Marines can go. We do not know what will happen in 24 hours. They have options also. We can make a decision tomorrow if we want to. But we should have orders ready to go so that they can move within 24 hours. That would be for the HOLT, the Marines, and the B-52's.
Rumsfeld:	When would it start, then?

Kissinger: At 2200 hours tomorrow. I think that when we move, we should hit the mainland as well as the island. We should hit targets at Kompong Som and the airfield and say that we are doing it to suppress any supporting action against our operations to regain the ship and seize the island.

If the B-52's can do it, I would like to do it tomorrow night. Forty-eight hours are better militarily. But so much can happen, domestically and internationally. We have to be ready to take the island and the ship and to hit Kompong Som.

President: I think we should be ready to go in 24 hours. We may, however, want to wait.

Schlesinger: We will be prepared to go on the morning of the 15th. We will see if we can get the Marines on the HOLT. At first light, we will have plans to go to the island. Simultaneously, we will go for the ship.

We will have the B-52's at Guam ready to go for Kompong Som But I think there are political advantages to using the aircraft from the CORAL SEA. You will have more problems on the Hill with the B-52's from Guam.

Vice President: Why?

Schlesinger: The B-52's are a red flag on the Hill. Moreover, they bomb a very large box and they are not so accurate. They might generate a lot of casualties outside the exact areas that we would want to hit.

President: Let's see what the chiefs say is better, the aircraft from the carrier or the B-52's. It should be their judgment.

Kissinger: But the CORAL SEA would delay us 24 hours.

Rumsfeld: But do we have to wait for the CORAL SEA actually to arrive?

Scowcroft: No. Their planes can operate at considerable distance.

President: On the 15th, we can use the B-52's from Guam. On the 16th, we also have the aircraft from the CORAL SEA.

Jones:	Except, if you use the CORAL SEA, it limits some assets. Everybody is now on alert. We can do it when you say. We are ready to go.
Rumsfeld:	Is it not possible that the CORAL SEA aircraft could strike Cambodia even when the CORAL SEA is still hours away?
Schlesinger:	I'm not sure it would be close enough. Let me check.
Rumsfeld:	The CORAL SEA could be there near that time.
Schlesinger:	Let me check.
President:	You may have an operational problem. If you have to turn the carrier into the wind in order to dispatch and recover aircraft, you may lose time.
Schlesinger:	Yes, but if you go for the 15th, you do not need its presence so soon if you can use the aircraft from a distance.
Kissinger:	What do we have on the CORAL SEA?
Jones:	We have fighter aircraft, including F-4's and A-7's.
Kissinger:	Would they be more accurate than the B-52's?
Jones:	Not necessarily. It depends on the type of target.
Buchen:	I see two problems:
	-- The first is Cooper-Church Amendment.
	-- The second is international law.
President:	On international law, I do not think we have a problem. They have clearly violated it.
Buchen:	We have the right of self-defense, but only self-defense. The Cooper-Church Amendment says no actions in Indochina.
Kissinger:	I think you can legitimately say that our aircraft are suppressing hostile action against our operation.

TOP SECRET/SENSITIVE

President:	We cannot be that concerned in this instance.
Marsh:	This afternoon, we had the NSC prepare a paper saying what we would do. It showed that you would use force in general terms. The reaction from the people we talked to was very favorable.
Clements:	I hate to have us lose sight of our objectives in this case. Those objectives are to get the Americans and the ship. If we want to punish people, that's another thing. I think that dropping a lot of bombs on the mainland will not help us with the release of the Americans.
President:	I think we have to assume that the Americans were taken from the island and that some were killed. This is tragic, but I think that we have to assume that it happened. Does anybody disagree?
	(General expressions of agreement.)
Vice President:	At a briefing yesterday, Congressman Zablocki, one of the proponents of the War Powers Act, said that he would tell the press that the U.S. could bomb the hell out of them.
Schlesinger:	We are not inhibited by the War Powers Act, only by Cooper-Church.
Colby:	We think there are about three T-28's at Kompong Som airfield. They could use them. So there is a potential threat at Kompong Som against our forces.
President:	Can we verify this?
Colby:	This is from a photograph taken on the 12th.
Rumsfeld:	How are those aircrafts equipped?
Colby:	With bombs and guns.
Kissinger:	I think the worst stance is to follow Phil's concern. If we only respond at the same place at which we are challenged, nobody can lose by challenging us. They can only win.

TOP SECRET /SENSITIVE - XGDS

This means, I think, that we have to do more. The Koreans and others would like to look us over and to see how we react. Under certain circumstances, in fact, some domestic cost is to our advantage in demonstrating the seriousness with which we view this kind of challenge.

President: Phil and I have argued for years.

Buchen: I have to state the problems that we face.

President: In this daylight cycle, unless something unusual comes up, we will try to prevent boats going to and from the island.

Kissinger: The latest intelligence shows that there are several small patrol boats near the island in the cove. I think we should sink them.

President: I agree.

Schlesinger: There are four boats.

President: I think we should sink any boats that can be used to try to move the Americans.

Rumsfeld: But not the ones that carry Americans.

Schlesinger: I disagree with Henry in one case. The legal situation in Indochina is unique. We should emphasize that. The restraints of our actions are different from the restraints anywhere else.

Kissinger: I would hit, and then deal with the legal implications.

President: Bill (Colby) should verify that the T-28's are there. At the second daylight cycle, we are prepared to do more. The HOLT will be there and the Marines will be ready to go on it and to be put on the island, with the B-52's and perhaps the aircraft from the CORAL SEA prepared to strike Kompong Som. But, unless there is some unusual development, the actual action will take place 24 hours later.

TOP SECRET/SENSITIVE - XGDS

Schlesinger: On the 16th.

Kissinger: You can decide it then.

President: The preferable time is 24 hours later.

Kissinger: That is when the best forces will be available. But that has
                    to be weighed against other considerations for the extra 24 hours
                    that you lose. I remember 1969, when the EC-121 was shot
                    down off Korea. We assembled forces like crazy. But in the
                    end, we did not do anything. Maybe we shouldn't have. We
                    will never know.

Colby: There is one other justifiable target in the Kompong Som
                    area. The old Cambodian Government had 25 patrol boats in
                    the Ream Naval Base.

                    (The President, Kissinger, and Schlesinger almost simul-
                    taneously remark along the lines that that might be a worth-
                    while target.)

Schlesinger: But this sort of thing would require the gunships out of
                    Thailand.

Kissinger: I think we should do something that will impress the Koreans
                    and the Chinese. I saw Teng Hsiao-Ping's comments in Paris.

President: Are there an airfield and a naval base there at Kompong Som?

Colby: Yes.

President: Why not hit both of them? There would be as many objections
                    to hitting one as two of them.

Schlesinger: The question is whether you use the B-52's or the carrier
                    aircraft. The B-52's may represent the best image for what
                    Henry is trying to accomplish. But, for Congress and others,
                    other aircraft would be better.

President: Bill has to verify what there is at the airport.

Schlesinger: We'll put some T-28's on the base.

TOP SECRET/SENSITIVE - XGDS

President: Tomorrow, we will still have the options as to what we should do.

Jones: On Guam, if we are to do anything, we have to start pretty soon. But there are lots of press there.

Rumsfeld: You would be launching at about 4:00 p.m. tomorrow.

Kissinger: How long does it take to load?

Jones: There are many planes to load and to get ready.

Kissinger: Is the first thing tomorrow still time enough?

Jones: I'm not sure.

President: Are there any others in the Far East?

Jones: Only at Utapao.

President: We do not want that.

Rumsfeld: It should not take long to calculate the answer on the question of using the CORAL SEA.

Vice President: Everybody wants to know when you are moving. In New York, where I just was, people expect you to be doing things. So any steps you take in preparation will be understood.

President: How many B-52's would you use?

Jones: Perhaps 6 or 9.

President: Let's say 9. How many do you have on Guam?

Jones: I am not sure. About 20 or more.

President: Every time I have looked at a B-52 base, they are always doing something. It should not be that unusual. I think you should load them, and get them ready.

Jones: There are about 50 reporters on Guam right now, because of the refugees.

TOP SECRET/SENSITIVE - XGDS

Kissinger: Can you tell the commander to shut up?

Schlesinger: It will get out, no matter how hard you try.

Vice President: Perhaps it would be good to have it get out. I don't think we
                  should cavil.

President: Let's have them get ready to carry out the mission if we
                  decide to do it.

Hartmann: I am not an expert on military affairs. I am just an old retired
                  captain in the Reserve. I have been listening in terms of what
                  the American public wants. I think the American public wants
                  to know what you are going to do.

                  This crisis, like the Cuban missile crisis, is the first real
                  test of your leadership. What you decide is not as important
                  as what the public perceives.

                  Nothing, so far as I know, has gone out to the public so far,
                  except that we are taking steps. It may be that we should let
                  the public know something of the steps that you are taking.
                  The public will judge you in accordance with what you do. We
                  should not just think of what is the right thing to do, but of what
                  the public perceives.

Kissinger: I would say nothing until afterwards. That will speak for
                  itself. Then you can explain what you have been doing.

                  If you say something now, everybody will be kibitzing.

President: But the press should know of the NSC meeting.

Hartmann: I think we should consider what the people think we are doing.

Rumsfeld: The delay worries me.

Hartmann: Yes.

Kissinger: If we are going to do an integrated attack, I think we have to
                  go in 22 hours. We should not wait for a later cycle.

	I cannot judge if there would be a problem in taking the island. We're saying that it will be one annihilating blow. I cannot judge if 270 Marines can do it.
Rumsfeld:	There would 500.
Kissinger:	But there will be 270 for four hours. They will have the HOLT support. Perhaps they will also have some support from the CORAL SEA.
President:	Do we have Marines on the CORAL SEA?
Jones:	I'm not sure.
Kissinger:	If the CORAL SEA can launch against Kompong Som, it can launch against the island. We have to be sure that the landing has a chance of success.
Jones:	The probability that the Americans are gone causes the problem. I think we have a high probability.
Kissinger:	Then my instinct is with Rummy. We should go tomorrow night or earlier.
President:	Everything will be ready. But, if you do it in the next cycle, you have the problem of Thailand.
Kissinger:	The ideal time would be Thursday night. But I am worried that in the next 48 hours some diplomatic pressure will occur, or something else. So we have to weigh the optimum military time against the optimum political time. For foreign policy and domestic reasons, tomorrow is better.
President:	The Thai will be upset.
Kissinger:	That is correct, but they will also be reassured.
Rumsfeld:	Can we be sure there is anybody on the island? We might just take a walk.
Kissinger:	If the Americans are on the mainland, then we have to rethink.

TOP SECRET /SENSITIVE - XGDS

Rumsfeld:	If we look at this tonight, we will know tomorrow.
President:	If Jones goes back to the Pentagon tonight with the orders to prepare, we will have details tomorrow.
Jones:	Everything is now moving, except the B-52's.
Ingersoll:	What is the flying time of the B-52's?
Kissinger:	About 6 hours.
Jones:	Maybe longer.
Schlesinger:	Can we tanker them out of Guam?
Jones:	Yes.
Kissinger:	What will we say about the boats that have been sunk?
Buchen:	We have to make a report to the Hill.
Schlesinger:	It may not get out that quickly.
President:	My answer would be, that we have ordered that no enemy boats should leave the island or go out to it, but that if they did, they would be sunk.
Kissinger:	I think a low-key press statement can be issued, saying what has happened. We should tell the truth. We should say it in a very matter-of-fact way, at a DOD briefing.
Schlesinger:	It will not stay low-key.
President:	The order was issued that no boats should leave.
Kissinger:	We should say nothing about the riot control agents. We should say that there were Americans possibly being moved, and that lives were at stake. Some Americans are still on the island. In pursuit of these objectives, the following boats were sunk.
	One other reason is that it is not inconceivable that the Khmers will cave, and they should come in response to something that we had done.

Schlesinger: Should we say that they were sunk from aircraft from
                  Thailand? That is your problem.

Kissinger: I am worried about it getting out of hand. We will look sneaky
                  and furtive about something we should be proud of.

                  But the Thai thing does give me trouble. I think the Thai
                  military will love it. But the Thai Government will say that it
                  does not like it.

                  The Liberals on the Hill will put forward a recommendation to
                  withdraw our forces from Thailand. They will match this with
                  some requests from the Thai Government.

Rumsfeld: I think that is a good issue.

Hartmann: Bob Byrd, whom I regard as a good antenna of sentiment, says
                  that we should act.

Marsh: Case says we should go in.

Vice President: In our statement, should we not call them launches?

Schlesinger: The boats are of different sizes.

Kissinger: I would urge that the spokesman make a short announcement at
                  noon tomorrow. He should explain why we are doing it. He
                  should say that it was ordered by you, executed by the National
                  Security Council, and then answer no other questions. This
                  would be noon. By 8 o'clock, we will have decided the other.
                  That will add to your strength.

                  (General concurrence.)

END OF MEETING

THE WHITE HOUSE

WASHINGTON

TOP SECRET/SENSITIVE

3540   MINUTES

NATIONAL SECURITY COUNCIL MEETING

Date: Wednesday, May 14, 1975

Time: 3:52 p. m. - 5:42 p. m.

Place: Cabinet Room, the White House

Subject: Seizure of American Ship by Cambodian
                   Authorities

Principals

The President
The Vice President
Secretary of State Henry A. Kissinger
Secretary of Defense James Schlesinger
Acting Chairman, Joint Chiefs of Staff General David C. Jones, USAF
The Director of Central Intelligence William Colby

Other Attendees

State: Deputy Secretary of State Robert Ingersoll

Defense: Deputy Secretary of Defense William Clements
                   Admiral James L. Holloway

WH: Donald Rumsfeld
                   John Marsh
                   Robert Hartmann
                   Philip Buchen

NSC: Lt. General Brent Scowcroft
                   W. R. Smyser

DECLASSIFIED • E.O. 12958 Sec. 3.6
With PORTIONS EXEMPTED
E.O. 12958 Sec. 1.5 (a)(b)(c)(d)

TOP SECRET/SENSITIVE - XGDS   MR 91-20, #4 NSC ltr. 3/19/96

By KBH ;NARA, Date 3/20/96

96

President: Bill (Colby), can we have your report on the latest situation?

Colby: Mr. President, we have some new information on the status of Khmer Communist forces in the Kompong Som - Koh Tang area.

The most recent reconnaissance concerning naval craft indicates that there are 24 armed ships in the vicinity of Kompong Som -- 13 coastal patrol boats, 10 riverine patrol boats, and one submarine chaser.

In addition, there are 3 utility launching craft (LCUs) at Kompong Som, and one LCM at Ream.

As for air strength, our preliminary analysis of 12 May···········showed three T-28 fighters and a total of six transport aircraft at Kompong Som airfield next to the port. There is also a substantial remaining number of some 100 T-28 aircraft left at Pochentong Airfield near Phnom Penh when it fell.

For air defense, the Communists have apparently deployed antiaircraft artillery near Kompong Som and Ream. Preliminary analysis of 13 May photography shows that there is one 37-mm antiaircraft position just south of Kompong Som, and two 37-mm positions southeast of Ream.

These weapons are some threat to aircraft flying within 3 nautical miles of their location, and under 14,000 feet.

In ground strength, KC combat forces at Kompong Som total some 2,000 troops. This force could be quickly augmented by the remaining 14,000 troops scattered throughout southwestern Cambodia.

                          ···
··
···
··

. . . .
. . . .
. . . .

Photo-reconnaissance of 13-14 May identified a probable 105-mm howitzer position and a possible coastal artillery position of unidentified caliber just south of Ream.

We have now observed one more large landing craft (LCU) at Kompong Som than reported in last night's briefing. This ship could transport 800 troops. This gives the KC the ability to move about 2,400 troops simultaneously.

These landing craft, if unopposed, could reach Koh Tang Island in a little over 4 hours.

The Cambodians have apparently transported at least some of the American crew from Koh Tang Island to the mainland, putting them ashore at Kompong Som port at about 11:00 last night, Washington time.

Kissinger: How do you know that?

Colby: From observation.

President: Of the boat last night?

Clements: That would be just the pilot report.

Colby: There is some more information.

. . . .
. . . .
. . . .
. . . .
. . . .
. . . .

Bringing at least some of the crew ashore suggests that the Cambodians appreciate the value of the American crew as hostages.

offering hope that they will be kept alive by
their captors to preserve their usefulness
as bargaining chips.

The Americans taken ashore may have been
transported further inland by the Cambodians,
and at present there is no way of telling
where they may be.

. . . .
. . . .
. . . .
. . . .
. . . .
. . . .

Of the five Cambodian gunboats that were
deployed as of last night (Washington time)
around Koh Tang Island, three have been
sunk by American aircraft.

At latest report, only one gunboat remained
a little over a mile south of the island.

. . . .
. . . .
. . . .
. . . .
. . . .
. . . .
. . . .
. . . .
. . . .
. . . .
. . . .

Around midnight (Washington time), a U.S.
tanker enroute to Bangkok reported that a
Swedish-registered refrigerator ship near
Panjang Island, well south of Koh Tang, had
been attacked and shot at by a Cambodian
boat. At 5:00 a.m. a U.S. reconnaissance
aircraft observed the ship. It showed no
sign of distress, and now appears on its

TOP SECRET/SENSITIVE - XGDS

normal course to Bangkok. A small boat,
not believed to be a gunboat, was sighted
3 miles away, following the ship's same
course and speed. According to press
reports from Thailand, a Panamanian
freighter was detained for about two hours
in the same area today.

President: Is the HOLT there now?

TOP SEGRET/SENSITIVE - XGDS

Jones:	Yes. The WILSON is there too.
President:	Is this also a destroyer or a destroyer escort?
Admiral Holloway:	This is a destroyer. It will be on station by 1750 Eastern Daylight Time. That means we will have two ships on station before we begin our operations.
Kissinger:	Why are we not sinking the boats?
Jones:	The report we have did not indicate it.
Kissinger:	What mission has been given to the HOLT and to the WILSON?
Jones:	The WILSON is just coming on station. We will instruct it.
Kissinger:	Is the HOLT instructed to stop ship movement to the island?
Jones:	The HOLT is now about 12 miles out beyond the island. It is not able to stop movement to and from the island. The reason it is that far out is that we did not want to tip our hand to the operation.
President:	I had the impression that the HOLT would station itself between the ships and the land. I am amazed at this.
Jones:	It is night, Mr. President. I do not recall any specific instructions to this regard.
President:	It does no good to have the destroyer 12 miles out. It can't stop a boat. Why did we hurry to get it there if it is going to stay that far out?
Jones:	We got it there because we wanted it to help in the operations we will conduct.

TOP ~~SECRET~~/SENSITIVE - XGDS

Rumsfeld:	How about the T-28's that are now at Phnom Penh airport? Could they help oppose our operation at Kompong Som?
Colby:	Yes, but they could not remain in the air for long at that distance from their base.
Jones:	They are not a real factor.
Rumsfeld:	I am thinking of the airport. If they could use it, then we would have a stronger argument to hit the airport.
Jones:	Theoretically they could, but they would not have much time on station.
President:	When does the CORAL SEA get there? What about the HANCOCK or the OKINAWA?
Admiral Holloway:	CORAL SEA aircraft are now within the range of the objective area. So it's on station.
	The HOLT is also on station. She stayed out beyond the island because of the plan to put Marines on her. That is why she is over the horizon.
	The CORAL SEA is within the range of tactical air and can put them in. The HANCOCK could arrive on the scene around noon of the 16th, D. C. time. She is loaded with helicopters.
	The WILSON will be on station this evening.
President:	So, as of now, the HOLT is there, the CORAL SEA is ready, and the WILSON will be there soon.
Admiral Holloway:	In two hours.
President:	What is the recommendation of the Defense Department now regarding operations?

TOP ~~SECRET~~/SENSITIVE - XGDS

Schlesinger: Dave (Jones), please give it.

Jones: (Showing a chart) We recommend that we land
                     tonight on the island and on the ship. We can
                     do it with high assurance of success. We have
                     the B-52's on alert but we do not recommend
                     using them. From the targeting standpoint,
                     it represents overkill. We might use them for
                     political or diplomatic reasons, though that
                     would seem mixed.

President: Are all the chart numbers in our time?

Jones: Yes.

                     We would send people as follows:

                         The Marines to recapture the boat and to
                     dismantle any explosive agents.

                         The helicopters can go at first light. They
                     can get people onto the Holt. It would take
                     two hours for people to get organized and cross
                     to the MAYAGUEZ. They could start out with
                     riot control agents. This probably would not
                     incapacitate them long, perhaps for about 10
                     minutes. The HOLT would then come along-
                     side and all the Marines would come over and
                     hopefully seize control of the vessel. Our
                     Marines would inspect it, so would an OD
                     team. Then it would be moved out.

President: The helicopters come from where?

Jones: From Utapao.

                     Next, the tactical air. We have tactical air on
                     the scene now. We have gunships, fighters, etc.
                     We can suppress fire. We have instructions to
                     minimize fire in case the Americans are there,
                     but to protect the people who are landing.

TOP SECRET/SENSITIVE - XGDS

Eight helicopters with 175 Marines aboard
will land on the island around sunrise. There
is a four-hour recycle time to Utapao. The
next wave of 235 or more would then come to
give us over 600 Marines on the island by dark.

The 175 can secure themselves, with gunships
and tactical air. When the second group
arrives, we can cut off the neck of the island
and move out.

President: I understand our time for this is 1845, but that
it is already the 15th over there. Is that 0645
or 0745 over there?

Jones: It is about 0545. It is around sunrise.

Here is a picture of the island. The Marine
in charge has reconnoitered it.

A close check indicates an open area with
trails leading into the woods. This is the
preferred landing zone. Also, they might
land on the beach. It is wide enough. It is
the only opening on the island. Later, we
would want to cut the island in two.

With somewhat over 600 Marines by nightfall,
we should have a good feel for what is there.

We can perhaps withdraw the next day. We
could bring the Marines out to the CORAL SEA.
This gets them out of Thailand. Or, of course,
we could go back by Thailand.

Tactical air based in Thailand would provide
most of the cover. It has the gunships and the
riot control agents.

That is the operation as we recommend it, as
a joint recommendation from all the Joint
Chiefs.

TOP SECRET/SENSITIVE - XGDS

President: What about the CORAL SEA and B-52's?

Jones: There are three targets:

                        -- First, the airfield at Kompong Som.
                        -- Second, the naval port.
                        -- Third, the regular port.

                        There is not much to hit on the airfield. There
                        is not much around the naval port. Greater
                        targeting is around the other port. We have
                        found two ships of unidentified registry, with
                        other craft around also. There are about 10
                        boats there. Eight of them look like fast patrol
                        craft; one is unknown; one other is a medium
                        landing craft.

President: Where are they located?

Jones: They are along one dock.

                        There are buildings, POL, and other things in
                        the area.

                        If we choose to apply the B-52's, we could put
                        three on one target, three on the other, and six
                        on a third. This would cover the area of the
                        targets.

President: Does this include the breakwater also?

Jones: We would cover the breakwater in one portion
                        of the target area. But it would be very difficult
                        to damage it. You would have to have a direct
                        hit.

                        The B-52's would take about six hours from
                        Guam. They fly at a high altitude so there is
                        no threat to them.

Vice President: I thought they would be on their way by now.

TOP SECRET/SENSITIVE - XGDS

President:	No.
Schlesinger:	No. We just put them in readiness.
	With a unit of three aircraft, there would be about 125 weapons. The concentration is in the center. They would probably not hit the breakwater.
Jones:	As for the CORAL SEA, it has about 48 aircraft. About 100 smart bombs are available, such as laser guided or Walleyes. They could be used with great precision. We would first send armed reconnaissance and then go for heavy targets like construction, POL, the warehouses, etc.
Admiral Holloway:	We have 21 F-4's, 24 A-7's, and 6 A-6's. There are 81 guided munitions on the CORAL SEA. They are about halfway split between laser and the Walleyes.
President:	What will be the extent of the damage from the CORAL SEA as compared with the B-52's?
Jones:	With the bombs from the carrier you could take out key targets. With the B-52's, you get more bombs, interdiction of the runway and of the port, etc. We would get additional buildings, including collateral damage.
	The key targets you could get from the CORAL SEA. With B-52's, you will get mass.
President:	What would be the altitude?
Admiral Holloway:	About 6000.
Kissinger:	How is the weather?
Admiral Holloway:	It is now suitable. It might be cloudy from time to time, but not for long.

TOP SECRET/SENSITIVE - XGDS

Jones:	The prediction is for patchy areas.
	With the CORAL SEA, we would have a continuous flow shifting from target to target.
Kissinger:	How long will the operation continue?
Jones:	From about 2250 tonight until the end of the day (6:00 a.m. tomorrow).
Kissinger:	How many aircraft?
Jones:	About 70 percent of the aircraft. We would use a lot at first, and less later.
President:	They could reload and come back.
Jones:	That's right. They could recycle.
Rumsfeld:	What is the purpose of having it go 8 hours?
Jones:	To hit all the targets. It could be less.
Kissinger:	Would we keep it up while the Marines are on the island?
Admiral Holloway:	The operation on the island is being supported from Thailand. We would have, from the CORAL SEA, a number of aircraft and targets.
	You would have, with those aircraft, enough to hit all the targets?
Jones:	Not the breakwater or the runway, but everything else.
Vice President:	But they would have time to get all the ships into action. As it stands now, the B-52's would not get there until later.
Jones:	We could start from the CORAL SEA earlier.

TOP SECRET/SENSITIVE - XGDS

Kissinger:	I have a question. You are landing on the island at 6:45 a.m. and on the ship at 8:45 a.m.; could they not sink the ship?
Jones:	As for the island, our timing decision is based on the capacity of the helicopters and on the cycles we need to run. It is already sliding slightly.
Kissinger:	This helps you with the bombing.
Schlesinger:	That has already slid.
Vice President:	Then you won't get all the Marines from Thailand?
Schlesinger:	We cannot. There are 1200 of them.
President:	Is this your recommendation on how it should be handled, and is it just a matter of time?
Jones:	We would need to get the order out as soon as possible.
President:	They should launch both operations as quickly as possible.
Admiral Holloway:	At first light.
Jones:	That's right. But that may be a moot question. We will have good communications in order to be able to follow everything.
Clements:	On the HOLT, let's be specific. We are supposed to have real time voice, as well as two-minute interval coded communication.
President:	How soon do you estimate that the three helicopters, with 63 Marines, will be airborne?
Jones:	It should be within an hour.

TOP SECRET/SENSITIVE - XGDS

President:	They are about 40 minutes behind your schedule.
Jones:	They should still make it.
Kissinger:	They are leaving simultaneously.
Jones:	The HOLT is first.
	(At this point, Admiral Holloway leaves the room to communicate instructions.)
President:	Now, regarding the B-52's and the CORAL SEA.
Jones:	There are various possible times on this.
Marsh:	Are you taking the island to get it or the people?
Schlesinger:	Because of the people there.
Rumsfeld:	We will plan to take off from the island in 24 hours.
Kissinger:	I would not answer how long we will stay there. We should say that we will try to find our people. We are not sure how long it may be.
Rumsfeld:	Privately, we should say we will not stay long enough so that we would lose face and have to get off too late.
Kissinger:	There is no point in staying on the island after we have searched it for our men. But I think we should not assure anybody ahead of time when we will leave. We will move at our own pace.
Schlesinger:	What about any prisoners we take?
Kissinger:	I would keep them.
Colby:	Remembering what happened at Son Tay, I would say that we are planning to look for people who might possibly be there. We should not be too positive that they are there.

President: The point is that we are going there to get our people, not the island.

Jones: With the CORAL SEA, one suggestion that has been made is to issue an ultimatum that would say that within so many hours, unless you tell us you are releasing the Americans, there would be air strikes. We could also do that with the B-52 strikes.

Rumsfeld: Regarding the ultimatum, I think there are three ways to do it:

-- First, publicly.
-- Second, privately or diplomatically.
-- Third, you can get into a taffy pull with the people on the scene.

I think one and three are bad ideas. The best is the second. It must be specific and must have a diplomatic initiative.

Kissinger: We sent a message to the Secretary General today. We could not get a better way to communicate with the Cambodians.

That message was delivered at one o'clock.

We thought of giving an ultimatum in Peking, but it is too complicated in terms of the time involved.

Schlesinger: How about a local ultimatum?

Kissinger: I have no objection. But I do not believe that our action should be dependent on an ultimatum.

Fundamentally, the purpose of our strikes is to protect our operations. I could be talked into taking out the 100 aircraft at Phnom Penh, but I do not want to upset people too much.

TOP SECRET/SENSITIVE - XGDS

But we should move massively and firmly. We should say that we are going to protect the operation to get out our people.

Buchen:
I do not agree. If they are not there on the island, you then issue the ultimatum.

President:
Supposing we do not find them all? If the operation is carried out in proper time sequence, they will land on the island at 1845 and on the HOLT earlier. (Points to General Jones' chart) On the schedule you have there, the CORAL SEA is about two hours after the HOLT, and about 4 hours after the island operation. In that space of time they can find out whether the Americans are on the ship or on the island.

Kissinger:
The first group cannot search.

President:
No, but it can perhaps find out if the Americans are there. That gives us some flexibility.

But I do not think we should delay. I think we should go on schedule. Then, whether or not we find the Americans, you can strike.

Buchen:
But an ultimatum may be the only way to get the Americans out.

Kissinger:
Rather than have an ultimatum, I would advance the strikes.

I think it is essential in situations of this kind to make clear that it is we who define the hazards. We can argue that we are doing this to protect our operation. What we have to get across to other countries is that we will not confine ourselves to the areas in which they challenge us.

So I think we should do the strikes at the time of the operation. Then, if we have not found our people, we can mine or do other things.

	We can also issue an ultimatum. We can say that the 100 aircraft was a protective operation. Of course, we would have some difficulties with people on the Hill and with others.
Colby:	The problem is that the KC could put 2,400 people on that island within 4 hours, if they are not blocked.
President:	So we have two reasons to speed up the CORAL SEA operations, so that its first attack coincides with the attack on the island and on the ship. If we use the CORAL SEA, you are then using it to protect the people on the operation. Second, if you use the CORAL SEA with the smart bombs, you are hitting military targets and you will not possibly do harm to Americans.
Rumsfeld:	There are only 80 smart bombs.
Jones:	But we have other armaments.
Buchen:	You have two neutral ships. With an ultimatum, they have a chance to get out.
Jones:	I suggest we expedite the CORAL SEA as soon as possible. It cannot go before the other operations, but at the same time. It would go after mobile targets at first, and other targets later.
Rumsfeld:	The logic is to protect the operation.
Buchen:	But we should avoid the neutral ships.
President:	If they are Cambodian ships, we should sink them.
Schlesinger:	The leak regarding the B-52's is not too bad. It shows that the President will use them if necessary.

TOP SECRET/SENSITIVE - XGDS

President:	I think you should reexamine the CORAL SEA operation with the expectation to keep it going. Henry, what do you think?
Kissinger:	My recommendation is to do it ferociously. We should not just hit mobile targets, but others as well.
Schlesinger:	We will destroy whatever targets there are.
President:	And they should not stop until we tell them.
Buchen:	You have the requirement for consultation with Congress. If you hit buildings, you might hit Americans.
Schlesinger:	I think they would have moved the Americans 20 miles inland as soon as possible.
Admiral Holloway:	If we now go to use the CORAL SEA it will hit before we take the ship. The first wave will hit targets connected with the operation. Later waves will hit other targets, including the three that we have discussed: the airfield and the ports.
Schlesinger:	They cannot fracture the runways.
President:	Can you get the boats?
Schlesinger:	That is possible.
President:	I think we should hit the planes, the boats, and the ships if they are Cambodian.
Schlesinger:	We will make a positive identification that they are Cambodian.
Admiral Holloway:	On the first operation, the fighters will come back and report. First, you can go for the runways; second you can come back with the required strikes.

TOP SECRET/SENSITIVE - XGDS

Schlesinger: How soon?

Holloway: Three hours.

Schlesinger: That would be about 7 o'clock.

Kissinger: They should not strike at the mainland before the HOLT can get to the ship.

Schlesinger: So we will go with a 2045 time.

Admiral Holloway: O.K.

(Admiral Holloway leaves again to pass on instructions.)

Schlesinger: Is there any change in our estimate regarding the forces on the island?

Colby: No.

Hartmann: Do we have any estimate of American casualties?

Jones: It is very hard to make a precise estimate. We do not know what there is. Saying that there would be ten people killed would be too precise.

Schlesinger: It might be 20 to 30.

Clements: Sooner or later you will get a linkage with the 23 already lost at NKP.

President: Any other questions?

Schlesinger: We are in position to do the SAR operation. If we hit again Kompong Som, will our people go in over land if they are hit?

Jones: We will have SAR aircraft. They could go down over land. It is conceivable.

TOP ~~SECRET~~/SENSITIVE - XGDS

President:	What is the distance between the targets and Kompong Som itself?
Colby:	About 15 kilometers.
Jones:	About 10 miles.
Rumsfeld:	Did you say that the Marines could be recovered on the CORAL SEA? Is this an option?
Jones:	No plan is yet finalized.
Kissinger:	They could go on the HANCOCK.
Rumsfeld:	Our preferred option is not to have them return to Thailand.
President:	According to the schedule, the HANCOCK will arrive at 0400 on Friday. It could be the recovery vessel for the Marines being taken off.
Schlesinger:	Augmenting the B-52 picture of being ready is that we are continuing to amass forces.
Rumsfeld:	We should not announce the termination.
President:	Will the WILSON link with the HOLT?
Jones:	Yes; also the CORAL SEA. The HANCOCK may be delayed. Even so, we will not take the Marines back to Thailand.
Rumsfeld:	Did you decide on an ultimatum after the strikes?
Kissinger:	We could use bullhorns to inform the Cambodians on the island. They should not negotiate. They should just state our demands. I think that once we start we should finish and get out.

TOP SECRET/SENSITIVE - XGDS

Ingersoll:	Shouldn't we remove the Marines out of Thailand once the operation has been launched?
Schlesinger:	It is not necessary.
Ingersoll:	We will have riots tomorrow.
Jones:	We have 1200 at Utapao. I suggest we undertake an airlift to get them out, once we decide we do not need them.
Kissinger:	Then we can announce that we have withdrawn them.
Buchen:	I have not understood how Henry (Kissinger) is planning to proceed.
Kissinger:	I think it will not work unless we hit. Then we can give an ultimatum that is credible. We have many things we can still do later. We can mine, or we can take out the planes at Phnom Penh. Then we will be in a long test. We will not have gained by not hitting Kompong Som.
Rumsfeld:	Tomorrow Congress is back in session.
President:	We have a lot of activity going. Let's see it then.
Kissinger:	We should not give the impression that we will stop.
Hartmann:	How will the Cambodians know what to do if they decide to let our people go?
Jones:	We will have a bullhorn. We can tell them what to do.
Kissinger:	The odds are that the people of the island have no orders and will sit tight.

TOP SECRET/SENSITIVE - XGDS

Clements:	I don't think the Americans are there anyway.
Kissinger:	They could be. We do not know.
President:	We are speculating on how many there were in the ship that got away.
Colby:	The pilot said he saw eight or so. He said there were others in the HOLT. He speculated it might be the full 39.
Jones:	We should word our release carefully so we say that we want to remove the Americans and get information on their whereabouts. There may also be value in capturing Cambodians.
Kissinger:	The problem is that we do not know that they are not there. Taking the island if they are not there is easier to explain than failing to take it if they are.
Hartmann:	Could a gunboat carry 39 people?
Colby:	Yes.
Jones:	We should say that we wanted to get the Americans. Even if we did not get them, it would be useful to talk to the Cambodians to find out what they know.
Kissinger:	We should have one clear line of this.
Colby:	We need to be braced against that pilot.
Schlesinger:	We have an obligation to get the Americans or to see if they are there.
Rumsfeld:	We need to make plans on press handling between now and midnight.

TOP SECRET/SENSITIVE - XGDS

Hartmann:	We should talk a little about Congressional consultation.
	Last night, we gave the leadership information on your actions. They agreed. They said that they were advised, but not consulted. We reported the attacks to them. Again, they supported you. Today, in the House, people are saying that there was no consultation under the War Powers Act.
	I have a summary of the Congressional response. I also have a summary of the House and Senate responses to our statements. During the afternoon, it was agreed to provide limited briefings to the House and Senate Foreign Affairs Committees. They want more information. We are sticking to the leadership. We have not expanded on the earlier material.
	The question now is what notification and consultation should proceed. There is a suggestion that you call Mansfield and Albert, but then others will be mad.
	We can bring the people over here, or we can call them.
President:	What does the law say?
Buchen:	The law says to consult before the introduction of forces and then to consult regularly. There is also a requirement for a report 48 hours after an action. We have to get that report in tonight.
Kissinger:	When did this action start, from the legal standpoint?
Buchen:	When you got the gunships in.
Kissinger:	Maybe you should get the leadership in tonight.

Buchen: That is what the Congress really wants.

President: How soon could they be down here?

Marsh: By 6:30 p. m.

Rumsfeld: As I understand it, consultation means telling
                   them in time so that they can oppose the action.
                   But we cannot worry about it, though they will
                   complain that it is not consultation.

Kissinger: I think we should give them the history of the
                   diplomatic effort. We should tell them that there
                   was no response and that we had to go ahead.
                   I do not think we should give them details on
                   our strikes.

President: We should say that we will land on the ship and
                   on the island.

Rumsfeld: From the political standpoint, we should get
                   your friends and brief them, so that they can
                   stand up and fight for you.

President: Jack (Marsh), can you ask them to come down
                   here? Whom would you ask?

Marsh: I would ask the leadership, such as the Speaker,
                   the Floor leaders, the Whips, and others. I
                   would also get the Foreign Affairs and Armed
                   Services Committee leaders and ranking Minority
                   members of both Houses.

Rumsfeld: I would do Anderson separately, perhaps at
                   7 o'clock.

Schlesinger: The plans regarding air strikes should be
                   presented to show that the targets will be
                   carefully selected. We should not just talk
                   about "a few" strikes, but about "selective"
                   strikes.

TOP SPCRDT/SENSITIVE - XGDS

I would recommend that the Republican leadership be among the group you are briefing.

Kissinger: But we must ask them to keep quiet. They
will be briefed before the operation starts.

Vice President: Perhaps 10 o'clock would be better.

Kissinger: How about 10 o'clock?

President: Would it be to our benefit to delay?

Buchen: I would not.

Marsh: The statute says to consult before initiation
of action.

Vice President: You have already done that.

Marsh: But we have not yet told them that we are
executing.

Vice President: What if the group is opposed? What should
the President do?

Kissinger: He would have to go ahead anyway.

Vice President: I was asked today by a business group when
you would react. They applauded when I said
that you would be firm.

President: I have had similar reactions.

Kissinger: What about informing the public? Should we
use national television?

Hartmann: Perhaps after it's over.

Kissinger: Let us do the beginning low key, and then go
to a fuller description. Perhaps we should
just do a brief announcement at first.
(To Schlesinger) I thought your statement
read well.

TOP SEGRET/SENSITIVE - XGDS

Rumsfeld:	You do not want to look as if, in being firm, you are being crimped by the Congress.
	Regarding the B-52's, the Congress would say you should not use them. Then you stand them down, as if in response to Bella Abzug. Should we perhaps stand them down now?
Kissinger:	I would ignore Bella and then explain the B-52's. If it works, it will not matter. If not, we will have other things to worry about. You will look implacable and calm and in control.
	Perhaps you should give a ten-minute speech.
Hartmann:	How about other countries?
Kissinger:	That is a good idea.
Rumsfeld:	You should let NATO know, for once.
Hartmann:	Are there any press on board?
Kissinger:	(To Ingersoll) We should get Sisco to organize messages. We should not use SEATO.
Vice President:	I think that's good.
President:	What do we want when the leadership is here?
Kissinger:	I think we should have no military men, but just Jim and myself. I could brief on the diplomatic steps. You would say what you have ordered.
Schlesinger:	What should we say?
Kissinger:	We should tell them about the island, about the ship, and about the related strikes on military targets to make the operation succeed.
Rumsfeld:	The first question will be, will the Marines land on the island.

TOP SECRET/SENSITIVE - XGDS

Kissinger:	We should not say yet.
Vice President:	They will know about the ship three hours in advance. They can scuttle it.
Kissinger:	Is it better to wait until 10 o'clock?
Buchen and Rumsfeld:	No.
President:	You go ahead.

TOP SECRET/SENSITIVE - XGDS

MEMORANDUM

3415X

NATIONAL SECURITY COUNCIL

~~CONFIDENTIAL~~

May 16, 1975

MEMORANDUM FOR THE RECORD

PARTICIPANTS: President Ford
                  Vice President Rockefeller
                  Dr. Henry A. Kissinger, Secretary of State
                    and Assistant to the President for
                    National Security Affairs
                  James R. Schlesinger, Secretary of Defense
                  Bipartisan Leadership (List attached)

DATE AND TIME: Wednesday, May 14, 1975
                  6:40 p.m. - 8:00 p.m.

PLACE: The Cabinet Room
                  The White House

SUBJECT: The MAYAGUEZ Incident

The President: I thought that it was important that I ask you down here
and fill   you in on a little of the history of the events this week and
tell you of the decisions I made an hour ago. I felt this was the best
way under the circumstances that I could comply with the War Powers
Act and inform you of the actions I feel are necessary to take.

Let me give you a brief chronology of the events since last Monday. We
were notified by the shipping company early Monday morning that their
ship had been taken. I was informed of this at my 7:40 a.m. intelligence briefing. I convened a meeting of the National Security Council
at noon that day and I directed that the Department of State immediately
convey a message to the Government of Cambodia demanding the release
of the ship. At 4:30 Monday afternoon, the Acting Secretary of State
called in the head of the PRC liaison office to read him a similar
statement asking him to transmit it to the Cambodian Government.
This message demanded the immediate release of the vessel and the

~~CONFIDENTIAL~~ XGDS

crew and said that if they were not released, the Government of Cambodia would be responsible for the consequences. The Chief of the Liaison Office did not accept the message, but we are confident that he communicated its contents to Peking. To make sure, however, that the message got through, we instructed our Liaison Office in Peking to deliver the same message to the Cambodian embassy in Peking. This was done at midnight our time Monday.

Also on Monday evening we learned that the Cambodians were moving the ship to a small island off the coast. The following morning we learned the Cambodians were moving the crew members from the ship to Koh Tang Island. The ship was anchored about two miles from the island, which is a small island about 1/2 mile wide and three miles long. The ship is still dead in the water near the island. (Secretary Kissinger points out these locations on the large map.)

On Tuesday morning at a second NSC meeting, I ordered American military forces in the area to maintain strict surveillance over the ship and to prevent any movement of boats from the ship to the mainland and the island. Our forces were to use the minimum force necessary. During this time we carefully covered the entire area with air surveillance.

After ordering that action, I asked Max Friedersdorf and Jack Marsh to inform the Congressional leadership of these decisions. At 8:30 p.m. last night, there were indications that the Cambodians were moving the captive crewmen from the ship to the mainland. I had ordered our planes to take warning measures against any such movements and to prevent them if necessary. During the course of the night, three Cambodian launches were destroyed after they disregarded such warnings; four other boats were damaged and one reached the port of Kompong Som, which is the old port of Sihanoukville. This boat possibly had some American captives aboard. Kompong Som is roughly 20 miles from where the ship is anchored. Also, I should mention that during the attempts to stop or destroy the Cambodian boats, some of our planes received small arms fire.

At another NSC meeting last night that lasted until 1:00 a.m., I ordered the following actions:

-- a Marine group would be made ready to retake the MAYAGUEZ.

-- Another Marine group would be made ready to seize Koh Tang Island.

-- The aircraft carrier CORAL SEA, on its way to Australia, would be turned around and headed toward the area of the ship's capture.

-- The destroyer escort HOLT was told to move into the area with the destroyer WILSON following behind it.

-- The helicopter carrier HANCOCK was also ordered to move into the area.

-- B-52 forces were alerted for action.

Another NSC meeting was held at 3:30 this afternoon. Just before this meeting, we notified the Congress of the results of last night's action. At noon today, we reiterated our message to the Cambodians through the United Nations Secretary General. As a result of this afternoon's NSC meeting, I have ordered the following actions, and let me say that it is of maximum importance that nothing be said to the press as you leave the White House since for the next few hours the actions I have ordered will not be started or completed, and any discussion of these actions could endanger the forces involved.

-- I have ordered a U.S. Marine group to land on the destroyer escort WILSON, which will then move alongside the MAYAGUEZ and the Marines will board and retake it.

-- Another group of Marines will land on Koh Tang Island.

-- To protect these Marine forces, aircraft from the CORAL SEA will attack selective targets, including the airfield at Kompong Som and the major naval air station at Ream. The purpose of these strikes is to protect our Marine forces moving against the island and retaking the MAYAGUEZ.

Our anticipation is that all three of these activities will occur at the same time within a couple of hours from now. Henry, do you have anything to add at this point?

Secretary Kissinger: The only thing I can add is that, at your orders, we did publish the note given to the Secretary General of the UN, believing that this was the quickest way to communicate its contents

to Peking. We also urged the UN Secretary General to use his influence to get the Cambodians to release the ship. At this point we have heard nothing from the Cambodians. I would also point out that when we delivered our note to the Cambodian embassy in Peking we also delivered a copy of it to the Chinese Ministry of Foreign Affairs. It was returned 24 hours later, and we think that its contents were transmitted to the Cambodians but the PRC would not want to be in a position of appearing to assist us in this effort.

Secretary Schlesinger: The Marine attack group will land by helicopter on the destroyer at daybreak. The group will also contain interpreters, a crew to run the ship, and a demolition team. At the same time, the first wave of Marines will land on the island. All of this will be underway as of 9:00 p.m. tonight.

Speaker Albert: Was there any danger that the U.S. crew might be on some of the Cambodian boats that were destroyed.

The President: We have no sure way of knowing where the crew is or whether any of the crew members were on the boats attacked.

Question: Which way were the boats going?

The President: Most were moving from the island to the mainland. They refused to follow the warnings they were given.

Senator Scott: The Deputy Secretary of State made a distinction in his testimony before our committee this afternoon about the ships which were attacked. The one which was sunk did not appear to have many people on it. The other ship had lots of people visible on the deck so the planes did not sink it.

Secretary Kissinger: The attack on that ship was stopped when the pilot thought he saw Americans or at least Caucasians on the deck.

The President: However, we all have to keep in mind that these planes were flying very fast and at relatively high altitudes.

Question: Is there any possibility that the MAYAGUEZ had picked up any Vietnamese refugees from off the shore of Vietnam?

Secretary Schlesinger: We have some indications of Vietnamese in the area, but we don't know that there were any on the ship.

126

Senator Mansfield: Mr. President, why are we again going into the mainland of Asia, especially at a time when we almost have the boat in our custody once again. I am deeply concerned by this aspect of your decision.

The President: Let me explain the basis for my decision. There are warplanes at the Kompong Som airport and at Ream, which is a major naval station. The actions I have ordered are to make sure that whatever forces they have in the area cannot be used against our Marines moving to take the ship and the island. I am told that they have some 2400 troops also at Kompong Som.

Senator Mansfield: Are any of the Americans being held on the mainland?

The President: We have only sketchy knowledge of their whereabouts.

Senator Mansfield: Are there armed Cambodians aboard the ship now? What happened to the Americans on the ship?

Secretary Schlesinger: We have to presume that there are armed Cambodian forces on the ship.

The President: We really don't know where the Americans are -- if they are on the island or on the ship.

Senator Byrd: Could we have intercepted the Cambodian boats?

The President: No, we could not. We had only aircraft in the area. We had no surface vessels in the area. The destroyer HOLT arrived there only several hours later.

Question: Do we have intercepted messages of the presence of Americans on the boats we sunk?

Secretary Schlesinger: We have some radio intercepts, but they are ambiguous and not at all clear.

Question: What about a Swedish vessel reported captured in the same area?

Secretary Schlesinger: We have reports it was stopped but it is now proceeding unimpeded.

Senator Eastland: Mr. President, nobody will agree with me, but I'm for bombing the hell out of them.

Senator Byrd: What about reports of the Thais calling for the removal of our Marines?

The President: Thailand was the only place we could carry out military operations against the island or the ship. We have no intention of returning those Marines to Thailand. They will go to our ships after the operation is completed.

Secretary Kissinger: The Thais did not give us an exact time limit for the Marines' removal. ....
....
....

The President: The Marines will be recovered by the HANCOCK and the CORAL SEA.

Representative O'Neill: What was the nature of the U.S. ship? What cargo was it carrying and where was it when it was captured?

The President: It was a commercial cargo ship carrying a normal cargo.

Secretary Kissinger: The MAYAGUEZ was seized 60 miles off the coast of Cambodia in the regular shipping lanes.

The President: There is an interesting fact about the island involved. It has been disputed by the Cambodians and the Vietnamese. There are also indications that oil might be there and, therefore, there is some speculation the Cambodians want to assert their authority at an early point.

An important point in this whole matter is that we have had no word from the Cambodians.

Senator Stennis: Are all the Marines in Thailand being used in this operation?

The President: Not all of them, but none of the Marines used in the operation will be returning to Thailand.

Senator Mansfield: What about the cargo on that ship. There have been some rumors on the Hill about what it may have been carrying.

Secretary Schlesinger: There was some military PX cargo within the normal commercial cargo aboard the ship, but the nature of the cargo is not an item of dispute in this matter.

The Vice President: Mr. President, you will want to mention that the objective of putting the Marines on the island is to get any of the American captives who may be held there.

The President: Yes, we want to ensure that we get any of our captives held there.

Question: Are the Americans on the island? We certainly can't allow them to be taken off the ship to the mainland.

The President: We have to find out where the Americans are being held. We will be here most of the night as this operation proceeds.

Question: Are there any inhabitants on the island?

The President: We don't know. Our intelligence speculates that there are some Cambodians on the island.

Question: Has the surveillance of the ship been continuous since it was taken?

The President: We don't know precisely when the air surveillance started. It has been 24 hours a day since at least Monday afternoon.

Secretary Schlesinger: All the evidence we have indicates that the Cambodians consider the Americans a valuable asset. We have evidence that they are trying to take care of them, to protect them as a valuable asset. We doubt that they are inclined to dispose of their captives.

Secretary Kissinger: They are valuable to the Cambodians as hostages.

The President: I want to reiterate that we are hitting the selected military targets on the mainland to ensure that the Cambodians cannot attack us.

Question: Shouldn't we wait until we are attacked before hitting the mainland?

Secretary Schlesinger: We have already been fired upon.

Question: Will you report to the Congress within 48 hours?

The President: We will respond in writing as the War Powers Act requires.

Senator McClellan: Mr. President, why are we attacking the mainland first? Isn't this provocative? Shouldn't we wait until we are attacked?

The President: It is my judgment that we have to take these actions to protect our troops in their operation against the island and the ship. We would be negligent to do otherwise.

Senator McClellan: I think this is using too much force without really knowing whether it is needed or not.

Representative O'Neill: It was reported on the Hill that the ship was a Pentagon charter.

Secretary Schlesinger: It was not.

Speaker Albert: It was said on the floor this morning that the law was not being complied with and the War Powers Act was not being followed. I was told repeatedly to tell you to send someone up to brief the House.

The President: We are faced with the fact that the Cambodians have seized a U.S. ship and American citizens. As Commander-in-Chief I have the right to use appropriate military force to recover them. We did give proper notice and we waited until today to take action against the Cambodians. I believe that regardless of the 1973 law, I have the authority as Commander-in-Chief to take this action. Of course, the War Powers Act requires that I report and we have scrupulously done that. We have twice telephoned some 20 members of the Congress on what we have done and we will file the required written report within the 48-hour rule.

Question: Why didn't you send someone to the Hill to inform us of the decisions you were about to make?

The President: We only ordered these actions at 10 minutes to 6 this evening. Our first obligation was to the Congressional leadership and that was why we invited you here immediately. We will report fully to the Congress in writing. Depending upon what happens tonight, we will do more to keep you informed if necessary.

Representative O'Neill: It is a fact that some of the Congressional leaders were briefed late this afternoon.

Senator Sparkman: Our Committee met this afternoon. We discussed this matter thoroughly and we have unanimously adopted a statement which condemns the Cambodian seizure of the ship; that expresses support for the President's use of diplomatic means to secure the release of the ship; that we support the President in his exercise of power to effect that release within the framework of the War Powers Act; and that we urged the Cambodians to release the ship.

The President: Thank you, John.

Question: Were the Cambodians given a specific deadline?

Secretary Kissinger: No, because this would let them calculate the timing of any countermeasures we might take. But the UN Secretary General told them in the open cable that we would respond if this ship was not released immediately. I want to emphasize the President's request that you not give out the details of his decisions because this would endanger our Marines and our planned operations. We need the element of surprise, so please don't describe the steps the President has ordered.

Question: Did China cooperate?

Secretary Kissinger: They did what we expected. They kept the note 24 hours and then returned it, saying they couldn't deliver it. We assume they communicated the message. We also gave a copy to the Embassy of Cambodia in Peking. As you know there are no foreign embassies in Phnom Penh except for the North Vietnamese, North Korean's and the Chinese. Obviously, we felt the Chinese were the best channel to use.

Question: When did the time start running in the 48-hour notification requirement?

Phil Buchen: We believe that time started when the ships were interdicted, so we plan to get the report to you by 6:15 a.m. tomorrow. We assume there will be someone there to receive it.

Senator Stennis: You said that your attack on the mainland is solely to protect your Marine operations?

The President: Yes, it is just to neutralize the Cambodian forces, including their aircraft and their ships.

Senator Mansfield: I must express my deep misgivings that we are again attacking the Indochina mainland. I am convinced that the reaction will not be good.

Senator Case: I must point out that although the Case-Church Amend-③
ment prohibits U. S. military action in Indochina, I disagree with
Senator Mansfield, and I do not believe that the Amendment does apply
to the purpose of rescuing American citizens. I believe this distinction
must be made clear.

Senator Byrd: One last question. Why were the leaders of Congress, ④
the Majority Leader, the Speaker, etc., not consulted about this at
least at the time the decision was still being made? We are being
told only after the fact. You are not required to do this in advance,
but it certainly would be better if we did wait until we were attacked
before hitting the mainland. You will be charged with overreacting and
it would have been better if the leaders of Congress would have been
consulted in advance on this decision.

The President: This is a proper question, Bob. As Commander-in- ⑤
Chief, I have to act to protect our citizens. I acted in a proper
exercise of my authority within the War Powers Act. I did have
within the NSC the advice of the Joint Chief of Staff and my other
advisors. It is my judgment and my understanding of my responsibility
that I had to weigh the risk of doing too little to avoid any danger to
the limited number of Marines going in on the first wave. I did not
want to be criticized for doing too little to protect our initial marine
forces.

Senator Byrd: Let me respectfully press this. I know you are doing ⑥
what you think best and I certainly don't question your authority to do
it, but I want to know why the leaders were not brought in in advance
of your decision?

The President: We have a government of separation of powers. The ⑦
President has the authority to act. I have an obligation to act. We
have lived within the law of the War Powers Act. We may have
differences over judgments and decisions, but I would never forgive
myself if I had let our Marines be attacked by the 2400 Cambodian
soldiers.

Senator Eastland: How much time did you have during this decision-making?

The President: We met at 3:30 this afternoon. We had to decide quickly
and give the signal early enough to provide time for the Marines to move
at first light.

I appreciate your all coming down here and I can assure that we will keep you posted throughout the night. I hope we can all pray for the best result of this operation.

Question: When will the public know?

Secretary Kissinger: DOD will make an announcement at 10:00 p.m.

Representative Rhodes: Mr. President, this operation is well planned, it is well conceived, and it is the right thing to do.

The President: Thank you.

PARTICIPANTS

SENATE

Bob Byrd
Cliff Case
John Eastland
Bob Griffin
John McClellan
Mike Mansfield
High Scott
John Sparkman
John Stennis
Milt Young

HOUSE

Speaker Albert
Bill Broomfield
Al Cederberg
Bob Michel
Thomas Morgan
Tip O'Neill
Mel Price
John Rhodes
Bob Wilson

Invited but regretted

Senator Strom Thurmond
Rep. John McFall
Rep. George Mahon

501

TOP SECRET/SENSITIVE

MINUTES

NATIONAL SECURITY COUNCIL MEETING
PART I OF III

Date: Thursday, May 15, 1975

Time: 4:02 p.m. - 4:20 p.m.

Place: Cabinet Room, The White House

Subject: Seizure of American Ship by Cambodian
                Authorities

Principals

The President
Secretary of State Henry A. Kissinger
Secretary of Defense James Schlesinger
Chairman of the Joint Chiefs of Staff General David C. Jones
The Director of Central Intelligence William Colby

Other Attendees

State: Deputy Secretary of State Robert Ingersoll

Defense: Deputy Secretary of Defense William Clements

WH: Donald Rumsfeld
                Robert Hartmann

NSC: Lt. Gen. Brent Scowcroft
                W. Richard Smyser

TOP SECRET/SENSITIVE - XGDS

DECLASSIFIED
E.C 12356, Sec. 3.4
MR 92-10 #26 NSC ltr 10/7/94
By KBH NARA. Date 2/6/95

President: Will you tell me where we stand at this time?

Colby: I can give you a report on foreign reaction. I think it would
                  be better if George could give you a wrap-up on our operation.

President: Please go ahead.

Colby: Mr. President, we have no reactions from Communist
                  authorities in Phnom Penh to the U.S. military operation
                  beyond what we had last night. In his statement on Phnom
                  Penh radio at that time, Information Minister Hu Nimm was
                  noticeably defensive in rationalizing the seizure of the vessel.

                  Although he did claim that the MAYAGUEZ was on an intelligence
                  mission, he stated several times that his government had no
                  desire to stage "provocations" and that the MAYAGUEZ had
                  only been halted for "questioning."

                  In the aftermath of the U.S. military operation, the Thai
                  cabinet today apparently decided to expel a "senior member
                  of the U.S. mission," and to recall the Thai ambassador in
                  Washington for consultations.

                  Thai newspapers today are also urging that the government:

                  -- publicize all agreements between the U.S. and Thailand, and

                  -- immediately close down all U.S. bases in Thailand.

                  Leftist politicians are now holding a rally in Bangkok. They
                  reportedly intend to demand that all U.S. troops leave
                  Thailand within 10 days.

                  The political left apparently believes that the time is right to
                  create a political crisis for the Khukrit government.

                  Organizers of the demonstration plan to move crowds to both
                  the prime minister's office and the U.S. embassy.

                  The Thai military leaders, on the other hand, have privately
                  continued to support the U.S. actions.

TOP SECRET /SENSITIVE - XGDS

In Peking's first reaction to the U.S. military action, Vice Premier Li Hsien-nien has accused the U.S. of an "outright act of piracy."

Speaking at a banquet in Peking today, Li said that "when an American ship invaded Cambodia's territorial waters, Cambodia took legitimate measures against the ship to safeguard her state sovereignty." Li added that "the U.S. went so far as to make an issue of the matter" and bombed Cambodian territory and ships.

Li said the American action "should be condemned by world public opinion."

Hanoi radio has characterized the operation as a "flagrant act of piracy" which shows that the U.S. still has not "learned from its defeats in Vietnam and Cambodia."

The new government in Saigon has not commented, but it can be expected to parrot Hanoi's line.

Soviet media continue to report the events surrounding the MAYAGUEZ incident from foreign wire services without editorial comment.

East European commentary remains muted. The Yugoslav press has even referred to the MAYAGUEZ as a "kidnapped" U.S. vessel.

The Cuban press has so far treated U.S. actions in a factual manner, but we have no comment since the U.S. operation was completed.

A Japanese Foreign Ministry spokesman has stated that "a container ship on open waters must not be subject to seizure" and that his government viewed the U.S. military action as "limited."

In most major Western countries there has been little official reaction.

British and West German press comment has been generally supportive.

TOP SECRET /SENSITIVE - XGDS

	Press reaction from South Korea, Taiwan, and Australia has been favorable.
Ingersoll:	Bill Rogers spoke to the OAS Ministers while they were here, including the one from Panama. He said they were very pleased.
President:	Jim, I would like to congratulate you and your whole Department for a job well done.
	Have we had any report on the damage so far?
Jones:	Not yet. We can summarize the claims, but we are not sure that they are accurate. Here is a photograph. It is the first one that has yet been received here. It shows the buildings around the airport before and after they were damaged. We understand that the damage reported on the aircraft was extensive.
President:	Which airport was this?
Jones:	The airport near Kompong Som, called Ream.
Kissinger:	Were any boats sunk?
Jones:	Yes, but we don't yet know how many.
	We have no Navy reports yet, just the Air Force. We need to survey all the aircraft involved in the operation.
Kissinger:	Were the aircraft used land aircraft?
Jones:	No, only the CORAL SEA aircraft were used against Kompong Som. There were four waves. The first was armed reconnaissance. They did not expend ordnance. They found the shipping of other countries and did not want to take the risk. The three subsequent waves went against the airport, against the POL facilities, and against support facilities.
	We put 240 Marines on the island, in total. We put 40 aboard the ship.

We lost three helicopters in the operation.   The equipment took a lot of battle damage.

Our casualties were 1 killed in action, 1 missing, and 30 wounded.   That is considerably lighter than we thought last night.

President: Are all the Marines now on the CORAL SEA or on the HANCOCK?

Jones: They are on the CORAL SEA.   We had a reserve of 1,000 on Thailand.   But when the ship's crew was returned, we stopped any more Marines going to the island.   Then we put in another 80 in order to help the Marines that were there to extricate themselves.

President: I heard that the Marines on the HOLT had gone to the island.

Jones: No, they did not have their full equipment.

Clements: How many helicopters were inoperative?

Jones: We got down to four Air Force helicopters and three from the CORAL SEA.   So there were only a few for the Marines who were left there.   We thought we might have to keep people overnight on the island.   But that was only the impression in Washington.   They continued the flow of helicopters and they also used several boats from the destroyer, so that they were able to extricate all the Marines.

Kissinger: How many Cambodians were on the island?

Jones: We do not know, but they were obviously well armed with supplies.   They put up a lot of fire against the helicopters.

President: That is probably why they moved the ship to that island from that other one where they had it.

Kissinger: Where did the boat carrying the crew come from?

Jones: From Kompong Som.

TOP SECRET/SENSITIVE - XGDS

Kissinger:	This indicates that the operation was really centrally controlled.
Jones:	They brought a message that they had been sent out on a Thai fishing vessel in order to be returned, and they asked us to stop the bombing. We had one or two more runs, but we stopped shortly thereafter.
Kissinger:	How many aircraft were used altogether?
Jones:	About 32 to 40.
Schlesinger:	Not the 81 that had been on the carrier.
President:	Henry, would you step out for a moment?
	(At this point, the President and the Secretary of State stepped out for about 3 minutes. They then returned.)
President:	Jim, I would like a full factual report giving a summary and chronology of what happened. It should include orders, summary results, photographs, etc., and indications of what we did when.
	Where is the ship now?
Jones:	She is on her way to Singapore. We towed her for some distance but then she was able to get up steam and she wanted to go to Singapore.
President:	It was a job well done. Let us now go on to the next item on our agenda.

80-187

CINCPAC

COMMAND HISTORY

1975

Appendix VI — The SS MAYAGUEZ Incident

COPY _1_ OF _65_ COPIES

TOP SECRET

APPENDIX C

COMMANDER IN CHIEF PACIFIC
COMMAND HISTORY

1975

Appendix VI — The SS MAYAGUEZ Incident

Prepared by the Command History Branch
Office of the Joint Secretary
Headquarters CINCPAC, FPO San Francisco 96610

CAMP H. M. SMITH, HAWAII
1976

i

TABLE OF CONTENTS

APPENDIX VI

THE SS MAYAGUEZ INCIDENT

SECTION I--INTRODUCTION

(U)   The Cambodian seizure of the United States vessel, MAYAGUEZ, on
12 May 1975 was a significant incident viewed in the context of the international situation when it occurred. Cambodia and Vietnam had just fallen to
communist control the previous month and the PUEBLO incident of 1968 was still
a fresh memory. It was apparent, at the time, to national leadership from the
President on down that this test of United States willpower called for quick,
firm, and decisive action which would help to reaffirm America's determination
in the eyes of her opponents and allies as well as the American public.
Admiral Noel Gayler, Commander in Chief Pacific at the time of the incident,
commented on the successful joint Service recovery operation:[1]

> Cambodian adventurism tested the United States with
> the seizure of the merchant ship MAYAGUEZ on the high seas
> in May. The recovery operation has left no doubt as to our
> resolve and capabilities in that part of the world. Our
> Marines, sailors and airmen again met the challenge.
> Stories of their courage abound - from the Marine who
> directed air strikes while swimming off-shore after his
> helicopter was shot down, to the sailors in the motor
> whaleboat who took on dug-in heavy weapons with small arms,
> to the Air Force pilots who forced their way into the landing
> zones while taking hits.

During the period immediately following the incident, detailed reports
were prepared independently by participants up to and including the Joint
Chiefs of Staff. In addition, every aspect of the incident was subjected to
exhaustive Congressional scrutiny to include a full-scale General Accounting
Office (GAO) investigation, the unclassified findings of which were released
to the public in October 1976. Although these findings were critical of
certain aspects of MAYAGUEZ recovery operations, overall military participation
was described as follows:[2]

----

1. CINCPAC Command History 1975, Vol. I, p. v.
2. The Seizure of the MAYAGUEZ--A Case Study of Crisis Management, Report of
    The Comptroller General of the United States, May 11, 1976, p. 56.
    hereinafter referred to as The Comptroller General MAYAGUEZ Report.

1

• Finally, assembling, under severe time constraints, the various military assets scattered throughout the Pacific area was generally accomplished in an efficient and effective manner.

• Command and control of, and communications between, multiservice assets was established expeditiously. The performance of U.S. Forces was inspiring.

(U)   This monograph will not attempt to recount all the details of the MAYAGUEZ operation already available in existing reports. Instead, it will attempt to tie together loose ends and present an overview of the MAYAGUEZ operation from the CINCPAC unified command level. This overview will stress the important military aspects of the operation to include command and control, intelligence/reconnaissance, and planning and execution. In covering these aspects, further emphasis will be placed on CINCPAC's "lessons learned," which should provide valuable insight, and hopefully foresight, for reference in coping with possible future crisis action situations. As CINCPAC has noted, "...with full benefit of hindsight we could have done a number of things better. Life is like that, and there is no reason we should not acknowledge it."[1]

----

1.   CINCPAC 131338Z Feb 76.

SECTION II--NOTIFICATION

(C) Cambodia had fallen to the communists on 17 April 1975 and the fall of the Republic of Vietnam followed closely behind on 30 April 1975. On 12 May 1975 the American Embassy in Vientiane advised that the Pathet Lao had moved quickly to exploit the virtual disappearance of the Vientiane side and to exert control over government operations, commercial activities, and movement of persons there. In the wake of these events, most United States Forces had departed the immediate area except for those in Thailand. In the midst of this situation, the MAYAGUEZ incident tested the United States crisis action capabilities.[1]

(U) It was 0718 Zulu (Z) hours on 12 May 1975 when Mr. John Neal of Delta Exploration Company in Jakarta, Indonesia received a "Mayday" (distress) call from the United States merchant ship MAYAGUEZ:[2]

> Have been fired upon and boarded by Cambodian armed
> forces at 9 degrees 48 minutes north/102 degrees 53 minutes
> east. Ship is being towed to unknown Cambodian port.

(C) CINCPAC received this information at 0914Z hours 12 May 1975 in a message from the American Embassy, Jakarta. This notification was similarly received by the White House, the National Security Agency (NSA), the Central Intelligence Agency (CIA), the Defense Intelligence Agency (DIA), and the National Military Command Center (NMCC) at the Pentagon. Based on the message, CINCPAC contacted the Joint Chiefs of Staff (JCS) and discussed assets available to reconnoiter the scene of the incident; thus, initial preparations for the MAYAGUEZ operation were begun, pending the outcome of State Department attempts to make contact through diplomatic channels. As the situation developed, diplomatic channels were determined at executive level to be unsatisfactory and military means were employed to recover the MAYAGUEZ and release her crew.[3]

(C) The MAYAGUEZ seizure, which began the chain of events leading to military action, was not a totally isolated incident, lacking any indications as to its possible occurrence. CINCPAC observed that adequate and timely warning was provided

----

1. CINCPAC Command History 1975, Vol. II, pp. 607, 609, 617.
2. Op. Cit., The Comptroller General MAYAGUEZ Report, p. 89. [All times will be shown in Greenwich Mean or Zulu time; for Cambodian (G) time, add 7 hours; for Hawaii (W) time, subtract 10 hours.]
3. Jakarta 0356/120903Z May 75.

3

SECTION III--COMMAND AND CONTROL

Command Relationships

(the communications aspects of command and
control will be discussed in detail later in this section).

In conference, the local on-scene commander, who was Commander, U.S.
Support Activities Group/7th Air Force (COMUSSAG/7AF), assumed the responsibility for planning and directing operations to recover the MAYAGUEZ and cause
the release of her crew. Based upon this understanding, COMUSSAG/7AF, in his
initial planning guidance to subordinate and supporting units, interpreted
command and control relationships as follows:[1]

> ...The international implications of this operation
> make restraint imperative. Complete command and control must
> be maintained by COMUSSAG/7AF, who will be acting upon
> direction from the National Military Command Center....

CINCPAC's execution message, authorizing implementation of COMUSSAG/
7AF's initial planning guidance, clarified the command and control relationship as it was to apply throughout the MAYAGUEZ operation until its termination
on 15 May 1975:[2]

> ...Command and control will be maintained by CINCPAC,
> who will be acting under direction from JCS (NMCC).

In accordance with this relationship, COMUSSAG/7AF, under CINCPAC's
operational command, planned and directed MAYAGUEZ operations on the scene.
Air Force and Marine assets were placed under the operational control of,
and Naval assets (minus the Marines) supported, COMUSSAG/7AF. Command
relationships were again spelled out, using different wording, in COMUSSAG/
7AF's final operation plan:[3]

> ...overall control of the operation will be as directed
> by CINCPAC and approved by the JCS. CINCPAC will have

---

1. COMUSSAG/7AF 131748Z May 75.
2. CINCPAC 132051Z May 75 and 152330Z May 75.
3. COMUSSAG/7AF 141730Z May 75 (EX).

5

operational control over all PACOM designated forces.
CINCSAC will have operational control over the B-52 strike
force. COMUSSAG/7AF will act as the coordinating authority
for the operations of supporting forces.

Command relationships are depicted on the following chart.

(U)   Although Naval forces committed to the MAYAGUEZ operation were not
under the operational control of COMUSSAG/7AF, it was noted that no requests
made by the local command were denied by these forces. As the Commander in
Chief Pacific Fleet (CINCPACFLT) noted, "the execution requirements for
MAYAGUEZ did not provide sufficient time to prepare and promulgate a detailed
OPORDER..."; however, CINCPACFLT did advise that "unless otherwise directed,
task force units assigned to subject operation in Gulf of Thailand should plan
on operating in support of COMUSSAG/7AF with direct liaison authorized all
concerned." The Commander, Seventh Fleet further passed on CINCPACFLT
instructions for participating task force units to respond to directions and
tasking from COMUSSAG/7AF.[1]

Communications

---

1. Ibid.; CINCPACFLT 131857Z May 75 and 140505Z Jun 75 (EX); COMSEVENFLT
142326Z May 75.
2. J3 Discussion Topic, undated, Issue: Lessons Learned Recent Contingency
Operations, for discussion at CINC conference held 14 Aug 75 at LANTCOM.

6

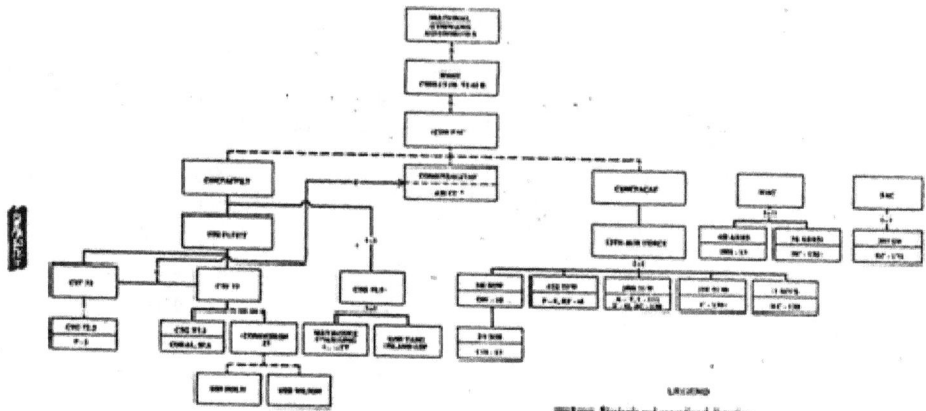

COMMAND RELATIONSHIPS

in Hawaii; and COMUSSAG/7AF in Thailand. This arrangement emphasized operational control and real time reporting and information gathering.[1]

(S) The communications conference permitted direct control by Washington decision-makers over events halfway around the world. On the other hand, [2] An example was COMUSSAG/7AF's interpretation of command and control relationships in his initial planning guidance. Furthermore,

(S) The PACOM Required Operational Capabilities for Secure Voice and Data Conferencing and Communications for Remote Force/Joint Task Force Operations, included in the PACOM Command and Control System Master Plan submitted to the JCS on 29 January 1975, recommended use of inherent satellite broadcast capability to satisfy conferencing requirements and proposed that an operational test bed be established in PACOM to resolve operational and technical questions. The experience gained through extensive use during the EAGLE PULL, FREQUENT WIND, and MAYAGUEZ operations led CINCPAC to further emphasize the following requirements:[3]

(S) Tactical communications established between the on-scene commander and subordinate and supporting units during the MAYAGUEZ operation were characterized

----

1. CINCPAC 131338Z Feb 76.
2. Op. Cit., The Comptroller General MAYAGUEZ Report, pp. 33-35; J6/Memo/ 0027-75 of 11 Jun 75, Subj: Lessons Learned-SS MAYAGUEZ/Koh Tang Island; J3/Memo/00566-75 of 8 Sep 75, Subj: SS MAYAGUEZ & Koh Tang Island Operation.
3. J6/Memo/0027-75 of 11 Jun 75, Subj: Lessons Learned-SS MAYAGUEZ/Koh Tang Island; CINCPAC 191623Z Jun 75 (EX).

8

It was monitored

, and patched   Enemy forces could just
as easily have monitored the same net.

                                                                    capability did
_exist from the ABCCC to USSAG, and to Naval units only, through the   i

        The Marine Ground Security Force (GSF), landed on Koh Tang Island to
free the MAYAGUEZ crew, lost its   capability in a helicopter crash,
and thus its   Therefore, the GSF
was forced to
i

        As a result of the
        during the MAYAGUEZ operation, CINCPAC further emphasized the following
requirements:[4]

---

1. Ibid.
2. Ibid.
3. CINCPAC 191623Z Jun 75 (EX).
4. Ibid.

9

151

(U) Communications nets involved in the MAYAGUEZ operation are depicted on the following chart.

(C) In commenting to the JCS on interrelated command and control and communications requirements for further contingency/noncombatant emergency evacuation (NEMVAC) operations, CINCPAC noted that, in the case of the MAYAGUEZ operation,

thus providing a clearer tactical picture to the on-scene commanders. The plot could have easily been remoted to the rear echelon headquarters and the.

Reporting

(S) The existence of unilateral Service reporting channels to the JCS during the MAYAGUEZ operation permitted the forwarding of conflicting reports, which had to be referred back to CINCPAC for resolution. The primary example of this was casualty reporting, where receipt and release of fragmentary and unverified information at Office of the Secretary of Defense level gave the appearance of inaccurate casualty reporting. This problem was partially related to the nature of the   means of communication in use (for details see communications section), which, lacking specific procedures, allowed for ad hoc inquiries from higher authority and discrepancies between voice and hard copy reporting.[2]

(C) Interface between intelligence and operational reporting was an area that witnessed highly effective innovations as well as need for refinement (for details see communications and intelligence/reconnaissance sections).

(C) In addition to report-related observations found in the communications and intelligence/reconnaissance sections of this monograph, CINCPAC noted, in general, that channels must go through the unified commander to insure coordinated and accurate reporting to all concerned. CINCPAC, realizing that official casualty figures had to be reported through Service channels,

---

1. Ibid.; J6/Memo/0027-75 of 11 Jun 75, Subj: Lessons Learned-SS MAYAGUEZ/ Koh Tang Island Operation.
2. J1/Memo/311-75 of 18 Jul 75, Subj: SS MAYAGUEZ/Koh Tang Island Operation; CINCPAC 191623Z Jun 75 (EX).

SECRET

10

COMMUNICATIONS

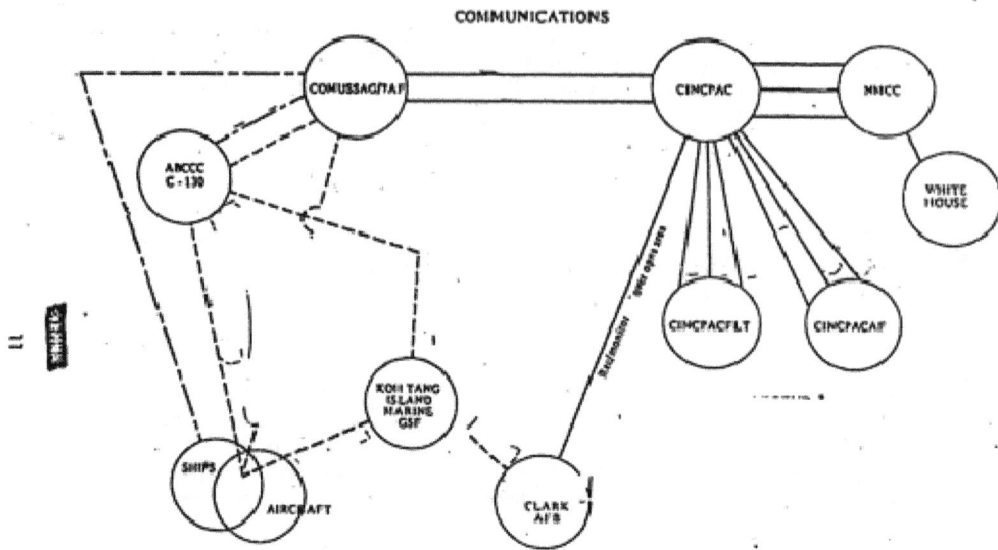

Adapted from J620 Chart dated 8 Jul 76 and J6 Memo/0027-75,
11 Jun 75, Subj: SS/Mayaguez/Koh Tang Island Operation.

153

recommended a change to JCS Publication 6 to provide force status and
identity (FORSTAT) casualty reporting from unit level to the unified command
to allow monitoring.[1]

---

1. J1/Memo/311-75 of 18 Jul 75, Subj: SS MAYAGUEZ/Koh Tang Island Operation.

12

SECTION IV--INTELLIGENCE/RECONNAISSANCE

(S) Upon notification of the MAYAGUEZ incident, the Deputy Director for Operations, National Military Command Center requested CINCPAC to launch reconnaissance aircraft from U-Tapao, Thailand. This initial request was followed by further guidance:[1]

- CINCPAC provide continuous P-3 surveillance over the Gulf of Siam north of 8 degrees north and east of 101 degrees east, no closer than 12 nautical miles to the Cambodian mainland, islands excluded.

- CINCPAC provide photo coverage of Phnom Penh, Sihanoukville, and the islands of Poulo Wai at first satisfactory light, regardless of cloud cover. (The platform was not specified.)

- ___   provide   (OLYMPIC MEET) coverage of Poulo Wai at ___ also within the 12 nautical mile restriction.

(S) From this guidance, CINCPAC further instructed CINCPACFLT to report sightings of Cambodian naval units as well as the captured MAYAGUEZ, and obtain photos of Cambodian naval units as feasible. This mission was, in turn, passed to the Commander, Philippine Air Patrol Group (CTG 72.3), who had P-3 aircraft located at his primary base of operations, Cubi Point, Republic of the Philippines, and at his logistic base and refueling stop, U-Tapao Royal Thai Naval Air Station, Thailand. At 0166Z hours, 13 May a P-3 aircraft reported positive identification of the MAYAGUEZ at 9°56' N, 102°58' E.[2]

(S) The platform, mechanics of film processing, and exploitation procedures for photo reconnaissance were not addressed by the JCS, but after a telephone exchange between CINCPAC J2 and the Defense Intelligence Agency (DIA) the DIA provided processing, duplicating, and disseminating instructions to CINCPAC, SAC, and the SAC Reconnaissance Center, with information copies to Air Force

----

1. After Action Report, US Military Operations, SS MAYAGUEZ/Koh Tang Island, 12-15 May 1975, prepared by the JCS, Tab D, Encl 9, p. 1 (hereinafter referred to as JCS After Action Report); JCS 8233/121944Z May 75.
2. U.S. Naval Institute Proceedings, Vol. 102/11/885, Nov 76, p. 94, "'Mayday' for the MAYAGUEZ," by Commander J.A. Messegee, USN (hereinafter referred to as Proceedings); Op. Cit., JCS After Action Report, Tab D, Encl 9, p. 1; CINCPAC 122104Z May 75.

13

headquarters, COMUSSAG, CINCPACAF, and the 432d Tactical Fighter Wing (TFW) at Udorn, Thailand. The DIA message cited the JCS message as having directed ____(OLYMPIC MEET) and ____ (FACE VALUE) missions against Cambodian targets; the FACE VALUE missions were to be processed and exploited by the 432d TFW at Udorn, while OLYMPIC MEET mission materials were to be delivered to the ____ The remainder of the DIA message named specific exploitation objectives, but did not address the JCS-directed P-3 reconnaissance.[1]

(S) This omission was apparently resolved (possibly through operational channels) because, approximately three hours after the DIA message, CINCPAC J2 directed COMUSSAG, CINCPACAF, and CINCPACFLT to follow the DIA instructions for processing and distributing the FACE VALUE and OLYMPIC MEET missions. CINCPAC also directed CINCPACFLT to forward unprocessed P-3 mission imagery to the 432d Reconnaissance Technical Squadron (RTS) at Udorn for initial processing and rapid readout. The 432d RTS was to prepare the Initial Photo Interpretation Report (IPIR) and dispatch it to specified addressees as "Special USN P-3 Coverage." A duplicate positive was to be sent to the Fleet Air Intelligence Service Center (FAISC) Pacific, and the original negative to Fleet Intelligence Center Pacific in Hawaii.[2]

(S) Because the Navy P-3 unit at U-Tapao, Thailand had not been an addressee on the CINCPAC message, COMUSSAG retransmitted the message to the U-Tapao-based P-3 unit, but apparently too late. A little more than six hours after the dispatch of the CINCPAC message, COMUSSAG was informed that the first P-3 film had been sent to the FAISC Pacific at Cubi Point, Philippines for processing.[3]

(S) Subsequent imagery was handled as instructed, however, and, when the operation to recover the MAYAGUEZ and her crew was authorized, CINCPAC provided film handling instructions for fleet tactical aerial photo reconnaissance operations. When IPIRs of Koh Tang Island indicated possible helicopter crash imagery, CINCPAC directed COMUSSAG to provide the most recent photography to the Commander Task Unit 72.3.5 (P-3s) at U-Tapao for possible resumption of Marine personnel recovery operations. Throughout the MAYAGUEZ operation, flash precedence COMPASS LINK ____ was employed. Expedited Armed Forces Courier Service, requested by CINCPAC on 13 May 1975,

----

1. J23 HistSum May 75, with 12 attached msgs, second of which was JCS 8223/ 121944Z May 75; DIA (DC-SC) 05216/122108Z May 75 (BOM).
2. CINCPAC 130239Z May 75.
3. COMUSSAG/7AF 131253Z May 75, which cited several undated phonecons and COMUSSAG INCR 130755Z May 75.

was cancelled on 20 May, and on 21 May CINCPAC directed CINCPACFLT, CINCPACAF, and COMUSSAG to revert to normal film handling procedures.[1]

(S) With the photo reconnaissance platform specified as RF-4C, CINCPAC instructed COMUSSAG/7AF to provide photo coverage of Phnom Penh, Sihanoukville, Hon Panjang Island (09°18' N, 103°28' E), and the island groups in the vicinity of 09°58' N, 102°53' E (Poulo Wai). Flights over Phnom Penh and Sihanoukville were restricted to a minimum altitude of 6,000 feet, while flights over the islands were restricted to a minimum of 4,500 feet. The Essential Elements of Information (EEI) included merchant ships, naval craft, and paratroop landing/drop zones. After the MAYAGUEZ was located and under observation, CINCPAC requested initial imagery of Koh Tang Island and daily coverage until after the execution of contemplated recovery operations. Flights in the vicinity of Koh Tang Island were restricted to a minimum altitude of 6,500 feet. The EEI now included:[2]

- Pier facilities.

- Gun emplacements.

- Fortifications.

- Small boat locations.

- Troop concentrations.

- Evidence of ship/shore personnel movement to/from MAYAGUEZ.

- One-time readout of building locations/helicopter landing areas.

(S) Photo reconnaissance instructions were subsequently amended, as required, and included RF-4C coverage following each tactical air strike in support of recovery operations as well as Navy missions over the Kompong Som area. In both cases the minimum altitude restriction of 6,500 feet applied.[3]

(TS) In the midst of this reconnaissance activity, the location of the MAYAGUEZ crew was of crucial importance to operational decisions. The

-----

1. J23 HistSum May 75; CINCPAC 130241Z May 75, 142145Z May 75, 152333Z May 75, 161511Z May 75, 162226Z May 75, 200037Z May 75, and 210113Z May 75.
2. CINCPAC 122137Z May 75 and 132346Z May 75.
3. CINCPAC 140325Z May 75, 142110Z May 75, 150040Z May 75, and 150045Z May 75.

above-listed EEI included the requirement to report evidence of personnel movement to/from the MAYAGUEZ and, in conjunction with preliminary actions to isolate Koh Tang Island and the MAYAGUEZ, the JCS emphasized that:[1]

> It is particularly important to get maximum information on any outgoing boat to determine if there are Americans aboard and to report such when requesting authority to sink, although this will be difficult to accomplish. Deck loading probably will be required on the small boats as they did in taking personnel, believed to be Americans, from the ship to the island.

The knowledge that personnel, believed to be Americans, had been taken from the MAYAGUEZ to Koh Tang Island was based on P-3 aircraft (LY499) reports that one gunboat and one tugboat were observed along side the MAYAGUEZ and that personnel were being transferred from the MAYAGUEZ to the tugboat. The P-3 further reported that the gunboat and tug with personnel on board departed the MAYAGUEZ heading toward shore, and that the personnel seated on deck with heads on knees appeared to be Caucasian. COMUSSAG/7AF followed the progress of this movement:[2]

Time	Observation
131018Z May	Boat which had been tied to starboard side of MAYAGUEZ has started to move toward the island with a lot of people on board.
131024Z May	Small fishing-type vessel which was tied to port side of MAYAGUEZ is now-moving toward island. The boat appears to have Caucasian personnel on board....
131033Z May	Ground fire was received by JUMBO 01 as he made low visual reconnaissance pass near the island. No hits. Personnel are disembarking on the island.
131115Z May	Report from KING 22, HC-130. Two small boats off-loading personnel on island and they are moving toward the interior of the island.

---

1. JCS 9376/131905Z May 75.
2. PATRON FOUR 131024Z May 75; CTG 72.3 131050Z May 75; COMUSSAG/7AF 131105Z May 75, 131115Z May 75, 131118Z May 75, 131135Z May 75, and 131245Z May 75.

131227Z May   Summary of situation. The MAYAGUEZ is still in the
water. All personnel appear to have been transferred
to the island...both small boats are at the island....

(U)   The above indications, which led to the conclusion that the MAYAGUEZ
crew was being held on Koh Tang Island, prompted the actions taken to isolate
the island and the MAYAGUEZ. The objective was to prevent the crew and ship
from being taken to mainland Cambodia, thus avoiding a situation similar to
the PUEBLO affair of 1968.[1]

(S)   The only other indication as to the possible location of the
MAYAGUEZ crew during the incident, prior to their release, came about 0103Z
hours 14 May, when a P-3 observed a "...fishing boat, with possible Caucasians
huddled in the bow..." heading from Koh Tang Island toward the Cambodian
mainland. Other United States Forces in the area at that time, which had also
observed the boat, included four A-7, two F-4, one C-130, two F-111, and one
KC-135.[2]

(S)   The flight of A-7s from the 347th TFW was directed to orbit and
maintain contact with what they described as "...a fishing vessel of approximately 40 foot length with approximately 30-40 people of undetermined race
aboard, seated on deck." They remained on station for two hours and tracked
the vessel until it entered the harbor around Kompong Som and docked at 0315Z
hours 14 May. At the same time, the flight of F-4s from the 388th TFW
reported observing the A-7s attempting to impede the progress of a boat
carrying 30-40 people on deck "...thought possible to be Caucasians...." The
F-4s were forced to leave the area early to refuel, but not before they had
attempted to turn the boat by firing in front of it. COMUSSAG/7AF reported
that "...one thirty foot craft with approximately 40 people aboard..." was
maintaining course toward Kompong Som harbor in spite of attempts to turn it
by firing in front of it and making multiple CBU-30 (riot control agent)
passes over it. This boat "...was not taken under direct attack because of
the probability of Americans being aboard...."[3]

(S)   In summary, the MAYAGUEZ crew was not positively identified until
they came alongside the USS WILSON in a Thai fishing boat about 0308Z on
15 May during the assault on Koh Tang Island. The balance of indications
favoring the existence of at least some of the crew remaining on the island

---

1. Op. Cit., JCS After Action Report, p. 1.
2. PATRON FOUR 140140Z May 75.
3. 347TFW 140707Z May 75; 388TFW 140355Z May 75, 140535Z May 75, 140550Z
   May 75; PATRON FOUR 140242Z May 75, 140323Z May 75; USSAG/7AF 140235Z
   May 75; Op. Cit., JCS After Action Report, p. 2.

17

was weighted by "...an intelligence source of higher classification..." which indicated that the Khmer Communists intended to take them to Koh Tang Island. The subsequent Koh Tang Island phase of the MAYAGUEZ operation was based on this conclusion.[1]

(U)   On the afternoon of 14 May Marine Major Randall Austin, who led the assault on Koh Tang Island, conducted an aerial reconnaissance of the island in a U.S. Army U-21 aircraft, but he noted, "unfortunately, we were limited to a minimum altitude of 6,000 feet and could not see the necessary detail." This restriction was apparently locally established. Evidence leading to this conclusion can be found in Navy Commander J.A. Messegee's (CTG 72.3) recollections of the initial P-3 reconnaissance to locate the MAYAGUEZ:[2]

*   *   *   *   *

In addition to no air cover, we also were concerned about the antiaircraft (AA) armament on the Cambodian gunboats, inasmuch as we had lost a P-3 to this type of boat during the Vietnam War. Although our best intelligence indicated the boats' heaviest weapons were 20mm, one publication indicated they had 40mm. This discrepancy caused me to set a 6,000-foot minimum altitude restriction on our aircraft when in the vicinity of a possible gunboat and to require a one-mile minimum offset. We were to learn that these restrictions did not hamper our ability to visually monitor gunboat movements, except during periods of low cloudiness. At these minimums, however, we could not discern specific details, such as the lettering on the bow and stern of the MAYAGUEZ.

(U)   Commander Messegee went on to say, however, that he later directed passes as low as 300 feet, and there was no indication that a 6,000-foot minimum remained in effect for P-3s beyond the initial sortie cited.[3]

(S)   Also important was the need for accurate information on the enemy situation, both on Koh Tang Island and on the Cambodian mainland. CINCPAC observed that, to this end, photo reconnaissance provided little order of

----

1. CINCPAC 131338Z Feb 76; PATRON FOUR 150258Z May 75 and 150327Z May 75.
2. NAVY TIMES, 27 Aug 75, p. 15, "The Assault on Koh Tang"; Draft narrative of interview by Colonel Savoy with Major Austin, undated, Subj: Koh Tang Assault/Operation MAYAGUEZ; USSAG/7AF & JCRC History, 1 Apr-30 Jun 1975, dated 22 Aug 75, p. 91; Op. Cit., Proceedings, p. 94.
3. Op. Cit., Proceedings, p. 95.

battle (OB) information on the island because of the dense jungle cover. Photo reconnaissance by _____ was not timely enough for use in such a fast-moving situation. As noted above, the Marine GSF commander's visual reconnaissance proved unsatisfactory to obtain OB information, and _____ ___ _____ collection resources provided no OB intelligence due to a _____

(S) Intelligence shortly after the fall of Cambodia (17 April 1975) reported the existence of 18-20 people on the island at that time. IPAC disseminated this information by an intelligence spot report (SPOTREP) on 13 May. In a second SPOTREP, following closely behind the first, IPAC estimated the maximum of one Khmer Communist company (90-100 men) reinforced with a heavy weapons squad to be on the island; however, this report apparently did not reach the Marine GSF commander prior to the assault on the island, although it did reach the transporting helicopter commander and others. According to Major J.B. Hendricks, Operations Officer of the Second Battalion of the Ninth Marine Regiment (2/9), from which the Koh Tang Island assault force was drawn, their briefings informed them "...that there were 20-30 Khmer Rouge irregulars on the island, possibly reinforced by whatever naval support personnel that were there associated with the gunboats sighted in the area." A DIA appraisal which appeared in the JCS after action report on the incident estimated approximately 150-200 Khmer Communists on the island at the onset of the operation; however, there was no indication that this specific appraisal was generally available prior to the assault.[2]

(S) Available maps were considered insufficient to plan an amphibious assault or direct naval gunfire in support of the Koh Tang Island phase of the MAYAGUEZ operation. Topographic maps at 1:50,000 or 1:100,000 scale did not extend to the island. The current nautical chart of the island was approximately 1:240,000 scale and there was a Joint Operations Graphic (JOG) at 1:250,000 scale. Standard Naval combat charts were only produced for high priority or training areas; however, other limited areas could have been mapped by the Defense Mapping Agency in 48 hours, exclusive of shipping time, for an amphibious assault.[3]

(S) During the MAYAGUEZ operation the use of intelligence collection media for timely operational reporting (see also communications section) proved an important source of U.S. force data.

----

1. CINCPAC 191623Z Jun 75 (EX).
2. Op. Cit., Proceedings, p. 104, and JCS After Action Report, Tab B, pp. 1-2; CONIPAC 131823Z May 75 and 132144Z May 75; CINCPAC 131338Z Feb 76.
3. J3/Memo/00566-75 of 8 Sep 75, Subj: SS MAYAGUEZ/Koh Tang Island Operation; CINCPAC 191623Z Jun 75 (EX).

19

From there, CINCPAC received them via operational communications, at times well ahead of COMUSSAG/7AF voice reports. There was some difficulty correlating operations and intelligence reports because of this time differential.[1]

(C) As a result of experience gained from the MAYAGUEZ operation, CINCPAC directed a feedback system to ensure acknowledgement of critical intelligence by commanders directly concerned, and further emphasized:[2]

•

• The need for accurate photos, charts, and maps of the area for Naval gunfire, close air and assault support forces.

• The need to maintain tactical reconnaissance forces in vital areas to provide timely coverage in fast-moving situations.

• The need for COMPASS LINK or a similar system to _____ to Washington, theater commanders, and for possible press releases.

•

• The need to develop procedures to rapidly introduce photography from various sources, such as P-3, into other reconnaissance distribution systems in the immediate area of operations.

---

1. J6/Memo/0027-75 of 11 Jun 75, Subj: Lessons Learned-SS MAYAGUEZ/Koh Tang Island Operation.
2. J3 Discussion Topic, undated, Issue: Lessons Learned Recent Contingency Operations, for discussion at CINC conference held 14 Aug 75 at LANTCOM; CINCPAC 191623Z Jun 75 (EX).

SECRET

20

SECTION V--PLANNING AND EXECUTION

Planning

(S) As CINCPAC's on-scene commander during the MAYAGUEZ operation, COMUSSAG/7AF was tasked to develop, submit for approval, and execute a multi-Service air, air assault, and surface plan for the recovery of the MAYAGUEZ and an assault on Koh Tang Island in little over 16 hours. Time constraints did not provide sufficient time for detailed operation orders.[1]

(S) The initial operational concept involved use of the nearest available assets, Air Force security police. They were to make a helicopter assault directly on to the MAYAGUEZ at first light on 14 May; however, as the situation developed, incoming Marines replaced the security police in what was planned to be a simultaneously executed two-phase operation to recover the MAYAGUEZ and release her crew, supported by air strikes on mainland Cambodia.[2]

(S) Actions taken at the direction of the JCS in support of the evolving operational concept included:[3]

> • CINCPAC move all available helicopter assets in Thailand to U-Tapao.

> • CINCPAC move 75 USAF security police from Nakhon Phanom to U-Tapao.

> • CINCPAC move two reinforced platoons of Marines from Cubi Point to U-Tapao via MAC airlift.

> • CINCPAC place one Okinawa-based Marine battalion on advanced deployability posture for movement to U-Tapao via MAC airlift.

> • CSAF task MAC to provide appropriate support to CINCPAC as required and move appropriate MAC airlift to Kadena AB in preparation to lift Okinawa-based Marines.

---

1. J5/Memo/00131-75 of 17 Jul 75, Subj: SS MAYAGUEZ/Koh Tang Island Operation.
2. USSAG/7AF and JCRC History, 1 Apr-30 Jun 1975, dated 22 Aug 75, pp. 87-89.
3. JCS 9179/131610Z May 75.

(S) Based on these JCS instructions, CINCPAC further tasked COMUSSAG/7AF to move the helicopter assets and security police in Thailand to U-Tapao; CINCPACFLT to move the Marines from Cubi Point and Okinawa to U-Tapao; and CINCPACAF to preposition the required airlift in Okinawa. In addition, the following taskings had already been directed:[1]

• USS CORAL SEA [CVA-43] and escorts (TG 77.5) from the vicinity of Indonesia (about 950 miles away) to the vicinity of Kompong Som.

• USS HOLT, Destroyer Escort (DE-1074), and USS VEGA from about 100 miles off the Philippine coast (southwest of Subic Bay) to the scene of the incident.

• USS WILSON, Guided-Missile Destroyer (DDG-7), enroute from Kaohsiung, Republic of China, bound for Subic Bay, Republic of the Philippines to the vicinity of Koh Tang Island.

• USS OKINAWA, enroute to Okinawa, return to the Philippines to reconstitute an Amphibious Ready Group (ARG) (USS OKINAWA, USS DULUTH, USS BARBOUR COUNTY, and USS MT. VERNON) and prepare to proceed to the scene. (This unit was not deployed.)

(S) The essence of COMUSSAG/7AF's initial operational concept was as follows:[2]

• Arrive on station at first light, 2300Z 13 May/ 0600G 14 May.

• Effect recovery of the ship and, if possible, the ship's crew.

• USAF tactical aircraft air-drop riot control agents (RCA) on the ship to immobilize any personnel on board.

• Use all CH-53 helicopter assets available in Thailand and all but two of the available HH-53 assets.

---

1. Op. Cit., JCS After Action Report, Tab D, Encl 9, p. 1; The Comptroller General MAYAGUEZ Report, pp. 36-38; and Proceedings, pp. 97, 108; CINCPAC 131737Z May 75.
2. COMUSSAG/7AF 131748Z May 75.

22

• At ten minute intervals, in a single helo-lift, offload, from a hover, 125 USAF security police, 2 explosive ordnance personnel, 2 paramedics, and 1 Army captain interpreter onto the MAYAGUEZ.

(S) During the deployment of helicopters and 100 USAF security police from Nakhon Phanom to U-Tapao, which began at 1300Z hours 13 May, one CH-53 crashed because of mechanical failure, killing 18 security police and 5 crew members.[1]

(S) At 2051Z hours 13 May, CINCPAC directed COMUSSAG/7AF to modify the concept by substituting USMC Ground Security Force (GSF) personnel for the USAF security police, and emphasized that command and control would be maintained by CINCPAC. No execute order was issued.[2]

(TS) At 0645Z hours 14 May the JCS notified CINCPAC:[3]

Higher authority has directed that all necessary preparations be made for potential execution early on the 15th to seize the MAYAGUEZ, occupy Koh Tang Island, conduct B-52 strikes against the port of Kompong Som and Ream Airfield, and sink all Cambodian small craft in target areas.

(TS) CINCPAC was now tasked to plan for and execute, when directed, the following operations:[4]

• USS HAROLD E. HOLT seize SS MAYAGUEZ using ships company and or augmenting Marines at U-Tapao.

• Occupy Koh Tang Island with Marine forces at U-Tapao supported by Air Force helo assets and tactical air and naval gunfire support as available and required.

• Sink all Cambodian small craft in the target areas of Koh Tang, Poulo Wai, Kompong Som, and Ream.

(TS) CINCSAC was tasked to conduct conventional B-52 strikes against the port of Kompong Som and Ream Airfield from Guam.[5]

---

1. USSAG/7AF & JCRC History, 1 Apr-30 Jun 1975, dated 22 Aug 75, p. 88.
2. CINCPAC 132051Z May 75.
3. JCS 1109/140645Z May 75 (EX).
4. Ibid.
5. Ibid.

23

(TS) CINCPAC then tasked COMUSSAG/7AF to provide the detailed plans required by the JCS by 1300Z hours 14 May. CINCPAC further specified that, in planning, maximum emphasis should be placed on use of the USS CORAL SEA for close air support and minimum reliance on the availability of Thai-based strategic and tactical air. Although not mentioned, this specification was probably in deference to Thai sensitivities; however, as the situation actually evolved, this specification was not adhered to.[1]

(TS) During the new planning phase, participating units provided input to the plan that was finally submitted. There was general agreement on the need for simultaneously boarding the MAYAGUEZ and helo assaulting Koh Tang Island; however, views differed on the method for boarding the MAYAGUEZ. CINCPACFLT's concept, which was finally executed, was to transfer the boarding party by helicopter to the USS HOLT. The Marine task force commander (CTF 79.9) and COMUSSAG/7AF initially envisioned inserting the boarding party by helicopter directly onto the MAYAGUEZ in a manner similar to COMUSSAG/7AF's previous concept (see page 23). The concept submitted in COMUSSAG/7AF's final plan agreed with CINCPACFLT on the method for boarding the MAYAGUEZ; but, in an apparent oversight in the employment paragraph to the same plan, insertion on the MAYAGUEZ was specified to be by helicopter. CINCPAC approved the final plan, subject to the boarding party boarding from the USS HOLT and clarification that supporting strategic air B-52D air strikes were to be as directed by the JCS. CINCPAC directed that the Marines be put aboard the HOLT and the HOLT brought alongside the MAYAGUEZ because it was unknown if any Cambodians were on the MAYAGUEZ. It was simpler, with fewer risks, to board the MAYAGUEZ from the HOLT than from helicopters.[2]

(TS) The following were the key elements of the final operational concept developed to recover the SS MAYAGUEZ and influence the outcome of U.S. initiatives to secure the release of the ship's crew:[3]

- Begin a simultaneous two-phase assault at sunrise 15 May local time (approximately 2300Z 14 May 1975).

- Using eight USAF CH/HH-53 helicopters, execute a combat assault on Koh Tang Island, with 175 Marines in the initial wave, subsequent buildup to a total of 625 Marines on the island, and rescue members of the SS MAYAGUEZ that may be found there.

----

1. CINCPAC 140750Z May 75.
2. CINCPACFLT 141254Z May 75; CTF 79.9 141400Z May 75; COMUSSAG 141515Z May 75; CINCPAC 142112Z May 75 and 131338Z Feb 76.
3. COMUSSAG/7AF 141730Z May 75 (EX).

24

• Using three USAF helicopters, insert 48 Marines, 12 USN/MSC personnel, and explosive ordnance team and a Cambodian linguist on the USS HOLT, close with the SS MAYAGUEZ, and board and secure her.

• Close air support and area coverage against all Cambodian small craft would be provided by USAF and USN tactical air. Naval gunfire support would be available, and B-52 strikes or Naval tactical air would be directed against possible reinforcing mainland Cambodian targets.

Subsequent operations followed this concept closely, with tactical air from the USS CORAL SEA being substituted for B-52s in the mainland strikes.[1]

Experience gained in planning for the MAYAGUEZ operation highlighted the need to maintain and follow adequate, current crisis action procedures in responding to quick-breaking situations. Realizing the impracticality of attempting to prepare explicit plans for every possible crisis situation, and the fact that sufficient planning time would hardly ever be available, CINCPAC observed that those options most likely to be executed should be clearly identified early in the planning process to prevent subordinate commands from "spinning their wheels," planning for options that had little likelihood of being executed. Overall, the requirement for U.S. military assets worldwide to be strategically mobile and instantly responsive was emphasized.[2]

Observing the interrelated plans and operations process, CINCPAC stressed the need to increase the number of joint incident exercises with more imaginative and realistic scenarios, commencing with PACOM Command Post Exercises (CPXs), moving, with JCS concurrence, to higher-level politico-military games (possibly inter-departmental), and then frequent, full-fledged exercises with force participation.[3]

Execution

The MAYAGUEZ/Koh Tang Island Operation

The operation began with the first insertion of Marines on Koh Tang Island at about 2255Z 14 May (0555G 15 May) and the landing of the boarding

---

1. Op. Cit., JCS After Action Report, Tab A, p. 2.
2. J5/Memo/00131-75 of 17 Jul 75, Subj: SS MAYAGUEZ/Koh Tang Island Operation.
3. CINCPAC 191623Z Jun 75 (EX).

167

party on the USS HAROLD E. HOLT at about 2305Z 14 May (0605G 15 May). Although the USS HOLT met no opposition, and the boarding party was in complete control of the MAYAGUEZ within about two hours (0128Z 15 May), the Marine GSF and transporting USAF helicopters met fierce opposition from the beginning. Their ordeal lasted about 14 hours (last Marines extracted at about 1310Z 15 May). The MAYAGUEZ crew had been identified as safe aboard the USS WILSON within about 4 hours (0308Z 15 May) after the initial assault on the island; however, because of the strong enemy opposition encountered on the island, reinforcements were required to stabilize the situation and successfully extract the Marines.[1]

(Ø) During the initial insertion of Marines on Koh Tang Island, concern for the safety of the MAYAGUEZ crew, believed to be on the island, precluded landing zone preparation by air strikes or naval gunfire. Even after confirmation of the crew's recovery, fast A-7 Forward Air Controllers (FACs) were unable to pinpoint locations of friendly units and suppress enemy fire because of the confines of, and confusing situation on, the battlefield. It was not until 0930Z 15 May that two OV-10 "Nail" slow FACs, with loitering ability, were on station to pinpoint friendly positions for effective close air support. Also, it was not until 0735Z 15 May that the first helicopter was able to recover to the CORAL SEA rather than return to U-Tapao (helicopters used were a mix of HH-53 air-refuelable "Jolly Green," and CH-53 non-air-refuelable "Knife" aircraft).[2]

(Ø) In summary, the Koh Tang Island phase of the MAYAGUEZ operation involved the insertion of 231 Marines and subsequent evacuation of 227 (there were three missing in action and one killed in action left on the island) in the face of severe enemy fire. A total of 15 USMC, USAF, and USN personnel were killed in action, 49 wounded in action, and 3 Marines missing in action. Participating USAF helicopters incurred three combat losses, four were severely damaged, and six received minor damage.[3]

(Ø) As a result of the experience gained from executing the Koh Tang Island phase of the MAYAGUEZ operation, CINCPAC made the following additional observations relative to the means available to support the assault:[4]

---

1. Assault on Koh Tang, DCS/Plans and Operations, HQ PACAF, 23 Jun 75, pp. 23, 1-1, 1-3; PATRON FOUR 150327Z May 75; COMUSSAG/7AF 150215Z May 75.
2. Assault on Koh Tang, DCS/Plans and Operations, HQ PACAF, 23 Jun 75, pp. 2, 4, 18, 28, 29, 1-2.
3. Ibid., USSAG/7AF & JCRC History, 1 Apr-30 Jun 1975, dated 22 Aug 75, p. 99.
4. J3/Memo/00566-75 of 8 Sep 75, Subj: SS MAYAGUEZ/Koh Tang Island Operation; CINCPAC 191623Z Jun 75 (EX).

26

• Helicopter availability dictated the size and composition of forces; thus, the initial insertion was marginal in size, and rapid buildup ashore was not possible due to limited lift capability. Once the CORAL SEA was within 10 miles of the island, and shuttle distance was reduced, adequate support was available for the extraction phase. As we approach reduced force levels in the theater, particular attention must be paid to airmobile support from all services which provides flexibility to force composition.

• Troop lift helicopters should be air refuelable and equipped with fire preventive foam in external fuel tanks, as well as other hardening measures (losses were greater among CH-53s).

• We should use helicopters and low speed FACs to coordinate tactical air assets whenever the tactical environment permits.

Supportive Air Strikes Against the Cambodian Mainland

(S) Air strikes in support of the MAYAGUEZ operation were conducted against mainland Cambodian targets as directed by the JCS, the final decisions resting with higher authority. Cyclic strikes from the USS CORAL SEA against targets in the Kompong Som area were scheduled with first time-on-target about 0045Z 15 May, which closely coincided with the recovery of the MAYAGUEZ. In the midst of the initial execution of the operation, a Foreign Broadcast Information Service report out of Bangkok quoted a Cambodian Government press release to the effect that they intended to release the MAYAGUEZ and crew. This was being discussed by CINCPAC and the NMCC when, about 0044Z 15 May, word was received from the White House to cancel the CORAL SEA strike; however, by 0052Z 15 May word was received to again proceed with the CORAL SEA strikes as planned. The first wave did not expend any ordnance. Then, right after the MAYAGUEZ had been searched and found empty, CINCPAC received information from an unknown Cambodian station saying, "Let the Americans go. We do not want to become prisoners ourselves." This supported the belief that at least some Americans could still be on Koh Tong Island, and shortly after this, the second wave of CORAL SEA aircraft arrived over the mainland to attack Ream Airfield. By 0308Z 15 May the release of the MAYAGUEZ crew had been confirmed and at 0329Z 15 May CINCPAC reported to the NMCC that the crew members had told the WILSON personnel that as a "condition for release they promised air strikes would cease." CINCPAC now queried the JCS as to whether

27

or not the third wave should continue on course. The Chairman, JCS discussed this with the Secretary of Defense, and the third and final strike was directed and carried out.[1]

Finally, at 0455Z 15 May, the JCS notified all participants in the MAYAGUEZ operation:[2]

Immediately cease all offensive operations against Khmer Republic related to seizure of MAYAGUEZ. Disengage and withdraw all forces from operation area as soon as possible consistent with safety/self-defense.

CINCPAC noted that "...the threat of bombing of the Cambodian mainland did, in fact, influence the Cambodian's decision to release the crew..." as was verified by the captain of the MAYAGUEZ.[3]

---

1. JCS Report, Strike Operations Against Mainland Targets During Operations to Recover SS MAYAGUEZ and Crew, dated 19 May 1975.
2. JCS 2396/150455Z May 75.
3. CINCPAC 131338Z Feb 76.

28

170

UNCLASSIFIED

SECTION VI--SUPPLEMENTARY BIBLIOGRAPHY

(U)   The following are additional references which, though not cited, helped to provide the full breadth of perspective necessary to write this monograph.

Carlile, Donald E., LTC, USA, "The MAYAGUEZ Incident--Crisis Management," Military Review, Vol. LVI, No. 10, October 1976, pp. 3-14.

Commander in Chief U.S. Pacific Fleet, Command History of the Commander in Chief U.S. Pacific Fleet, 1 January 1975-31 December 1975, Makalapa, Hawaii, 7 September 1976. (SECRET)

Headquarters, 1st Battalion, 4th Marines, 3rd Marine Division (-)(Rein), FMF, After Action Report, Recovery of the SS MAYAGUEZ, 12 November 1975. (CONFIDENTIAL)

Headquarters, Pacific Air Force, History of Pacific Air Forces, 1 July 1974-31 December 1975, Vol. I, Hickam AFB, Hawaii:Office of PACAF History, 30 July 1976. (TOP SECRET)

Rowan, Roy, The Four Days of MAYAGUEZ, New York:W.W. Norton and Co., Inc., 1975.

Smith, James E., LTC, USAF, "The MAYAGUEZ Incident," a case study submitted to the faculty of the Air War College, Maxwell AFB, Alabama, April 1976. Defense Supply Agency, Defense Documentation Center file number ADC006284. (SECRET)

U.S. House of Representatives, Seizure of the MAYAGUEZ, Part I, Hearings before the Committee on International Relations and its Subcommittee on International Political and Military Affairs, 94th Congress, First Session, May 14 and 15, 1975. Washington:U.S. Government Printing Office, 1975.

U.S. House of Representatives, Seizure of the MAYAGUEZ, Part II, Hearings before the Subcommittee on International Political and Military Affairs of the Committee on International Relations, 94th Congress, First Session, June 19 and 25, and July 25, 1975. Washington:U.S. Government Printing Office, 1975.

UNCLASSIFIED

THIS PAGE INTENTIONALLY LEFT BLANK

Command Relationships

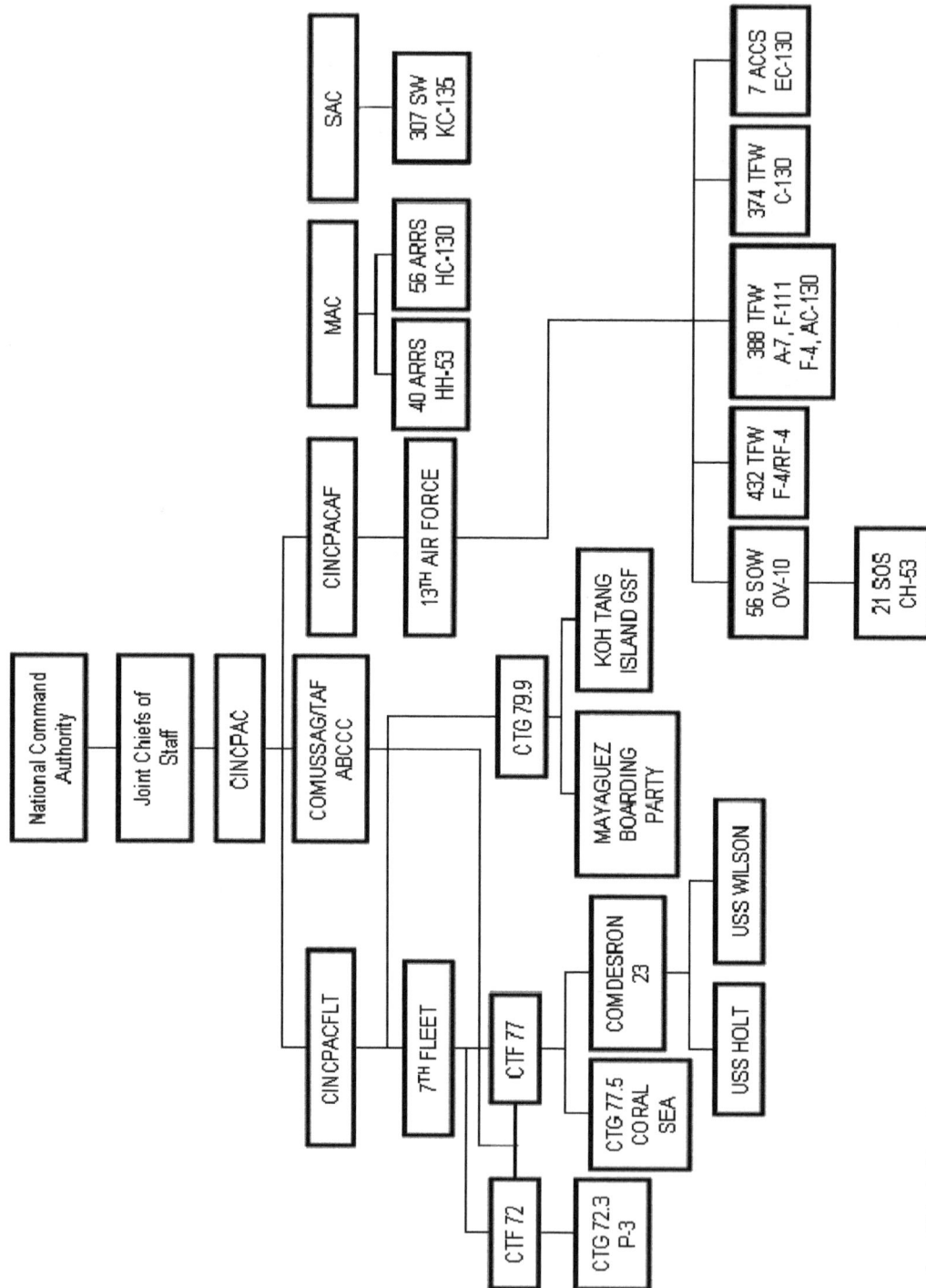

- National Command Authority
- Joint Chiefs of Staff
- CINCPAC
  - COMUSSAG/TAF ABCCC
    - CTG 79.9
      - MAYAGUEZ BOARDING PARTY
      - KOH TANG ISLAND GSF
  - CINCPACAF
    - 13TH AIR FORCE
      - 56 SOW OV-10
        - 21 SOS CH-53
      - 432 TFW F-4/RF-4
      - 388 TFW A-7, F-111 F-4, AC-130
      - 374 TFW C-130
      - 7 ACCS EC-130
  - MAC
    - 40 ARRS HH-53
    - 56 ARRS HC-130
  - SAC
    - 307 SW KC-135
  - CINCPACFLT
    - 7TH FLEET
      - CTF 77
        - CTG 77.5 CORAL SEA
        - COMDESRON 23
          - USS HOLT
          - USS WILSON
      - CTF 72
        - CTG 72.3 P-3

*Adapted from Commander in Chief Pacific Command Overview, *The SS Mayaguez Incident.* Command History Branch, Office of the Joint Secretary, Appendix VI. San Francisco, CA. 1976.

THIS PAGE INTENTIONALLY LEFT BLANK

LIST OF REFERENCES

Argyris, Chris. *Personality and Organization.* New York: Harper and Row, 1957.

Wilson, James Q. *Bureaucracy: What Government Agencies Do and Why They Do It.* New York: Basic Books, 1989.

United States Marine Corps Doctrinal Publication 6: *Command and Control.* Department of the Navy: PCN 142 000001 00, October 4, 1996.

THIS PAGE INTENTIONALLY LEFT BLANK

BIBLIOGRAPHY

Allison, Graham & Philip Zelikow. Essence of Decision Making: Explaining the Cuban Missile Crisis. 2nd Ed. New York: Addison-Wesley Educational Publishers, Inc., 1999.

Argyris, Chris. Integrating the Individual and the Organization. New York: John Wiley & Sons, Inc., 1964.

Bolman, Larry G. and Terrence E. Deal. Reframing Organizations: Artistry, Choice, and Leadership. 3rd Ed. San Francisco: Jossey-Bass, 2003.

Commander in Chief Pacific Command. The SS *Mayaguez* Incident. Command History Branch, Office of the Joint Secretary, Appendix VI, Overview. San Francisco, CA. 1976.

Comptroller General of the United States. Seizure of the *Mayaguez*: Parts II-I. 94th Congress, 2nd Session. Washington, D.C.: U.S. Government Printing Office. 1976.

Fairhurst, Gail T., and Robert A. Sarr. The Art of Framing: Managing the Language of Leadership. San Francisco: Jossey-Bass, 1996.

Galbraith, Jay R., Diane Downey and Amy Kates. Designing Dynamic Organizations: A Hands on Guide for Leaders at All Levels. New York: American Management Association, 2002.

Guilmartin, John F., Jr. A Very Short War: The *Mayaguez* and the Battle of Koh Tang. College Station: Texas A&M University Press, 1995.

Heffron, Florence A. Organization Theory and Public Organizations: The Political Connection. NJ:Apprentice Hall, 1989.

Jones, Michael O. Studying Organizational Symbolism: What, How, Why? Thousand Oaks, CA: Sage Publications, 1996.

Kotter, John P. The General Managers. New York: Free Press, 1982.

Kotter, John P. Power and Influence: Beyond Formal Authority. New York: Free Press, 1985.

Martinez, J. Carlos, and Jon. C. Jarillo. "The evolution of research on coordination mechanisms in multinational research." Journal of International Business Studies, 1989: 489-514.

Mintzberg, Henry. "Organization Design: Fashion or Fit?" Harvard Business Review, January-February (1981): 1-16.

Mintzberg, Henry. and Quinn, James B. The Strategy Process: Cases, Concepts, Cases. 2nd ed. Englewood Cliffs, NJ: Prentice Hall, 1991.

National Defense University. Strategic Leadership and Decision Making. http://www.au.af.mil/au/aw. Accessed April 1, 2006.

National Security Council Memorandum for the Record. Wednesday, May 14, 1975, 6:40pm-8:00pm. Gerald Ford Library.

National Security Council Minutes. Tuesday, May 13, 1975, 10:40pm-12:25am. Gerald Ford Library.

National Security Council Minutes. Wednesday, May 14,1975, 3:52pm-5:42pm. Gerald Ford Library.

National Security Council Minutes. Thursday, May 15, 1975, 4:02pm-4:20pm. Gerald Ford Library.

Pfeffer, Jeffrey. Managing with Power: Politics and Influence in Organizations. Boston, MA: Harvard Business School Press, 1992.

Principia Cybernetica Web. http://pespmc1.vub.ac.be/ASC/LAW_VARIE.html. Accessed Aug 24, 2006.

Quinn, Kenneth. *Mayaguez* Paper. Kenneth Quinn to General Scowcroft. 25 Aug 75. "*Mayaguez* Performance Evaluation – Memoranda 6/75-10/75," Box 8. National Secruity Adviser Staff Assistant John K. Matheny Files. Gerald R. Ford Library.

Russo, J. Edward and Paul J.H. Schoemaker. Decision Traps: Ten Barriers to Brilliant Decision-Making and How to Overcome Them. New York: Doubleday, 1989.

Rowen, Roy. The Four Days of the *Mayaguez*. New York: W.W. Norton & Company, 1975.

Seized at Sea: Situation Critical: The Story of the *Mayaguez* Crisis. DVD. Produced, directed, and written by Brian Kelly. Alexandria, VA: Henninger Productions, 2000.

United States Joint Forces Command. Joint Center for Operational Analysis. http://www.jfcom.mil/about/fact_jcoa.htm. Accessed August 23, 2006.

United States Department of Defense News Release. "MIA Marines Identified from the *Mayaguez* Incident." http://www.defenselink.mil/releases/2000/b05182000_bt260-00.html. Accessed August 20, 2006.

Wilderom, Celeste P.M., Mark Peterson, and Neal Ashkanasy, eds. Handbook of Organizational Culture and Climate. Thousand Oaks, CA: Sage Publications, Inc., 2000.

Zegart, Amy B. Flawed by Design. Stanford, CA: Stanford University Press, 1999.

THIS PAGE INTENTIONALLY LEFT BLANK

INITIAL DISTRIBUTION LIST

1.   Defense Technical Information Center
      Ft. Belvoir, Virginia

2.   Dudley Knox Library
      Naval Postgraduate School
      Monterey, California

REPORT DOCUMENTATION PAGE		READ INSTRUCTIONS BEFORE COMPLETING FORM
1. REPORT NUMBER	2. GOVT ACCESSION NO.	3. RECIPIENT'S CATALOG NUMBER
4. TITLE (and Subtitle) Chaos Theory: The Mayaguez Crisis		5. TYPE OF REPORT & PERIOD COVERED Study Project
		6. PERFORMING ORG. REPORT NUMBER
7. AUTHOR(s) Lieutenant Colonel Theodore H. Mueller		8. CONTRACT OR GRANT NUMBER(s)
9. PERFORMING ORGANIZATION NAME AND ADDRESS U.S. Army War College Carlisle Barracks, PA 17013		10. PROGRAM ELEMENT, PROJECT, TASK AREA & WORK UNIT NUMBERS
11. CONTROLLING OFFICE NAME AND ADDRESS Same		12. REPORT DATE March 1990
		13. NUMBER OF PAGES 92
14. MONITORING AGENCY NAME & ADDRESS(If different from Controlling Office)		15. SECURITY CLASS. (of this report) Unclassified
		15a. DECLASSIFICATION/DOWNGRADING SCHEDULE

16. DISTRIBUTION STATEMENT (of this Report)

Approved for public release; distribution is unlimited.

17. DISTRIBUTION STATEMENT (of the abstract entered in Block 20, if different from Report)

18. SUPPLEMENTARY NOTES

19. KEY WORDS (Continue on reverse side if necessary and identify by block number)

20. ABSTRACT (Continue on reverse side if necessary and identify by block number)
The emerging science of Chaos may be applicable to sciences other than just those that are classical. Characterized by a nonlinear notion that a small input can have a disproportionately large output, the phenomenon is referred to as the "butterfly" effect--the flapping of a butterfly's wings in Hong Kong might affect the weather in New York. The effects are often seen in many sciences to include political science. The military has as a corollary, the "for the loss of a nail" affect. This nonlinear phenomenon has occurred often in history--wars have been started because of some otherwise insignificant

DD FORM 1473 EDITION OF 1 NOV 65 IS OBSOLETE

event. The phenomenon, however, has not been studied in detail as a relationship unto itself. Chaos Theory predicts that when circumstances are in a
near chaotic state, the addition of another input, albeit however minor, can
result in a major, wholly disporportionate output. The world and national
situations in 1975 were uniquely unsettled and in some ways, unprecedenced,
when a small Cambodian force seized a U.S. merchant vessel, the Mayaguez.
Instead of handling the matter purely as a routine diplomatic matter, the U.S.
responded with a combat assault within hours of the seizure. The crew and
ship were captured. This paper explores the possibility that the response
was due to more than just the seizure. It suggests that the political, social,
and economic events that preceded the seizure may have significantly
contributed to a feeling of "crisis," and, in the jargon of Chaos Theory,
became the "almost intransitive" event that precipitated the U.S. reaction.

USAWC MILITARY STUDIES PROGRAM PAPER

CHAOS THEORY THE THE MAYAGUEZ CRISIS

An Individual Study Project
Intended for Publication

by

Lieutenant Colonel Theodore H. Mueller

Dr. Michael I. Handel
Project Adviser

U.S. Army War College
Carlisle Barracks, Pennsylvania 17013
15 March 1990

ABSTRACT

AUTHOR: Theodore H. Mueller, LTC (P), SC

TITLE: Chaos Theory and the Mayaguez Crisis

FORMAT: Individual Study Project Intended for Publication

DATE: 15 March 1990   PAGES: 85   CLASSIFICATION: Unclassified

The emerging science of Chaos may be applicable to sciences other
than just those that are classical.   Characterized by a non-linear
notion that a small input can have a disproportionately large output,
the phenomenon is referred to as the "butterfly" effect---the flapping
of a butterfly's wings in Hong Kong might effect the weather in New
York.   The effects are often seen in many sciences to include
political science.   The military has as a corollary, the "for the loss
of a nail" effect.   This non-linear phenomenon has occured often in
history---wars have been started because of some otherwise
insignificant event.   The phenomenon, however, has not been studied in
detail as a relationship unto itself.   Chaos Theory predicts that when
circumstances are in a near chaotic state, the addition of another
input, albeit however minor, can result in a major, wholly
disproportionate output.   The world and national situations in 1975
were uniquely unsettled and in some ways, unprecedenced, when a small
Cambodian force seized a U.S. merchant vessel, the Mayaguez.   Instead
of handling the matter purely as a routine diplomatic matter, the U.S.
responded with a combat assault within hours of the seizure.   The crew
and ship were recaptured.   This paper explores the possibility that
the response was due to more than just the seizure.   It suggests that
the political, social, and economic events that preceded the seizure
may have significantly contributed to a feeling of "crisis", and, in
the jargon of Chaos Theory, became the "almost intransitive" event
that precipitated the U.S. reaction.

TABLE OF CONTENTS

INTRODUCTION

Time and circumstances can sometimes catapult the most
unlikely event onto the world's center stage. The smallest
event can erupt into an international crisis; a few have
caused wars i.e., a pistol fired by Gavrilo Princip led to
the outbreak of World War I. The emerging science of chaos
refers to this phenomenon as the "butterfly effect"---the
flapping of a butterfly's wings in Hong Kong might effect
the weather in New York. Directly applicable to the
physical sciences, the phenomenon might also apply to
political science. Even in political science the effects of
the phenomenon are not unknown. It has been characterized
as the "loss of a nail effect"---for the want of a nail the
shoe was lost, for the want of a shoe the horse was lost,
etc. The results are experienced almost immediately---the
causes evaluated mostly in hindsight.

The seizure of the U.S. merchant ship, Mayaguez, by
Cambodian forces as the catalyst, the ensuing international
intrigue that erupted as a byproduct, and the dramatic U.S.
response that erupted as the result, may exemplify a
political type of chaos [1].

The purpose of this paper is to review issues surrounding the Mayaguez seizure, relate the circumstances prompting these issues to the emerging science of chaos and to focus upon implications that might be applicable for the future.

THE CRISIS

Prior to the time of its seizure the _Mayaguez_ was
destined to be no more than a footnote in history as the
world's first containerized cargo ship. During a few days
in May 1975, the world's attention focused on it for a
different reason; its name became banner headlines across
the world. The aftermath resulted in the name _Mayaguez_
earning a solid, albeit dubious, place in history, different
from its previous status.

On May 12, 1975, Cambodian naval forces seized the U.S.
merchant ship, _Mayaguez_. The reason for its seizure was not
immediately known nor were explanations forthcoming from the
Cambodian Government. Throughout the duration of the
seizure, no direct contact was ever made between the
governments of U.S. or Cambodia. U.S. officials, aware of
the killing of millions of Cambodians by the newly placed
government, feared for the safety of the crew. Comparisons
were also made between it and the seizure of another U.S.
ship, the _Pueblo_, in 1968. A variety of diplomatic actions
were quickly initiated in an effort to secure the immediate

release of the ship and its 40 crew members. When
diplomatic efforts failed, the United States initiated
military action against Cambodia to secure the same end.

The military action was based on a hastily drawn plan
developed from incomplete, inaccurate, and conflicting
intelligence. The plan was further encumbered by time and
availability of forces constraints. Regardless, it was
approved with minor modification by the Commander-in-Chief
Pacific (CINCPAC) after it had also received scrutiny and
ultimately the approval of the military and political
leaders in Washington D.C. However, before the plan could
be implemented, Cambodia announced through a commercial
radio broadcast that the ship had been released. No
specific mention of the crew was made in the broadcast.
U.S. Government officials seized upon this lack of reference
to the crew. President Ford used it as the sole
justification for implementing the military plan against
Cambodia; an assault that began less than 29 hours after the
initiation of diplomatic efforts to resolve the crisis.
Prior to its implementation, U.S. authorities made no effort
to rectify or clarify what may have been an oversight by the
Cambodians in not mentioning the crew.

U.S. intelligence located at least part of the crew at
Tang, an island about sixty miles off the Cambodian coast.
One hundred seventy-five Marines aboard eight U.S. Air Force

4

helicopters assaulted the island on the morning of May 15th.
The attacking force suffered heavy casualties almost
immediately.   At about the same time as the assault, and
for reasons unrelated to it, all the Mayaguez crew members
were released and a short time later are taken aboard the
U.S.S. Wilson. In a classic intelligence miscue, the crew
members were never on Tang island. The assault on the
island was not necessary.

The crew was rescued from a Thai fishing boat at 10:00
a.m. on May 15,1975. This equates to 11:00 p.m., May 14,
1975 Washington time.   At 12:50 a.m. (Washington time) on
May 15th, an hour and fifty minutes after the crew members
were recovered, the Secretary of Defense ordered cessation
of all offensive operations [2].

After the crisis it was discovered that the Cambodians
had released the crew at the same time the ship was
released. In fact, the crew members were enroute to the
vicinity of the Mayaguez even before the U.S. assault
started. Although U.S. authorities were unaware that the
crew had been released with the ship, this information did
become known and the crew was actually in U.S. custody
before the final phase of the assault---the bombing of the
Cambodian mainland---was completed.   Also, U.S. authorities
knew more than 14 hours before the assault that a senior
diplomat representing a foreign government, whose identity

5

remains classified, was using its influence with Cambodia to seek an early release of the ship and crew. The diplomat had passed word to U.S. authorities that the ship and crew were expected to be released soon [3].

Regardless of the knowledge that the crew was already safely in U.S. custody and that a foreign government was actively working to resolve the crisis, President Ford directed that the bombing of the mainland proceed. The result destroyed or severely damaged 12 "old propeller-driven Cambodian aircraft," hangers, fuel storage facilities, and an anti-aircraft site at Ream Airfield, barracks and fuel storage facilities at Ream Naval Base, and two warehouses, an unused oil refinery, and a railroad marshalling yard building at Kompong Som port complex [4]. All of these facilities were on the Cambodian mainland miles from the marine assault at Koh Tang (Koh means island in the Thai language). The bombing has been criticized as unnecessary and without legitimate purpose. It therefore can be asked, "Why did the bombing take place?" "What military or political purposes were served?"

Reasons for the release of the crew members are not readily apparent. It is possible that the crew was released because of the third country influence. It is also possible that the continued heavy U.S. presence of U.S. Air Force reconnaissance and fighter aircraft near Cambodia since the

seizure had simply unnerved the Cambodians into releasing
the crew. Others support the Cambodian view that the
seizure had been the result of an overly zealous Cambodian
officer who acted without authority and the Cambodian
Government acted quickly to rectify the situation.

Some U.S. politicians later claimed the bombing
constituted a purely "retaliatory" action and served no
useful military purpose. President Ford was heavily
criticized for ordering the bombing. Both Congress and the
press expressed consternation over the decision. Elizabeth
Holtzman of New York stated the following in the
Congressional Record:

> "The bombing of the mainland, from approximately 8:45
> to midnight on May 14 raises other questions.
> Although this bombing was supposedly related either to
> the recovery of the Mayaguez crew or the protection of
> the Marines invading Koh Tang Island, it makes no sense
> with regard to either purpose. At the time of the
> bombing, the President believed that at least part of
> the crew was in the vicinity of Kompong Som. If the
> bombing was related to the recovery of the crew, why
> was it directed at an area in which they might have
> been held? And why did it continue for an hour after
> the crew was recovered?
>
> If on the other hand, the bombing was intended to
> support the invasion and prevent Cambodian
> reinforcement of Koh Tang Island, its timing seems
> wrong. Why, for example, was it timed to begin with
> the recapture of the Mayaguez, rather than with the
> beginning of the island invasion?   Since no attempts
> at reinforcement were reported, why was the bombing
> needed at all?   Why were an oil depot and a naval base
> bombed after earlier bombings had destroyed Cambodian
> boats and planes in the area?   Finally, if the bombing
> was intended to protect our Marines on the island, why
> did it end while they were still pinned down by enemy
> fire, not to be rescued until nine hours later?

7

The bombing of Kompong Som, therefore, seems to have
had no military purpose directly related to the
recovery of the Mayaguez and its crew or to the
protection or rescue of the Marines.   It was
apparently punitive, part of the President's effort to
make a show of force regardless of the needless
destruction caused." [5]

In the aftermath of the assault, some 65 hours after

the crisis began, 41 U.S. Marines were killed or missing and

another 50 were wounded; ten of eleven helicopters were

destroyed or damaged, while the U.S. Government suffered

strained relations with Thailand, its only ally in southwest

Asia.   Cambodia also suffered significant personnel and

property losses.

The Mayaguez crisis is studied at the U.S. Army War

College as a classic case of crisis management.   But is the

real and only issue crisis management?   Are there other

important issues worthy of study?

Essentially, the seizure of the Mayaguez pitted United

States and Cambodia against each other over matters of

national will and international law.   From a different

perspective, the incident led to questions about U.S. crisis

management procedures, not the least of which is, Was the

incident a crisis?.   The actions taken by the respective two

governments, particularly those of the United States, raised

major issues of diplomacy, expediency, and political

precedent.   The encompassing issue then was the rationale

for the unusually strong and quick reaction of the United

8

States to an otherwise minor incident---one that ordinarily should have been handled through routine diplomatic channels. Perhaps Carl von Clausewitz anticipated such occurrences in international affairs when he wrote in his classic, On War;

> "The same political object can elicit differing reactions from different people, even from the same people at different times...Between two peoples and two states, there can be such tensions, that the slightest quarrel can produce a wholly disproportionate effect---a real explosion [6].

CHAOS THEORY

National events during early 1975 were unprecedented. International events, too, were dramatic and extraordinary. Reactions to events at the national and international level remained within the bounds of expectant behavior, that is, both routine and unusual events resulted in characteristic responses by the participants. However, the rational, predictable behavior that characterized most diplomatic occurrences was abruptly violated by the actions that followed the seizure of the Mayaguez. The U.S. reaction may have been the result of the chaos it was experiencing and witnessing. If so, then it should have been predicted.

Classical science and political science are about cause and effect, characterized by a largely linear relationship. Non-classical science or chaos recognizes a less obvious relationship between cause and effect. It is generally characterized as a non-linear relationship. In this regard, the situation in 1975 could be called chaotic---effects were obvious, causes were not. If there was a relationship

10

between the seizing of the Mayaguez and the ensuing strong reaction by the U.S. and the generally chaotic political conditions that existed in the U.S., then it was general, non-specific and non-linear. Even from a cursory view, the war-like response by the U.S. exceeded the concept of proportionality.

As a premise, classical science anticipates that apples fall because of gravity; appearance and features of animals result from predetermined genetic structure; and, rational governments act within a prescribed set of norms. Order and structure are the basis of teaching and understanding. Science relies heavily upon the ability to duplicate experiments and derive consistent outcomes. A given action elicits a given response. At sea level water boils at one-hundred degrees and freezes at zero degrees Celsius. Change parameters and the results of the experiment change as well; water at a lower barometric pressure boils faster. Water at a higher barometric pressure freezes faster. Still, for classical science the results are largely anticipated and verifiable through repeated experiments.

The emerging science of Chaos, however, views the progression of water freezing to be constant, in the classical sense, until the very narrow range of temperature when the water turns into ice. At that time chaos develops. This phenomenon, a rapid and disproportional consequence of

11

a minor increase in input, manifests itself in many other physical occurrences as well; smoke from a cigarette rises in a tight column until a point where it spreads out into an undefined cloud; iron goes from "un"magnetized to magnetized at some undetermined point; and, two colors mix but retain their respective color characteristics until some point when a new color develops. In each of these cases, a normal pattern of behavior ensued until the very brink of uncertainty---or chaos--was reached. At that very narrow moment, the addition of just one more input into a defined universe---a butterfly flapping its wings, a loss of a nail, or the seizure of a merchant ship---pushed the consequences into chaos. There is an abrupt transition into this mysterious turbulence instead of a linear accumulation of input.

Edward Lorenz of the Massachusetts Institute of Technology called this behavior "almost intransitivity." It is evident when a system displays one sort of behavior for a long period of time and then suddenly and abruptly it shifts into a different representative behavior. Both behaviors exhibit a different type of behavior [7]. Progression no longer remains linear, but becomes nonlinear; some say less predictable. But is the system and the reaction really unpredictable? Chaos recognizes these exceptional happenings and finds a coarse order and discipline to the structure---order masquerading as randomness. There are two

12

natural kinds of behavior, one stable and observable over a long period of time, the other completely different, occurs less often, but is just as natural and observable [8].

Under a Bell-shaped curve, normal, or so-called Gaussian distribution, in principle, every phenomenon can be explained. Standard deviations from the center of the norm explain most observed results and account for most happenings. Researchers, economists, and politicians speak of these as probabilities. Usually though, regardless of how certain they may be of an outcome, some percentage is left for chance, luck, or "unforeseen circumstances." Seldom is anything so certain that the chance for a predictable outcome is absolute, certain, and guaranteed.

In Figure 1, the center area of the distribution curve reflects the "range of expectant behavior;" the range where most occurrences are probable. Whether hard science, economics, or politics, every action within this range elicits a comparable and somewhat predictable reaction. Raymond Cohen in his book, Threat Perception in International Crisis, calls this mutual expectation "rules of the game." He says,

> "Rules point the way to a predetermined rendezvous. If
> the signpost should be knocked down or altered,
> travelers journeying apart will be unable to arrive at
> a common destination; coordinated behavior becomes
> impossible. But rules also perform a second,
> complementary boundary function: they demarcate the
> territory of the permissible from that of the

13

forbidden. And just as an infringement of "rules of the game" removes the only means of tacit restraint between them, it also removes the only means for tacit restraint between them."[9]

In figure 1, the width of the boundaries change as the range of available alternatives change. Significantly, the range of expectant behavior between like entities, animals within a species, elements within a compound, or nations within a political setting, may differ.

In a political sense, Great Britain could be characterized as having a relatively narrow range---political reactions are generally predictable, proportionate, reflect a mature outlook, and seldom go beyond the accepted range of expectant behavior. Libya, on the other hand, exhibits the perception of a wider range of expectant behavior. Responses run the gamut from reasonably assumed political behavior to outright, unpredictable terrorism to declared, open hostilities. In the case of both Great Britain and Libya, a dramatic event happened that changed their respective range of expectant behavior---Great Britain's became wider because of the Falkland Islands conflict; Libya's became more narrow after the U.S. air attack on its territory.

Stable Range of Expectant Behavior

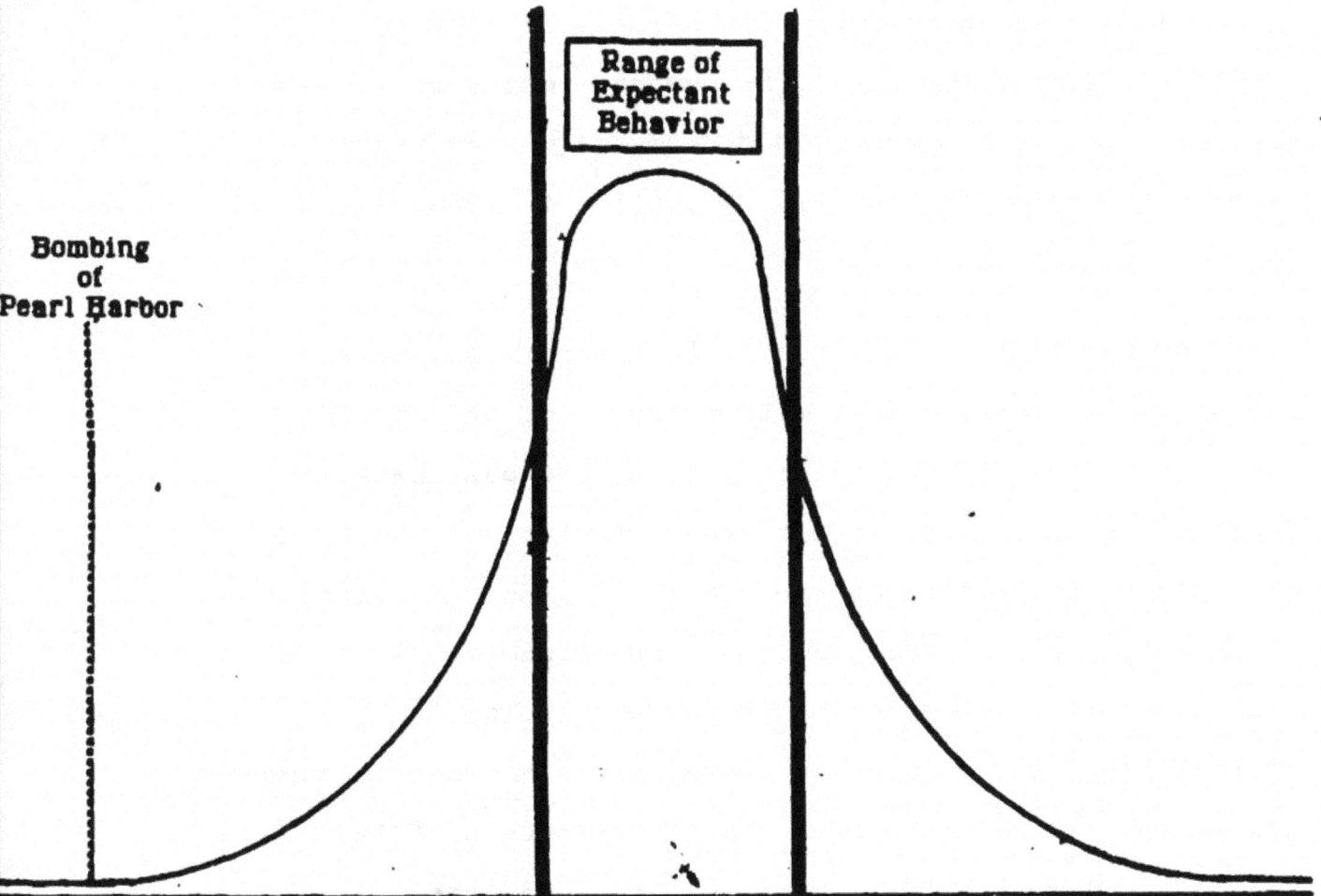

Figure 1

In dealing in the international arena, value lies in correctly assessing the political ranges of other countries for any period of time. This serves diplomatic relations well and allows outstanding issues to be resolved usually within the range of expectant behavior. Failure to accurately assess the political responsiveness of a nation to a given event has produced dire consequences---even war: Germany in World War I and II, Argentina in 1980, and Egypt in 1967, to name a few.

The reaction of one country to that of another should, therefore, ordinarily fall within its range of expectant behavior. Custom, international laws, and past behavior greatly influence, if not dictate, the width of the range. Dimensions, quantified by the number of possible reactions to any given event, are generally understood by all. In fact, nations are dependent upon understanding, appreciating, and respecting these norms in order to conduct diplomacy. If all adhere to the disciplines of this political discourse then there are few surprises.

Even if a catastrophic event occured---one that fell outside the range of expectant behavior---such as the bombing of Pearl Harbor in 1941---a response that was expected and predictable should normally result. Some may say that given the growing hostile political relations

16

between the U.S. and Japan, that a hostile act should, in fact, have been anticipated. On the other hand, the attack was not adequately anticipated. Until it actually happened, both the U.S. and Japanese governments continued to play a diplomatic intrigue. In response to the bombing, the U.S. reacted predicability, forcibly, and as expected; the hostile act was returned in kind---a state of war existed.

Although the action taken by Japan against the U.S. was beyond the range of expectant behavior, the U.S. response to it was not. Responses of this type are similar to that of other nations that have a capability to respond---generally characterized as "tit for tat." When something happens out of the ordinary there is a tendency to return to the status quo or the expectant behavior range. Or to put it another way, there is a tendency to return to equilibrium. For instance, a pendulum clock is, as Dr. Lorenz would call it, an "intransitive system." It will swing rhythmically until it is disrupted by some outside force---a bump. It will then swing wildly or slow down at the onset of an influence and exhibit a pattern that is beyond the range of expectant behavior. Soon after, however, it will almost as rapidly return to its characteristic, precision rhythm. The aberration, though not expected, only temporarily disrupts the system. Classical science like political science expects harmony and strives to maintain it.

17

Explanations of most scientific and political
situations focus on effects that are regulated, predictable,
and largely linear. Given an approximate knowledge of a
system's initial condition and an understanding of the
natural laws that effect it, it is possible to calculate the
approximate behavior of the system. That is, small changes
produce small effects and large changes produce large
effects such as the U.S. response to the bombing of Pearl
Harbor. Embassy personnel deported by one country for
spying result in an equal number deported from the other,
and so on. These action reflect some general law of
proportionality.

The science of chaos, on the other hand, addresses
occurrences where small changes result in gross effects.
There is essentially a non-linear relationship between
action and reaction. Consequences of actions (or
non-action, as the case may be) are represented in the
extreme tails of the normal distribution curve. Although
they seldom occur, they can and do. Their occurrence, like
the chaotic behavior of the bumped pendulum clock, are
generally short-lived and are prone to return to a state of
equilibrium or status quo. When results are determined to
be complex then there is a tendency to search for complex
causes; however, when random relationships are suspected
between the input and the output of a system, there is an
assumption that randomness would have to be incorporated

18

Into any realistic theory by "artificially adding noise"
[10]. Clausewitz refers to this as the friction in war–"the
force that makes the apparently easy so difficult" [11].

The science of chaos has one other important aspect.
Unlike quantum mechanics or political science, Chaos Theory
attempts to <u>predict</u> an outcome. Generally, the theory
provides that given a general circumstance or situation that
is near chaotic, any stimulus, however minor or routine,
however distant in relation to the environment, is likely to
cause the situation to become even more chaotic. The theory
also considers short bursts of chaos such as the pendulum
clock example or the eleven year cycle of intense solar
activity. Both support short bursts of chaos separated by
long intervals of regular behavior... a return to
equilibrium. So even within chaos there is order.

Dr. Edward Lorenz first began developing the Theory of
Chaos in the 1960's. He constructed a computer weather
model that reduced the physics of the atmosphere to a few
mathematical equations. These equations, temperature,
pressure, etc., were used to simulate weather. When Dr.
Lorenz attempted to repeat one forecast, however, he entered
data into the computer rounded off to three decimal places
rather than the usual six. The results were dramatic.
They clearly did not relate to the previous outcome. In the
jargon of Chaos Theory, the weather forecast displayed a

19

"sensitive dependence on initial conditions"[12]. The apparent minor change of rounding to three decimal places rather than six produced a major and totally different outcome. It is not inconceivable that this phenomenon could apply to political science, as well. True Chaos Theory is supported by complex mathematical formulas and references to partial dimensions; however, political science currently lacks this sophistication. As the science of Chaos develops further there will undoubtedly be an effort to associate the mathematics to all the sciences, political science included. For now, the basic theory will suffice to explain the general association with political science.

POLITICAL CHAOS

With regard to the political setting on May 12, 1975,
extraordinary and unprecedented events were evident.
President Nixon, on the verge of impeachment, became the
nation's first deposed president by resigning nine months
previously; John N. Mitchell, John D. Erlichman, and H.R.
Halderman, former high ranking members of the Nixon
Administration, were convicted and sentenced to
two-and-a-half to eight years in prison for their roles in
the Watergate cover-up; Robert C. Mardian was also convicted
and is given a 10-month to three year sentence; worldwide
inflation contributed to dramatic increases in the cost of
fuel, food, and materiels; oil-producing nations raised
prices, heightening inflation; economic growth slowed to
near zero in most industrialized nations; Dow Jones stock
exchange index fell to 663 in 1974, the lowest level since
1970; Saigon, in the aftermath of the United States' first
military and political defeat, fell to the Communists twelve
days before the Mayaguez incident; and, Cambodia fell to the
Communists only twenty-nine days earlier. President Ford

became the United States' first appointed president and granted former President Nixon a pardon for any criminal offenses committed while in office---widespread protests developed. The President later granted a limited amnesty to Vietnam War draft evaders and military deserters. These and other events contributed to a political atmosphere within the U.S. of self doubt and suspicion.

As president, Ford was yet unproven as a leader. Secretary of State Henry Kissinger, lingering in the failed military and diplomatic resolution of Vietnam had failed to secure a second disengagement of forces between Egypt and Israel in the Sinai in March. The United States, like most other economies of the world, still suffered from the impact of the oil embargo of 1974. The status of the United States as an economic and world leader was clearly at a low ebb [13]. Table 1 depicts some of the major events of the period.

Cambodia, too, was experiencing internal turmoil. A long and especially violent war had just been concluded. Cambodian President Lon Nol fled besieged Phnom Penh before the Communist takeover; the U.S. Embassy closed and the last Americans left Cambodia. Khmer Rouge insurgents, flush with their recent victory, set up headquarters in Phnom Penh.

22

Table 1
Significant Events Prior to the Mayaguez Incident
(1974 through mid-1975)

Worldwide inflation helped to cause dramatic increases in cost of fuel, food, and materials

Oil-producing nations boosted prices, heightening inflation

Economic growth slowed to near zero in most industrialized nations

Terrorism continued in Northern Ireland and spreads to England

Tower of London and the Houses of Parliament were bombed

Greek-led Cypriot rebels overthrew the government

India became the sixth nation to explode a nuclear device

Maurice H. Stans, former U.S. Secretary of Commerce, became the third member of the Nixon cabinet to be convicted of violating campaign laws during the 1972 Nixon re-election campaign

John N. Mitchell, John D. Erlichman, and H.R. Haldeman, senior-level members of the Nixon Administration, were convicted and sentenced for their roles in Watergate.

Communist forces overran South Vietnam

Cambodian President Lon Nol fled besieged Phnom Penh before Communist takeover; U.S. Embassy closed

Unemployment rate in the U.S. reached 9.2%, highest since 1941

Eastern Airlines jet crashed at New York's Kennedy International Airport---America's worst domestic airline crash

W.T. Grant stores, billions in debt, filed bankruptcy

New York City appealed to Federal government for cash to avert default

Two assassination attempts were made on the life of President Ford

U.S. ended two decades of military involvement in Vietnam

The new government, though less than a month old, attempted to establish its nationalism and legitimacy by renouncing Vietnam and Thailand claims to the islands of Tang, Poulo Wai and Rong Sam Lem and announcing a twelve mile territorial limit. The islands located up to sixty miles off the coast of Cambodia, were claimed by Cambodia as a historical right. Figure 2 shows the general location of the Mayaguez during the crisis and the location of the islands. An ongoing, sometimes hostile, dispute existed between Cambodia and the nations of Vietnam and Thailand.

The new Cambodian government in Phnom Pehn also lacked credibility in the international community. It had few diplomatic missions in other countries. Cambodia, geographically located in a region of intense and prolonged warfare, genuinely felt threatened by outside forces.

Cambodia's population, weary of war, was adjusting to the hardships of postwar. People were forcibly relocated from the cities where there was safety during the war to the countryside where there was more food. In short, the Cambodian government faced difficult and unprecedented times. Externally, the government faced outrage and consternation about alleged atrocities conducted against its people during the war. Internally, the government attempted

Figure 2

Location of the Mayaguez

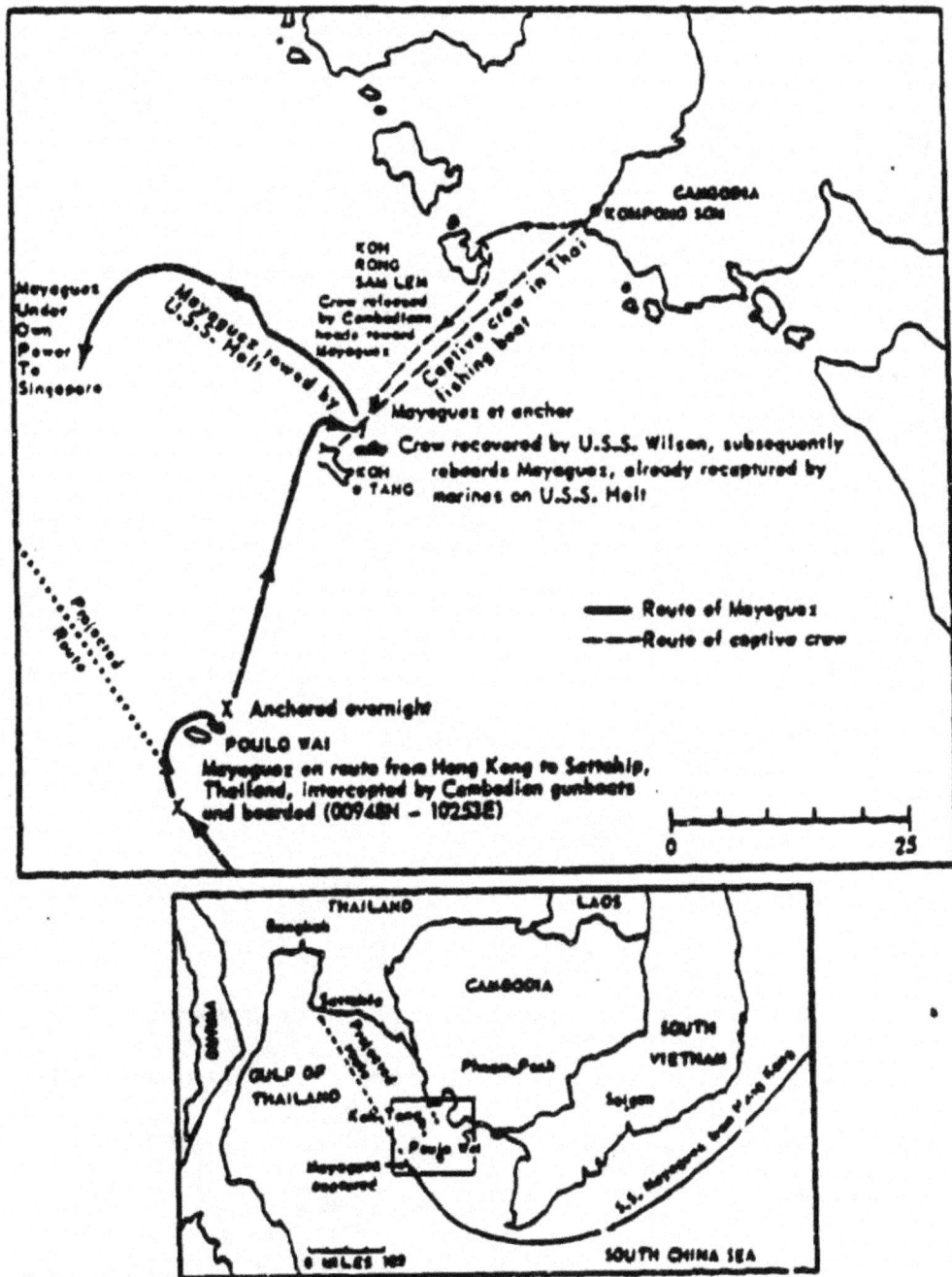

Report of the Comptroller General of the United States,
"The Seizure of the Mayaguez---A Case Study of Crisis Management,
4 October 1976, page 64.

to rebuild its economy and to structure its government to function in an international political environment .

The circumstances in evidence for the United States and Cambodia in the mid-70's had both contrasts and similarities. The respective situations, though different, shared a similarity of being considered extreme, even chaotic.

If the Theory of Chaos applies equally to politics as it does to the classical science, then the chaotic political conditions that existed, could easily be further exacerbated by only a minor discord, i.e., the butterfly effect. Only a catalyst was needed, one that would serve to catapult the already wild U.S. political situation into a temporary state of chaos.

The enormous military power of the United States presented an especially volatile and dangerous situation to the world. In Chaos Theory the use of military means to solve an otherwise minor political problem cannot be ruled out. Indeed, Clausewitz viewed war as, "a true political instrument, a continuation of political activity by other means"[14]. It is, "a part of man's social existence"[15], that "the only source of war is politics"[16]. Implicit in his statements is that war is an act of choice; not "merely added violence to perfidy"[17]. Regardless, history

vividly documents the use of military power as an element of
political power even among civilized states.   Many use war
often to further or protect national interests. Others,
like the U.S., have initiated it less often.

    While Cambodia had the military means to inflict harm
to its own people, without external help, it lacked the
ability to conduct a formidable military capability beyond
its territory.   Its inferior military power, a few propeller
driven aircraft and five U.S. manufactured patrolboats,
would be particularly inadequate against that of the United
States---a case of the sparrow challenging the eagle.
Therefore, a real military response by Cambodia to be
considered a threat against the U.S. would be improbable.

    In response to a highly abnormal situation, one that
bordered on the extremes of possibilities, Chaos Theory
would predict abnormal consequences. If applied to the
political situation evident in mid-1975, the otherwise minor
incident like the seizing of the Mayaguez, could, like the
flapping of a butterfly's wings, produce a dramatic and
unfortunate response. If the military might of the United
States was unleashed as a consequence of an otherwise minor
event such as the seizing of the Mayaguez,, the response
could be tragic.   However, the response would not be
unexpected. Time and circumstances were ripe for an
eventful happening.

The seizure of the Mayaquez set into motion a series of events that produced a major and uncharacteristic response by the United States---one that without the Theory of Chaos could not have been expected.   Figure 3 represents a graphic portrayal of the relative domestic situation in mid-1975.   The seizure of the Mayaquez was within the range of expectant behavior because the action was not extraordinary or exceptional.   Seizures of U.S. ships by foreign nations had occured before, but in those incidences the recovery had been handled as a routine matter through diplomatic channels.

Relative Range of Expectant Behavior
at the Time of the Mayaguez

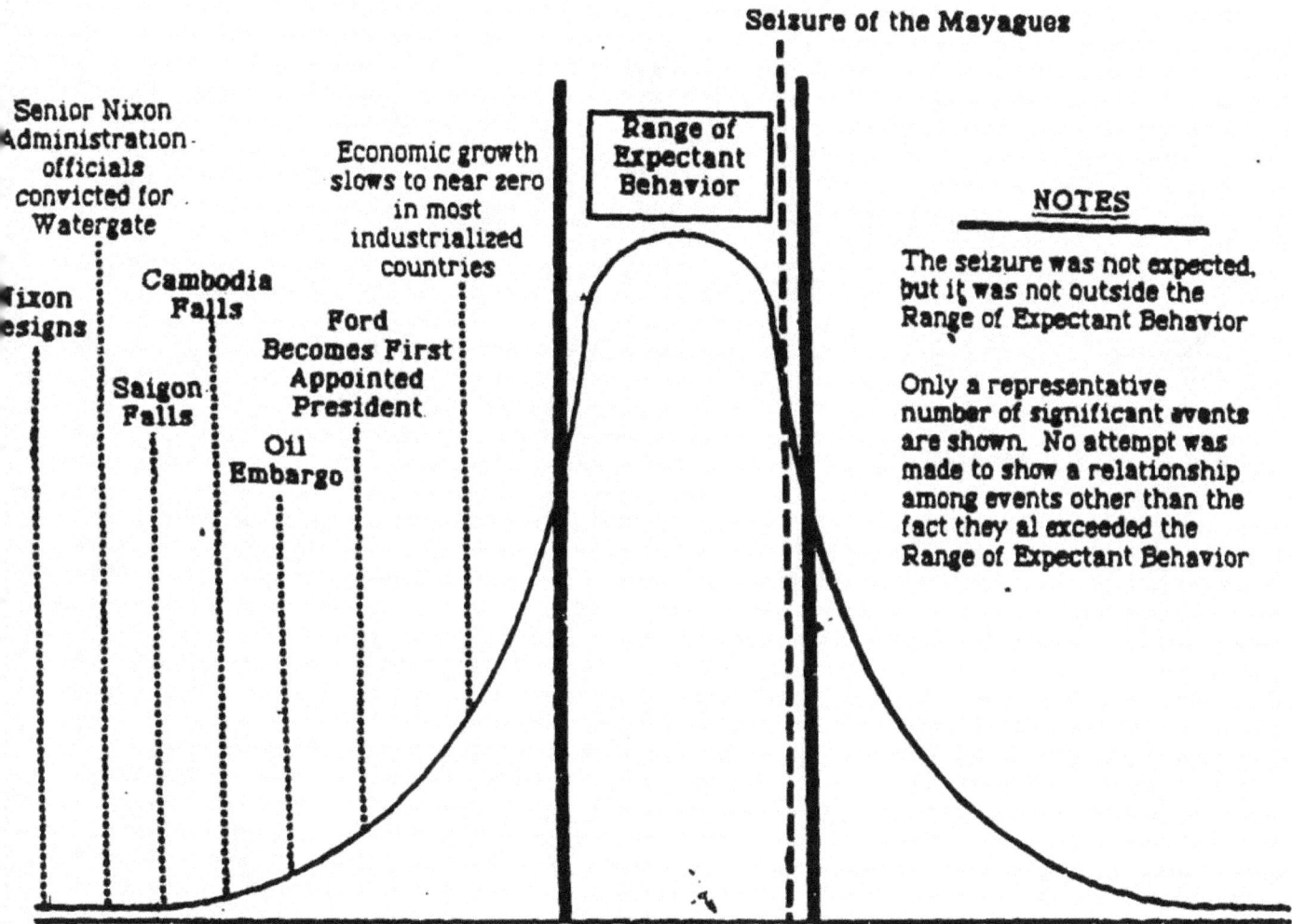

Seizure of the Mayaguez

Senior Nixon Administration officials convicted for Watergate

Nixon resigns

Cambodia Falls

Saigon Falls

Oil Embargo

Economic growth slows to near zero in most industrialized countries

Ford Becomes First Appointed President

Range of Expectant Behavior

NOTES

The seizure was not expected, but it was not outside the Range of Expectant Behavior

Only a representative number of significant events are shown. No attempt was made to show a relationship among events other than the fact they al exceeded the Range of Expectant Behavior

Figure 3

THE SEIZURE

At 2:18 pm on May 12, 1975, a representative of the Sea
Land Service Corporation, located in Jakarta, Indonesia,
received a Mayday message from one of the company's ships,
the Mayaguez. The ship had been sailing in the Gulf of
Thailand about sixty miles from the Cambodian coast eight
miles from Poulo Wai, one of the islands claimed by both
Cambodia and Vietnam. The Khmer Rouge forces maintained a
garrison on Poulo Wai and took direct action to enforce the
newly announced 12-mile territorial sea limit. The United
States, aware of the active enforcement of what Cambodia
claimed as a sovereign right and aware, too, of recent
seizures of foreign vessels, did not regard the situation
with great concern. Although the U.S. Defense Mapping
Agency Hydrographic Center has responsibility for
broadcasting warnings to U.S. shipping, it had not issued
any about Cambodian actions [18]. It would be two days
after the seizure of the Mayaguez before a warning to
mariners would be broadcast. Not-surprisingly, Congress

30

soon made this apparent lapse in responsibility the subject
of a Congressional Hearing.

Information concerning Cambodian motivations prior to
the first National Security Council Meeting, held about
seven hours after news of the seizure was received in
Washington, included the knowledge that:

1.   Ten days prior to the seizure Cambodia had seized
and later released a group of Thai fishing boats.

2.   Eight days previously, Cambodian patrol boats had
fired upon and unsuccessfully attempted to capture a
South Korean ship.

3.   Six days earlier, six vessels fleeing from South
Vietnam and a South Vietnam government boat were seized
by Cambodia.

4.   Five days earlier, Cambodia had stopped, seized,
and searched a Panamanian ship. It was released 36
hours later.

5.   Five days previously, Cambodian officials were
focusing interest on controlling certain outlying
islands because of possible petroleum reserves.

6.   Three days earlier there was evidence that
Cambodia planned to enforce by seizing all foreign
ships, a 90 mile territorial limit [19].

With regard to the Mayaguez, Cambodian officials later
claimed that the ship was actually "two and a half to three
miles from the island" instead of the eight miles claimed by
U.S. authorities [20]. Also, that United States observation
aircraft had flown over Cambodia daily since the Communist
overthrow in April and that small boats carrying Thai and
Cambodian agents with U.S. radio equipment and bombs had
been caught in Cambodian waters [21]. U.S. authorities

31

acknowledged the reconnaissance flights, but denied any other intelligence activities involving ships. Suspicions about foreign vessels entering its territorial waters were justified and, for Cambodia, cause for alarm. It was these suspicions that encouraged the Cambodian seizure of the Mayaguez.

The Mayday message received from the Mayaguez stated that the ship had been fired upon and boarded by Cambodian naval forces and that it was being towed to an unknown Cambodian port. Captain Miller, Captain of the Mayaguez, later stated during the hearings of the Subcommittee on International Political and Military Affairs that addressed, "Seizure of the Mayaguez", that his ship was boarded by seven armed insurgents and a young boy. The young boy carried an eight-foot shoulder rocket launcher. Captain Miller also stated that none of the insurgents spoke any English. In fact two days lapsed before any communications beyond hand signals were possible.

President Ford called the Cambodian seizure an "act of piracy". The Cambodian government had a different view. Ieng Sary, a Cambodian Deputy Premier, stated four months later, the seizure was made by a local commander without the knowledge of the Phnom Penh Government [22]. He further stated that after his government found out about the incident from an American radio broadcast, the local

32

commander was "under instructions to release the Mayaguez immediately"[23]. A public announcement to that effect was made over commercial radio and monitored by the U.S. Before the local commander could act, however, U.S. officials, reacting to the order from President Ford, had already set into motion a military plan to recapture the ship and its crew.

Cambodian forces had actually released the crew members before the planned U.S. military action; however, some senior U.S. military officials claim that this information was not properly disseminated to decision makers until after the military action was completed. Others claim that they were aware of it, but a decision had been made to continue with the military action for "demonstration purposes"[24]. Press Secretary Ron Nessen announced at a news briefing on May 14, 1975, the President's decision to use "military measures" to obtain the release of the Mayaguez and crew and that operations would stop "promptly" once Cambodia issued a statement to release the crew members [25]. Elizabeth Holtzman, (D-N.Y.), in a prepared statement to the International Political and Military Affairs Committee on June 25, 1975 stated:

> "On the basis of information currently available, it
> appears that the President's chief concern in this
> matter was to make a show of force in Asia, a show
> perhaps prompted by a desire to obliterate the memory
> of our defeat in Indochina. This conclusion about
> President Ford's intent is justified, in the first

place, by his tardy and utterly inadequate efforts at securing the release of the crewmen through diplomacy. Although he was reportedly notified of the seizure of the Mayaguez at approximately 6:30 a.m. on March 12 (sic), the President did not attempt to make diplomatic contact with the Cambodian government until 4:30 p.m., 10 hours later.

At no time did President Ford have any assurance that any message had been received by the Cambodian government before the invasion and bombing began. In fact, at no time did American authorities initiate any direct contact with Cambodia, by radio or otherwise. Moreover, despite receiving a Cambodian message announcing the release of the Mayaguez as the invasion was beginning, President Ford continued the invasion and waited more than an hour to reply"[26].

One can only guess the actual reason for the U.S. delay in ceasing military action. Regardless of the reason, the seizure acted as a trip wire. It set into motion a series of events that caused the Mayaguez to become the focal point of two nations. One, the United States, considered to be the most militarily powerful nation on earth, had recently suffered a humiliating political failure in a costly and unpopular war. It had also suffered embarrassment over the Watergate scandal---conviction of senior government officials, and a deposed president. The other, Cambodia, had an unproven communist government that was but three weeks old and had reached only a fragile peace with its people. These two unlikely nations, David and Goliath, now clashed in a battle of wills over a ship...a ship with 40 Americans aboard...a ship that had been in the wrong place at the wrong time.

34

U.S. Army Colonel, Zane Finklestein, legal adviser to the Chairman, Joint Chiefs of Staff, equated the seizure situation to "two blind men in a dark room looking for a black cat that wasn't there"[27]. On the surface, the situation appeared to be routine, but for the U.S., uncertainty about the real purpose of the seizure and a still burning embarrassment about recent challenges to its leadership, caused strong action to be taken quickly.

THE SHIP

Only when the Vietnam war broke out did the _Mayaguez_
reach its full potential as a containerized ship.   Its two
large on-board cranes, used to load and unload the ship's
maximum load of 274 containers, made it ideal to operate
from Asian ports.

The _Mayaguez_ sailed with her forty crew members from
Hong Kong on the morning of May 7, 1975. Loaded with 184
35-foot and 40-foot containers, she steamed to her
destination, Sattahip, Thailand, at 12.5 knots.
Seventy-seven of the containers carried military supplies.
The others contained general cargo such as food, shoes,
furniture, and clothing [28]. Neither the ship nor its crew
were armed.

Captain Miller later told a congressional hearing panel
that the Cambodians had no way of knowing that the _Mayaguez_
was an American ship because "we don't fly the flag at sea".
Based on this, plus the fact none of the Cambodians spoke
English it appears the seizure of the _Mayaguez_ was more of a

target of opportunity than a deliberate attempt to embarrass the United States.

After the ship was taken, questions immediately arose. Why had the ship been taken? Was it involved in any intelligence gathering activities for the U.S.? Or was it just what it appeared---an unarmed cargo ship under contract to the U.S. government on a routine voyage in the Gulf of Thailand? Should the seizure be handled through diplomatic channels? How could the crew be saved? The principle issues the U.S. to took from a position of strength were, What's happened?, Why did it happen?, and What comes next?[29].

Secretary of State Kissinger said in a speech the day after the seizure, "The United States will not accept harassment of its ships on international sea lanes" [30]. President Ford later said that the United States' slow reaction to the Pueblo incident that began on January 23, 1968 and the similarities of it to the Mayaguez crisis provided a "benchmark" from which to proceed [31]. Secretary of Defense James Schlesinger does not recall President Ford talking much about the Pueblo, nor does he remember it figuring in his own thoughts [32]. However, in contrast to the seizure of the U.S. intelligence ship, Pueblo, and the Gulf of Tonkin incident in August, 1964, when North Vietnamese patrol boats allegedly fired on two

37

U.S. destroyers, the Mayaguez seizure did not involve U.S. Navy ships. It was a commercial ship of private U.S. ownership. This fact made the incident more akin to the seizure of an American tuna boat by Ecuador for fishing within a claimed 200 mile limit or of the U.S. seizure of a Russian vessel for fishing within the U.S. claimed limit than it did to a deliberate act of war.

For both military and commercial reasons, the United States officially recognizes territorial claims only up to three miles; however, in the past it has claimed exclusive jurisdiction over mineral rights as far as 200 miles from the coast [33]. Only five days after the seizing of the Mayaguez, the U.S. Coast Guard seized a Polish fishing trawler off the California coast for operating within the 12-mile fishing limit claimed by the United States. The situation was resolved, within the range of expectant behavior, that is, in a court of law.

With regard to the Mayaguez, the central issues under international law became the "right of passage" against the right to declare and enforce an economic territorial limit. A third factor addressed the right to inspect a ship suspected of engaging in a belligerent action---spying, of making warlike actions---or of disturbing any mineral or fishing rights claimed by the nation. Or even when hostile actions are not suspected, the right of a nation to

38

"inspect" ships that transgress its claimed territorial limit.

As the Mayaguez situation started to unfold, more questions arose. President Ford felt that strong action had to be taken. The National Security Council agreed. However, the lack of credible information about Cambodia and its intentions left the U.S. with few options and little time. The real crisis developed when U.S. authorities "realized there was nothing that we could do"[34]. Some action had to be taken. Along with the advice of the National Security Council and that of Dr. Kissinger, who was given the role of "preeminent hawk [35]," President Ford assumed direct control of the situation and at the first meeting of the National Security Council, directed several diplomatic overtures to be taken [36]:

o   A public statement demanding the immediate release of the Mayaguez was released at 1:50 p.m., May 12. This is significant for two reasons: the statement was not issued until after the first meeting of the NSC and 10 hours after the seizure; and only included the release of the ship and did not specify the crew. (This latter point is particularly important.   It was the failure of the Cambodians to specifically mention the crew when the release of the ship was announced

39

that President Ford cited as justification for
continuing the military action against Cambodia.)

o   An attempt was made to deliver a message through
the People's Republic of China Liaison Office in
Washington, D.C. to the Cambodians at 4:30 p.m., May
12.

o   An attempt to deliver messages to the Cambodian
Embassy and the Foreign Ministry of the People's
Republic of China in Peking was made at 12:10 a.m., May
13. George Bush, later to become President of the
United States, was the U.S. Liaison Officer to China at
the time.

o   The United States formally sought the assistance
of U.N. Secretary General Waldheim in securing the
release of the ship and crew between 1 and 2 p.m., May
14.

o   A response was made at 9:15 p.m. on May 14 to a
Cambodian radio broadcast that military operations
would cease only when the Cambodians stated they would
return the crew.

The diplomatic efforts directed by President Ford to
resolve the crisis were heavily criticized as only token
efforts and lacking in good faith. It was generally felt
that insufficient time had been allowed for diplomatic

resolution. Even before the military assault began,
Congress expressed concern about the use of diplomacy as the
preferred course of action. Senator Robert Taft Jr. (R -
Ohio) urged that the United States "try all kinds of
sanctions before resorting to force". Senator Hubert
Humphrey (D - Minn) urged the government to "stop, look and
listen" before it resorts to force". And Senator Jacob
Javits (R - N.Y.) said that Americans should "keep our
shirts on and see if they return the ship" [37]. Others in
Congress shared President Ford's outrage and pushed for
direct military intervention. With little else to go on,
Congressmen generally expressed fears of getting involved in
anything that resembled a another Vietnam and equated the
situation to that of the Gulf of Tonkin incident.

CHAIN OF COMMAND

Once the crisis began, President Ford became the focal point for decision making. He was both a fill-in Vice President then a fill-in President. Former President Johnson characterized him as someone who "could not walk and chew gum at the same time [38]." President Ford undoubtedly saw the seizure both as a personal challenge as a former Navy officer and as a possible opportunity to establish his political credentials. The fact the following year was a presidential election year and there was obvious political gain to be had could not have been missed as well. More fundamentally, the Mayaguez incident offered Ford a chance to erase some of the memories of the evacuation of Saigon by helicopters. It offered him a chance to demonstrate the leadership to be President. As the minority leader of the House of Representatives during the Vietnam conflict, Ford had been outspoken and always called for stronger measures [39]. Now he had his chance to act.

With regard to Presidential micromanagement, President Ford's deep involvement in the Mayaguez incident ranks at the

42

very top of a list of previous and subsequent military actions
that includes Beirut, Grenada, and Panama [40]

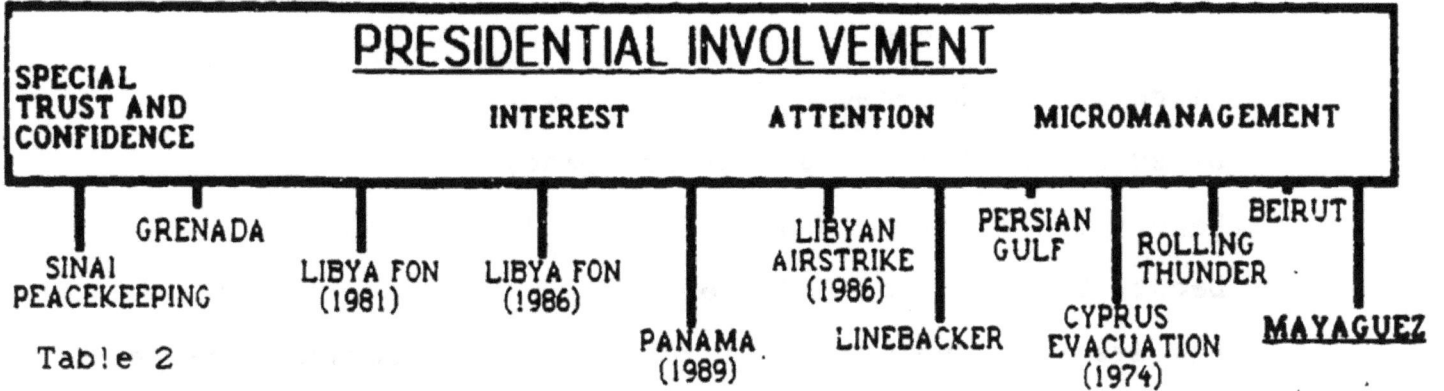

PRESIDENTIAL INVOLVEMENT

SPECIAL TRUST AND CONFIDENCE	INTEREST	ATTENTION	MICROMANAGEMENT

GRENADA		LIBYAN AIRSTRIKE (1986)	PERSIAN GULF	BEIRUT
SINAI PEACEKEEPING	LIBYA FON (1981)	LIBYA FON (1986)			ROLLING THUNDER	
Table 2		PANAMA (1989)	LINEBACKER	CYPRUS EVACUATION (1974)	MAYAGUEZ

Others within President Ford's advisory council, to include
Secretary of Defense Schlesinger, Secretary of State Kissinger,
and acting Chairman of the Joint Chiefs of Staff, Air Force
General Jones (General George S. Brown, the chairman, was in
Europe on official business), saw a challenge to American power
and to the principle of freedom of the seas. Clearly, the
incident provided a chance to demonstrate the military
establishment's competence, and as a consequence, to lift
military and public morale. Kissinger may have had a deeper,
more personal interest. He, more so than anyone else, was
closely linked to the fall of Saigon a few weeks earlier. So,
the president and his primary advisors, appeared to be primed for
the strong response that followed. They were united in their
effort.

The participants differed slightly during the various
meetings of the National Security Council (NSC), but generally
included:

43

President

Vice President

Secretary of State

Secretary of Defense

Director, Central Intelligence Agency

Deputy Secretary of State

Deputy Secretary of Defense

Assistant to the President for National Security Affairs

Acting Chairman, Joint Chiefs of Staff, General David Jones

Assistant to the President, Donald Rumsfeld

Deputy Assistant for National Security Affairs

Senior NSC Staff Officer for East Asia, Richard Smyser

Counselor to the President, John Marsh

Counselor to the President, Robert Hartman

At the time of the crisis, Henry Kissinger held both the post of Secretary of State and Assistant to the President for National Security Affairs. At each NSC meeting, the Deputy Secretary of State presented the views of the Department of State while Dr. Kissinger acted as Assistant to the President for National Security Affairs [41].

As for the decision making process, President Ford followed an established procedure: he listened to options suggested by the other members of the National Security Council; consulted with them and received assurances that the information was current and correct, made his decision; and, lastly, he conferred further with the National Security Council, presented the rationale for his decision, and sought concurrence. "In every instance, the answer was unanimous agreement to every decision [42].

Military orders were then issued from President Ford through Lieutenant General Scowcroft, the President's Deputy Assistant for National Security Affairs, to Secretary of Defense Schlesinger, General David C. Jones to the Commander-in-Chief Pacific (CINCPAC). CINCPAC had planning and operational responsibility for the entire operation.

The National Security Council met a total of four times during the crisis. The first meeting, about seven hours after Washington received notice about the seizure, was on Monday, May 12th at noon. The meeting lasted forty-five minutes. The second meeting was the following day. It started at 10:30 and lasted one hour. The third meeting was held the night of May 13th at 10:40 p.m. It lasted about two hours. The final meeting was held on the afternoon of May 14th at 3:52 p.m. That meeting lasted until 5:40 p.m.

As indicated in Figure 4, CINCPAC, located in Hawaii, exercised different control measures over each of the services. There was no centralized military command authority over all the services. The local U.S. commander, an Air Force general, was directed by CINCPAC to develop the plan for the rescue operation.

U.S. MILITARY
CHAIN OF COMMAND
During Mayaguez Crisis

Figure 4

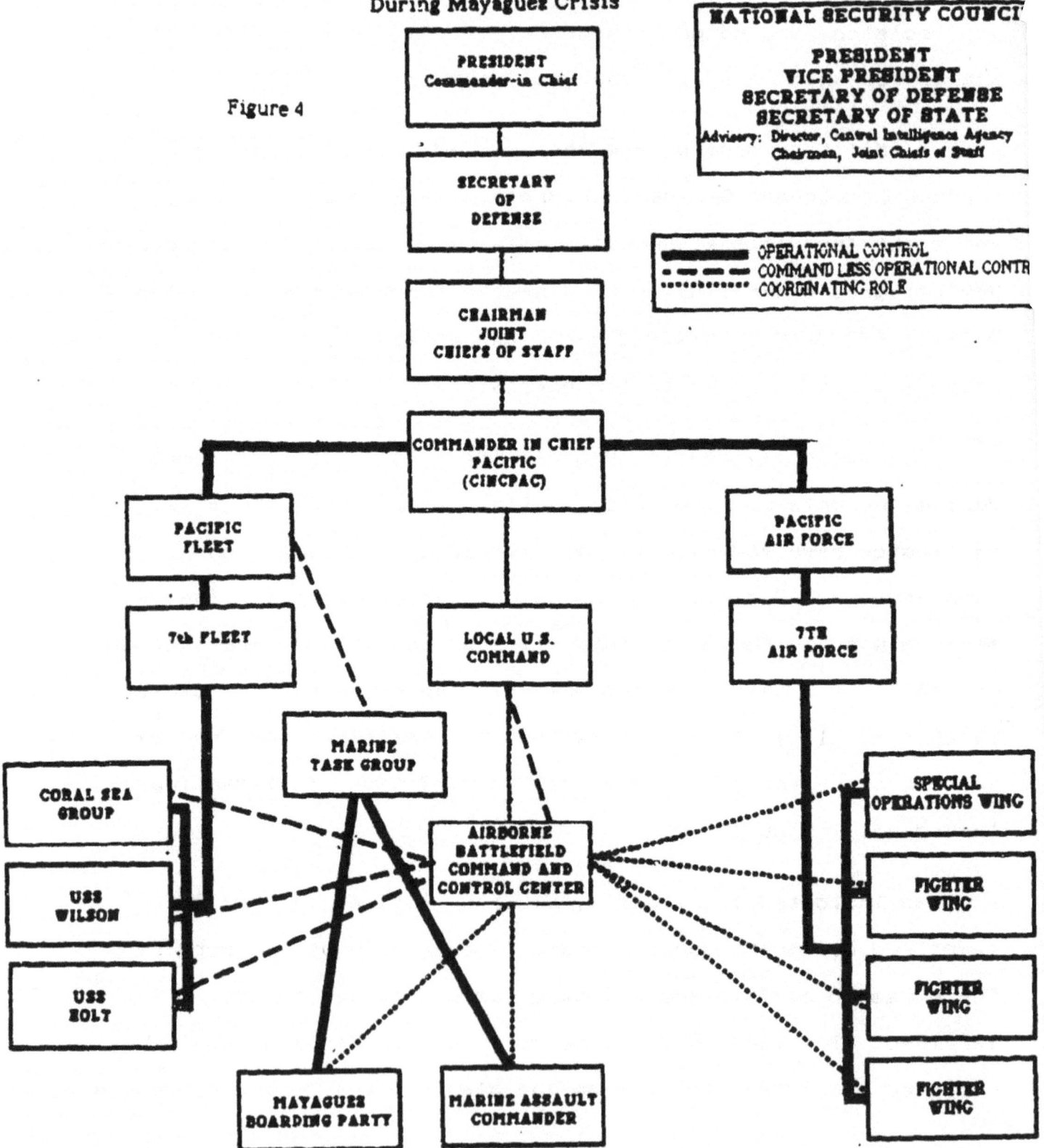

Modified from a chart contained in The Comptroller General of the United States, "The Seizure of the Mayaguez---A Case Study of Crisis Management", 4 October 1976, page 86.

Control by CINCPAC over Naval operations was through the CINCPAC Fleet and the 7th Fleet. Significantly, CINCPAC Fleet exercised no operational control (OPCON) over the participating naval units---the U.S.S. Holt, the U.S.S. Wilson, and the Coral Sea Group. CINCPAC Fleet's mission was to train, equip, provide, administer, and discipline the naval forces involved. Its job was to support, not to fight.

Marines would normally come under Navy control. However, once the Marine Task Group arrived in the "Mayaguez" theater of operations, it came under the control of the U.S. Air Force commander based in Thailand. This local U.S. command controlled all Marine forces once the operation began.

Control of the air forces was not as awkward. The Commander, 7th Air Force and the local U.S. commander were the same individual. Once orders were received from CINCPAC they were passed to the operational wings by the Commander, 7th Air Force/local U.S. commander. Command authority was not an issue with the Air Force.

Finally, the airborne battlefield command and control center, was essentially a communications link. It had no real authority of its own. It merely relayed information and attempted to understand and influence the combat situation as it developed. Since the plan called for the

47

airborne battlefield command and control center to orbit in an about ninety nautical miles from Koh Tang, this was not an easy task.

During the operation, radio links brought the sounds of the assault wave to the White House and to the Pentagon. President Ford could hear the helicopters and the "pings" of bullets from Khmer Rouge rifles [43]. The rapidity of communications did have one undesirable feature---it encouraged centralized decision making. In fact, during the incident, the communications network was utilized by the president to exercise direct control over the use of military force. For example, the communications capability allowed President Ford to decide whether to attack a vessel heading toward the Cambodian mainland which was suspected of carrying Mayaguez crew members.

Later, he was able to cancel and then reinstate the initial air strikes against Kompong Som [44]. The president, in fact, had better communications than the U.S. commanders in the vicinity of Tang Island during the combat operations. This was in spite of the use of an on-scene C-130 communications relay aircraft. At the operational level, the lack of radio interoperability posed a major problem for controlling the forces and understanding the situation as it unfolded.

Communications normally follow the same channels as the chain of command in military operations. However, the lack of reliable communications within the combat area and the relatively good communications between the combat forces and Washington D.C., allowed, if not encouraged, active participation by personnel in Washington. There was a communications and, by inference, a control void to fill. It was filled. The ability to monitor and communicate with the combatants from Washington minimized opportunities for local commanders to take total control. In addition, the likelihood of questioning decisions made by Washington were for all practical purposes eliminated.

Within the State Department problems were also evident. Lower level officers with long experience in Cambodia were excluded from contributing or otherwise participating in the crisis management [45]. President Ford,

> "seems to have struck in Southeast Asia not as a last resort after exhaustive diplomacy, not in some genuinely informed calculus of the adversary's intentions, but by what must have been a largely intuitive judgment that he had no other choice" [46].

War Powers Act

Passed over President Nixon's veto in November 1973, the War Powers Resolution attempts to restrict the president's authority to involve the U.S. in armed conflict or in situations likely to involve such conflict. It was passed in response to the U.S. involvement in the Vietnam War. The act explicitly requires the President to report to Congress, within forty eight hours of their deployment, any commitment of troops to actual or imminent hostilities or any introduction of troops into he territory, air space, or waters of a foreign nation while they are equipped for combat. The act further requires that the President consult with Congress prior to so acting. Congress is required to approve or disprove the continued use of troops within sixty days of their commitment. If Congress fails within sixty days (or ninety days if the President certifies that troop safety requires the added time) the continued use of the forces, the President must withdraw them.

Although President Ford notified Congress in accordance with the War Powers Resolution, he did so only in "accordance with my desire that Congress be informed on this matter"[47]. There has was a reluctance of President Ford and President Nixon before him, and President Carter after him, to full accept the requirements of the War Powers Resolution. Special reluctance has been over adhering to the "consultation" provision.

Although President Ford made indirect contact with congressional leaders several times throughout the crisis, according to several Senate leaders, the letter of the law was not upheld. Senator Mike Mansfield of Montana said, "I was not consulted. I was notified after the fact about what the Administration had already decided" [48]. Representative John B. Anderson of Illinois, the third-ranking Republican in the House, said he was disappointed that Mr. Ford had done no more than "calling up and saying here's what we've decided" [49]. Consultation with Congress occurred at 2:30 a.m.---four hours before the advanced notification would have expired under the terms of the War Powers Resolution. Whatever the political rhetoric, President Ford's actions avoided a legal confrontation with Congress.

The following documents the various contacts made by the President, his staff, and executive branch officials with Congress during the Mayaguez crisis [50]:

May 13 (5:50 p.m.-11 p.m.) The President directed that
White House staff officers contact ten House and eleven
Senate Members regarding the planned military measures
to prevent the Mayaguez and its crew from being
transferred to the Cambodian mainland. The action was
also designed to prevent Cambodian reinforcements of
Koh Tang Island where the Marine assault was to take
place.

May 14 (11:50 a.m.-12 noon) 11 House and 11 Senate
Members were notified that three Cambodian vessels had
been sunk and four others damaged. This action was
taken to prevent removal of the Mayaguez crew to the
mainland of Cambodia.

May 14 (2 p.m.-5 p.m.) Deputy Assistant Secretary of
State for East Asian and Pacific Affairs and Deputy
Assistant Secretary of Defense for International
Security Affairs briefed the House International
Relations Committee on the status of the crisis.
Other briefings were made by the Legal Advisor, Office
of Chairman, Joint Chiefs of Staff and the National
Intelligence Officer for South and Southeast Asia,
Central Intelligence Agency.

May 14 (6:30 p.m.) The congressional leadership was
personally briefed by the President about his specific
orders for the recapture of the ship and crew.

Although the War Power Resolution specifically says
that "the President in every possible instance shall consult
with Congress before introducing U.S. armed forces into
hostilities or into situations where imminent involvement in
hostilities is clearly indicated", the wording left room for
interpretation: it is qualified by the phrase "in every
possible instance" and the word "consult" is not defined.
The wording also leaves unanswered, the manner by which the
President is to "consult" with Congress. For the most part,
President Ford "consulted" through his staff to the
Congressional leaders.

    Once the crisis was over, congressional discussions
about President Ford's compliance or non-compliance with the
requirements of the War Powers Resolution were not
particularly harsh nor prolonged. The apparent success and
the short duration of the commitment of military forces
undoubtedly had something to do with limiting congressional
concern. Even when briefed personally by the President the
day before the assault, there was no objection expressed by
the congressional leadership. The majority of congressmen
hailed the President for the quick, decisive daring of the
operation; only a few asked whether he exceeded his
authority.

THAI REACTION

The military plan to retake the <u>Mayaguez</u> and free its
crew required the use of nearby forces. Sufficient forces
were not available in nearby Thailand, the planned staging
area. So plans were made to fly ground forces to Thailand.
Premier Kukrit Pramoj of Thailand stated that if the U.S.
military assault force, 1000 U.S. Marines, came to Thailand
then Thailand, "cannot be friends with the United States any
more [51]." U.S. diplomatic and military officials in
Bangkok refused to comment regarding the prime minister's
proclamation.

On the morning of May 13, 1975 at the second NSC
meeting, it was announced that the Thai Prime Minister had
emphasized that Thailand would not permit use of its bases
for U.S. action against Cambodia.

The U.S. Charge d'Affairs informed the Thai Government
that the United States would inform it before initiating any
action involving U.S. planes based in Thailand. It was
then reported by the U.S. Charge d'Affairs in Thailand to

54

the Secretary of State, that the U.S. should "play by the rules" or stand to lose Thai support and cooperation [52].

Within six hours after the second NSC meeting, the Chairman, Joint Chiefs of Staff directed that two Marine platoons from the Philippines, and a Marine battalion from Okinawa be moved to Utapao, Thailand Air Base. The Thai Government promptly protested this action pending arrival of the U.S. Marines.

U.S. Marines arrived in Thailand the next day. The Premier charged that the arrival of the marines violated Thai sovereignty and that the troops were to leave Thailand immediately. In a diplomatic message to President Ford, Prime Minister Khukrit Pramoj wrote the following:

> "...The Thai Government considers that this action (the arrival of the Marines) by the United States Government is not consistent with the goodwill existing between Thailand and the United States, and unless these forces which have entered against the wishes of the Thai Government are withdrawn immediately, the good relations and cooperation existing between the Thailand and the United States would be exposed to serious and damaging consequences" [53].

The U.S. ignored the Prime Minister's demand and the troops left Thailand only after the military operation had been concluded two days later.

On May 19, 1975, U.S. Charge d'Affairs Edward Masters delivered to the Foreign Minister of Thailand, Chatchai Choonavan in Bangkok, a diplomatic note. It stated that:

55

"The United States regrets the misunderstandings that have arisen between Thailand and the United States in regard to the temporary placement of marines at Utapao to assist in the recovery of the S.S. Mayaguez. The United States wishes to express its understanding of the problem caused the Royal Thai Government..."[54]

The U.S. Embassy in Thailand reported the view that if U.S. Marines were withdrawn speedily, U.S. relations with would eventually recover from the Mayaguez crisis.

A search of all unclassified published sources failed to substantiate a statement by Ron Rowan in his book, The Four Days of Mayaguez, that "privately", Thailand had given its concurrence to the staging of the marines in Thailand [55]. Mr. Rowan cites a private conversation with President Ford as one of his sources for his book. His conclusion carries with it the following: U.S./Thai relations remained strong after the crisis; Thailand, suffering an uneasy relationship with its Asian neighbors, was naturally hesitant about openly welcoming U.S. involvement; and, Thailand was able to reap the dividends of being a protected U.S. ally. In addition, Thailand and Cambodia relations were strained over the disputed islands.

The Cost

The captain and thirty-nine crewmen of the Mayaguez
were freed. Of the one hundred seventy-nine marines who
participated in the operation, fifteen were killed during
the assault, three others were missing and presumed dead,
and another twenty-three lost their lives in a related
helicopter crash in Thailand. Fifty additional marines
were wounded [56]. Reportedly, the Cambodian death toll was
at 25 [57].

Two other factors are worthy of mention: the use or
riot agents by the United States; and, the use of a 15,000
pound bomb, the BLU 82, on Tang Island.

President Ford authorized the use of riot control
agents at the first meeting of the NSC. They were
authorized in an effort to recover the ship and crew.
However, gas agents were used at least twice: the first time
to stop a Thai vessel from reaching the Cambodian mainland
with the crew of the Mayaguez on it. This operation was
unsuccessful. Secondly, gas was used when the Marines

57

assaulted the Mayaquez during the combat assault. This
operation was not needed as the ship was empty. The use of
gas, though ineffective, did beg questions about the
rationale for its use.

When asked about riot control agents and the possible
violation to the Geneva Protocol that prohibited the use of
gas, the Department of Defense offered the following:

> "The United States has ratified the Geneva Protocol of
> 1925, but in our view that Protocol does not extend to
> the use of riot control agents.
>
> In ratifying the Geneva Protocol, the President
> announced that the United States would, as a matter of
> national policy, renounce the first use in war of riot
> control agents except their use, upon approval of the
> President, in defensive military modes to save lives,
> such as their use in rescue missions in remotely
> isolated areas.
>
> The use of riot control agents in the Mayaquez incident
> was specifically authorized by the President, and was
> deemed necessary to facilitate the rescue of the
> Mayaquez crew in an area which at that moment was
> remotely isolated from U.S. forces. Accordingly, the
> action was consistent with U.S. policy in the use in
> war of riot control agents." [58]

The use of BLU 82, commonly called the "Daiseycutter",
was also questioned. The bomb, the largest non-nuclear bomb
in the U.S. arsenal, was developed during the Vietnam
conflict for blasting out landing zones from thick jungle.
During the Mayaquez incident, it was dropped on Tang Island
as the last of the Marines were evacuating the island after
the assault. Purportedly, it was dropped to eliminate enemy
weapons fire that could not be suppressed by other means.

Three BLU 82 bombs were available and ready for use during the Marine assault. A decision by the Marine Task Group Commander before the assault allowed that the BLU 82 would not be used unless its use was specifically requested by the on-the-ground assault commander. He never requested its use. He was not informed that a decision had been made to drop the bomb nor had he requested its use at any time. An Inquiry into the Mayaguez Incident determined that "the decision to use the weapon was probably made in Washington" [59]. The use of this extremely lethal weapon against Cambodian forces cannot be justified for military reasons.

In all, the use of riot control agents and the BLU 82 bomb served no useful purpose except to further support the perception of chaos and its consequences.

INTELLIGENCE

Intelligence was faulty. The Central Intelligence Agency (CIA) and the Defense Intelligence Agency (DIA) provided widely varying and contradictory analysis. The military operation called for marines to assault Tang Island. One thousand marines had been placed in Thailand as a "ready reserve" for that purpose. One hundred and seventy-five were thought to be sufficient. This number was deemed an acceptable risk. It was also in accordance with marine doctrine which calls for an initial three to one superiority over enemy troops. Coincidentally, the number was also the approximate number of troops that could be carried by the maximum available helicopters.

The number of enemy forces on Tang Island was based on an initial CIA estimates that placed the enemy strength at about 20 irregulars and their families [60]. DIA, however, estimated the enemy strength to be as high as 200 Khmer Rouge soldiers armed with automatic weapons, mortars, and recoilless rifles [61]. This latter estimate proved to be

very accurate---but it was not believed. The reasons for
the significant discrepancy between estimates are not
contained in unclassified sources; however, they can be
assumed: responsibility was credited to DIA for the
inaccurate estimates of Viet Cong and North Vietnamese
forces during the recently concluded Vietnam War; therefore,
there may have been a reluctance to believe DIA again.

The Marine Ground Commander later reported the
estimated enemy strength at about "150 professional
soldiers, well-equipped with small arms, machine guns,
recoilless rifles, and mortars" [62]. For reasons unknown,
the earlier DIA estimate was not made known to him. This
ratio of marines (175) to enemy forces (150) was not in
accordance with corps doctrine, but because of the nature of
the operation and the expectation of initial surprise, it
constituted an acceptable risk.

During the combat assault the marines discovered
that the Mayaguez crew actually were never on Tang Island.
The crew had been taken from the ship when it was seized,
to the mainland and subsequently to Rong Island, some 30
miles from the action---almost 24 hours earlier [63]. This
information should have been known, but because of faulty
intelligence, it was not. Air reconnaissance was available
but its effectiveness was diminished because of the dense

vegetation on Tang Island.   Photos of the island were
taken, but they too proved to be of little value.

Intelligence sufficient to conduct an assault on Tang
Island was limited.   All available Cambodian refugees in
the Utapao Air Base area were located and queried about the
island.   One former Cambodian naval officer, who said he
had been on the island some time before the crisis, alleged
that there would probably be no more than twenty to thirty
people on the island with no organized regular units there
[64].   The fact there were no tactical maps available
compounded the problem [65].   Given the high U.S. presence
in Southeast Asia, particularly in nearby Vietnam, the lack
of maps of the general area as almost implausible.

One U.S. Air Force RF-4 aircraft was allowed to fly 16
reconnaissance flights over Tang Island to take pictures;
however, it was limited to above 6,000 feet because of
possible hostile fire. A total of 5000 to 6,000 pictures
were taken.   Significantly, of 1,000 pictures taken at
about the time the fishing boat reached Kompong Som near the
Cambodian mainland,, several showed a "fishing boat with
approximately 29 possible people on deck."   This same boat
had "probable boxes" and drums or barrels in front of the
pilot house.   The boat from which the crew was eventually
recovered also, had drums or barrels in front of the pilot
house.   The crew later confirmed that they had been taken to

Kompong Som harbor by a Thai fishing boat [66]. Had the photo analyst been instructed to look for possible caucasians, the crew may have been spotted on the fishing boat and the attack on Tang Island avoided. This observation was made in the Comptroller General's report after the crisis and after examining the film taken [67].

A U.S. Air Force drone is an unmanned aircraft equipped with high resolution cameras. It was not used for intelligence gathering, though it was available. Specially equipped to take photographs at low altitudes in a hostile environment, the use of the drone was rejected because: at least 24 hours are required to make it operational; the air space was already saturated with other aircraft; and, the drone's flight route must be preprogramed and works best against stationary targets [68].

The intelligence passed to the President and the NSC was equally poor. As the various intelligence agencies attempted to acquire the most current and accurate information, information was often passed before it could be verified and authenticated. Some critical, and as it turned out, accurate, intelligence about the number and capabilities of the forces on Tang Island never reached the assault force. It differed with other official intelligence sources. This led to contradictory intelligence recommendations. As a consequence, poor decisions resulted.

63

In his book, Leaders and Intelligence, Dr. Michael
Handel states, "The first major difference (between highest
political strategic level and those on the operational or
lower level) is that decisions and intelligence estimates at
the highest political and strategic level are seldom
produced under pressure of time because they are mainly
concerned with long-range trends" [69]. This statement is
certainly true with regard to planned operations and to the
probabilistic range of expectant behavior. However, a
danger arises when a senior political leader, such as the
President, becomes directly involved in tactical decisions.
Dr. Handel agrees that because of the very nature of crisis
management, when a political leader becomes intimately
involved in operational details, he can be inclined to make
decisions based on operational intelligence and loose sight
of strategic objectives. Clausewitz comments:

> In (tactics), one is carried away by the pressures of
> the moment, caught up in a maelstorm when resistance
> would be fatal, and, suppressing incipient scruples,
> one presses boldly on. In strategy, the pace is much
> slower. There is room for apprehensions, one's own and
> those of others; for objections and remonstrations and,
> in consequence, for premature regrets [70].

Operational or tactical intelligence, because of its
perishable nature, requires a quick, decisive determination
for its use. Usually, the political leader is in the worst
position to use it effectively. There is a military
perception that politicians should not involve themselves
the operational details. Churchill, the First Lord of the

64

Admiralty and "meddling civilian" was, after all, sacrificed after the disastrous Dardanelles campaign of 1915. He had thrust the campaign upon a "somewhat uneager staff"[71]

RESULTS

The success of the rescue operation can be debated.
Although the captain and the 39 crewmen were returned and
the ship recovered, an equal number of American marines were
killed and a greater number were wounded during the
operation. President Ford and the military were praised for
the decisive and deliberate action to rescue the ship and
crew. However, if the goal of the exercise was to improve
U.S. morale, then the exercise was indeed successful. In a
Gallup Opinion Poll, conducted June, 1975, President Ford's
popularity improved from 39% before the Mayaguez incident to
51% after [72]. Decision Research Corporation directly
addressed Ford's handling of the Mayaguez affair. The poll
showed that 75% approved. "The success generated a moral
uplift for the American people, restored a belief in
American credibility, and demonstrated a strategic resolve
worthy of a great power"[73].

Indirect affects were also in evidence. They, too,
reflect an apparent success. Capitalizing on the success of
the rescue, President Ford made his first visit to Europe as

President of the United States three weeks after the crisis. The visit included a summit with NATO heads of government, talks on the Middle East with Egyptian President Sadat, and meetings with the governments of Spain and Italy:

> "Mr. Ford's travels come at a pregnant time.   He leaves an America somewhat doubtful about its world role as it absorbs the sudden, final collapse in Indochina. He faces a Western Europe hungry for reassurance, but again somewhat doubtful of America's present will and capacity to back up that reassurance." [74]

In response to a question about the value of his handling of the Mayaguez incident in reassuring Europe of America's resolve, President Ford said,

> "I am sure that both domestically in the United States, as well as worldwide, the handling of the Mayaguez incident should be a firm assurance that the United States is capable and has the will to act in emergencies, in challenges. I think this is a clear, clear indication that we are not only strong but we have the will and the capability of moving." [75]

Other indirect repercussions included a defeat in the House of Representatives of an amendment that would have forced withdrawal of 70,000 U.S. military personnel on a worldwide basis. Senator Mike Mansfield publicly stated that [because of the Mayaguez incident] he was reassessing his position regarding support for the troop withdrawal and wondered if it was not the time to perhaps keep America's strength overseas. This position was echoed by Congressman O'Neill of Massachusetts [76].

Internationally, the retaking of the Mayaguez caused few repercussions except within the Communist community.

Deputy Premier Teng Hsiao-ping, Chief of Staff of China's Armed Forces is quoted as saying even before the U.S. action, "If the U.S. intervenes, there is nothing we can do" [77]. Pravda, the official Communist news agency, stated that the American ship seizure was well within international waters [78]. This implied that the U.S. actions were justified. However, the Thai government formally protested the use of its territory by the U.S. forces. An American embassy official in Thailand remarked, "It was a ham-handed operation. It would seem that no one in Washington gave any thought to the Thai feelings"[79]. Regardless, the event did not appear to have any lasting negative effect.

If, on the other hand, the U.S. action was to serve notice to the rest of the world that the U.S. would and could respond to protect its interests, the success may not be as obvious. As a Thai official put it: "The Americans have shown that they will respond when an American ship is in trouble. That is hardly any comfort to us because we are an independent nation, not an American ship"[80].

The decision-making process has also been called into question. The President was criticized by members of Congress for his handling of the crisis. Senator Robert C. Byrd of West Virginia, the Senate Democratic whip, voiced the concern of some members of Congress over what he characterized as "the failure to ask as least some of the

leaders to participate in the decision-making process" (81).
Others may wonder why the President would be so intimately
involved in the tactical planning and decision making
process.

SUMMARY AND APPLICATIONS

In relating the decisions and the actions taken by the
U.S. government in the Mayaguez crisis to the unique
national and international environment and the Theory of
Chaos, there is ample evidence to suggest that a
relationship exists. But, before too much is drawn from
this conclusion, it is important to note that Chaos Theory
relies on the environment of the time, not the crisis
itself, to function. Unlike other models, Chaos Theory does
nor depend on blocs, capabilities or special relationships
among nations to explain actions. Nor does it differentiate
between large and small nations. The satisfying aspect is
that it allows anticipation or prediction.

With regard to the unique case of the Mayaguez, the
unique environment in which it was set lends its
consequences to support Chaos Theory.

The complex and highly unusual national and
International setting in the mid-70's that presented an
political climate in the U.S. of uncertainty;

70

the technological capabilities that allowed the
President to actively monitor the on-going combat
operations and thereby encouraged a centralized
decision making;

the lack of reliable intelligence which encouraged
decision makers to believe the intelligence that best
supported the desired course of action and ignore
intelligence to the contrary;

the President's cursory acknowledgment and token
adherence to the War Powers Resolution that minimized
Congressional input into the decision making process;

the bombing of the Cambodian mainland that begged
questions of necessity and real purpose and violated
the unwritten code of proportionality;

the early authorization by the President on use of riot
agents;

the "Washington decision" to drop the BLU 82, the
largest non nuclear bomb in the U.S. arsenal; and,

the apparent desire by Washington to "punish" the
Cambodians

The reactions by the U.S. suggests a behavior that goes
beyond that expected of a rational and politically mature
nation. They went beyond the "range of expectant behavior"

that had been in evidence prior to the incident. The reaction, particularly with regard to the dropping of the BLU 82, was not proportional to the situation. In fact the reaction is bias toward political chaos; a reaction, given the environment of the time, that Chaos Theory predicts in such circumstances.

The events of May 1975, widened the "range of expectant behavior" for the United States. Figure 5 reflects this change. No longer would a military reaction by the U.S. to a world event be totally unexpected. A degree of uncertainty has been introduced for the future. Indeed, a U.S. precedence had been set. The later excursion into Grenada, the raid into Libya, and the invasion of Panama serve to highlight the fact that once a precedence has been set, similar actions are more apt to happen. Neither the world nor the U.S. Congress reacted as violently or as surprised to these events as they did to the violent and destructive U.S. response to the Mayaguez crisis.

Relative Change in Range of Expectant Behavior

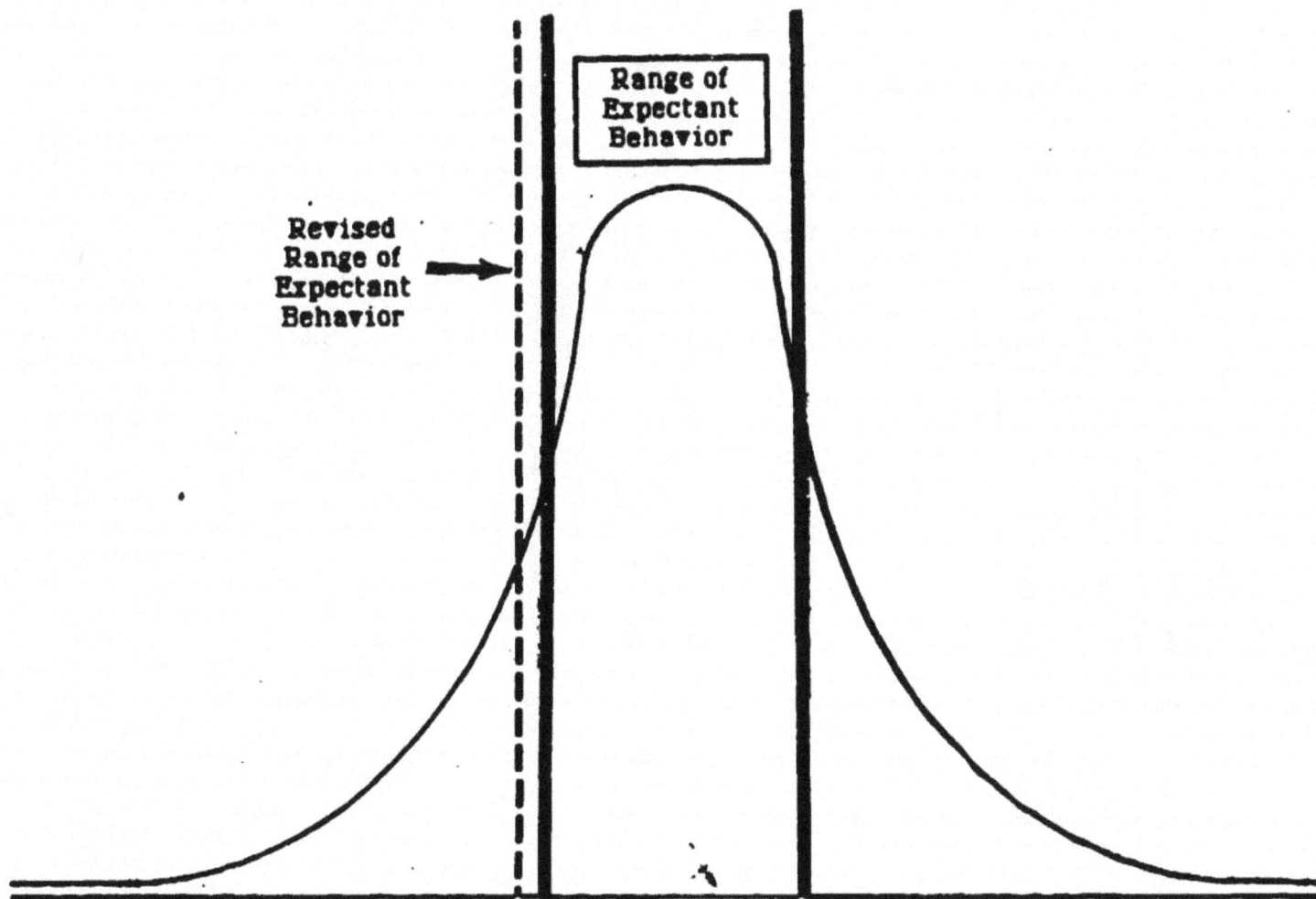

Figure 5

The U.S. reaction to the seizure of the Mayaguez can be
explained in many ways. This paper suggests that the
application of the Theory of Chaos is one way. Other
theories can also serve to explain the events. In
hindsight, they like Chaos Theory, are as accurate. Their
shortcoming then, is that, unlike Chaos Theory, they do not
pretend to predict.

Figure 6 depicts model of crisis management. Within
the time a crisis develops and until the time action is
taken, certain factors become important. Ideally, such
factors as intelligence, forces, weather, etc., reach
maturity at the time a course of action is initiated.
Because crisis' are usually time-sensitive, simultaneous
maturity for all elements may not be possible. Immaturity
of any element, such as inadequate intelligence or lack of a
sufficient resources, or helicopters in the case of the
Mayaguez rescue, create risk. This risk must be judged by
the decision maker, and with proper counsel, determined to
be acceptable or unacceptable. Like Chaos Theory or the
'loss of a nail' metaphor, a single, seemingly insignificant
factor, can foretell doom. Conversely, a positive result is
just "plain dumb luck". The driving forces in crisis
management then, are like the three-dimensional situation or
stool in Figure 7. These dimensions, time, threat, and

74

Figure 6

Model of Crisis Management

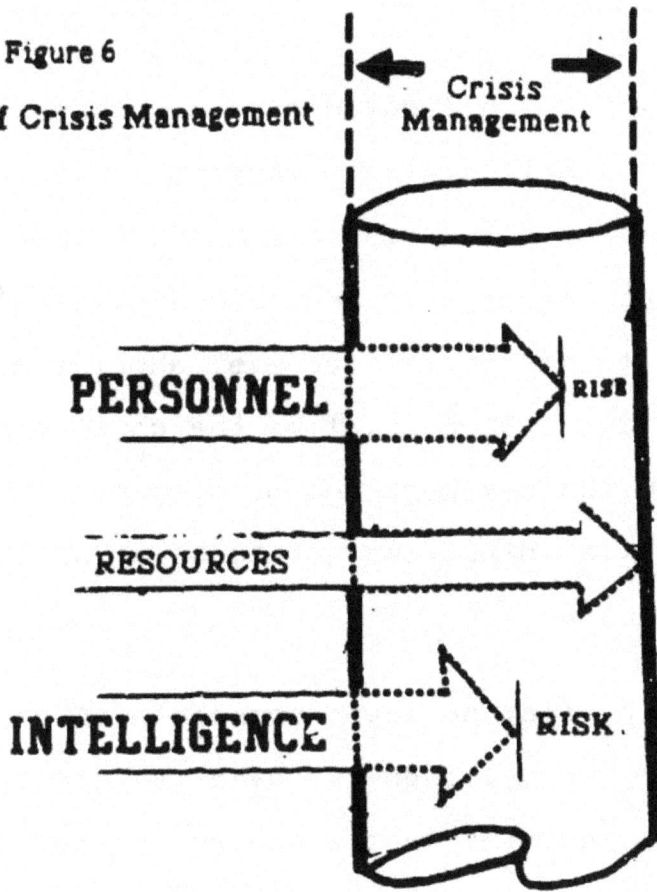

PERSONNEL

RESOURCES

INTELLIGENCE

RISK

RISK

Crisis Management

Crisis Management

Crisis Management

THREAT   TIME   SURPRISE

Figure 7

This drawing is a visual representation of the properties Charles F. Hermann associates with crisis management in "International Crisis as a Situational Variable", International Politics and Foreign Policy, edited by James N. Rosenau, New York, The Free Press, 1969, page 415.

Driving Forces in Crisis Management

75

surprise, relate to eight classifications described by
Charles F. Hermann [82].   All relate to varying differences
in the three variables.   The situation that most closely
approximates the Mayaguez incident is the "circumstantial
situation"---low threat to national interests, short time
for reaction, and surprise.   However, like the conclusion
that can be deduced from the Mayaguez facts, Hermann
considers the circumstantial situation not to be a justified
crisis[83].

If there is value in relating the response taken by the
U.S. Government to Chaos Theory, then the benefits for the
future are significant.   Inherent in the theory is its
universality.   Chaotic changes like those on-going through
the disintegration of communism in the Soviet Union and
Eastern Europe, may be cause for alarm for Soviets, former
communist bloc countries and the rest of the world.

The recent clashes between Armenians and Azerbaijanis
in the Soviet Union's southern republic of Azerbaijan are
another problem that contributes to a extraordinary
situation for the Soviet Union.   It is but one more factor
that contributes to the possibility of a chaotic reaction by
the Soviets.   Former Secretary of State Henry Kissinger said
of the conflict that the Kremlin currently is using more
force than needed to quell the clashes [84].   Political
rhetoric or prophecy?   If it is reality, then does the

76

action by the Soviet Union betray logic and exceed the range
of expectant behavior? Any action taken by the Soviets
could produce an increase in world tension. The catalyst to
cause a chaotic response could be small in the eyes of the
world, but perceived as justification of significant action
by the Soviets. The dramatically changing events in eastern
Europe and those clashes between various ...ctions within the
Soviet Union are happening too rapidly to ignore from a
Chaos Theory point of view.

History is replete with cases where political
motivation caused an otherwise unimportant event to become a
crisis. The North Korean invasion of South Korea on June
24, 1950 may be such an example. It may also be an example
where chaos politics affected the judgment of decision
makers. Hermann character.zes the North Korean attack on
his situational cube as a true crisis situation---high
threat, short time, and surprise [85]. This conclusion is
shared by a majority of historians; however this conclusion
m / not be complete.

The chaotic nature of the international events that
existed prior to the North Korean attack were not unlike the
chaos evident during the Mayaguez incident twenty-five years
later. The Cold War was worsening; the Russians recently
developed their own atomic bomb; the effects of a deep
recession were still lingering in the U S . President

Truman's popularity was at an all time low of 37 per cent; and the Administration had been denounced by the press for "losing" mainland China to the Communists [86]. Also, critical Senate and House elections were at risk in the up-coming November elections. Though not directly related to each other, these events, nevertheless, presented a chaotic environment.

Significantly, in 1948, President Truman had agreed with a top secret chiefs of staff paper provided that South Korea was not vital to U.S. interests. He reaffirmed this position in June of 1950 that Korea "is of little strategic value to the United States and that commitment to United States use of military forces in Korea would be ill-advised" [87]. Still, President Truman made decisions as a result of the North Korean invasion that led to the U.S. involvement in the Korean War. The implication is that because world and national events were chaotic, invasion of a country twice rejected to be of strategic value to the U.S. produced a chaotic response from the U.S.

Responses to a chaotic situation that has been exasperated by a surprising event, are most dangerous when the situation is considered a crisis. Even when an event does not qualify as a crisis, as in Hermann's criteria, decision-makers may make it so. When the amount of time available is linked to an event that demands action or to the existence of an unique and unacceptable situation, the possibility of a chaotic response increases.

CONCLUSION

The application of the Theory of Chaos to political
science has a potential worthy of study. Given its current
theoretical application lacks an exact mathematical
measurement that classical sciences enjoy; however, the
basic theory does hold promise.

Does Chaos Theory suggest a better method of dealing
with political chaos? Perhaps. Instead of formulating
detailed contingency plans for as many scenarios as
possible, it appears to be better to gather a crisis
management team or cell of experts to handle all unforeseen
crisis. The routine management of crisis' could produce
better and less reactionary responses. With some logic it
would be possible to develop a crisis template or computer
model as a tool to better manage crisis situations. This
approach is not unlike the approach suggested by Neustadt
and May in their book, Thinking in Time [88]. They propose
to "disassemble" a crisis situation into Known, Presumed,
and Unclear and write down what is known about each.
Writing these makes it harder to "deceive yourself---or

anybody else." Both the Neustadt and May approach and the
formulation of a crisis management team attempt to reduce a
crisis management analysis to an objective evaluation. If
this is done chances increase for a rational decision. And,
unless external factors preclude handling of the situation
by the team, such as President Ford's active involvement in
the Mayaguez crisis, then management will not be by
exception, but become more routine. Even if some high
authority does take direct control, at least the means to
acquire information and intelligence and the means to
disseminate instructions is firmly in place. As more
thought is given to the association between Chaos Theory and
disproportionate responses to non-threatening events, other
alternatives will undoubtedly surface.

The word Mayaguez means "a place of many streams". In
this regard, its namesake, the Mayaguez has become a part of
political history because of those four days in May. Its
significance as a ship is the same as before. However, its
significance to political science has been increased by its
association to Chaos Theory. The actions that transpired
during May, 1975, like its name implies, the Mayaguez became
and remains, "a place of many interests". The actions taken
by the United States as a result of the seizure introduced a
wider "range of expectant behavior" to U.S. alternatives.
The concept of Chaos Theory helps to explain, but not

81

justify, unusual actions.   There is no doubt that the
theories of chaos may have application in political science.

NOTES

1 James Gleick, <u>Chaos---Making of A New Science</u> (New York: Penguin. 1987). 5.

2 Comptroller General of the United States Report. "The Seizure of the <u>Mayaguez</u>---A Case Study in Crisis Management." 4 October. 1976: 94.

3 Ibid.. 60.

4 Ibid.. 97.

5 Elizabeth Holtzman, Representative in Congress from the State of New York, <u>Hearings of the Subcommittee on International Political and Military Affairs</u>, 25 June 1975: 174.

6 Carl von Clausewitz, <u>On War</u>, ed. Michael Howard and Peter Paret (Princeton: Princeton University Press, 1976). 81.

7 Gleick, 170.

8 Ibid., 169.

9 Raymond Cohen, <u>Threat Perception in International Crisis</u> (Madison: Wisconsin Press, 1979), 188.

10 Gleick, 8.

11 von Clausewitz, 120.

12 "The Mathematics of Mayhem," <u>The Economist</u>, 8 Sept. 1984: 87.

13 Richard G. Head, Frisco W. Short, and Robert C. McFarland. Crisis Resolution: Presidential Decision Making in the Mayaguez and Korean Confrontations (Boulder: Westview, 1978). 102.

14 von Clausewitz, 87.

15 Ibid., 149.

16 Ibid., 605.

17 Bernard Brodie, War & Politics (New York: MacMillan, 1973). 2.

18 Report of the Comptroller of the United States, "System to Warn U.S. Mariners of Potential Political/Military Hazards: S.S. Mayaguez, A Case Study," 11 February 1976: 6.

19 Comptroller General of the United States Report. op. cit., 66.

20 "Cambodia Too Weak To Resist U.S. Official Says." New York Times, 14 May 1975, late ed.: A-18.

21 Message by Cambodian Government to Secretary General of the United Nations. 20 May 1975.

22 Thomas Butson and Byrant Rollins, "Phnom Penh's Version of the Mayaguez Story," New York Times. 14 May 1975: 4.

23 Ibid.

24 Anthony Lewis, "Watch What I Do," New York Times, 10 Nov. 1975: 10.

25   Statement by White House Press Secretary Ron Nessen. 14 May 1975.

26   Prepared statement, Comptroller General of the United States Report: 174.

27   Video taped interview with Colonel Zane Finklestein. 6 July 1979.

28   Phillip Shabecoff, "White House Says Cambodia Seized a U.S. Cargo Ship," New York Times. 13 May 1975: 19.

29   Video taped interview. loc. cit.

30   "Story of The Rescue of Merchant Vessel Mayaguez." U.S. News & World Report. 26 May 1975:   20.

31   Roy Rowan, The Four Days of Mayaguez (New York: Norton, 1975), 68.

32   Richard E.Neustadt and Ernest R. May, Thinking in Time (New York: The Free Press, 1986), 61.

33   Robert C. Zelnick, "How Much of Ocean Can a Nation Claim? Mayaguez Heats Territorial Sea Limit Debate," Christian Science Monitor, 19 May 1975:   1.

34   Video tape interview. loc. cit.

35   Godfrey Sperling, "Manipulating Mayaguez News Coverage," Christian Science Monitor. 27 May 1975:   35.

36   Comptroller General of the United States Report, op. cit., 66.

37 Congressional Record, 13 May 1975: 14140.

38   Neustadt,   59.

39   Rowan,   68.

40   Mr. W.H. Parks, Legal Advisor on International Law
to the Chairman, Joint Chiefs of Staff, in a speech
presented at the U.S. Army War College, 14 March 1990.

41   Comptroller General of the United States Report,
op. cit., 112.

42   Sperling, loc. cit.

43   "The Mayaguez---What Went Right, Wrong," U.S. News
and World Report, 2 June 1975: 29.

44   Comptroller General of the United States Report,
op. cit., 85.

45   Charles H. Wilson, "What To Make of the Mayaguez,"
New Republic, 14 June 1975: 25.

46   Ibid., 27.

47   President Ford's Letter to the Speaker of the House
and the President Pro Tempore of the Senate, 15 May 1975.

48   David E. Rosenbaum, "Members of Congress Generally
Endorse the Military Action Against Cambodia," New York
Times, 16 May 1975: 8.

49   Ibid.

50   Comptroller General of the United States Report,
op cit., 70.

51   "Thailand Reports Marines Arrive In Ship's
Seizure," New York Times, 14 May 1975: 1.

52   Comptroller General of the United States Report,
op. cit., 119.

53 Aide memoire presented by Thailand Prime Minister
Khukrit Pramoj to the United States Charge d'Affairs at 4:00
p.m., 14 May 1975.

54 United States diplomatic note to the Thai
Government, 19 May, 1975.

55 Rowan, 92.

56 "The Mayaguez - What Went Right, Wrong?", loc. cit.

57 Ibid.

58 Statement submitted by the Department of Defense
for Robert S. Ingersoll, Acting Secretary of State,
12 Sept 1975.

59 Comptroller General of the United States Report,
op. cit., 94.

60 Head, 120.

61 Comptroller General of the United States Report,
op. cit., 90.

62 "The Mayaguez Operation," Center for Naval
Analysis, 1 July 1977: 8.

63 Captain Charles T. Miller, Captain of the
Mayaguez, testimony at Congressional Hearings of the
Subcommittee on International Political and Military
Affairs, 25 July 1975: 189-197.

64 J. M. Johnson, et al., "Individual Heroism Overcame
Awkward Command Relationships, Confusion and Bad
Information Off the Cambodian Coast," Marine Corps Gazette,
61 (October 1977): 27.

65   Richard A. Gabriel, Military Incompetence: Why the
American Military Doesn't Win (New York: Hill & Wang,
1985), 74.

66   Comptroller General of the United States Report,
op. cit., 77.

67   Ibid.

68   Ibid., 82.

69   Michael I. Handel, ed., Leaders and Intelligence
(London: A. Wheaton & Company, 1989), 17.

70   Howard, 178.

71   Brodie, op. cit., 14.

72   Gallup Opinion Index - Political, Social, and
Economic Trends, Report no. 120, June 1975: 12.

73   Phillip Shabecoff, "Ford Is Backed," New York
Times, 15 May 1975: 1.

74   "Interview with European Journalists,"
Presidential Documents: Gerald R. Ford, 1975, Vol. 11,
No. 21: 545.

75   Ibid.

76   Ibid.

77   "Worldgram," U.S. News & World Report,
 26 May 1975: 37.

78   Ibid.

79   "Thailand: Another U.S. Ally Lost?," U.S. News &
World Report, 26 May 1975: 22.

80   Ibid.

81 Shabecoff. loc. cit.

82 Charles F. Hermann. "International Crisis,"
International Politics and Foreign Policy. ed.. James N.
Rosenau (New York: Free Press, 1969). 415.

83 Ibid.. 418.

84 Gene Kramer. "Back German Reunification, Kissinger
Urges U.S.," Harrisburg Sunday Patriot News.
28 January 1990: A-8.

85 Rosenau. op. cit.. 413.

86 Neustadt. op. cit.. 35.

87 Ibid.

88 Neustadt. op. cit.. 45-90.

END

FILMED

DATE: 7-90

DTIC

The Mayaguez Incident
Omnibus

Contents

Articles

References

Article Licenses